BRILLIANT CAREERS

BRILLIANT CAREERS

*The Virago Book of
Twentieth-Century Fiction*

Edited by
Kasia Boddy, Ali Smith
and
Sarah Wood

A *Virago* Book

Published by Virago Press 2000

This collection and introduction copyright ©
Kasia Boddy, Ali Smith and Sarah Wood 2000

The moral right of the authors has been asserted.

Copyright Acknowledgements on page 509
constitute an extension of this copyright page

Photograph credits:

My Corsage, 1931 by James VanDerZee,
Copyright © Donna Mussenden VanDerZee;
Morgan State University graduates,
Copyright © Dudley M. Brooks;
'Aunt and nephew' copyright © Lennie Goodings

A CIP catalogue record for this book
is available from the British Library

ISBN 1 86049 842 6

Typeset in New Baskerville by M Rules

Printed and bound in Great Britain by
Clays Ltd, St Ives plc

Virago Press
A Division of
Little, Brown and Company (UK)
Brettenham House
Lancaster Place
London WC2E 7EN

Here comes the twenty-first century,
It's going to be much better for a girl like me.

Blondie

To all the twentieth-century girls

Contents

Contents

Acknowledgements and thanks

Thank you Lennie Goodings, Elise Dillsworth, Sajidah Ahmad and Patricia James at Virago.

Thank you Alexandra Pringle, Ursula Owen, Isobel Murray, Lizbeth Goodman, Charlotte Mitchell.

Introduction

Literary anthologies are a peculiarly artificial species. It's in their nature to create unlikely bedfellows, and to benefit from the unusual or timely comparisons their juxtapositions create. It's in their nature to be selective, to have to leave people out, and to cause uproar because they have.

But they make a species which (when they work, and in the best tradition of artifice) doesn't just mimic but actually recreates the life.

Our criteria for choosing passages for this anthology were these: we wanted one fiction extract to represent, chronologically, each year of the twentieth century. Each was to have been written by a woman, in English, and published or republished by Virago. Where there was a year of the century not covered by Virago reprints, we would choose something representative from elsewhere – this happened in only six instances. It has been the power and the blessing of the Virago Modern Classics list to make available to us, since the late 1970s, books which may otherwise have disappeared off the face of the earth (at least as far as the reading public was concerned). The Classics list demonstrates, as it announces on the inside covers of the reprints, 'the existence of a female tradition in fiction'. The passages we have selected from this huge and necessary act of positive discrimination always, without fail, illuminate three things: the period, how it was lived, and what its literature was making of it.

As you read your way through these hundred extracts from 1901 to 2000, the twentieth century in all its changes and its repetitions, its constraints and its liberations, its violences, its nostalgias and its hopes, will pass before your eyes.

Kasia Boddy, Ali Smith and Sarah Wood

1900s

1901

Miles Franklin

———

Stella Maria Sarah Miles Franklin was born in 1879 near Tumut, New South Wales, into a pioneering family and lived on her father's station Brindabella until poverty forced the family to decamp. The publication of what has been called 'the very first Australian novel', *My Brilliant Career*, which she wrote when she was still in her mid-teens, made her famous. This notoriety (even though the publishers had already removed much of the novel's satire on Victorian values and institutions) left her so uneasy that she gave instruction that the novel not be republished until ten years after her death. Franklin was also annoyed to have had her gender revealed, despite her androgynous choice of name, by the Australian writer Henry Lawson's preface to the novel.

A vibrant, politically active spirit, she lived for the rest of her life in Sydney, Melbourne, London and the USA. She wrote freelance journalism, five more novels under this name and six under the pseudonym Brent of Bin Bin. She actively promoted Australian literature, and left her estate to fund the prestigious Miles Franklin Award. She died in 1954.

Virago published *My Brilliant Career* in 1980.

from

My Brilliant Career

'Boo, hoo! Ow, ow; Oh! oh! Me'll die. Boo, hoo. The pain, the pain! Boo, hoo!'

'Come, come now. Daddy's little mate isn't going to turn Turk like that, is she? I'll put some fat out of the dinner-bag on it, and tie it up in my hanky. Don't cry any more now. Hush, you must not cry! You'll make old Dart buck if you kick up a row like that.'

That is my first recollection of life. I was barely three. I can remember the majestic gum-trees surrounding us, the sun glinting on their straight white trunks, and falling on the gurgling fern-banked stream, which disappeared beneath a steep scrubby hill on our left. It was an hour past noon on a long clear summer day. We were on a distant part of the run, where my father had come to deposit salt. He had left home early in the dewy morning, carrying me in front of him on a little brown pillow which my mother had made for the purpose. We had put the lumps of rock-salt in the troughs on the other side of the creek. The stringybark roof of the salt-shed which protected the troughs from rain peeped out picturesquely from the musk and peppercorn shrubs by which it was densely surrounded, and was visible from where we lunched. I refilled the quart-pot in which we had boiled our tea with water from the creek, father doused our fire out with it, and then tied the quart to the D of his saddle with a piece of green hide. The green-hide bags in which the salt had been carried were hanging on the hooks of the pack-saddle which encumbered the bay pack-horse. Father's saddle and the brown pillow were on Dart, the big grey horse on which he generally carried me, and we were on the point of making tracks for home.

Preparatory to starting, father was muzzling the dogs which had just finished what lunch we had left. This process, to which the dogs strongly objected, was rendered necessary by a cogent reason. Father had brought his strychnine flask with him that day, and in hopes of causing the death of a few dingoes, had put strong doses of its contents in several dead beasts which we had come across.

Whilst the dogs were being muzzled, I busied myself in plucking ferns and flowers. This disturbed a big black snake which was curled at the butt of a tree fern.

'Bitey! bitey!' I yelled, and father came to my rescue, despatching the reptile with his stock-whip. He had been smoking, and dropped his pipe on the ferns. I picked it up, and the glowing embers which fell from it burnt my dirty little fat fists. Hence the noise with which my story commences.

In all probability it was the burning of my fingers which so indelibly impressed the incident on my infantile mind. My father was accustomed to take me with him, but that is the only jaunt at that date which I remember, and that is all I remember of it. We were twelve miles from home, but how we reached there I do not know.

My father was a swell in those days – held Bruggabrong, Bin Bin East, and Bin Bin West, which three stations totalled close on 200,000 acres. Father was admitted into swelldom merely by right of his position. His pedigree included nothing beyond a grandfather. My mother, however, was a full-fledged aristocrat. She was one of the Bossiers of Caddagat, who numbered among their ancestry one of the depraved old pirates who pillaged England with William the Conqueror.

'Dick' Melvyn was as renowned for hospitality as joviality, and our comfortable, wide-veranda'ed, irregularly built, slab house in its sheltered nook amid the Timlinbilly Ranges was ever full to overflowing. Doctors, lawyers, squatters, commercial travellers, bankers, journalists, tourists, and men of all kinds and classes crowded our well-spread board; but seldom a female face, except mother's, was to be seen there, Bruggabrong being a very out-of-the-way place.

I was both the terror and the amusement of the station. Old boundary-riders and drovers inquire after me with interest to this day.

I knew everyone's business, and was ever in danger of publishing it at an inopportune moment.

In flowery language, selected from slang used by the station hands, and long words picked up from our visitors, I propounded

unanswerable questions which brought blushes to the cheeks of even
tough old wine-bibbers.

Nothing would induce me to show more respect to an appraiser of
the runs than to a boundary-rider, or to a clergyman than a drover. I
am the same to this day. My organ of veneration must be flatter than
a pancake, because to venerate a person simply for his position I
never did or will. To me the Prince of Wales will be no more than a
shearer, unless when I meet him he displays some personality apart
from his princeship – otherwise he can go hang.

Authentic record of the date when first I had a horse to myself has
not been kept, but it must have been early, as at eight I was fit to ride
anything on the place. Side-saddle, man-saddle, no-saddle, or astride
were all the same to me. I rode among the musterers as gamely as any
of the big sunburnt bushmen.

My mother remonstrated, opined I would be a great unwomanly
tomboy. My father poohed the idea.

'Let her alone, Lucy,' he said, 'let her alone. The rubbishing con-
ventionalities which are the curse of her sex will bother her soon
enough. Let her alone!'

So, smiling and saying, 'She should have been a boy,' my mother let
me alone, and I rode, and in comparison to my size made as much
noise with my stock-whip as any one. Accidents had no power over me,
I came unscathed out of droves of them.

Fear I knew not. Did a drunken tramp happen to kick up a row, I
was always the first to confront him, and, from my majestic and roly-
poly height of two feet six inches, demand what he wanted.

A digging started near us and was worked by a score of two dark-
browed sons of Italy. They made mother nervous, and she averred
they were not to be trusted, but I liked and trusted them. They carried
me on their broad shoulders, stuffed me with lollies and made a general pet of me. Without the quiver of a nerve I swung down their
deepest shafts in the big bucket on the end of a rope attached to a
rough windlass, which brought up the miners and the mullock.

My brothers and sisters contracted mumps, measles, scarlatina, and
whooping-cough. I rolled in the bed with them yet came off scot-free.
I romped with dogs, climbed trees after birds' nests, drove the bul-
locks in the dray, under the instructions of Ben, our bullocky, and
always accompanied my father when he went swimming in the clear,
mountain, shrub-lined stream which ran deep and alone among the
weird gullies, thickly carpeted with maidenhair and numberless other
species of ferns.

My mother shook her head over me and trembled for my future, but father seemed to consider me nothing unusual. He was my hero, confidant, encyclopedia, mate, and even my religion till I was ten. Since then I have been religionless.

Richard Melvyn, you were a fine fellow in those days! A kind and indulgent parent, a chivalrous husband, a capital host, a man full of ambition and gentlemanliness.

Amid these scenes, and the refinements and pleasures of Caddagat, which lies a hundred miles or so farther Riverinawards, I spent the first years of my childhood.

1902

Charlotte Mew

Charlotte Mew was born into a middle-class family in Bloomsbury, London, in 1869. A melancholy, eccentric-seeming figure, she and her sister, to whom she was exceptionally close, spent their lives under the terrifying threat of an inherited mental instability. After the death of her father, Mew helped support the impoverished family by writing; her early works were published in *The Yellow Book*. When her first innovative and powerful collection of poems, *The Farmer's Bride*, was published in 1916, it drew high praise from writers like Thomas Hardy, Virginia Woolf and May Sinclair (whom a besotted Mew once chased upstairs and round a bedroom, in a story Sinclair dined out on more than once). But it sold very few copies and in the end Mew treated her own work with cavalier disdain, using manuscript pages to light cigarettes with, and sending back her civil pension, which Hardy and other admiring writers had procured for her, because she felt she simply wasn't writing enough to deserve it. Charlotte Mew committed suicide, by drinking disinfectant, not long after the death of her sister, in London in 1928.

Virago published *The Collected Poems and Prose of Charlotte Mew*, edited by Val Warner, in 1981.

from

'In the Curé's Garden'

Idiscovered it in summer. I do not know what it is like in spring; golden with daffodils, perhaps, and haunted by hidden violets, walled in by lilac trees, and sweetened with the scent of may.

I can imagine it to be the first meeting-place of budding things, a garden of the resurrection, where the birds re-assemble to recapture last year's song, and mate again, and build their nests anew.

Then, when the trees are leafless, or just starting into bud, one must see the convent on the hill more plainly, and hear less clearly, above the birds' busy twitter, the bell tinkle across the fields. Then, in the skeleton poplar avenue, one may be able even to distinguish the figures of the good Sisters of our Lady of Compassion, as they pace slowly up and down. Today, one cannot catch a glimpse of them, but only now and then the outline of the distant walls, between green branches where they part.

In spring, Père Laurent says the garden has an air *plus béni, l'odeur plus fraîche, et plus consacré au repos.*

I can believe it; in these August days, the scents are heavy, insistent, almost over-sweet; the colours, fiercely brilliant, still more luminous at early twilight, in the narrow walks where among roses the carnations bloom. Was not their odour almost passionate? I asked him once, in one of our little discursive talks, and were they not *par excellence* the flowers of seduction and desire?

Par excellence, he agreed; adding that yet it was well they should be there, diffusing their distracting fragrance; they were reminders of the world, the flesh: *fleurs des sens, fantômes de la chair, toujours tentant et qui doivent toujours être crucifiées.*

This sultry afternoon, however, it was not Père Laurent whom I had come to see. I passed him in the village and he stopped me to say that I should assuredly find Anita, if I were bound that way; that she would 'make his amend' for absence, and if I were pleased to loiter, he would return later to smoke a pipe with me. I was content with the proposed 'amend'.

Though both could speak it (the Curé had taught Anita; where he himself had learned it I do not know), they 'loved not the English', and would sometimes slip suddenly for relief or emphasis into the more natural tongue.

'Ah,' Anita would cry, vainly seeking expression for a too subtle phrase, 'here is one of the things you cannot say. It suffices only that you think it; but in your language – truly a great one, but *lourd*, you pardon me? it is a thought *enterrée*; do you call it dumb?

I thrust open the little gate through which the Curé's mutinous flowers were pushing, peeping into the white forsaken road to catch the gallant glances of some passer-by. There were so few to pass, the truants might peer safely as Anita, who cared so much less than they for passers-by. At most, they would only encounter some straggling figure, following half-a-dozen dreamy cows; a straying child, or a boy whistling, who would smite their flushed faces as he went past them with his swinging hand. And later, towards evening, Père Laurent himself, leisurely walking homeward – a sombre figure, the last gleams of sunlight catching the silver buckles of his shoes.

The low white house of the Curé hid itself in summer-time behind the garden, modestly leaving welcome to the flowers. As I strolled in, I could see, beyond lines of pink and crimson blossom, the ponderous figure of Henriette taking in the clothes, which dry so quickly in this summer sun. Her voice disturbed the slumbrous stillness of the sunshine; she was singing in her unmelodious alto, *O que j'aime les militaires!*

I sat down on the little bench under the chestnut tree, where Père Laurent was wont to bring his books and smoke peacefully, till the twilight dimmed their pages, with Anita sitting smiling over her *méditations* by his side. I did not mean to seek her this afternoon; she was probably in the kitchen, devising some simple surprise for the Curé's evening meal. By-and-by she would saunter along the scented path and find me, and I awaited the child's greeting, the accustomed: 'Ah! it is you, monsieur? a thousand welcomes,' and the gracious wave of the little hand. How long was it, I began to wonder, since that little hand had held me here? Only a few weeks in fact, and yet it seemed for a sweet eternity that I had loitered in the Curé's garden, to learn how bare a place without Anita the wider world might be. I found, not indeed a thousand, but one generous welcome here; always the wish on Père Laurent's lips that I would remain so long as I was not weary, always a smile to second it from the happy, musing child.

A step stole softly up behind me, and the 'thousand welcomes' was in my ear.

'Where did you spring from?' I asked, springing up myself, as the girl before me rose and stood still as the sunshine under the green shade. 'I imagined you in the kitchen, helping or hindering Henriette, and you appear, like an angel, suddenly to disperse my earthly dreams.'

'Henriette is *méchante* today,' she explained; 'it is the washing that discomposes her. I have taken myself away.'

'That is not pretty in you; you should have more sympathy.'

'*Vous êtes bien sympathique*,' she returned, laughing, 'because you do not live always with Henriette.'

'Then if you are tired of Henriette, perhaps you are pleased to see me? I have no washing; I am prepared to be very gay.'

'Am I not always enchanted to see you?' she questioned simply.

'You are the friend of *le petit père*, and you speak of something new – something original; Henriette, all the days, and the years, says always the same. That wearies sometimes. *Dieu me pardonne!* Truly I have my meditations, and they do not tire, but sometimes – sometimes,' she said with a little gesture of unusual abandonment, 'it is too warm for them, I become confused; you understand?'

This little person of seventeen was curiously indifferent to her loveliness; the wonderful dreaming eyes had never lodged a conscious glance, the delicate fruit-like skin flushed only under the sun's too ardent gaze. She accepted what she called *un compliment* with the prettiest air of indulgence; it pleased the giver, it was therefore but natural she should be pleased.

Very early I had dispensed with *compliments*, and spoke with her more simply, choosing phrases fitted to a child.

'Yet you would be sorry,' I said, 'to lose Henriette, to go away from her; you would miss her scolding and her care?'

'Yes,' she admitted, 'I should be desolated; but', and her face took on a serious, almost exalted look, 'some day it may happen that it must be.'

'When you marry, perhaps?' I ventured. 'Perhaps she would not leave you; she would want to go with you.'

'That is not what I meant,' she said. 'It is not of marriage that I think.'

'In your meditations?'

'Truly no.'

'Is it then a forbidden thought?'

'*Une pensée défendue? Peut-être.*' She paused to consider, clasping her hands, glancing reflectively upwards at the motionless, dazzling sky.

'It is of the world,' she replied at last, 'which we do not figure to ourselves, *le petit père* and I.'

It was thus she always spoke of him, in distinction, as she had explained to me, from '*le grand Père, c'est Dieu*'. The two were inseparable in her thoughts; she included them habitually in every consideration; and though she had mentioned once, with a touch of hesitancy, '*un autre, bien différent; je ne l'ai jamais vu*', of him she never spoke again. What place he claimed in her musings, I could not conjecture, but it was clear and not remarkable that he was the least real of the three.

'Would you not like to see this world?' I asked at length, while she unclasped her hands and, seating herself on the bench beside me, took out a little book which she always carried, a tiny volume of devotions, bound in old morocco, and richly tooled in faded gold.

At my question she put it down, and faced me with one of her serenest smiles.

'It has not occupied my thoughts,' she said. 'Is it truly very beautiful? You must know, you who have seen it all.'

'It is not so beautiful as your garden,' I answered, returning the fresh interrogative glance; 'but it is full of faces, and voices, and wonderful churches with arches so high that your eyes grow tired in looking up at them; there are great *salons*, where ladies dance in marvellous costumes, and streets with tall houses, where carriages are always rolling up and down.'

'It is then a spectacle very amusing,' she conceded; 'but there would appear to be too much of distraction, too little of peace. Is it not so?'

Taking lightly one of the little hands lying upon her knee, 'Anita,' I said, 'if some one should offer to show it you really, would you like that? would you go?'

'*Véritablement?*' She had read no second meaning in my question, and looked into my eyes with frank, friendly negation. 'No, Monsieur Vidal, it would not be possible, it is not my destiny.'

1903

Gertrude Stein

———

Gertrude Stein was born in Pittsburgh in 1874. An experimenter, inventor and mentor of modernism and postmodernism, a re-maker of language, a modern original, she began writing her huge 1925 novel, *The Making of Americans*, as early as this draft in 1903, the year after she and her brother Leo moved from the USA to Paris. In France her literary salon, her friendships with artists like Picasso, Gauguin and Matisse, and her love of modern art, made not just for an extraordinarily prescient collection of twentieth-century work but for a writing style that took literal account of cubism and avant-gardism. Her love of art and her love for Alice B. Toklas, her partner, sustained her and her writing for nearly thirty years. A novelist, poet, essayist, dramatist and short-story writer, Stein made up her own genres. She died in 1946.

Virago published the first draft of *The Making of Americans* in *Fernhurst, Q.E.D. and Other Early Writings* in 1995.

from

The Making of Americans

The wedding time drew quickly on through all this sharp endeavour of making her new home just what it should be for her life to come. Julia thought more of her ideals these days than of her man and truly this man had meant to her always ideals rather than a creature to be known and loved. She had made him to herself as she was now to make her home an inharmonious unreality by bringing complicated natural tastes to the simplicities of fitness and of decoration of a self-digested older world.

I say again this was all twenty years ago before the passion for the simple line and toned green burlap on the wall and wooden panelling all classic and severe. But the moral force was making then as now in art all for the simple line, though then it had not come to be as now alas it is, that natural sense for gilding and white paint and complicated decoration in design all must be suppressed and thrust away and thus take from us all the last small hope that some day something real might spring from crudity and luxury of ornament. In those days there was still some freedom left to love elaboration in good workmanship and ornate rococoness of complication in design and all the houses of one's friends and new school rooms and settlements in slums and dining halls and city clubs had not yet taken on this modern sad resemblance to a college woman's college room.

Julia's new house was in arrangement a small edition of her mother's but here there were no bourgeois riches to be found. The parlor walls in place of light-blue silk brocade were covered with modern sombre tapestry, the ceiling all in tone, the chairs as near to good colonial as modern imitation can effect and all about dark aesthetic ornaments from China and Japan. Pictures there were none but carbon photographs closely framed in dull and wooden frames.

The dining room was without brilliancy in its aesthetic aspiration; the chairs were made after some old French fashion not very certain what and covered with dull tapestry copied without life from old designs, the room was generally all green with simple oaken woodwork underneath. The living room was a prevailing red, that certain shade of red, like that certain shade of green dull without hope the shade that so completely bodies forth the ethically aesthetic aspiration of the spare American emotion. Here were some more carbon photographs hung upon the wall sadly framed in painted wooden frames the etchings one or two of Whistler and of Seymour Haydon had not yet arrived, these were a later stage in decoration nor were there any prints upon the walls, nothing but photographs and family portraits of the elder Herslands. Built in couches and open book-cases and a fire place with really burning logs finished out the room.

These were triumphant days for Julia. Every day she led her family a new flight and they followed after agape with wonder disapproval and with pride. The mother began to lose all sense of her creation of this original and brilliant daughter and was almost ready to admit her obedience and defeat. She still resisted somewhat but was swollen visibly with admiration and with pride. The father who had always been convinced and proud even when he disapproved the opinions of his daughter, now took a solid satisfaction in the completeness of her resolution. After all to know well what one wanted and to win it for oneself by steady fighting was to him the best act that a man or woman could affect and well had his favourite daughter accomplished her end. He still shook his head at her literary notions as he called them and at all her new-fangled ways of doing things but he was so proud of her and of them all that his head shake carried even less conviction than before.

Bertha Dehning was always convinced and overcome by her brilliant elder sister though often slowly and with no great understanding of what it was about. The boy George admired and followed gladly with strong sympathy after his sister's lead and the little Hortense by herself worshipped from afar.

Altogether these last weeks were brilliant days for Julia.

But through all this pride in domination and in the admiration of her family and their friends there was always somewhere in the background of her sense a vague uncertainty of her understanding and

her right. She did not think much in these days about the man she
was to marry but she felt him somehow in her way, an unknown force
that might attack her unawares in spite of all the wisdom and experience of her life that she felt so strongly in her mind.

A few weeks before her marriage day Julia's diffuse and vague dis-
trust received a sharper edge. Hersland was talking of their life to
come, their prospects and his hopes. 'I've some good schemes, Julia
in my head,' he said, 'and I mean to do big things and with a safe man
like your father to back me through I think I can.' Julia somehow was
startled, 'What do you mean?' she said. 'Why,' he went on, 'I want to
do some things that have big money and big risks in them and a man
as well known as your father for wealth and reliability for a father-in-
law will do all that I need. Of course you know Julia,' he added simply
enough, 'you must not talk to him now about such things. You are my
wife now, my own darling and you and I will live our lives together
always loving and believing in the same good thing.'

He said it simply enough and he was safe. Julia would not speak of
such things to her father now. No torment of doubt, no certainty of
misery could bring her to such dubious questioning at this late date.
He was safe then, though very simply now, again and yet again he
helped to make that sharp uncertainty for her more dreadful and
more sure. He was in no wise different in his ways or in his talk than
he had always been only she seemed to see now as dying men are said
to see, clearly and freely things as they were and not as she had wished
them. Face to face with nakedness in the soul of a man poorly made
by God she shuddered and grew sick.

And then she would remember suddenly what she had really
thought he was and then she felt, she knew, that all that former
thought was truer, better judgment than this sudden sight and so she
dulled her momentary clearing mind and hugged her old illusions to
her breast.

'He didn't mean it like that,' she said over to herself, 'he couldn't
mean it like that. He only meant that papa will help him along in his
career and of course papa will. Oh I know he didn't really mean it like
that. Anyhow I will ask him what he really meant.'

She asked him then and he freely made her understand just what
it was he meant. It sounded better then, a little better as he told it
more at length but it left her a foreboding sense that perhaps the
world had meanings in it that would be hard for her to understand
and judge but now she had to think that it was all as it had a little
sounded good and best. She had to think it so else how could she

marry him and how could she not marry him. She had to marry him
and so she had to think it so and she would think it so and did.

In a few days more the actual marrying was done and their new life
together always doing things and learning things was at last begun.

1904

Violet Hunt

—————

Isobel Violet Hunt was born in Durham in 1862, daughter of the pre-Raphaelite painter A. W. Hunt and the novelist and suffrage supporter Margaret Raine Hunt. She grew up in aesthetic circles; her girlhood poems, for instance, were read for her by Christina Rossetti. Against her father's wishes (he wanted her to be a painter), she became a novelist, and was soon feted as a typical New Woman whose novels spoke frankly for their time about sexual politics and relationships. Her own too-well-publicised love affair with the married writer Ford Madox Ford brought her almost as much outraged scandal as her later books about the pre-Raphaelites.

   Hunt spent the modernist years working on the *English Review*, her books admired by friends like D. H. Lawrence, Rebecca West and Ezra Pound. She never married. Later in life, with Gaudier-Brzeska's huge sculpture of the head of Pound dominating the neighbourhood in her London front garden, and with a house full of beloved cats, she suffered the symptoms of advanced syphilis, and finally died in 1942.

from

The Celebrity at Home

This is the first time she has ever been in love, she says, and it hurts – women. It doesn't hurt a man who loves in vain, only clears up his ideas a little, and shows him the kind of girl he really does want when the first choice refuses him. A refusal from first choice only sends him straight off with his heart in his mouth to second choice, who is waiting for the chance of him. I am sure that is the way most marriages are made – hearts on the rebound. The first girl is a true benefactor to her species, and gets her fun and her practice into the bargain. Ariadne has now reduced this to a system, from novels. In refusing, you must remember to hope after you have said that it can never be, that you will at least always be friends. With regard to accepting, she thinks and I think, that the nicest way is to hide your burning face on the lapel of his coat and say nothing, and then when you come up again the rough stuff of his coat has made you blush, a thing neither Ariadne nor I have ever been able to manage for ourselves.

Novels tell you all sorts of things, for instance, when and what to resent, otherwise you might say thank you! for what is really an affront. Out on the Cliff Walk the other day, it came on to rain, and a man offered to lend Ariadne his umbrella, and see her to her own door. A harmless, nay useful proposal. But my sister knew – from novels – that that sort of thing leads to all sorts of wickedness, and that she must unconditionally, absolutely refuse. She was broken-hearted at having to sacrifice her best hat, but bravely bowed and refused his offer, and went off in the rain, feeling his disappointed eyes right through the back of her head, and hearing the plop-plop of the rain-drops on the crown of her hat all the way home. But she had behaved well. That was her consolation.

[. . .]

I am not quite sure that Simon can fall in love, it is the dull men who do that best, not the universal favourites. But if Simon has any love latent, I am anxious to get it all for Ariadne.

She hates herrings now, and doesn't care for cream. She lives principally on jam-tarts and cheese-cakes. It is the proper thing to go about eleven in the morning to that shop on the quay and eat tarts and cheese-cakes standing, and watch people pass, and the bridge opening and shutting to let tall funnels go through. Ariadne sometimes has to wade through half-a-dozen tarts before Simon and Lady Scilly and the dogs and the rest of them come round the corner of Flowergate, and surely it is a pity to spoil your complexion for the sake of any young man in the world? No digestion could stand the way Ariadne treats hers for long. She plays it very low down on her constitution generally. She won't go to bed till awfully late, but sits by the window telling her sorrow to the sea and the stars, and writing poems to the harbour-bar, that never moans that I know of. Luckily, as yet, it doesn't show in her face that she has been burning the midnight oil, or candles. She burns three short fours a night sometimes that she buys herself. She has made three pounds altogether by writing poems that Mr Aix puts in an American paper for her. She doesn't let Simon know that she publishes, for it would discredit her in his eyes. He says there's no harm in girls scribbling if they like, but he is jolly well glad his sister doesn't.

1905

Edith Wharton

———

Edith Wharton was born Edith Newbold Jones to rich parents in New York in 1862. She spent much of her childhood in Europe and was educated privately, could read French, German and Italian and was writing short novels and poems when she was in her teens. She married Teddy Wharton in 1885; they settled in France in 1907, but it was a difficult and thwarted marriage (he suffered all his life from bad mental health and she from nervous illnesses) and they divorced in 1913. After this she lived solely in Europe, visiting America only once more in 1923 to become the first woman ever to receive an honorary degree from Yale. She died in France in 1937.

Wharton published over twenty novels and novellas in her lifetime, and many short stories, as well as autobiography and non-fiction. Her first book, co-written with Ogden Codman Jr, was an analysis of taste, fashion and social mores, *The Decoration of Houses*, in 1897, and her first collection of short stories came out in 1899. *The House of Mirth* was her first bestseller.

Virago published *The House of Mirth* in 1990.

from

The House of Mirth

They turned into Madison Avenue and began to stroll northward. As she moved beside him, with her long light step, Selden was conscious of taking a luxurious pleasure in her nearness: in the modelling of her little ear, the crisp upward wave of her hair – was it ever so slightly brightened by art? – and the thick planting of her straight black lashes. Everything about her was at once vigorous and exquisite, at once strong and fine. He had a confused sense that she must have cost a great deal to make, that a great many dull and ugly people must, in some mysterious way, have been sacrificed to produce her. He was aware that the qualities distinguishing her from the herd of her sex were chiefly external: as though a fine glaze of beauty and fastidiousness had been applied to vulgar clay. Yet the analogy left him unsatisfied, for a coarse texture will not take a high finish; and was it not possible that the material was fine, but that circumstance had fashioned it into a futile shape?

As he reached this point in his speculations the sun came out, and her lifted parasol cut off his enjoyment. A moment or two later she paused with a sigh.

'Oh dear, I'm so hot and thirsty – and what a hideous place New York is!' She looked despairingly up and down the dreary thoroughfare. 'Other cities put on their best clothes in summer, but New York seems to sit in its shirt-sleeves.' Her eyes wandered down one of the side-streets. 'Some one has had the humanity to plant a few trees over there. Let us go into the shade.'

'I am glad my street meets with your approval,' said Selden as they turned the corner.

'Your street? Do you live here?'

She glanced with interest along the new brick and limestone house-fronts, fantastically varied in obedience to the American craving for novelty, but fresh and inviting with their awnings and flower-boxes.

'Ah, yes – to be sure: *The Benedick*. What a nice-looking building! I don't think I've ever seen it before.' She looked across at the flat-house with its marble porch and pseudo-Georgian façade. 'Which are your windows? Those with the awnings down?'

'On the top floor – yes.'

'And that nice little balcony is yours? How cool it looks up there!'

He paused a moment. 'Come up and see,' he suggested. 'I can give you a cup of tea in no time – and you won't meet any bores.'

Her colour deepened – she still had the art of blushing at the right time – but she took the suggestion as lightly as it was made.

'Why not? It's too tempting – I'll take the risk,' she declared.

'Oh, I'm not dangerous,' he said in the same key. In truth, he had never liked her as well as at that moment. He knew she had accepted without afterthought: he could never be a factor in her calculations, and there was a surprise, a refreshment almost, in the spontaneity of her consent.

On the threshold he paused a moment, feeling for his latch-key.

'There's no one here; but I have a servant who is supposed to come in the mornings, and it's just possible he may have put out the tea-things and provided some cake.'

He ushered her into a slip of a hall hung with old prints. She noticed the letters and notes heaped on the table among his gloves and sticks; then she found herself in a small library, dark but cheerful, with its walls of books, a pleasantly faded Turkey rug, a littered desk, and, as he had foretold, a tea-tray on a low table near the window. A breeze had sprung up, swaying inward the muslin curtains, and bringing a fresh scent of mignonette and petunias from the flower-box on the balcony.

Lily sank with a sigh into one of the shabby leather chairs.

'How delicious to have a place like this all to one's self! What a miserable thing it is to be a woman!' She leaned back in a luxury of discontent.

Selden was rummaging in a cupboard for the cake.

'Even women,' he said, 'have been known to enjoy the privileges of a flat.'

'Oh, governesses – or widows. But not girls – not poor, miserable, marriageable girls!'

'I even know a girl who lives in a flat.'

She sat up in surprise. 'You do?'

'I do,' he assured her, emerging from the cupboard with the sought-for cake.

'Oh, I know – you mean Gerty Farish.' She smiled a little unkindly. 'But I said *marriageable* – and besides, she has a horrid little place, and no maid, and such queer things to eat. Her cook does the washing and the food tastes of soap. I should hate that, you know.'

'You shouldn't dine with her on wash-days,' said Selden, cutting the cake.

They both laughed, and he knelt by the table to light the lamp under the kettle, while she measured out the tea into a little teapot of green glaze. As he watched her hand, polished as a bit of old ivory, with its slender pink nails, and the sapphire bracelet slipping over her wrist, he was struck with the irony of suggesting to her such a life as his cousin Gertrude Farish had chosen. She was so evidently the victim of the civilisation which had produced her, that the links of her bracelet seemed like manacles chaining her to her fate.

She seemed to read his thought. 'It was horrid of me to say that of Gerty,' she said with charming compunction. 'I forgot she was your cousin. But we're so different, you know: she likes being good, and I like being happy. And besides, she is free and I am not. If I were, I daresay I could manage to be happy even in her flat. It must be pure bliss to arrange the furniture just as one likes, and give all the horrors to the ash-man. If I could only do over my aunt's drawing-room I know I should be a better woman.'

'Is it so very bad?' he asked sympathetically.

She smiled at him across the teapot which she was holding up to be filled.

'That shows how seldom you come there. Why don't you come oftener?'

'When I do come, it's not to look at Mrs Peniston's furniture.'

'Nonsense,' she said. 'You don't come at all – and yet we get on so well when we meet.'

'Perhaps that's the reason,' he answered promptly. 'I'm afraid I haven't any cream, you know – shall you mind a slice of lemon instead?'

'I shall like it better.' She waited while he cut the lemon and dropped a thin disk into her cup. 'But that is not the reason,' she insisted.

'The reason for what?'

'For your never coming.' She leaned forward with a shade of perplexity in her charming eyes. 'I wish I knew – I wish I could make you out. Of course I know there are men who don't like me – one can tell that at a glance. And there are others who are afraid of me: they think I want to marry them.' She smiled up at him frankly. 'But I don't think you dislike me – and you can't possibly think I want to marry you.'

'No – I absolve you of that,' he agreed.

'Well, then—?'

He had carried his cup to the fireplace, and stood leaning against the chimney-piece and looking down on her with an air of indolent amusement. The provocation in her eyes increased his amusement – he had not supposed she would waste her powder on such small game; but perhaps she was only keeping her hand in; or perhaps a girl of her type had no conversation but of the personal kind. At any rate, she was amazingly pretty, and he had asked her to tea and must live up to his obligations.

'Well, then,' he said with a plunge, 'perhaps *that's* the reason.'

'What?'

'The fact that you don't want to marry me. Perhaps I don't regard it as such a strong inducement to go and see you.' He felt a slight shiver down his spine as he ventured this, but her laugh reassured him.

'Dear Mr Selden, that wasn't worthy of you. It's stupid of you to make love to me, and it isn't like you to be stupid.' She leaned back, sipping her tea with an air so enchantingly judicial that, if they had been in her aunt's drawing-room, he might almost have tried to disprove her deduction.

'Don't you see,' she continued, 'that there are men enough to say pleasant things to me, and that what I want is a friend who won't be afraid to say disagreeable ones when I need them? Sometime I have fancied you might be that friend. I don't know why, except that you are neither a prig nor a bounder, and that I shouldn't have to pretend with you or be on my guard against you.' Her voice had dropped to a note of seriousness, and she sat gazing up at him with the troubled gravity of a child.

'You don't know how much I need such a friend,' she said. 'My aunt is full of copy-book axioms, but they were all meant to apply to conduct in the early fifties. I always feel that to live up to them would include wearing book-muslin with gigot sleeves. And the other women – my best friends – well, they use me or abuse me; but they don't care a straw what happens to me. I've been about too long – people are getting tired of me; they are beginning to say I ought to marry.'

There was a moment's pause, during which Selden meditated one or two replies calculated to add a momentary zest to the situation; but he rejected them in favour of the simple question: 'Well, why don't you?'

She coloured and laughed. 'Ah, I see you *are* a friend after all, and that is one of the disagreeable things I was asking for.'

'It wasn't meant to be disagreeable,' he returned amicably. 'Isn't marriage your vocation? Isn't it what you're all brought up for?'

She sighed. 'I suppose so. What else is there?'

'Exactly. And so why not take the plunge and have it over?'

She shrugged her shoulders. 'You speak as if I ought to marry the first man who came along.'

'I didn't mean to imply that you are as hard put to it as that. But there must be some one with the requisite qualifications.'

She shook her head wearily. 'I threw away one or two good chances when I first came out – I suppose every girl does; and you know I am horribly poor – and very expensive. I must have a great deal of money.'

1906

E. Nesbit

———

Edith Nesbit was born in Dymchurch, Kent, in 1858. A tomboyish girl, she grew up with a healthy disrespect for convention, and married Hubert Bland when she was seven months pregnant. They were founder members of the Fabian Society, and in a life that swung dangerously close to poverty many times, Nesbit kept their increasingly bohemian family (complete with her own and Hubert's lovers, and not just her own children but the children of Hubert's mistresses) afloat with income from her journalism, from writing verses for greetings cards which she decorated, and from her fiction – she wrote her first novel, *The Prophet's Mantle*, jointly with Hubert in 1885. Her children's fiction finally made her enough money for comfort; since *The Railway Children* was first published in 1906, it has never been out of print. Regardless of her Fabian and bohemian lifestyle, Nesbit saw no use for women's suffrage (ripping off petticoats to stop the train is as far and as practical as she got when it came to women's emancipation), though she numbered among her friends the more vocal suffragists Charlotte Perkins Gilman and Olive Schreiner. Nesbit died of lung cancer in 1924.

from

The Railway Children

The mouth of the tunnel was some way from Three Chimneys, so Mother let them take their lunch with them in a basket. And the basket would do to bring the cherries back in if they found any. She also lent them her silver watch so that they should not be late for tea. Peter's Waterbury had taken it into its head not to go since the day when Peter dropped it into the water-butt. And they started. When they got to the top of the cutting, they leaned over the fence and looked down to where the railway lines lay at the bottom of what, as Phyllis said, was exactly like a mountain gorge.

'If it wasn't for the railway at the bottom, it would be as though the foot of man had never been there, wouldn't it?'

The sides of the cutting were of grey stone, very roughly hewn. Indeed, the top part of the cutting had been a little natural glen that had been cut deeper to bring it down to the level of the tunnel's mouth. Among the rocks, grass and flowers grew, and seeds dropped by birds in the crannies of the stone had taken root and grown into bushes and trees that overhung the cutting. Near the tunnel was a flight of steps leading down to the line – just wooden bars roughly fixed into the earth – a very steep and narrow way, more like a ladder than a stair.

'We'd better get down,' said Peter; 'I'm sure the cherries would be quite easy to get at from the side of the steps. You remember it was there we picked the cherry blossoms that we put on the rabbit's grave.'

So they went along the fence towards the little swing gate that is at the top of these steps. And they were almost at the gate when Bobbie said:

'Hush. Stop! What's that?'

'That' was a very odd noise indeed – a soft noise, but quite plainly to be heard through the sound of the wind in the branches, and the hum and whir of the telegraph wires. It was a sort of rustling, whispering sound. As they listened it stopped and then it began again.

And this time it did not stop, but it grew louder and more rustling and rumbling.

'Look' – cried Peter, suddenly – 'the tree over there!'

The tree he pointed at was one of those that have rough grey leaves and white flowers. The berries, when they come, are bright scarlet, but if you pick them, they disappoint you by turning black before you get them home. And, as Peter pointed, the tree was moving – not just the way trees ought to move when the wind blows through them, but all in one piece, as though it were a live creature and were walking down the side of the cutting.

'It's moving!' cried Bobbie. 'Oh, look! and so are the others. It's like the woods in *Macbeth*.'

'It's magic,' said Phyllis, breathlessly. 'I always knew the railway was enchanted.'

It really did seem a little like magic. For all the trees for about twenty yards of the opposite bank seemed to be slowly walking down towards the railway line, the tree with the grey leaves bringing up the rear like some old shepherd driving a flock of green sheep.

'What is it? Oh, what is it?' said Phyllis; 'it's much too magic for me. I don't like it. Let's go home.'

But Bobbie and Peter clung fast to the rail and watched breathlessly. And Phyllis made no movement towards going home by herself.

The trees moved on and on. Some stones and loose earth fell down and rattled on the railway metals far below.

'It's *all* coming down,' Peter tried to say, but he found there was hardly any voice to say it with. And, indeed, just as he spoke, the great rock, on the top of which the walking trees were, leaned slowly forward. The trees, ceasing to walk, stood still and shivered. Leaning with the rock, they seemed to hesitate a moment, and then rock and trees and grass and bushes, with a rushing sound, slipped right away from the face of the cutting and fell on the line with a blundering crash that could have been heard half a mile off. A cloud of dust rose up.

'Oh,' said Peter, in awestruck tones, 'isn't it exactly like when coals come in? – if there wasn't any roof to the cellar and you could see down.'

'Look what a great mound it's made!' said Bobbie.

'Yes, it's right across the down line,' said Phyllis.

'That'll take some sweeping up,' said Bobbie.

'Yes,' said Peter slowly. He was still leaning on the fence.

'Yes,' he said again, still more slowly.

Then he stood upright.

'The 11.29 down hasn't gone by yet. We must let them know at the station, or there'll be a most frightful accident.'

'Let's run,' said Bobbie, and began.

But Peter cried, 'Come back!' and looked at Mother's watch. He was very prompt and businesslike, and his face looked whiter than they had ever seen it.

'No time,' he said; 'it's ten miles away, and it's past eleven.'

'Couldn't we,' suggested Phyllis, breathlessly, 'couldn't we climb up a telegraph post and do something to the wires?'

'We don't know how,' said Peter.

'They do it in war,' said Phyllis; 'I know I've heard of it.'

'They only *cut* them, silly,' said Peter, 'and that doesn't do any good. And we couldn't cut them even if we got up, and we couldn't get up. If we had anything red, we could go down on the line and wave it.'

'But the train wouldn't see us till it got round the corner, and then it could see the mound just as well as us,' said Phyllis; 'better, because it's much bigger than us.'

'If we only had something red,' Peter repeated, 'we could go round the corner and wave to the train.'

'We might wave, anyway.'

'They'd only think it was just *us*, as usual. We've waved so often before. Anyway, let's get down.'

They got down the steep stairs. Bobbie was pale and shivering. Peter's face looked thinner than usual. Phyllis was red-faced and damp with anxiety.

'Oh, how hot I am!' she said; 'and I thought it was going to be cold; I wish we hadn't put on our –' she stopped short, and then ended in quite a different tone – 'our flannel petticoats.'

Bobbie turned at the bottom of the stairs.

'Oh, yes,' she cried, '*they're* red! Let's take them off.'

They did, and with the petticoats rolled up under their arms, ran along the railway, skirting the newly fallen mound of stones and rock and earth, and bent, crushed, twisted trees. They ran at their best pace. Peter led, but the girls were not far behind. They reached the corner that hid the mound from the straight line of railway that ran half a mile without curve or corner.

'Now,' said Peter, taking hold of the largest flannel petticoat.

'You're not' – Phyllis faltered – 'you're not going to *tear* them?'

'Shut up,' said Peter, with brief sternness.

'Oh, yes,' said Bobbie, 'tear them into little bits if you like. Don't you see, Phil, if we can't stop the train, there'll be a real live accident, with people *killed*. Oh, horrible! Here, Peter, you'll never tear it through the band!'

She took the red flannel petticoat from him and tore it off an inch from the band. Then she tore the other in the same way.

'There!' said Peter, tearing in his turn. He divided each petticoat into three pieces. 'Now, we've got six flags.' He looked at the watch again. 'And we've got seven minutes. We must have flagstaffs.'

The knives given to boys are, for some odd reason, seldom of the kind of steel that keeps sharp. The young saplings had to be broken off. Two came up by the roots. The leaves were stripped from them.

'We must cut holes in the flags, and run the sticks through the holes,' said Peter. And the holes were cut. The knife was sharp enough to cut flannel with. Two of the flags were set up in heaps of loose stones beneath the sleepers of the down line. Then Phyllis and Roberta took each a flag, and stood ready to wave it as soon as the train came in sight.

'I shall have the other two myself,' said Peter, 'because it was my idea to wave something red.'

'They're our petticoats, though,' Phyllis was beginning, but Bobbie interrupted.

'Oh, what does it matter who waves what, if we can only save the train?'

1907

Elinor Glyn

————

Elinor Glyn was born in Jersey in 1864 into comparative poverty, the daughter of a civil engineer. She was brought up in Canada by her aristocratic-minded French grandmother. Biographical dictionaries make much of Glyn's flaming red hair and searing green eyes, and her ability to make a truly dramatic entrance; she was, as she insisted, 'the first society woman to become a novelist'. When *Three Weeks* came out in 1907, the public went wild for its unheard-of daring mix of frankness, sex and intimacy. Five million copies sold and the novel was translated into nearly all European languages.

Glyn went to Hollywood, scripted, directed and appeared in many films (she created the It Girl blueprint for Clara Bow, taught Valentino how to really kiss a woman's hand – not on the back, but inside, in the palm), and was notorious for her salons, where she'd lie on a tiger skin much like the heroine of this provocative novel. Not content with simply being, as Sam Goldwyn said, 'synonymous with the discovery of sex appeal for the cinema', she worked as a war correspondent during the First World War, was one of the only two women present at the signing of the Treaty of Versailles, and came back to Britain after the war to open her own film company, for which she directed two sound movies. She died in 1943.

Virago published *Three Weeks* in 1996.

from

Three Weeks

'Now we will read fairy-tales, Paul.'

But Paul was too moved to speak. These rapid changes were too much for him, greatly advanced though he had become in these short days since he had known her. He leant back in his chair, every nerve in his body quivering, his young fresh face almost pale.

'Paul,' she cooed plaintively, 'to-morrow I shall be reasonable again, perhaps, and human, but to-day I am capricious and wayward, and mustn't be teased. I want to read about Cupid and Psyche from this wonderful "Golden Ass" of Apuleius – just a simple tale for a wet day – and you and – me!'

'Read then!' said Paul, resigned.

And she commenced in Latin, in a chanting, tender voice. Paul had forgotten most of the Latin he knew, but he remembered enough to be aware that this must be as easy as English to her as it flowed along in a rich rhythmic sound.

It soothed him. He seemed to be dreaming of flowery lands and running streams. After a while she looked up again, and then with one of her sudden movements like a graceful cat, she was beside him leaning from the back of his chair.

'Paul!' she whispered right in his ear, 'am I being wicked for you to-day? I cannot help it. The devil is in me – and now I must sing.'

'Sing then!' said Paul, maddened with again arising emotion.

She seized a guitar that lay near, and began in a soft voice in some language he knew not – a cadence of melody he had never heard, but one whose notes made strange quivers all up his spine. An exquisite pleasure of sound that was almost pain. And when he felt he could bear no more, she flung the instrument aside, and leant over his chair again – caressing his curls with her dainty fingers, and purring unknown strange words in his ear.

Paul was young and unlearned in many things. He was completely enthralled and under her dominion – but he was naturally no weakling of body or mind. And this was more than he could stand.

'*You* mustn't be teased. My God! it is you who are maddening me!' he cried, his voice hoarse with emotion. 'Do you think I am a statue, or a table, or chair – or inanimate like that tiger there? I am *not* I tell you!' and he seized her in his arms, raining kisses upon her which, whatever they lacked in subtlety, made up for in their passion and strength. 'Some day some man will kill you I suppose, but I shall be your lover – first!'

The lady gasped. She looked up at him in bewildered surprise, as a child might do who sets a light to a whole box of matches in play. What a naughty, naughty toy to burn so quickly for such a little strike!

But Paul's young, strong arms held her close, she could not struggle or move. Then she laughed a laugh of pure glad joy.

'Beautiful, savage Paul,' she whispered. 'Do you love me. Tell me that?'

'Love you!' he said. 'Good God! Love you! Madly, and you know it, darling Queen.'

'Then,' said the lady in a voice in which all the caresses of the world seemed melted, 'then, sweet Paul, I shall teach you many things, and among them I shall teach you how – to – LIVE.'

* * * * *

And outside the black storm made the darkness fall early. And inside the half-burnt logs tumbled together causing a cloud of golden sparks, and then the flames leapt up again and crackled in the grate.

1908

Jane and Mary Findlater

Mary Findlater was born in Lochearnhead, central Scotland, in 1865, and her sister Jane the year after. Their father was a Free Church minister and their mother a writer. The two sisters were so close that Mary chose to break her marriage engagement so as not to leave Jane; they saw themselves as 'halves of one whole'. Mary published a collection of poems in 1895, and Jane a well-received novel, *The Green Graves of Balgowrie*, the following year (she wrote it on old sheets of paper the local grocer didn't need, because the family was so poor after the death of their father).

The sisters went on to support their mother and sister on their combined writings, especially the three novels they produced together between 1908 and 1923; *Crossriggs* was the first of these. In 1904 they visited the USA, where they met William, Henry and Alice James, were entertained by Amy Lowell, dined with Frances Hodgson Burnett and preferred, they agreed, New England to New York.

They lived in Devon, Sussex and then Scotland again, and were rarely ever apart. After the First World War their work declined sharply in popularity. Jane died in 1946 and Mary outlived her by seventeen years, dying in 1963.

Virago published *Crossriggs* in 1986.

from

Crossriggs

About this time the exigencies of income made Alex place the whole household upon vegetarian diet. Mr Hope was delighted.

'We shall find health and happiness in it, dear Alex, I am persuaded; it is gratifying to see that you at last adopt my principles,' he said, and the girl smiled rather grimly, for with a searing wind blowing from the east, and bitter frost making hungry children ravenous, it seemed hardly the weather in which to begin a more ethereal diet. Matilda acquiesced in the new order a little reluctantly.

'I'm not quite sure how it will suit the children. *Can* cabbage be as nourishing as beef and mutton, in spite of all that dear Father says?' she hinted. 'Don't you think, Alex, that we might, just while the weather is so cold, run an account with the butcher?'

To this suggestion Alex would not pay heed for an instant.

'No – if we can't pay, we don't eat,' she said doggedly.

'But, my dear, consider the children,' Matilda objected.

'I don't care. We must try them on this sort of food, and if it hurts them I'll see if I can get a situation of some kind, that's all I can do, only, whatever happens, we mustn't get into debt.'

Matilda rather doubtfully agreed to this, and the vegetarian dinners were begun. They were not a success. The children, accustomed to lavish Canadian meals, did not approve of this simple diet, and in spite of all their mother's admonitions could not quite hide their feelings. One bitter day in January the family meal was little short of a tragedy. The cereal which formed its main constituent happened to be singed, and singed cereal is not very nice.

Poor little Mike, who was too young to speak anything but the whole truth, laid down his spoon and said plaintively, 'I want meat, please,' while the other children, after one pleading glance at their mother, gulped down the singed porridge with an expression of disgust. When dessert came they bit into their frozen apples with little squeals of pain, and tears were rapidly coming, when Alex made a timely suggestion that the apples might be roasted on strings before the fire. This saved the situation, though Old Hopeful protested that the 'raw juices' were much more beneficial. Alex produced a ball of twine, and made wonderful arrangements with hat-pins stuck into the old wooden mantelpiece, so that soon a row of apples was rotating before the fire, the sap bubbling with a delicious smell, while the children squatted on the hearthrug to watch.

'Oh, dear me!' Alex sighed, 'this isn't at all a successful day's feeding.'

She felt anxious and depressed as she watched the now happy children, who had already, with the blessedly short memory of childhood, forgotten all about the singed porridge.

'I'm going out, Matilda,' said Alex, rather abruptly, 'going alone, so you'll have to look after the chicks by yourself to-day.'

Matilda looked at her in surprise. 'Why, what mysterious errand are you going on?' she asked.

Alex did not answer, and left the room a few minutes later.

She went out, and took the solitary road which lies to the north of Crossriggs. In old coaching days this was one of the highways between England and Scotland, and many a merry coachload had passed along it. Now it is but little used; one may walk for a mile without meeting anything more interesting than a string of farm carts or a ploughman with his team.

It was a bitter afternoon, yet when Alex had walked for about a mile she sat down on one of the low dykes by the roadside, apparently forgetting the cold. Her thoughts were busy with something else, and suddenly she exclaimed aloud – 'I can't! I can't!' as if she were rejecting some suggestion that had come to her.

The sound of her own voice in that solitary place startled her. She looked up and shivered. The wind soughed across the empty fields with the low, gurgling note of winter's breath. She rose and stood wringing her hands together, as if in an agony of uncertainty. The next moment she began to walk swiftly along the road in the direction of Foxe Hall.

At the avenue gate she stopped and fumbled with the lock – turned back, as if uncertain whether to go through the gate, then opened it, and began to walk even more quickly along the dark, tree-bordered road. Once in sight of the house, however, Alex paused, and came up to the door in a more dignified manner.

She was going to call on Admiral Cassilis, though by this time she had almost got the length of praying that he should not be at home.

'Now then, Alexandra Hope, remember Cranmer or Latimer, or whoever it was, who said in the flames, *Play the man!* That's what you have to do!' she admonished herself.

The Admiral was at home. Alex followed the butler through the hall, where a large fire was burning – quite unnecessarily large, she thought bitterly, for there were not five little cold children squatting round it roasting apples on strings. 'If we only had fires like that at home!' she sighed.

'Miss Hope, sir,' the servant said, ushering her into the Admiral's study. Like the hall, the room was deliciously warm, and there was a pleasant scent of flowers in the air.

The Admiral did not smoke, and he was feverishly particular, so there was an indescribable atmosphere, perceptible only to the housekeeping sense of a woman, that meant well-kept rooms where dusting and cleaning go on continually. Alex was keenly sensitive to the beautiful side of life; even as she crossed the floor to greet the old man, she said to herself, 'How wonderfully soothing it must be to live in a well-kept house – heigh-ho for the dust and shabbiness and age of everything we possess – nothing fresh and delicious like this! But oh, it's ugly enough as far as taste goes!'

The Admiral rose to meet her, and stood with a hand on the back of his chair, afraid to step forward without guidance.

The dependence of the attitude struck Alex in a moment and smote her conscience.

'Fancy feeling envious of him – I who have such an excellent pair of eyes!' she thought.

The Admiral wore an expression of no small astonishment, though he said genially enough that he was glad to see her. Alex sat down, and without giving herself time to hesitate dashed at her subject.

'Yes, I'm glad you happened to be at home,' she said, 'for I've come to see you about business. I wondered if you really did want some one to read to you, because I know a person who would be glad to undertake to do so.'

'Ah – umph, I'm sure you're very kind to have remembered me,' the old man began, stroking down his stock and fingering his pearl pin as usual. 'But between ourselves, I fear that any person from the village would annoy me by provincialities of accent, faults of elocution, and so on. The fact is that I am particular about such matters. I like an educated voice – foolish perhaps – but the pleasure of hearing is one of the few still left to me, and it is essential to my enjoyment of reading aloud that I should hear the voice of an educated person. When my good William reads to me it is a continual annoyance to listen to his enunciation. You understand?'

'Yes, perfectly. This person I speak of *is* educated; has been very carefully taught to read aloud.'

'Then I am afraid the remuneration I am prepared to give would seem insufficient. Men of education, of course, naturally look for a good return for their talents. The fact is that I want a good thing cheap, Miss Hope – a difficult thing to get!' He laughed a dry old laugh as he spoke.

'I hope you don't mind my having asked you about it?' said Alex.

'Not at all – not in the least. The only hesitation I feel is about the quality of the reading. Have you heard this young person yourself?'

'No; but my Father, who is a great critic of elocution, has, and is quite satisfied.'

'Well, perhaps the young man would be willing to come up and let me hear him. But why is he anxious to get such a small unremunerative post? I trust he has no bad habits necessitating a stay in a quiet neighbourhood like ours?'

Alex laughed suddenly and merrily at this suggestion, and the laugh helped her.

'Might I ask, supposing the reader suited you, how much you would be prepared to give?'

'Hum – let me see. I had scarcely gone into the subject so exactly. What would he say to a shilling an hour, two hours a day?'

'Would you think two and sixpence a day too much?' Alex asked. Her voice trembled; this was dreadful.

The Admiral tried a little mental arithmetic before he answered, and in the meanwhile Alex sat holding on to the arms of her chair in desperate suspense.

'Well, two and sixpence a day – not a very large sum if the right person were to appear,' he announced at last. 'But who is the young man? You have not mentioned his name.'

Alex clenched her cold hands together and took the plunge.

'I will not keep you in the dark any longer,' she said. 'I was going to offer my own services; not that I am a very good thing, perhaps, but I want very much to earn a little money;' she paused, and tried to steady her trembling voice.

1909

Susan Glaspell

———

Susan Glaspell was born in Davenport, Iowa, the daughter of pioneer settlers, in 1876. Best known for her dramas, for starting New York's little-theatre movement and for founding the Provincetown Players with her husband George Cook and the playwright Eugene O'Neill, she began her writing career with fiction. *The Glory of the Conquered* was her first novel, a melodrama concerning the marriage of art, science and all-consuming love. She won the 1930 Pulitzer Prize for her play *Alison's House*, and was a tireless examiner, in all she wrote, of the conflict between personal desires, un-ideal realities and idealistic social values. She died in 1948.

from

The Glory of the Conquered

Georgia was to be married. It was the week before Christmas, and on the last day of the year she would become Mrs Joseph Tank. She had told Joe that if they were to be married at all they might as well get it over with this year, and still there was no need of being married any earlier in the year than was necessary. She assured him that she married him simply because she was tired of having paper bags waved before her eyes everywhere she went, and she thought if she were once officially associated with him people would not flaunt his idiosyncrasies at her that way. And then Ernestine approved of getting married, and Ernestine's ideas were usually good. To all of which Joe responded that she certainly had a splendid head to figure it out that way. Joe said that to his mind reasons for doing things weren't very important anyhow; it was doing them that counted.

Yesterday had been her last day on the paper. She had felt queer about that thing of taking her last assignment, though it was hard to reach just the proper state, for the last story related to pork-packers, and pork-packing is not a setting favourable to sentimental regrets. It was just like the newspaper business not even to allow one a little sentimental harrowing over one's exodus from it. But the time for gentle melancholy came later on, when she was sorting her things at her desk just before leaving, and was wondering what girl would have that old desk – if they cared to risk another girl, and whether the other poor girl would slave through the years she should have been frivolous, only to have some man step in at the end and induce her to surrender the things she had gained through sacrifice and toil. As she wrote a final letter on her typewriter – she did hate letting the old machine go – Georgia did considerable philosophizing about the irony of working for things only to the end of giving them up. She had waded through snowdrifts and been drenched in pouring rains, she had been frozen with the cold and prostrated with the heat, she had been blown about by Chicago wind until it was strange there was any of her left in one piece, she had had front doors – yes, and back doors too – slammed in her face, she had been the butt of the alleged wit of menials and hirelings, she had been patronized by vapid women as the poor girl who must make her living some way, she had been roasted by – but never mind – she had had a beat or two! And now she was to wind it all up by marrying Joseph Tank, who had made a great deal of money out of the manufacture of paper bags. This from her – who had always believed she would end her days in New York, or perhaps write a realistic novel exposing some mighty evil!

1910s

1910

Henry Handel Richardson

———

Ethel Florence Lindesay Richardson was born in Melbourne, Australia, in 1870. After her father's death, her mother sent her to a Presbyterian ladies' college, the experience of which later became this celebrated 1910 novel. In 1888 the family moved to Germany so that Richardson could study music in Leipzig, where she read Freud and absorbed the contemporary musical and intellectual stimuli, but eventually found that writing brought her more success. She chose to be pseudonymously male precisely because she wanted her novels 'to be considered masculine'. Her first novel, *Maurice Guest* (1908), explored gender reversal and was courageously experimental in form and in frankness; she wrote her acclaimed trilogy *The Fortunes of Richard Mahoney* between 1917 and 1929 and was Nobel Prize nominee in 1932.

She had moved to London in 1904 with her husband, J. G. Robertson, the first professor of German literature at the University of London; after his death in 1933 she moved to Sussex. Reclusive, and sustained by her lifelong interest in spiritualism, she began an auto-biography which was left unfinished at her death in 1946.

Virago published *The Getting of Wisdom* in 1981.

from

The Getting of Wisdom

My dear mother

I sent you a postcard did you get it. I told you I got here all right and liked it very much. I could not write a long letter before I had no time and we are only alowed to write letters two evenings a week Tuesday and Friday. When we have done our lessons for next day we say please may I write now and Miss Chapman says have you done everything and if we say we have she says yes and if you sit at Miss Days table Miss Day says it. And sometimes we haven't but we say so. I sit up by Miss Chapman and she can see everything I do and at tea and dinner and breakfast I sit beside Mrs Gurley. Another girl in my class sits opposite and one sits beside me and we would rather sit somewhere else. I dont care for Mrs Gurley much she is very fat and never smiles and never listens to what you say unless she scolds you and I think Miss Chapman is afraid of her to. Miss Day is not afraid of anybody. I am in the first class. I am in the College and under that is the school. Only very little girls are in the school they go to bed at half past eight and do their lessons in the dining hall. I do mine in the study and go to bed with the big girls. They wear dresses down to the ground. Lilith Gordon is a girl in my class she is in my room to she is only as old as me and she wears stays and has a beautiful figgure. All the girls wear stays. Please send me some I have no waste. A governess sleeps in our room and she has no teeth. She takes them out every night and puts them in water when the light is out. Lilith Gordon and the other girl say goodnight to her after she has taken them off then she cant talk propperly and we want to hear her. I think she knows for she is very cross. I don't learn latin yet till I go into the second class my sums are very hard. For supper there is only bread and butter and water if we don't have cake and jam of our own. Please send me some strawberry jam and another cake. Tell Sarah there are three servants to

*wait at dinner they have white aprons and a cap on their heads. They say will
you take beef miss*

I remain
your loving daughter
Laura.

Dear Pin

    *I am very busy I will write you a letter. You would not like being here I think
you should always stop at home you will never get as far as long division. Mrs
Gurley is an awful old beast all the girls call her that. You* WOULD *be frightened
of her. In the afternoon after school we walk two and two and you ask a girl to
walk with you and if you dont you have to walk with Miss Chapman. Miss
Chapman and Miss Day walks behind and they watch to see you dont laugh
at boys. Some girls write letters to them and say they will meet them up behind
a tree in the corner of the garden a paling is lose and the boys put letters in. I
think boys are silly but Maria Morell says they are tip top that means awfully
jolly. She writes a letter to boys every week she takes it to church and drops it
coming out and he picks it up and puts an answer through the fence. We put
out letters on the mantlepiece in the dining hall and Mrs Gurley or Miss
Chapman read the adress to see we dont write to boys. They are shut up she
cant read the inside. I hope you dont cry so much at school no one cries. Now
Miss Chapman says it is time to stop*

I remain
your afectionate sister
Laura.

    P.S. I took the red lineing out of my hat.

Warrenega
Sunday.

My dear Laura

    *We were very glad to get your letters which came this morning. Your postcard
written the day after you arrived at the College told us little or nothing. However
Godmother was good enough to write us an account of your arrival so that we
were not quite without news of you. I hope you remembered to thank her for driving in all that way to meet you and take you to school which was very good of
her. I am glad to hear you are settling down and feeling happy and I hope you
will work hard and distinguish yourself so that I may be proud of you. But there
are several things in your letters I do not like. Did you really think I shouldnt
read what you wrote to Pin. You are a very foolish girl if you did. Pin the silly
child tried to hide it away because she knew it would make me cross but I*

insisted on her showing it to me and I am ashamed of you for writing such non-sense to her. Maria Morell must be a very vulgar minded girl to use the expressions she does. I hope my little girl will try to only associate with nice minded girls. I didnt sent you to school to get nasty ideas put into your head but to learn your lessons well and get on. If you write such vulgar silly things again I shall complain to Mrs Gurley or Mr Strachey about the tone of the College and what goes on behind their backs. I think it is very rude of you too to call Mrs Gurley names. Also about the poor governess who has to wear false teeth. Wait till all your own teeth are gone and then see how you will like it. I do want you to have nice feelings and not grow rough and rude. There is evidently a very bad tone among some of the girls and you must be careful in choosing your friends. I am sorry to hear you are only in the lowest class. It would have pleased me better if you had got into the second but I always told you you were lazy about your sums – you can do them well enough if you like. You dont need stays. I have never worn them myself and I dont intend you to either. Your own muscles are quite strong enough to bear the weight of your back. Bread and water is not much of a supper for you to go to bed on. I will send you another cake soon and some jam and I hope you will share it with the other girls. Now try and be sensible and industrious and make nice friends and then I shant have to scold you

your loving mother
J.T.R.

P.S. Another thing in your letter I dont like. You say you tell your governess you have finished your lessons when you have not done so. That is telling an untruth and I hope you are not going to be led away by the examples of bad girls. I have always brought you children up to be straightforward and I am astonished at you beginning fibbing as soon as you get away from home. Fibbing soon leads to something worse.

P.P.S. You must have written your letter in a great hurry for your spelling is anything but perfect. You are a very naughty girl to meddle with your hat. Pin has written a letter which I enclose though her spelling is worse than ever.

Dear Laura

mother says you are a very sily girl to rite such sily letters I think you are sily to I shood be fritened of Mrs Girly I dont want to go to Skool I wood rather stop with mother and be a cumfert to her I think it is nauty to drop letters in Cherch and verry sily to rite to Boys boys are so sily Sarah sends her luv she says she wood not ware a cap on her hed not for annything she says She wood just as soon ware a ring thrugh her nose.

I remain
your luving sister
Pin.

Dear mother

*please please dont write to Mrs Gurley about the Tone in the College or not
to Mr Strachey either. I will never be so silly again. I am sorry my letters were
so silly I wont do it again. Please dont write to them about it. I dont go much
with Maria Morell now I think she is vulger to. I know two nice girls now in
my own class their names are Inez and Bertha they are very nice and not at all
vulger. Maria Morell is fat and has a red face she is much older than me and
I dont care for her now. Please dont write to Mrs Gurley I will never call her
names again. I had to write my letter quickly because when I have done my lessons it is nearly time for supper. I am sorry my spelling was wrong I will take
more pains next time I will learn hard and get on and soon I will be in the
second class. I did not mean I said I had done my lessons when I had not done
them the other girls say it and I think it is very wrong of them. Please dont write
to Mrs Gurley I will try and be good and sensible and not do it again if you
only wont write.*

> *I remain*
> > *your afectionate daughter*
> > *Laura.*

P.S. I can do my sums better now.

> *Warrenega*

My dear Laura

*My letter evidently gave you a good fright and I am not sorry to hear it for
I think you deserved it for being such a foolish girl. I hope you will keep your
promise and not do it again. Of course I dont mean that you are not to tell me
everything that happens at school but I want you to only have nice thoughts
and feelings and grow into a wise and sensible girl. I am not going to write a
long letter today. This is only a line to comfort you and let you know that I
shall not write to Mrs Gurley or Mr Strachey as long as I see that you are being
a good girl and getting on well with your lessons. I do want you to remember
that you are a lady though you are poor and must behave in a ladylike way.
You dont tell me what the food at the College is like and whether you have blankets enough on your bed at night. Do try and remember to answer the questions
I ask you. Sarah is busy washing today and the children are helping her by sitting with their arms in the tubs. I am to tell you from Pin that Maggy is
moulting badly and has not eaten much since you left which is just three weeks
today*

> *your loving*
> > *Mother.*

Friday

My dear mother

 I was so glad to get your letter I am so glad you will not write to Mrs Gurley this time and I will promise to be very good and try to remember everything you tell me. I am sorry I forgot to answer the questions I have two blankets on my bed and it is enough. The food is very nice for dinner for tea we have to eat a lot of bread and butter I dont care for bread much. Sometimes we have jam but we are not alowed to eat butter and jam together. A lot of girls get up at six and go down to practice they dont dress and have their bath they just put on their dressing gowns on top of their night gowns. I dont go down now till seven I make my own bed. We have prayers in the morning and the evening and prayers again when the day scholers come. I do my sums better now I think I shall soon be in the second class. Pins spelling was dreadfull and she is nearly nine now and is such a baby the girls would laugh at her.

       I remain
        your afectionate daughter
        Laura.

 P.S. I parssed a long sentence without any mistakes.

1911

Willa Cather

Willa Cather was born in Back Creek, Virginia, in 1873 into a farming family. When she was a child they moved to the wild west, to a ranch in Nebraska; Cather graduated from the University of Nebraska at nineteen and began teaching, writing journalism and editing *McClure's Magazine*. In 1911 she began her first novel, *Alexander's Bridge*, in serial form; it was published the year after. From then on she produced an astonishing range of novels, short stories, essays and poetry (her first book of poems had been published in 1903), all of which fast established her as one of the twentieth century's great American writers; novels like *O Pioneers!*, *My Ántonia*, *A Lost Lady* and *The Professor's House* built and sustained this reputation.

Although Cather herself was later a little scathing about early work like *Alexander's Bridge*, it represents well her romantic marriage of civilisation and exploration, and her complex views of the doomed relation between smoky old European and pure new American romanticisms.

Cather lived for much of her life with her companion Edith Lewis, and died in New York in 1947.

Virago published *Alexander's Bridge* in 1990.

from

Alexander's Bridge

It was a warm, smoky evening, and there was a grimy moon. He went through Covent Garden to Oxford Street, and as he turned into Museum Street he walked more slowly, smiling at his own nervousness as he approached the sullen grey mass at the end. He had not been inside the Museum, actually, since he and Hilda used to meet there; sometimes to set out for gay adventures at Twickenham or Richmond, sometimes to linger about the place for a while and to ponder by Lord Elgin's marbles upon the lastingness of some things, or, in the mummy room, upon the awful brevity of others. Since then Bartley had always thought of the British Museum as the ultimate repository of mortality, where all the dead things in the world were assembled to make one's hour of youth the more precious. One trembled lest before he got out it might somehow escape him, lest he might drop the glass from over-eagerness and see it shivered on the stone floor at his feet. How one hid his youth under his coat and hugged it! And how good it was to turn one's back upon all that vaulted cold, to take Hilda's arm and hurry out of the great door and down the steps into the sunlight among the pigeons – to know that the warm and vital thing within him was still there and had not been snatched away to flush Cæsar's lean cheek or to feed the veins of some bearded Assyrian king. They in their day had carried the flaming liquor, but to-day was his! So the song used to run in his head those summer mornings a dozen years ago. Alexander walked by the place very quietly, as if he were afraid of waking some one.

He crossed Bedford Square and found the number he was looking for. The house, a comfortable, well-kept place enough, was dark except for the four front windows on the second floor, where a low, even light was burning behind the white muslin sash curtains. Outside there were window boxes, painted white and full of flowers. Bartley was making a third round of the Square when he heard the far-flung hoof-beats of a hansom cab horse, driven rapidly. He looked at his watch, and was astonished to find that it was a few minutes after twelve. He turned and walked back along the iron railing as the cab came up to Hilda's number and stopped. The hansom must have been one that she employed regularly, for she did not stop to pay the driver. She stepped out quickly and lightly. He heard her cheerful 'Good-night, cabby,' as she ran up the steps and opened the door with a latchkey. In a few moments the lights flared up brightly behind the white curtains, and as he walked away he heard a window raised. But he had gone too far to look up without turning round. He went back to his hotel, feeling that he had had a good evening, and he slept well.

1912

Ethel M. Dell

Ethel M. Dell was born in Streatham, south London, in 1881, the younger daughter of a life-assurance salesman, and lived in Sevenoaks and Guildford for most of her life. She wrote as a child and adolescent, but it wasn't until she was in her thirties and after several rejections that her first book, *The Way of an Eagle*, was published. It was an immediate bestseller, reprinted twenty-seven times in the first two years, and she followed it with another thirty-six very successful sellers, most of them featuring black-hearted villains, tough-jawed, only slightly sadistic, chivalric heroes, and heroines who thrilled, panted and trembled to exactly this combination. The cocktail of desire and responsibility in her fiction, its reinforced social hierarchies, slightly risqué passion and inevitable happy endings, made her books immensely popular in the war years and after – there were reprints of many of her novels well into the 1950s.

Her writing made her wealthy, and since wealth left her uneasy, she gave away most of it to her family. She aptly married G. T. Savage, a lieutenant-colonel in the Royal Army Service Corps, lived quietly in the Home Counties surrounded by dogs, cars and her beloved gardens, and died in 1939.

Virago published *The Way of an Eagle* in 1996.

from

The Way of an Eagle

Suddenly, in short, painful tones the Brigadier began to speak.
'Sit down,' he said. 'I have sent for you to ask one among you to
undertake for me a certain service which must be accomplished, but
which I – ' he paused and again audibly caught his breath between his
teeth – 'which I – am unable to execute for myself.'

An instant's silence followed the halting speech. Then the young
officer who stood against the door stepped briskly forward.

'What's the job, sir? I'll wager my evening skilly I carry it through.'

One of the men in the shadows moved, and spoke in a repressive
tone. 'Shut up, Nick! This is no mess-room joke.'

Nick made a sharp, half-contemptuous gesture.

'A joke only ceases to be a joke when there is no one left to laugh,
sir,' he said. 'We haven't come to that at present.'

He stood in front of the Brigadier for a moment – an insignificant
figure but for the perpetual suggestion of simmering activity that per-
vaded him; then stepped behind the commanding officer's chair, and
there took up his stand without further words.

The Brigadier paid no attention to him. His mind was fixed upon
one subject only. Moreover, no one ever took Nick Ratcliffe seriously.
It seemed a moral impossibility.

'It is quite plain to me,' he said heavily at length, 'that the time has
come to face the situation. I do not speak for the discouragement of
you brave fellows. I know that I can rely upon each one of you to do
your duty to the utmost. But we are bound to look at things as they
are, and so prepare for the inevitable. I for one am firmly convinced
that General Bassett cannot possibly reach us in time.'

He paused, but no one spoke. The man behind him was leaning forward, listening intently.

He went on with an effort. 'We are a mere handful. We have dwindled to four white men among a host of dark. Relief is not even within a remote distance of us, and we are already bordering upon starvation. We may hold out for three days more. And then' – his breath came suddenly short, but he forced himself to continue – 'I have to think of my child. She will be in your hands. I know you will all defend her to the last ounce of your strength; but which of you' – a terrible gasping checked his utterance for many labouring seconds; he put his hand over his eyes – 'which of you,' he whispered at last, his words barely audible, 'will have the strength to – shoot her before your own last moment comes?'

The question quivered through the quiet room as if wrung from the twitching lips by sheer torture. It went out in silence – a dreadful, lasting silence in which the souls of men, stripped naked of human convention, stood confronting the first primæval instinct of human chivalry.

It continued through many terrible seconds – that silence, and through it no one moved, no one seemed to breathe. It was as if a spell had been cast upon the handful of Englishmen gathered there in the deepening darkness.

The Brigadier sat bowed and motionless at the table, his head sunk in his hands.

Suddenly there was a quiet movement behind him and the spell was broken. Ratcliffe stepped deliberately forward and spoke.

'General,' he said quietly, 'if you will put your daughter in my care, I swear to you, so help me God, that no harm of any sort shall touch her.'

There was no hint of emotion in his voice, albeit the words were strong; but it had a curious effect upon those who heard it. The Brigadier raised his head sharply, and peered at him; and the other two officers started as men suddenly stumbling at an unexpected obstacle in a familiar road.

One of them, Major Marshall, spoke, briefly, and irritably, with a touch of contempt. His nerves were on edge in that atmosphere of despair.

'You, Nick!' he said. 'You are about the least reliable man in the garrison. You can't be trusted to take even reasonable care of yourself. Heaven only knows how it is you weren't killed long ago. It was thanks to no discretion on your part. You don't know the meaning of the word.'

Nick did not answer, did not so much as seem to hear. He was standing before the Brigadier. His eyes gleamed in his alert face – two weird pin-points of light.

'She will be safe with me,' he said, in a tone that held not the smallest shade of uncertainty.

But the Brigadier did not speak. He still searched young Ratcliffe's face as a man who views through field-glasses a region distant and unexplored.

After a moment the officer who had remained silent throughout came forward a step and spoke. He was a magnificent man with the physique of a Hercules. He had remained on his feet, impassive but observant, from the moment of his entrance. His voice had that soft quality peculiar to some big men.

'I am ready to sell my life for Miss Roscoe's safety, sir,' he said.

Nick Ratcliffe jerked his shoulders expressively, but said nothing. He was waiting for the General to speak. As the latter rose slowly, with evident effort, from his chair, he thrust out a hand, as if almost instinctively offering help to one in sore need.

General Roscoe grasped it and spoke at last. He had regained his self-command. 'Let me understand you, Ratcliffe,' he said. 'You suggest that I should place my daughter in your charge. But I must know first how far you are prepared to go to ensure her safety.'

He was answered instantly, with an unflinching promptitude he had scarcely expected.

'I am prepared to go to the uttermost limit, sir,' said Nicholas Ratcliffe, his fingers closing like springs upon the hand that gripped his, 'if there is a limit. That is to say, I am ready to go through hell for her. I am a straight shot, a cool shot, a dead shot. Will you trust me?'

His voice throbbed with sudden feeling. General Roscoe was watching him closely. 'Can I trust you, Nick?' he said.

There was an instant's silence, and the two men in the background were aware that something passed between them – a look or a rapid sign – which they did not witness. Then reckless and debonair came Nick's voice.

'I don't know, sir. But if I am untrustworthy, may I die to-night!'

General Roscoe laid his free hand upon the young man's shoulder. 'Is it so, Nick?' he said, and uttered a heavy sigh. 'Well – so be it then. I trust you.'

'That settles it, sir,' said Nick cheerily. 'The job is mine.'

He turned round with a certain arrogance of bearing, and walked to the door. But there he stopped, looking back through the darkness at the dim figures he had left.

'Perhaps you will tell Miss Roscoe that you have appointed me deputy-governor,' he said. 'And tell her not to be frightened, sir. Say I'm not such a bogey as I look, and that she will be perfectly safe with me.' His tone was half-serious, half-jocular. He wrenched open the door, not waiting for a reply.

'I must go back to the guns,' he said, and the next moment was gone, striding carelessly down the passage, and whistling a music-hall ballad as he went.

1913

F. M. Mayor

Flora MacDonald Mayor was born in London in 1872 and grew up in Kingston Hill. Her father was a professor of classics at King's College, University of London, and her mother was a musician and linguist. In 1892, when university education was still relatively unusual for women, F. M. Mayor went to study at Newnham College, Cambridge, where she had a 'rapturous' time, maddening her parents with her love for acting and socialising; after Cambridge she maddened them even more by deciding to become an actress. In 1903, when the heart problems and severe bronchial asthma which dogged her life had put a stop to her acting ambitions, she became engaged to a young architect, but he died of typhoid fever within the year, leaving her depressed and semi-invalid.

Her first novel, *The Third Miss Symons*, came out to widespread admiration, but she did not publish again until after the First World War. Her second and third novels, *The Rector's Daughter* and *The Squire's Daughter*, came out in 1924 and 1929. Although her work was greatly admired by writers like Leonard and Virginia Woolf, E. M. Forster and Rebecca West, when she died in 1932 an obituary written about her by John Masefield simply didn't make it into the columns of *The Times*.

Virago published *The Third Miss Symons* in 1980.

from

The Third Miss Symons

Henrietta was eighteen when she left school. Minna and Louie had gone two or three years before, and by the time Henrietta came home, Minna was engaged to be married. There was nothing particular about Minna. She was capable, and clear-headed, and rather good-looking, and could dress well on a little money. She was not much of a talker, but what she said was to the point. On these qualifications she married a barrister with most satisfactory prospects. They were both extremely fond of one another in a quiet way, and fond they remained. She was disposed of satisfactorily.

Louie was prettier and more lively. She was having a gay career of flirtations, when Henrietta joined her. She did not at all want a younger sister, particularly a sister with a pretty complexion. Three years of parties had begun to tell on her own, which was of special delicacy. She and Henrietta had never grown to like one another, and now there went on a sort of silent war, an unnecessary war on Louie's side, for she had a much greater gift with partners than Henrietta, and her captives were not annexed.

But for her complexion there was nothing very taking in Henrietta. Whoever travels in the Tube must have seen many women with dark-brown hair, brown eyes, and too-strongly-marked eyebrows; their features are neither good nor bad; their whole aspect is uninteresting. They have no winning dimples, no speaking lines about the mouth. All that one can notice is a disappointed, somewhat peevish look in the eyes. Such was Henrietta. The fact that she had not been much wanted or appreciated hitherto began to show now she was eighteen. She was either shy and silent, or talked with too much positiveness for fear she should not be listened to; so that though she was not a failure at dances and managed to find plenty of partners, there were none of the interesting episodes that were continually occurring on Louie's evenings, and for a year or two her hopes were not realised. The Prince Charming she was waiting for came not.

Sometimes Louie was away on visits, and Henrietta went to dances without her. At one of these, as usual a strange young man was introduced. There was nothing special about him. They had the usual talk of first dances. Then he asked for a second, then for a third. He was introduced to her mother. She asked him to call. He came. He talked mostly to her mother, but it was clear that it was Henrietta he came to see. Another dance, another call, and meetings at friends' houses, and wherever she was he wanted to be beside her. It was an exquisitely happy month. He was a commonplace young man, but what did that matter? There was nothing in Henrietta to attract anyone very superior. And perhaps she loved him all the more because he was not soaring high above her, like all her previous divinities, but walking side by side with her. Yes, she loved him; by the time he had asked her for the third dance she loved him. She did not think much of his proposing, of their marrying, just that someone cared for her. At first she could not believe it, but by the end of the month the signs clearly resembled those of Louie's young men. Flowers, a note about a book he had lent her, a note about a mistake he had made in his last note; she was sure he must care for her. The other girls at the dances noticed his devotion, and asked Henrietta when it was to be announced. She laughed off their questions, but they gave her a thrill of delight. All must be well.

And if they had married all would have been well. There might have been jars and rubs, with Henrietta's jealous disposition there probably would have been, but they would have been as happy as the majority of married couples; she would have been happier, for to many people, even to some women, it is not, as it was to her, the all-sufficing condition of existence to love and be loved.

At the end of the month Louie came home. Henrietta had dreaded her return. She had no confidence in herself when Louie was by. Louie made her cold and awkward. She would have liked to have asked her not to come into the room when he called, but she was too shy; there had never been any intimacy between the sisters. Mrs Symons, however, spoke to Louie. 'A very nice young fellow, with perfectly good connections, not making much yet, but sufficient for a start. It would do very well.'

Louie would not have considered herself more heartless than other people, but she was a coquette, and she did not want Henrietta to be settled before her. The next time the young man came, he found in the drawing-room not merely a very much prettier Miss Symons, that in itself was not of much consequence, but a Miss Symons who was well aware of her advantages, and knew moreover from successful practice exactly how to rouse a desire for pursuit in the ordinary young man.

Henrietta saw at once, though she fought hard, that she had no chance.

'Are you going to the Humphreys to-morrow?' he said to Louie.

'If Henrietta's crinoline will leave any room in the carriage,' answered Louie, 'I shall try to get a little corner, perhaps under the seat, or one could always run behind. I crushed – see, what did I crush? – a little teeny-tiny piece of flounce one terrible evening; didn't I, Henrietta? And I was never allowed to hear the last of it.'

She smiled a special smile, only given to the most favoured of her partners. The young man thought how pretty this sisterly teasing was on the part of the lovely Miss Symons; Henrietta saw it in another light.

'My crinolines are not larger than yours, you know they are not.'

'Methinks the lady doth protest too much, don't you, Mr Dockerell?'

'And you always take the best seat in the carriage, so it is nonsense to say . . .'

He noticed for the first time how loud her voice was.

'Please let us change the conversation,' said Louie gently, 'it can't be at all interesting for Mr Dockerell. I am ready to own anything you like, that you don't wear crinolines at all, if that will please you.'

'If there is any difficulty, could not my mother take one of you to-morrow night?' (It was Louie he looked at.) 'She is staying with me for a week. Couldn't we call for you? It would be a great pleasure.'

'Oh, thank you,' began Henrietta.

'Really,' said Louie, 'you make me quite ashamed of my poor little joke. I don't think we have come quite to such a state of things that two sisters can't sit in the same carriage. I hear you are a most alarmingly good archer, Mr Dockerell, and I want to ask you to advise me about my bow, if you will be so kind.' To be asked advice, of course, completed the conquest.

Mr Dockerell had not been so much in love with Etta as with marrying. It took him a very short time to change, but when he had made his offer and Louie had discovered that he was too dull a young man for her, he did not transfer his affections back to Henrietta. She would gladly have taken him if he had. He left the neighbourhood, and not long after married someone else.

1914

Djuna Barnes

Djuna Barnes was born in 1892 in an artists' colony in Cornwall-on-Hudson, north of New York. She studied art in the early 1900s, then became a regular columnist on the *Brooklyn Daily Eagle* in 1913, shortly before she began publishing her short stories; 'The Terrible Peacock' is the earliest published of these.

She supported her mother and brothers with her income and was a pioneering journalist: to write about hunger-strikers being force-fed, for instance, Barnes insisted on being force-fed too to find out what it was like. In 1919–20 the Provincetown Players produced three of her one-act plays; that year she left the USA for Paris, where she lived for many years, writing, becoming one of the city's stylish expatriate figures. When her ten-year relationship with the artist and engraver Thelma Wood ended, Barnes transformed it into her great novel *Nightwood*, which T. S. Eliot, alarmed at the denseness of its allusive quality, edited severely before he published it at Faber and Faber in 1936.

Barnes moved back to the USA and became reclusive, living in a small apartment in Greenwich Village and surviving on the kindnesses of friends. She died in 1982.

Virago published Barnes's early stories in *Smoke* in 1985.

from

'The Terrible Peacock'

It was during the dull season, when a subway accident looms as big as a Thaw getaway, that an unusual item was found loose in the coffee.

Nobody seemed to know whence it had come. It dealt with a woman, one greater, more dangerous than Cleopatra, thirty-nine times as alluring as sunlight on a gold eagle, and about as elusive.

She was a Peacock, said the item, which was not ill-written – a slinky female with electrifying green eyes and red hair, dressed in clinging green-and-blue-silk, and she was very much observed as she moved languorously through the streets of Brooklyn. A Somebody – but who?

The city editor scratched his head and gave the item to Karl.

'Find out about her,' he suggested.

'Better put a new guy on,' said Karl. 'Get the fresh angle. I got that Kinney case to look after today. What about Garvey?'

'All right,' said the city editor, and selected a fresh piece of gum.

Garvey was duly impressed when Karl hove to alongside his desk and flung his leg after the item onto it, for Karl was the Star.

Rather a mysterious person in a way, was Karl. His residence was an inviolable secret. He was known to have accumulated money, despite the fact that he was a newspaperman. It was also known that he had married.

Otherwise, he was an emergency man – a first-rate reporter. When someone thought best to commit suicide and leave a little malicious note to a wife who raved three steps into the bathroom and three into the kitchen, hiccuping 'Oh, my God!' with each step, it got into Karl's typewriter – and there was the birth of a front-page story.

'So you're to look her up,' said Karl. 'She's dashed beautiful, has cat eyes and Leslie Carter hair – a loose-jointed, ball-bearing Clytie, rigged out with a complexion like creamed coffee stood overnight. They say she claws more men into her hair than any siren living or dead.'

'You've seen her?' breathed Garvey, staring.

Karl nodded briefly.

'Why don't *you* get her, then?'

'There are two things,' said Karl judicially, 'at which I am no good. One is subtraction, and the other is attraction. Go to it, son. The assignment is yours.'

He strolled away, but not too late to see Garvey swelling visibly at the implied compliment and caressing his beautiful, lyric tie.

Garvey didn't altogether like the assignment, nonetheless. There was Lilac Jane, you see. He had a date with her for that very night, and Lilac Jane was exceedingly desirable.

He was at that age when devotion to one female of the species makes dalliance with any others nothing short of treason.

But – he had been allotted this work because of his fascinations for slinky green sirens! Garvey fingered the tie again and withdrew his lavender scented handkerchief airily, as an altarboy swings a censer.

At the door he turned under the light and pushed back his cuff, and his fellow workers groaned. It was seven by his wristwatch.

Outside he paused on the corner near the chophouse. He looked up and down the gloomy street with its wilted florist-window displays and its spattering of grey house fronts, wishing there were someone with him who could be told of his feeling of competence in a world of competent men.

His eyes on the pavement, lost in perfervid dreams of Lilac Jane, he wandered on. The roaring of the bridge traffic disturbed him not, nor the shouts of bargemen through the dusk on the waterfront.

At last through the roseate visions loomed something green.

Shoes! Tiny shoes, trim and immaculate; above them a glimpse of thin, green stockings on trimmer ankles.

There was a tinkle of laughter, and Garvey came to himself, red and perspiring, and raised his eyes past the slim, green-clad body to the eyes of the Peacock.

It was she beyond question. Her hair was terribly red, even in the darkness, and it gleamed a full eight inches above her forehead, piled higher than any hair Garvey had ever seen. The moon shone through it like butter through mosquito netting.

Her neck was long and white, her lips were redder than her hair, and her green eyes, with the close-fitting, silken dress, that undulated like troubled, weed-filled water as she moved, completed the whole daring creation. The powers that be had gone in for poster effects when they made the Peacock.

She was handsome beyond belief, and she was amused at Garvey. Her silvery laugh tinkled out again as he stared at her, his pulse a hundred in the shade.

He tried to convince himself that this physiological effect was due to his newspaper instinct, but it is to be conjectured that Lilac Jane would have had her opinion of the Peacock had she been present.

'Well, young man?' she demanded, the wonderful eyes getting in their deadly work.

'I – I'm sorry – I didn't mean –' Garvey floundered hopelessly, but he did not try to escape.

'You were handing me bouquets by staring like that? That what you're trying to say?'

She laughed again, glided up to him and took his arm. 'I like you, young man,' she said.

'My nun-name is Garvey, and I'm on the – the *Argus.*'

She started at that and looked at him sharply. 'A reporter!'

But her tinkly laugh rang out again, and they walked on. 'Well, why not?' she said gaily.

Then, with entire unexpectedness: 'Do you tango?'

Garvey nodded dumbly, struggling to find his tongue.

'I *love* it!' declared the Peacock, taking a step or two of the dance beside him. 'Want to take me somewheres so we can have a turn or two?'

Garvey swallowed hard and mentioned a well-known resort.

'Mercy!' cried the green-eyed siren, turning shocked orbs upon him. 'I don't drink! Let's go to a tearoom – Poiret's.' She called it 'Poyrett's'.

Garvey suffered himself to be led to the slaughter, and as they went she chattered lightly. He drew out his handkerchief and dabbed gently at his temples.

'Gracious!' she drawled. 'You smell like an epidemic of swooning women.'

Garvey was hurt, but deep within himself he decided suddenly that scent was out of place on a masculine cold-assuager.

1915

Katherine Mansfield

———

Katherine Mansfield was born in Wellington, New Zealand, in 1888. She was educated in Wellington and in London. In 1909, pregnant with someone else's child, she married George Bowden, and left him that first night; while she was in Bavaria her child was still-born. She met John Middleton Murry; they cohabited for six years and married in 1918, and she lived for the rest of her short life between him and her friend and lover Ida Baker.

Mansfield's first volume of stories, *In a German Pension*, was published in 1911, *Prelude* in 1918, and *The Garden Party* in 1922. 'The Aloe' is the first version of 'Prelude', begun in 1915. Her writing transformed the short-story form; Virginia Woolf, who published Mansfield at the Hogarth Press and with whom she had enjoyed an enigmatic and uneasy friendship, said after Mansfield's death that it was 'the only writing I have ever been jealous of'.

Katherine Mansfield died in 1923 in France, at Fontainebleu, where she had come to the Russian guru Gurdjieff's community in the hope that he could cure her of the tuberculosis which finally took her life.

Virago published 'The Aloe' in 1985.

from

'The Aloe'

'Stand on your head on the verandah. That's quite flat,' said Lottie. 'No, smartie,' said Pip, 'you have to do it on something soft see? Because if you give a jerk – just a very little jerk and fall over like that bump yourself something in your neck goes click and it breaks right off. Dad told me . . .' 'Oh do let's have a game,' said Kezia – 'Do let's play something or other – ' 'Very well' said Isabel quickly 'we'll play hospitals. I'll be the nurse and Pip can be the doctor and you and Rags and Lottie can be the sick people' – But No, Lottie didn't not want to play that because last time Pip squirted something down her throat and it hurt awfully. 'Pooh!' said Pip 'it was only the juice out of a bit of orange peel – ' 'Well let's play ladies' said Isabel 'and Pip can be my husband and you can be my three dear little children – Rags can be the baby – ' 'I *hate* playing ladies' said Kezia 'because you always make us go to church hand in hand and come home again an go to bed' – Suddenly Pip took a filthy handkerchief out of his pocket – 'Snooker, here sir' he called, but Snooker as usual, began to slink away with his long bent tail between his legs. Pip leapt on top of him – and held him by his knees – 'keep his head firm Rags' he said as he tied the handkerchief round Snooker's head with a funny sticking up knot at the top. 'What ever is that for' – asked Lottie. 'It's to train his ears to grow more close to his head, see' said Pip. 'All fighting dogs have ears that lie kind of back and they prick up – but Snooker's got rotten ears they're too soft.' 'I know' said Kezia, 'they're always turning inside out I *hate* that.' 'Oh it isn't that' said Pip 'but I'm training his ears to look a bit more fierce see' – Snooker lay down and made one feeble effort with his paw to get the handkerchief off but finding he could not he trailed after the children with his head bound up in the dirty rag – shivering with misery. Pat came swinging by. In his hand he held a little tomahawk that winked in the sun. 'Come with me now' he said to the children 'and I'll show you how the Kings of Ireland chop off the head of a duck.' They held back – they didn't believe him it was one of his jokes, and besides the Trout boys had never seen Pat before – 'Come on now' he coaxed, smiling and holding out his hand to Kezia. 'A real duck's head' she said. 'One from ours in the paddock where the fowls and ducks are' – 'It is' said Pat. She put her hand in his hard dry one, and he stuck the tomahawk in his belt and held out the other to Rags – He loved little children. 'I'd better keep hold of Snooker's head, if there's going to be any blood about' said Pip – trying not to show his excitement 'because the sight of blood makes him awfully wild sometimes' – He ran ahead dragging Snooker by the knot in the handkerchief. 'Do you think we *ought* to' whispered Isabel to Lottie. 'Because we haven't asked Grandma or anybody have we?' 'But Pat's looking after us,' said Lottie.

At the bottom of the orchard a gate was set in the paling fence. On the other side there was a steep bank leading down to a bridge that spanned the creek and once up the bank on the other side you were on the fringe of the paddocks. A little disused stable in the first paddock had been turned into a fowl house. All about it there spread wire netting chicken runs new made by Pat. The fowls strayed far away across the paddock down to a little dumping ground in a hollow on the other side but the ducks kept close to that part of the creek that flowed under the bridge and ran hard by the fowl house – Tall bushes overhung the stream with red leaves and Dazzling yellow flowers and clusters of red and white berries, and a little further on there were cresses and a water plant with a flower like a yellow foxglove. At some places the stream was wide and shallow, enough to cross by stepping stones but at other places it tumbled suddenly into a deep rocky pool like a little lake with foam at the edge and big quivering bubbles. It was in these pools that the big white ducks loved to swim and guzzle along the weedy banks. Up and down they swam, preening their dazzling breasts and other ducks with yellow bills and yellow feet swam upside down below them in the clear still water. 'There they are' said Pat. 'There's the little Irish Navy, and look at the old Admiral there with the green neck and the grand little flag staff on his tail.' He pulled a handful of grain out of his pocket and began to walk towards the fowl house lazily, his broad straw hat with the broken crown pulled

off his eyes. 'Lid-lid lid lid-lid lid' he shouted – 'Qua! Qua Qua!'
answered the ducks, making for land and flopping and scrambling up
the bank – They streamed after him in a long waddling line – He
coaxed them pretending to throw the grain shaking it in his hands
and calling to them until they swept round him close round him
quacking and pushing against each other in a white ring – From far
away the fowls heard the clamour and they too came running across
the paddock, their heads crooked forward, their wings spread, turning in their feet in the silly way fowls run and scolding as they came.
Then Pat scattered the grain and the greedy ducks began to gobble –
Quickly he bent forward, seized two, tucked them quacking and struggling one under each arm and strode across to the children. Their
darting heads, their flat beaks and round eyes frightened the children – and they drew back all except Pip. 'Come on sillies' he cried,
'They can't hurt, they haven't got any teeth have they Pat – they've
only got those two little holes in their beaks to breathe through.'
'Will you hold one while I finish with the other' asked Pat. Pip let go
of Snooker – 'Won't I! Won't I! Give us one – I'll hold him. I'll not let
him go. I don't care how much he kicks – give us give us!' He nearly
sobbed with delight when Pat put the white lump in his arms – There
was an old stump beside the door of the fowlshed – Pat carried over
the other duck, grabbed it up in one hand, whipped out his little tomahawk – lay the duck flat on the stump and suddenly down came the
tomahawk and the duck's head flew off the stump – up and up the
blood spurted over the white feathers, over his hand – When the children saw it they were frightened no more – they crowded round him
and began to scream – even Isabel leaped about and called out 'The
blood the blood' – Pip forgot all about his duck – He simply threw it
away from him – and shouted 'I saw it, I saw it' and jumped round the
wood block –

Rags with cheeks as white as paper ran up to the little head and put
out a finger as if he meant to touch it then drew back again and again
put out a finger. He was shivering all over. Even Lottie, frightened
Lottie began to laugh and point at the duck and shout 'Look Kezia
look look look' – 'Watch it' shouted Pat and he put down the white
body and it began to waddle – with only a long spurt of blood where
the head had been – it began to pad along dreadfully quiet towards
the steep ledge that led to the stream – It was the crowning wonder.
'Do you see that – do you see it?' yelled Pip and he ran among the
little girls pulling at their pinafores – 'It's like an engine – it's like a
funny little darling engine – ' squealed Isabel – But Kezia suddenly

rushed at Pat and flung her arms round his legs and butted her head as hard as she could against his knees; 'Put head back put head back' she screamed – When he stooped to move her she would not let go or take her head away – She held as hard as ever she could and sobbed 'head back head back' – until it sounded like a loud, strange hiccough. 'It's stopped it's tumbled over it's dead' – said Pip. Pat dragged Kezia up into his arms. Her sunbonnet had fallen back but she would not let him look at her face. No she pressed her face into a bone in his shoulder and put her arms round his neck –

The children stopped squealing as suddenly as they had begun – they stood round the dead duck. Rags was not frightened of the head any more. He knelt down and stroked it with his finger and said 'I don't think perhaps the head is quite dead yet. It's warm Pip. Would it keep alive if I gave it something to drink – ' But Pip got very cross and said – 'Bah! you baby – ' He whistled to Snooker and went off – and when Isabel went up to Lottie, Lottie snatched away. 'What are you always touching me for Is a *bel*.'

'There now' said Pat to Kezia 'There's the grand little girl' – She put up her hands and touched his ear. She felt something – Slowly she raised her quivering face and looked – Pat wore little round gold earrings. How very funny – She never knew men wore earrings. She was very much surprised! She quite forgot about the duck. 'Do they come off and on,' she asked huskily?

1916

Catherine Carswell

———

Catherine Carswell was born in Glasgow in 1879. She studied English literature at Glasgow University, though women still weren't admitted to degrees, and travelled in Italy and France. In 1904 she married Herbert Jackson, who tried to kill her in 1905 when she announced her pregnancy; he was declared insane. Carswell began legal proceedings for the annulment of the marriage, and won the case in 1907, making legal history. In 1915 she married her second husband, Donald Carswell, and worked in Glasgow and London as drama and literary critic for the *Glasgow Herald* until an admiring review she wrote of D. H. Lawrence's banned novel *The Rainbow* lost her her job. In 1916 she and Lawrence exchanged manuscripts of *Women in Love* and *Open the Door!* (which wasn't published until 1920), and they discussed writing a novel together, Lawrence writing the male characters and Carswell the female. Her fiction clearly reveals Lawrence's literary influence.

Carswell's only other novel, *The Camomile*, came out in 1922, and for years she was forgotten as a novelist at all, remembered instead for her controversial biographies of famous men; Robert Burns and her friend D. H. Lawrence. She died in Oxford in 1946.

Virago published *Open the Door!* in 1986.

from

Open the Door!

At the School the fun was in full swing when Mildred's party arrived. A waltz came to an end as they were taking off their wraps, and Joanna thought Mrs Plummer would never stop re-arranging her hair, which stayed perfectly untidy in spite of prolonged fingering.

When at last they entered the dancing-room, the students were grouping themselves noisily for the foursome reel. Most of the dancers already stood facing one another, in two double lines which stretched from end to end of the long class-room; but still here and there some couples ran linked, laughing and sliding on the polished floor in a race for the few gaps left. Onlookers sat round on benches or on the floor. Many had kept on their overalls of holland or blue linen, and numbers of the girls were so young that their hair still hung over their shoulders. There was something easy-going, almost countrified about these dances. The sloping timbered ceiling, hung with a few lanterns of yellowish paper, made Joanna feel as if she were in a barn; and she thought that the easels and thrones stacked in each corner looked like farm implements.

And if it was a village festival, Mr Valentine Plummer united in himself the parts of the Squire and the Parson. He came effusively to greet the newcomers, pressed them to join in at once, and shepherded them to the far end of the room. 'There is always room at the top,' he said, cracking his little parsonish joke. But neither the Lovatts nor Mrs Plummer nor Pender could dance the reel.

Lawrence Urquhart glanced at Joanna.

'You, then, bella Signora!' exclaimed the Director jocosely. 'Come. Shall it be said that a Scotswoman refused to take part in a reel?'

'Will you?' asked Lawrence.

But Joanna shook her head, excusing herself.

'Ah! but do, do dance it!'

Not Lawrence this time but Louis Pender had spoken. He stood close to Joanna, and begged like a lively child who fears the loss of a long-promised treat. And Joanna, blushing deeply with pleasure, laughed and yielded.

She gave her hand to Urquhart who was clenching his black, mortified brows. Only to please this other was he accepted!

Although a couple was wanted almost where they stood, he set off with her to the far end of the room. It was some satisfaction to him that he was really dragging her there; but he suffered too all the way from the hateful reluctance of her body. She was humiliated by his knowledge that she desired to dance before the other man. But by her backward drag on his arm she thrust him down so far below herself that her humiliation was a triumph compared with his.

Still he plodded on, his head forward and hanging a little. And they had barely got to their places when the band let fly with the tune.

To Joanna's great astonishment Urquhart danced well. It was the last thing she had expected of him; but he sprang featly to music, and his body was delivered by the steady rhythm from all stiffness and self-consciousness. As he passed and re-passed her in the figure eight, taking first one of her hands and then the other; as he placed his own hands on his slight hips or raised them high above his head; as he swung his partners round, each time lifting them clean off the floor; above all as he came to go through his complicated steps facing Joanna, gravely leaping on his small Highland feet; the young man was wholly possessed. He had to the full that tranced and happy seriousness which is the spirit of a national dance.

From the outset he caught Joanna up into something of his own dignity, winning her surprised acknowledgment. Then, as the reel progressed, she began to lose all sense of identity. Every moment she became less herself, more a mere rhythmical expression of the soil from which they both had sprung. The memory dawned in her of some far back ancestress, of whom unheedingly she had heard her mother tell. Fresh, dim, sweet like dawn, she could see the Stirlingshire farmer's daughter carrying the milk-pails at sunrise and at sunset to the Castle on its hill. She could hear the swinging clink of the pails, could smell the spilt, clover-sweet milk, while the farmer's daughter gave her lips to the young, unknown Welsh soldier who kept the drawbridge. *She* was that lass, that meeting, without which her being would not have been. And soon she was not even these. Beneath the candid darkness of Lawrence Urquhart's face, soon she was no more than a field of barley that swings unseen in the wind before dawn.

But suddenly, though the music went on, and though her feet persisted in its rhythms, she was recalled into herself. Louis Pender, edging along by the wall, had come unknown to where she was dancing. And now that she had seen him, she knew nothing else but that he watched her through his glasses with his practised, unhappy eyes. She did not look at him, but his being there changed everything for her. It changed subtly the spirit of her dancing into a conscious revelation and a less conscious withholding. She became an appeal, a claim, a scarcely endurable excitement. She could not help herself.

1917

Mary Webb

Mary Webb (née Meredith) was born in Shropshire in 1881 and educated at home. At fourteen she took over running the household, after her mother was injured in a riding accident. A shy woman of poor health, she suffered from Graves' disease, which gave her a goitre and staring eyes, attributes she passed on to the naive, attractive, innocent and earthy heroines of her immensely popular fiction. She wrote poetry, short stories, essays and journalism as well as novels. She married Henry Webb in 1912 (he was an animist, as she was; her animist views deeply inform her fiction, where nature tends to become quasi-religious and mystical).

Gone to Earth came as close to being an anti-war novel as it dared in 1917, and her later novel *Precious Bane* won the Femina Vie Heureux Prize in the mid-twenties. Her fiction suffered a sharp decline in popularity after Stella Gibbons's *Cold Comfort Farm* lampooned it so successfully in 1932. Webb had by then died in Sussex in 1927.

Virago published *Gone to Earth* in 1979.

from

Gone to Earth

She went on, regardless of direction. At last she found an old pasture where heavy farm-horses looked round at her over their polished flanks and a sad-eyed foal rose to greet her. There she found button mushrooms to her heart's content. Ancient hedges hung above the field and spoke to her in fragrant voices. The glory of the may was just giving place to the shell-tint of wild roses. She reached up for some, and her hair fell down; she wisely put the remaining pins in the bag for the return journey. She was intensely happy, as a fish is when it plunges back into the water. For these things, and not the God-fearing comfort of the mountain, nor the tarnished grandeur of Undern, were her life. She had so deep a kinship with the trees, so intuitive a sympathy with leaf and flower, that it seemed as if the blood in her veins was not slow-moving human blood, but volatile sap. She was of a race that will come in the far future, when we shall have outgrown our egoism – the brain-less egoism of a little boy pulling off flies' wings. We shall attain philosophic detachment and emotional sympathy. We have even now far outgrown the age when a great genius like Shakespeare could be so clumsy in the interpretation of other than human life. We have left behind us the bloodshot centuries when killing was the only sport, and we have come to the slightly more reputable times when lovers of killing are conscious that a distinct effort is necessary in order to keep up 'the good old English sports'. Better things are in store for us. Even now, although the most expensively bound and the most plenti-ful books in the stationer's shops are those about killing and its thousand ramifications, nobody reads them. They are bought at Christmas for necessitous relations and little boys.

Hazel, in the fields and woods, enjoyed it all so much that she walked in a mystical exaltation.

Reddin in the fields and woods enjoyed himself only. For he took his own atmosphere with him wherever he went, and before his footsteps weakness fled and beauty folded.

The sky blossomed in parterres of roses, frailer and brighter than the rose of the briar, and melted beneath them into lagoons greener and paler than the veins of a young beech-leaf. The fairy hedges were so high, so flushed with beauty, the green airy waters ran so far back into mystery, that it seemed as if at any moment God might walk there as in a garden, delicate as a moth. Down by the stream Hazel found tall water-plantains, triune of cup, standing each above the ooze like candelabras, and small rough-leaved forget-me-nots eyeing their liquid reflections with complaisance. She watched the birds bathe – bull-finches, smooth-coated and well-found; slim willow-wrens; thrushes, ermine-breasted; lusty blackbirds with beaks of crude yellow. They made neat little tracks over the soft mud, drank, bathed, preened, and made other neat little tracks. Then they 'took off', as Hazel put it, from the top of the bank, and flew low across the painted meadow or high into the enamelled tree, and piped and fluted till the air was full of silver.

Hazel stood as Eve might have stood, hands clasped, eyes full of ecstasy, utterly self-forgetful, enchanted with these living toys.

'Eh, yon's a proper bird!' she exclaimed, as a big silken cuckoo alighted on the mud with a gobble, drank with dignity, and took its vacillating flight to a far ash-tree. 'Foxy ought to see that,' she added.

Silver-crested peewits circled and cried with their melancholy cadences, and a tawny pheasant led out her young. Now that the dew was gone, and cobwebs no longer canopied the field with silver, it was blue with germander speedwell – each flower painted with deepening colour, eyed with startling white, and carrying on slender stamens the round white pollen-balls – worlds of silent, lovely activity. Every flower-spike had its family of buds, blue jewels splashed with white, each close-folded on her mystery. To see the whole field not only bright with them, but brimming over, was like watching ten thousand saints rapt in ecstasy, ten thousand children dancing. Hazel knew nothing of saints. She had no words for the wonder in which she walked. But she felt it, she enjoyed it with a passion no words could express.

Mrs Marston had said several times, 'I'm almost afraid Hazel is a great one for wasting her time.' But what is waste of time? Eating and sleeping; hearing grave, sedulous men read out of grave, sedulous books what we have heard a hundred times; besieging God (whom we end by imagining as a great ear) for material benefits; amassing property – these, the world says, are not waste of time. But to drink at the stoup of beauty; to lift the leafy coverlet of earth and seek the cradled God (since here, if anywhere, He dwells), this in the world's eye is waste of time. Oh, filthy, heavy-handed, blear-eyed world, when will you wash and be clean?

Hazel came to a place where the white water crossed the road in a glittering shallow ford. Here she stayed, leaning on the wooden bridge, hearing small pebbles grinding on one another; seeing jewel-flashes of ruby, sapphire and emerald struck from them by the low sunlight; smelling the scent that is better than all (except the scent of air on a barren mountain, or of snow) – the scent of running water. She watched the grey wagtails, neat and prim in person, but wild in bearing, racing across the wet gravel like intoxicated Sunday-school teachers. Then, in a huge silver willow that brooded, dove-like, over the ford, a blackcap began to sing. The trills and gushes of perfect melody, the golden repetitions, the heart-lifting ascents and wistful falls drooping softly as a flower, seemed wonderful to her as an angel's song. She and the bird, sheltered under the grey-silver feathers of the tree, lived their great moments of creation and receptivity until suddenly there was a sharp noise of hooves, the song snapped, the willow was untenanted, and Reddin's horse splashed through the ford.

'Oh!' cried Hazel, 'what for did you break the song? A sacred bird, it was. And now it's fled!'

He had been riding round the remnant of his estate, a bit of hill sheep-walk that faced the Mountain and overlooked the valley. He had seen Hazel wander down the road, white-limbed and veiled in tawny hair. He thought there must be something wrong with his sight. Bare legs! Bare arms! Hair all loose, and no hat! As a squire-farmer, he was very much shocked. As a man, he spurred downhill at the risk of a bad fall.

Hazel, unlike the women of civilization, who are pursued by look-ing-glasses, was apt to forget herself and her appearance. She had done so now. But something in Reddin's face recalled her. She hastily took the butterfly out of her skirt and put on her shoes and stockings.

'What song?' asked Reddin.

'A bird in the tree. What for did you fritten it?'

Reddin was indignant. Seeing Hazel wandering thus so near his own domain, he thought she had come in the hope of seeing him. He also thought that the strangeness of her dress was an effort to attract him.

To the pure all things are pure.

'But you surely wanted to see me? Wasn't that why you came?' he asked.

'No, it wasna. I came to pick the little musherooms as come wi' the warm rain, for there's none like spring musherooms. And I came to see the flowers, and hearken at the birds, and look the nesses.'

'You could have lots of flowers and birds at Undern.'

'There's plenty at the Mountain.'

'Then why did you come here?'

'To be by my lonesome.'

'Snub for me!' He smiled. He liked opposition. 'But look here, Hazel,' he reasoned. 'If you'd come to Undern, I'd make you enjoy life.'

'But I dunna want to. I be Ed'ard's missus.'

'Be *my* missus!' At the phrase his weather-coarsened face grew redder. It intoxicated him.

He slipped off his horse and kissed her.

'I dunna want to be anybody's missus!' she cried vexedly. 'Not yourn nor Ed'ard's neither! But I *be* Ed'ard's, and so I mun stay.' She turned away.

'Good morning to you,' she said in her old-fashioned little way. She trudged up the road. Reddin watched her, a forlorn, slight figure armed with the black bag, weary with the sense of reaction. Reddin was angry and depressed. The master of Undern had been for the second time refused.

'H'm,' he said, considering her departing figure, 'it won't be asking next time, my lady! And it won't be for you to refuse.'

He turned home, accompanied by that most depressing companion – the sense of his own meanness. He was unable to help knowing that the exercise of force against weakness is the most cur-like thing on earth.

1918

Rebecca West

———

Cicely Isabel Fairfield was born in London in 1892. She was educated in Edinburgh and in London, where she went to the Academy of Dramatic Art. Her pen-name comes from the Ibsen play *Rosmersholm*, from the strong-minded character she once played. Already by the time she was a teenager, West was sending letters to the newspapers about suffrage, publishing essays in the *Freewoman* and upsetting her mother by being too involved with left-wing and suffragist meetings (her decision to use a pen-name at all stemmed from trying to calm her mother about having too public a daughter).

Her first book, *Henry James*, was published in 1916; *The Return of the Soldier* was her first novel. Later novels include *The Judge* (1922), *The Thinking Reed* (1936) and *The Fountain Overflows* (1954). Her irreverent criticism of an H. G. Wells novel led to their meeting and becoming lovers; she gave birth to his son in 1914. In 1930, she married Henry Maxwell. She spent her life writing witty and iconoclastic literary criticism, biography, travel writing, history and social polemic. In her later years she became virulently anti-communist, disapproving of the totalitarianism of all absolutes. She died in London in 1983.

Virago published *The Return of the Soldier* in 1980.

from

The Return of the Soldier

'Ah, don't begin to fuss!' wailed Kitty; 'if a woman began to worry in these days because her husband hadn't written to her for a fortnight—! Besides, if he'd been anywhere interesting, anywhere where the fighting was really hot, he'd have found some way of telling me instead of just leaving it as "Somewhere in France". He'll be all right.'

We were sitting in the nursery. I had not meant to enter it again after the child's death, but I had come suddenly on Kitty as she slipped the key into the lock and had lingered to look in at the high room, so full of whiteness and clear colours, so unendurably gay and familiar, which is kept in all respects as though there were still a child in the house. It was the first lavish day of spring, and the sunlight was pouring through the tall arched windows and the flowered curtains so brightly that in the old days a fat fist would certainly have been raised to point out the new translucent glories of the rose-buds; it was lying in great pools on the blue cork floor and the soft rugs, patterned with strange beasts; and it threw dancing beams, that should have been gravely watched for hours, on the white paint and the blue distempered walls. It fell on the rocking-horse which had been Chris's idea of an appropriate present for his year-old son and showed what a fine fellow he was and how tremendously dappled; it picked out Mary and her little lamb on the chintz ottoman. And along the mantelpiece, under the loved print of the snarling tiger, in attitudes that were at once angular and relaxed – as though they were ready for play at their master's pleasure but found it hard to keep from drowsing in this warm weather – sat the Teddy Bear and the chimpanzee and the woolly white dog and the black cat with the eyes that roll. Everything was there, except Oliver. I turned away so that I might not spy on Kitty revisiting her dead.

But she called after me:

'Come here, Jenny. I'm going to dry my hair.'

And when I looked again I saw that her golden hair was all about her shoulders and that she wore over her frock a little silken jacket trimmed with rosebuds. She looked so like a girl on a magazine cover that one expected to find a large '7d.' somewhere attached to her person. She had taken Nanny's big basket-chair from its place by the high chair and was pushing it over to the middle window.

'I always come in here when Emery has washed my hair; it's the sunniest room in the house. I wish Chris wouldn't have it kept as a nursery when there's no chance—'

She sat down, swept her hair over the back of the chair into the sunlight, and held out to me her tortoise-shell hairbrush.

'Give it a brush now and then like a good soul. But be careful. Tortoise snaps so.'

I took the brush and turned to the window, leaning my forehead against the glass and staring unobservantly at the view. You probably know the beauty of that view; for when Chris rebuilt Baldry Court after his marriage, he handed it over to architects who had not so much the wild eye of the artist as the knowing wink of the manicurist, and between them they massaged the dear old place into matter for innumerable photographs in the illustrated papers.

The house lies on the crest of Harrow-weald, and from its windows the eye drops to miles of emerald pastureland lying wet and brilliant under a westward line of sleek hills blue with distance and distant woods, while nearer it ranges the suave decorum of the lawn and the Lebanon cedar whose branches are like darkness made palpable, and the minatory gauntnesses of the topmost pines in the wood that breaks downward, its bare boughs a close texture of browns and purples, from the pond on the hill's edge.

That day its beauty was an affront to me, because like most Englishwomen of my time I was wishing for the return of a soldier. Disregarding the national interest and everything except the keen prehensile gesture of our hearts towards him, I wanted to snatch my cousin Christopher from the wars and seal him in this green pleasantness his wife and I now looked upon. Of late I had had bad dreams about him. By night I saw Chris running across the brown rottenness of No Man's Land, starting back here because he trod upon a hand, not even looking there because of the awfulness of an unburied head, and not till my dream was packed full of horror did I see him pitch forward on his knees as he reached safety – if it was that. For on the war-films I have seen men slip down as softly from the trench parapet, and none but the grimmer philosophers would say that they had reached safety by their fall. And when I escaped into wakefulness it was only to lie stiff and think of stories I had heard in the boyish voice, that rings indomitable yet has most of its gay notes flattened, of the modern subaltern.

'We were all of us in a barn one night, and a shell came along. My pal sang out, *"Help me, old man, I've got no legs!"* and I had to answer, *"I can't, old man, I've got no hands!"*'

Well, such are the dreams of Englishwomen to-day; I could not complain. But I wished for the return of our soldier.

So I said: 'I wish we could hear from Chris. It is a fortnight since he wrote.'

And then it was that Kitty wailed, 'Ah, don't begin to fuss,' and bent over her image in her hand-mirror as one might bend for refreshment over scented flowers.

1919

May Sinclair

May Sinclair was born in Liverpool in 1863; her father owned a shipping business. When the business went bankrupt, the family moved several times, settling in Devon. She went to Cheltenham Ladies' College when she was eighteen; her first and only formal education. From 1908 she was an active suffragist. She never married, and supported herself by writing reviews, translations, poetry, criticism and fiction; during the First World War she drove an ambulance in Belgium, earning herself the Iron Cross.

Her modernist criticism was seminal; she was among the first to write about the imagists and T. S. Eliot's early work; she is credited with coining the phrase 'stream of consciousness' in its literary usage with reference to Dorothy Richardson's prose. Her fiction, influenced by Freud and Richardson, made her critically acclaimed in her lifetime, though she was uneasy with this acclamation; she once sat next to Mark Twain at a literary dinner, after which he thanked her for her 'remarkably interesting silence'.

For the last fifteen years of her life she suffered from Parkinson's disease, and retired to Buckinghamshire, where she died in 1946.

Virago published *Mary Olivier: A Life* in 1980.

from

Mary Olivier: A Life

Dead people really did rise. Supposing all the dead people in the City of London Cemetery rose and came out of their graves and went about the city? Supposing they walked out as far as Ilford? Crowds and crowds of them, in white sheets? Supposing they got into the garden?

'Please, God, keep me from thinking about the Resurrection. Please God, keep me from dreaming about coffins and funerals and ghosts and skeletons and corpses.' She said it last, after the blessings, so that God couldn't forget. But it was no use.

If you said texts: 'Thou shalt not be afraid for the terror by night.' 'Yea, though I walk through the City of London Cemetery.' It was no use.

'The trumpet shall sound and the dead shall arise . . . Incorruptible.'

That was beautiful. Like a bright light shining. But you couldn't think about it long enough. And the dreams went on just the same: the dream of the ghost in the passage, the dream of the black coffin coming round the turn of the staircase and squeezing you against the banister; the dream of the corpse that came to your bed. She could see the round back and the curled arms under the white sheet.

The dreams woke her with a sort of burst. Her heart was jumping about and thumping; her face and hair were wet with water that came out of her skin.

The grey light in the passage was like the ghost-light of the dreams.

Gas light was a good light; but when you turned it on Jenny came up and put it out again. She said, 'Goodness knows when you'll get to sleep with *that* light flaring.'

There was never anybody about at bedtime. Jenny was dishing up the dinner. Harriet was waiting. Catty only ran up for a minute to undo the hooks and brush your hair.

When Mamma sent her to bed she came creeping back into the dining-room. Everybody was eating dinner. She sickened with fright in the steam and smell of dinner. She leaned her head against Mamma and whimpered, and Mamma said in her soft voice, 'Big girls don't cry because it's bed-time. Only silly baby girls are afraid of ghosts.'

Mamma wasn't afraid.

When she cried Mark left his dinner and carried her upstairs, past the place where the ghost was, and stayed with her till Catty came.

1920s

1920

Anzia Yezierska

———

Anzia Yezierska was born some time in the early 1880s in a village near Warsaw in Russian Poland, one of nine children. In the 1890s her family sailed to the USA and settled in Manhattan on the Lower East Side. At seventeen she worked in sweatshops and laundries, then won a scholarship, graduating from Columbia University in 1904. She taught domestic science for a few years after this, but was denied formal teaching qualifications, and, having married and annulled the marriage, she was forced by poverty to hand her daughter to her ex-husband, Jacob Gordon, a lawyer, to bring up.

When her first story, 'The Free Vacation House', was published, she dropped the name given to her by immigration officers, and went back to using her own, and in 1920, when her collection *Hungry Hearts* was published, it was bought by Samuel Goldwyn in Hollywood for the huge sum of $10,000 and brought her fame. She went to Hollywood to work on scripts, wrote more high-earning books, but by the Depression her luck changed, her reputation declined. She eked a living out of stories and reviews and wrote a fictionalised autobiography in 1950. She died in California in poverty in 1970.

Virago published *Hungry Hearts and Other Stories* in 1985.

from

'The Free Vacation House'

How came it that I went to the free vacation house was like this:
One day the visiting teacher from the school comes to find out
for why don't I get the children ready for school in time; for why are
they so often late.

I let out on her my whole bitter heart. I told her my head was on
wheels from worrying. When I get up in the morning, I don't know
on what to turn first: should I nurse the baby, or make Sam's breakfast, or attend on the older children. I only got two hands.

'My dear woman,' she says, 'you are about to have a nervous
breakdown. You need to get away to the country for a rest and
vacation.'

'Gott im Himmel!' says I. 'Don't I know I need a rest? But how? On
what money can I go to the country?'

'I know of a nice country place for mothers and children that will
not cost you anything. It is free.'

'Free! I never heard from it.'

'Some kind people have made arrangements so no one need pay,'
she explains.

Later, in a few days, I just finished up with Masha and Mendel and
Frieda and Sonya to send them to school, and I was getting Aby ready
for kindergarten, when I hear a knock on the door, and a lady comes
in. She had a white starched dress like a nurse and carried a black
satchel in her hand.

'I am from the Social Betterment Society,' she tells me. 'You want
to go to the country?'

Before I could say something, she goes over to the baby and pulls out the rubber nipple from her mouth, and to me, she says, 'You must not get the child used to sucking this; it is very unsanitary.'

'Gott im Himmel!' I beg the lady. 'Please don't begin with that child, or she'll holler my head off. She must have the nipple. I'm too nervous to hear her scream like that.'

When I put the nipple back again in the baby's mouth, the lady takes herself a seat, and then takes out a big black book from her satchel. Then she begins to question me. What is my first name? How old I am? From where come I? How long I'm already in this country? Do I keep any boarders? What is my husband's first name? How old he is? How long he is in this country? By what trade he works? How much wages he gets for a week? How much money do I spend out for rent? How old are the children, and everything about them.

'My goodness!' I cry out. 'For why is it necessary all this to know? For why must I tell you all my business? What difference does it make already if I keep boarders, or I don't keep boarders? If Masha had the whooping-cough or Sonya had the measles? Or whether I spend out for my rent ten dollars or twenty? Or whether I come from Schnipishock or Kovner Gubernie?'

'We must make a record of all the applicants, and investigate each case,' she tells me. 'There are so many who apply to the charities, we can help only those who are most worthy.'

'Charities!' I scream out. 'Ain't the charities those who help the beggars out? I ain't no beggar. I'm not asking for no charity. My husband, he works.'

'Miss Holcomb, the visiting teacher, said that you wanted to go to the country, and I had to make out this report before investigating your case.'

'Oh! Oh!' I choke and bit my lips. 'Is the free country from which Miss Holcomb told me, is it from the charities? She was telling me some kind people made arrangements for any mother what needs to go there.'

'If your application is approved, you will be notified,' she says to me, and out she goes.

When she is gone I think to myself, I'd better knock out from my head this idea about the country. For so long I lived, I didn't know nothing about the charities. For why should I come down among the beggars now?

Then I looked around me in the kitchen. On one side was the big wash-tub with clothes, waiting for me to wash. On the table was a pile of breakfast dishes yet. In the sink was the potatoes, waiting to be peeled. The baby was beginning to cry for the bottle. Aby was hollering and pulling me to take him to kindergarten. I felt if I didn't get away from here for a little while, I would land in a crazy house, or from the window jump down. Which was worser, to land in a crazy house, jump from the window down, or go to the country from the charities?

In about two weeks later around comes the same lady with the satchel again in my house.

'You can go to the country to-morrow,' she tells me. 'And you must come to the charity building to-morrow at nine o'clock sharp. Here is a card with the address. Don't lose it, because you must hand it to the lady in the office.'

I look on the card, and there I see my name wrote; and by it, in big printed letters, that word 'CHARITY'.

'Must I go to the charity office?' I ask, feeling my heart to sink. 'For why must I come there?'

'It is the rule that everybody comes to the office first, and from there they are taken to the country.'

I shivered to think how I would feel, suppose somebody from my friends should see me walking into the charity office with my children. They wouldn't know that it is only for the country I go there. They might think I go to beg. Have I come down so low as to be seen by the charities? But what's the use? Should I knock my head on the walls? I had to go.

When I come to the office, I already found a crowd of women and children sitting on long benches and waiting. I took myself a seat with them, and we were sitting and sitting and looking on one another, sideways and crosswise, and with lowered eyes, like guilty criminals. Each one felt like hiding herself from all the rest. Each one felt black with shame in the face.

We may have been sitting and waiting for an hour or more. But every second was seeming years to me. The children began to get restless. Mendel wanted water. The baby on my arms was falling asleep. Aby was crying for something to eat.

'For why are we sittin' here like fat cats?' says the woman next to me. 'Ain't we going to the country to-day yet?'

At last a lady comes to the desk and begins calling us our names, one by one. I nearly dropped to the floor when over she begins to ask: Do you keep boarders? How much do you spend out for rent? How much wages does your man get for a week?

Didn't the nurse tell them all about us already? It was bitter enough to have to tell the nurse everything, but in my own house nobody was hearing my troubles, only the nurse. But in the office there was so many strangers all around me. For why should everybody have to know my business? At every question I wanted to holler out: 'Stop! Stop! I don't want no vacations! I'll better run home with my children.' At every question I felt like she was stabbing a knife into my heart. And she kept on stabbing me more and more, but I could not help it, and they were all looking at me. I couldn't move from her. I had to answer everything.

When she got through with me, my face was red like fire. I was burning with hurts and wounds. I felt like everything was bleeding in me.

When all the names was already called, a man doctor with a nurse comes in, and tells us to form a line, to be examined. I wish I could ease out my heart a little, and tell in words how that doctor looked on us, just because we were poor and had no money to pay. He only used the ends from his finger-tips to examine us with. From the way he was afraid to touch us or come near us, he made us feel like we had some catching sickness that he was trying not to get on him.

The doctor got finished with us in about five minutes, so quick he worked. Then we was told to walk after the nurse, who was leading the way for us through the street to the car. Everybody what passed us in the street turned around to look on us. I kept down my eyes and held down my head and I felt like sinking into the sidewalk. All the time I was trembling for fear somebody what knows me might yet pass and see me. For why did they make us walk through the street, after the nurse, like stupid cows? Weren't all of us smart enough to find our way without the nurse? Why should the whole world have to see that we are from the charities?

When we got into the train, I opened my eyes, and lifted up my head, and straightened out my chest, and again began to breathe. It was a beautiful, sunshiny day. I knocked open the window from the train, and the fresh-smelling country air rushed upon my face and made me feel so fine! I looked out from the window and instead of seeing the iron fire-escapes with garbage-cans and bedclothes, that I always seen when from my flat I looked – instead of seeing only walls and wash-lines between walls, I saw the blue sky, and green grass and trees and flowers.

Ah, how grand I felt, just on the sky to look! Ah, how grand I felt just to see the green grass – and the free space – and no houses!

'Get away from me, my troubles!' I said. 'Leave me rest a minute.

Leave me breathe and straighten out my bones. Forget the unpaid butcher's bill. Forget the rent. Forget the wash-tub and the cook-stove and the pots and pans. Forget the charities!'

'Tickets, please,' calls the train conductor. I felt knocked out from heaven all at once. I had to point to the nurse what held our tickets, and I was feeling the conductor looking on me as if to say, 'Oh, you are only from the charities.'

By the time we came to the vacation house I already forgot all about my knock-down. I was again filled with the beauty of the country. I never in all my life yet seen such a swell house like that vacation house. Like the grandest palace it looked. All round the front, flowers from all colors was smelling out the sweetest perfume. Here and there was shady trees with comfortable chairs under them to sit down on.

When I only came inside, my mouth opened wide and my breathing stopped still from wonder. I never yet seen such an order and such a cleanliness. From all the corners from the room, the cleanliness was shining like a looking-glass. The floor was so white scrubbed you could eat on it. You couldn't find a speck of dust on nothing, if you was looking for it with eye-glasses on.

I was beginning to feel happy and glad that I come, when, Gott im Himmel! again a lady begins to ask us out the same questions what the nurse already asked me in my home and what was asked over again in the charity office. How much wages my husband makes out for a week? How much money I spend out for rent? Do I keep boarders?

We were hungry enough to faint. So worn out was I from excitement, and from the long ride, that my knees were bending under me ready to break from tiredness. The children were pulling me to pieces, nagging me for a drink, for something to eat and such like. But still we had to stand out the whole list of questionings. When she already got through asking us out everything, she gave to each of us a tag with our name written on it. She told us to tie the tag on our hand. Then like tagged horses at a horse sale in the street, they marched us into the dining-room.

There was rows of long tables, covered with pure-white oil-cloth. A vase with bought flowers was standing on the middle from each table. Each person got a clean napkin for himself. Laid out by the side from each person's plate was a silver knife and fork and spoon and tea-spoon. When we only sat ourselves down, girls with white starched aprons was passing around the eatings.

I soon forget again all my troubles. For the first time in ten years I sat down to a meal what I did not have to cook or worry about. For the first time in ten years I sat down to the table like a somebody. Ah, how grand it feels, to have handed you over the eatings and everything you need. Just as I was beginning to like it and let myself feel good, in comes a fat lady all in white, with a teacher's look on her face. I could tell already, right away by the way she looked on us, that she was the boss from this place.

'I want to read you the rules from this house, before you leave this room,' says she to us.

Then she began like this: We dassen't stand on the front grass where the flowers are. We dassen't stay on the front porch. We dassen't sit on the chairs under the shady trees. We must stay always in the back and sit on those long wooden benches there. We dassen't come in the front sitting-room or walk on the front steps what have carpet on it – we must walk on the back iron steps. Everything on the front from the house must be kept perfect for the show for visitors. We dassen't lay down on the beds in the daytime, the beds must always be made up perfect for the show for visitors.

'Gott im Himmel!' thinks I to myself; 'ain't there going to be no end to the things we dassen't do in this place?'

But still she went on. The children over two years dassen't stay around by the mothers. They must stay by the nurse in the play-room. By the meal-times, they can see their mothers. The children dassen't run around the house or tear up flowers or do anything. They dassen't holler or play rough in the play-room. They must always behave and obey the nurse.

We must always listen to the bells. Bell one was for getting up. Bell two, for getting babies' bottles. Bell three, for coming to breakfast. Bell four, for bathing the babies. If we come later, after the ring from the bell, then we'll not get what we need. If the bottle bell rings and we don't come right away for the bottle, then the baby don't get no bottle. If the breakfast bell rings, and we don't come right away down to the breakfast, then there won't be no breakfast for us.

When she got through with reading the rules, I was wondering which side of the house I was to walk on. At every step was some rule what said don't move here, and don't go there, don't stand there, and don't sit there. If I tried to remember the endless rules, it would only make me dizzy in the head. I was thinking for why, with so many rules, didn't they also have already another rule, about how much air in our lungs to breathe.

On every few days there came to the house swell ladies in auto-mobiles. It was for them that the front from the house had to be always perfect. For them was all the beautiful smelling flowers. For them the front porch, the front sitting-room, and the easy stairs with the carpet on it.

Always when the rich ladies came the fat lady, what was the boss from the vacation house, showed off to them the front. Then she took them over to the back to look on us, where we was sitting together, on long wooden benches, like prisoners. I was always feeling cheap like dirt, and mad that I had to be there, when they smiled down on us.

'How nice for these poor creatures to have a restful place like this,' I heard one lady say.

The next day I already felt like going back. The children what had to stay by the nurse in the play-room didn't like it neither.

'Mamma,' says Mendel to me, 'I wisht I was home and out in the street. They don't let us do nothing here. It's worser than school.'

'Ain't it a play-room?' asks I. 'Don't they let you play?'

'Gee wiss! play-room, they call it! The nurse hollers on us all the time. She don't let us do nothing.'

The reason why I stayed out the whole two weeks is this: I think to myself, so much shame in the face I suffered to come here, let me at least make the best from it already. Let me at least save up for two weeks what I got to spend out for grocery and butcher for my back bills to pay out. And then also think I to myself, if I go back on Monday, I got to do the big washing; on Tuesday waits for me the ironing; on Wednesday, the scrubbing and cleaning, and so goes it on. How bad it is already in this place, it's a change from the very same sameness of what I'm having day in and day out at home. And so I stayed out this vacation to the bitter end.

But at last the day for going out from this prison came. On the way riding back, I kept thinking to myself: 'This is such a beautiful vacation house. For why do they make it so hard for us? When a mother needs a vacation, why must they tear the insides out from her first, by making her come down to the charity office? Why drag us from the charity office through the streets? And when we live through the shame of the charities and when we come already to the vacation house, for why do they boss the life out of us with so many rules and bells? For why don't they let us lay down our heads on the bed when we are tired? For why must we always stick in the back, like dogs what have got to be chained in one spot? If they would let us walk around free, would we bite off something from the front part of the house?

'If the best part of the house what is comfortable is made up for a show for visitors, why ain't they keeping the whole business for a show for visitors? For why do they have to fool in worn-out mothers, to make them think they'll give them a rest? Do they need the worn-out mothers as part of the show? I guess that is it, already.'

When I got back in my home, so happy and thankful I was I could cry from thankfulness. How good it was feeling for me to be able to move around my own house, like I pleased. I was always kicking that my rooms was small and narrow, but now my small rooms seemed to grow so big like the park. I looked out from my window on the fire-escapes, full with bedding and garbage-cans, and on the wash-lines full with the clothes. All these ugly things was grand in my eyes. Even the high brick walls all around made me feel like a bird what just jumped out from a cage. And I cried out, 'Gott sei dank! Gott sei dank!'

1921

Dorothy Richardson

Dorothy Richardson was born in Berkshire in 1873; her father called her his 'son' and gave her the run of his library. She was privately educated, worked in Hanover, Germany, as a pupil-teacher and was a governess to a wealthy family in Finsbury Park, London, before taking a post as a Harley Street dentist's receptionist and supplementing her small income with journalism. She married Alan Odle in 1917 and they divided their lives between London and Cornwall until he died in the late forties.

Richardson didn't embark on *Pilgrimage*, the thirteen-volume experimental novel which she worked on intermittently for the rest of her life, until she was nearly forty. The original 'stream of consciousness' novel, its first volume, *Pointed Roofs* in 1915, anticipated the experimental forms of the more acknowledged modernists Joyce and Woolf; Woolf also credited Richardson with discovering what she called 'the psychological sentence of the feminine gender'. She died in Kent in 1957, having published twelve volumes of *Pilgrimage* between 1915 and 1938; another, *March Moonlight*, was posthumously published in 1967, shortly after which feminist critics in the 1970s rediscovered Richardson for the seminal force she was, and republished her work.

Virago published *Pilgrimage* in four volumes in 1979.

from

Deadlock

It was not only that it was her own perhaps altogether ignorant and lazy and selfish way of reading *everything* so that she grasped only the sound and the character of the words and the arrangement of the sentences, and only sometimes a long time afterwards, and with once-read books never, anything, except in books on philosophy, of the author's meaning . . . but always the author; in the first few lines; and after that, wanting to change him and break up his shape or going about for days thinking everything in his shape.

It was that there was nothing there. If there had been anything, reading so attentively, such an odd subject as Spanish literature, she would have gathered some sort of vague impression. But in all the close pages of cramped cruel pointed handwriting she had gleaned nothing at all. Not a single fact or idea; only Mr Lahitte; a voice like an empty balloon. The lecture was a fraud. *He* was. How far did he know this? Thinking of the audience, those few who could learn quickly enough to follow his voice, waiting and waiting for something but strings of superlatives, the same ones again and again, until the large hall became a prison and the defiant yellow-grey form a tormentor, and their impatience and restlessness turned to hatred and despair, she pitied him. Perhaps he had not read Spanish literature. But he must have consulted numbers of books about it, and that was much more than most people did. But what could she do? She glanced at her little page of notes. Break up sentences. Use participles instead of which. Vary adjectives. Have gaps and pauses here and there. Sometimes begin further off. What is picaresque? They had been written, enthusiastically, seeming like inspirations, in the first pages, before she had discovered the whole of the nothingness. Now they were only alterations that were not worth making; helping an imposition and being paid for it.

Stopford Brooke . . . Lecturing on Browning . . . blissful moonface with fringe of white hair, talking and talking, like song and prayer and politics, the past and the present showing together, Browning at the centre of life and outside it all over the world, and seeing forward to the future. Perfect quotations, short and long, and the end with the long description of Pompilia . . . rising and spreading and ceasing, not ending . . . standing out alive in the midst of a world still shaped by the same truths going on and on. 'A marvellous piece of analysis.' That young man had been waiting to say that to the other young man.

Introduce their philosophies of life, if any, she wrote; introduce quotations. But there was no time; quotations would have to be translated. Nothing could be done. The disaster was completely arranged. There was no responsibility. She gathered the accepted pages neatly together and began pencilling in improvements.

The pencilled sentences made a pleasant wandering decoration. The earlier ones were forgotten and unfamiliar. Re-read now, they surprised her. How had she thought of them? She had not thought of them. She had been closely following something, and they had come, quietly, in the midst of engrossment; but they were like a photograph, funny in their absurd likeness set there side by side with the photograph of Mr Lahitte. They were alive, gravely, after the manner of her graver self. It was a curious marvel, a revelation irrevocably put down, reflecting a certain sort of character . . . more oneself than anything that could be done socially, together with others, and yet not oneself at all, but something mysterious, drawn uncalculatingly from some fund of common consent, part of a separate impersonal life she had now unconsciously confessed herself as sharing. She remained bent motionless in the attitude of writing, to discover the quality of her strange state. The morning was raw with dense fog; at her Wimpole Street ledgers she would by this time have been cramped with cold; but she felt warm and tingling with life as if she had been dancing, or for a long while in happy social contact; yet so differently; deeply and serenely alive and without the blank anxious looking for the continuance of social excitement. This something would continue, it was in herself, independently. It was as if there were someone with her in the room, peopling her solitude and bringing close around her all her past solitudes, as if it were their secret. They greeted her; justified. Never again, so long as she could sit at work and lose herself to awake with the season forgotten and all the circumstances of her life coming back, as if narrated from the fascinating life of someone else, would they puzzle or reproach her.

She drew forth her first page of general suggestions, written so long ago that they already seemed to belong to some younger self, and copied them in ink. The sound of the pen shattered the silence like sudden speech. She listened entranced. The little strange sound was the living voice of the brooding presence. She copied the phrases in a shape that set them like a poem in the middle of the page, with even spaces between a wide uniform margin; not quite in the middle; the lower margin was wider than the upper; the poem wanted another line. She turned to the manuscript listening intently to the voice of Mr Lahitte pouring forth his sentences, and with a joyous rush penetrated the secret of its style. It was *artificial*. There was the last line of the poem summing up all the rest. Avoid, she wrote, searching; some word was coming; it was in her mind, muffled, almost clear; avoid – it flashed through and away, just missed. She recalled sentences that had filled her with hopeless fury, examining them curiously, without anger. Avoid ornate alias. So *that* was it! Just those few minutes glancing through the pages, standing by the table while the patient talked about her jolly, noisy, healthy, thoroughly *wicked* little kid, and now remembering every point he had made . . . extraordinary. But this was life! These strange unconsciously noticed things, living on in one, coming together at the right moment, part of a *reality*.

Rising from the table she found her room strange, the new room she had entered on the day of her arrival. She remembered drawing the cover from the table by the window and finding the ink-stains. There they were in the warm bright circle of midmorning lamplight, showing between the scattered papers. The years that had passed were a single short interval leading to the restoration of that first moment. Everything they contained centred there; her passage through them, the desperate graspings and droppings, had been a coming back. Nothing would matter now that the paper-scattered lamplit circle was established as the centre of life. Everything would be an everlastingly various joyful coming back. Held up by this secret place, drawing her energy from it, any sort of life would do that left this room and its little table free and untouched.

1922

Elizabeth von Arnim

Elizabeth von Arnim was born Mary Annette Beauchamp in Sydney, Australia, in 1866. She was educated in Ealing, London, and won prizes for music at school. She and her first husband, Count von Arnim, lived in Nassenheide, Pomerania, which inspired her extremely popular first book, *Elizabeth and her German Garden*. She wrote over twenty acclaimed books, signing many of them simply 'By Elizabeth'. A favourite theme was dreary or harsh marriage, or escapism from such a marriage or a similarly constraining lifestyle. After her first husband's death in 1910 she built the Chateau Soleil in Switzerland, where she entertained guests (such as H. G. Wells, with whom she had an affair) and relatives (such as Katherine Mansfield, her cousin). Her novels include *The Pastor's Wife* (1912), *Vera* (1921) and *Mr Skeffington* (1940). A second marriage, to Earl Russell, the brother of Bertrand Russell, was short-lived; they divorced in 1919. She moved to South Carolina on the outbreak of the Second World War, and died in 1941.

Virago published *The Enchanted April* in 1986.

from

The Enchanted April

Steadfast as the points of the compass to Mrs Arbuthnot were the great four facts of life: God, Husband, Home, Duty. She had gone to sleep on these facts years ago, after a period of much misery, her head resting on them as on a pillow; and she had a great dread of being awakened out of so simple and untroublesome a condition. Therefore it was that she searched with earnestness for a heading under which to put Mrs Wilkins, and in this way illumine and steady her own mind; and sitting there looking at her uneasily after her last remark, and feeling herself becoming more and more unbalanced and infected, she decided *pro tem*, as the vicar said at meetings, to put her under the heading Nerves. It was just possible that she ought to go straight into the category Hysteria, which was often only the antechamber to Lunacy, but Mrs Arbuthnot had learned not to hurry people into their final categories, having on more than one occasion discovered with dismay that she had made a mistake; and how difficult it had been to get them out again, and how crushed she had been with the most terrible remorse.

Yes. Nerves. Probably she had no regular work for others, thought Mrs Arbuthnot; no work that would take her outside herself. Evidently she was rudderless – blown about by gusts, by impulses. Nerves was almost certainly her category, or would be quite soon if no one helped her. Poor little thing, thought Mrs Arbuthnot, her own balance returning hand in hand with her compassion, and unable, because of the table, to see the length of Mrs Wilkins's legs. All she saw was her small, eager, shy face, and her thin shoulders, and the look of childish longing in her eyes for something that she was sure was going to make her happy. No; such things didn't make people happy, such fleeting things. Mrs Arbuthnot had learned in her long life with Frederick – he was her husband, and she had married him at twenty and was now thirty-three – where alone true joys are to be found. They are to be found, she now knew, only in daily, in hourly, living for others; they are to be found only – hadn't she over and over again taken her disappointments and discouragements there, and come away comforted? – at the feet of God.

Frederick had been the kind of husband whose wife betakes herself early to the feet of God. From him to them had been a short though painful step. It seemed short to her in retrospect, but it had really taken the whole of the first year of their marriage, and every inch of the way had been a struggle, and every inch of it was stained, she felt at the time, with her heart's blood. All that was over now. She had long since found peace. And Frederick, from her passionately loved bridegroom, from her worshipped young husband, had become second only to God on her list of duties and forbearances. There he hung, the second in importance, a bloodless thing bled white by her prayers. For years she had been able to be happy only by forgetting happiness. She wanted to stay like that. She wanted to shut out everything that would remind her of beautiful things, that might set her off again longing, desiring. . .

'I'd like so much to be friends,' she said earnestly. 'Won't you come and see me, or let me come to you sometimes? Whenever you feel as if you wanted to talk. I'll give you my address' – she searched in her handbag – 'and then you won't forget.' And she found a card and held it out.

Mrs Wilkins ignored the card.

'It's so funny,' said Mrs Wilkins, just as if she had not heard her, 'but I *see* us both – you and me – this April in the mediaeval castle.'

Mrs Arbuthnot relapsed into uneasiness. 'Do you?' she said, making an effort to stay balanced under the visionary gaze of the shining grey eyes. 'Do you?'

'Don't you ever see things in a kind of flash before they happen?' asked Mrs Wilkins.

'Never,' said Mrs Arbuthnot.

She tried to smile; she tried to smile the sympathetic yet wise and tolerant smile with which she was accustomed to listen to the necessarily biased and incomplete views of the poor. She didn't succeed. The smile trembled out.

'Of course,' she said in a low voice, almost as if she were afraid the

vicar and the Savings Bank were listening, 'it would be most beautiful – most beautiful—'

'Even if it were wrong,' said Mrs Wilkins, 'it would only be for a
month.'

1923

Rose Macaulay

Emilie Rose Macaulay was born in Rugby in 1881, and spent a
tomboyish childhood in England and Italy (she always believed she
might 'grow up to be a man', and in her early twenties was still endeav-
oring to join the Navy). She studied modern history from 1900 to
1903 at Somerville College, Oxford. In 1906 she published her first
novel, *Abbots Verney*, and over the next fifty years wrote, in her 'off-
hand, lightly-smiling manner' (as Katherine Mansfield said), over
twenty more plus volumes of poetry, travel writing, journalism, and
studies of writers including Milton and Forster. During the First World
War she worked as a clerk in the War Office dealing with applications
for Conscientious Objection; there she met the married ex-priest,
Gerald O'Donovan, with whom she was to have a clandestine relationship until his death in 1942. This relationship meant that Macaulay, an
'Anglo-Agnostic' as she put it, spent much of her life in a crisis of faith,
returning to religion later in the years before she died. These were also
the years of her most acclaimed novels, including *The Towers of Trebizond*
(1956). Macaulay lived for many years near Cambridge, was made
DBE in 1958, and died some months later.

Virago published *Told by an Idiot* in 1983.

from

Told by an Idiot

Meanwhile, the people settled down, were demobilised from the army, and from the various valuable services which they had been rendering to their country, and began to fall back into the old grooves, began to recover, at least partially, from the war. But the war had left its heritage, of poverty, of wealth, of disease, of misery, of discontent, of feverish unrest.

'Now to write again,' said Imogen, and did so, but found it difficult, for the nervous strain of the years past, and the silliness of the avocations she had pursued through them, had paralysed initiative, and given her, in common with many others, an inclination to sally forth after breakfast and catch a train or a bus, seeking such employment as might be created for her, instead of creating her own. The helpless industry of the slave had become hers, and to regain that of the independent and self-propelled worker was a slow business.

Further, she was absorbed, shaken and disturbed by a confusing and mystifying love into which she had fallen, blind and unaware, even before peace had descended. All values were to her subverted; she fumbled blindly at a world grown strange, a world as to whose meaning and whose laws she groped in the dark, and emotion drowned her like a flood

There revived in force about this time the curious old legend about the young The post-war young, they were now called, and once more people began to believe and to say that one young person closely resembles other young persons, and many more things about them.

'The war,' they said, 'has caused a hiatus, and thought has broken with tradition. Thus youth is no longer willing to accept forms and formulae only on account of their age. It has set out on a voyage of inquiry, and, finding some things which are doubtful and others which are insufficient, is searching for forms of expression more in harmony with the realities of life and knowledge.'

[. . .]

Never, perhaps, was thinking, writing and talking looser, vaguer, and more sentimental than in the years following the European war. It was as if that disaster had torn great holes in the human intelligence, which it could ill afford. There was much writing, both of verse and prose, much public and private speaking, much looking for employment and not finding it, much chat about the building of new houses, much foolish legislation, much murder and suicide, much amazement on the part of the press. Newspapers are always easily amazed, but since the war weakened even their intelligence there could not be so much as a little extra departure from railway stations on a Bank Holiday (surely most natural, if one thinks it out) without the ingenuous press placarding London with 'Amazing scenes.' The press was even amazed if a married couple sought divorce, or if it thundered, or was at all warm. 'Scenes,' they would say, 'scenes;' and the eager reader, searching their columns for these, could find none worthy of the name. One pictures newspaper reporters going about, struck dumb with amazement at every smallest incident in this amazing life we lead, hurrying back to their offices and communicating their emotion to editors, news editors and leader writers, so that the whole staff gapes, round-eyed, at the astonishing world on which they have to comment. An ingenuous race; but they make the mistake of forgetting that many of their readers are so very experienced that they are seldom surprised at anything

During these years, the sex disability as regards the suffrage being now removed, women stood freely for Parliament, but the electorate, being mostly of the male sex, showed that the only women they desired to have in Parliament were the wives of former members who had ceased to function as such, through death, peerage, or personal habits. Many women, including Stanley Croft, who, of course, stood herself, found this very disheartening. It seemed that the only chance for a woman who desired a political career was to marry a member and then put him out of action. Such women as were political in their own persons, who were educated and informed on one or more public topics, had small chance. 'We don't want to be ruled by the ladies,' the electorate firmly maintained. 'It's not their job. Their place is, etc.'

The world had not changed much since the reign of Queen Victoria.

And so, with the French firmly and happily settled in the Ruhr, their hearts full of furious fancies, declaring that it would not be French to stamp on a beaten foe, but that their just debts they would have, Germany rapidly breaking to pieces, drifting towards the rocks of anarchy or monarchy, and working day and night at the industry of printing million-mark notes, with Russia damned, as usual, beyond any conceivable recovery, with Italy suffering from a violent attack of Fascismo, with Austria counted quite out, with a set of horrid, noisy and self-conscious little war-born States in the heart of Europe, all neighbours and all feeling and acting as such, with Turkey making of herself as much of an all-round nuisance as usual, with Great Britain anxiously, perspiringly endeavouring both to arrest the progressive wreckage of Europe and to keep on terms with her late allies, and with Ireland enjoying at last the peace and blessings of Home Rule, Europe entered on her fifth year since the Armistice.

1924

Margaret Kennedy

Margaret Kennedy was born in Kensington, London, in 1896, daughter of a barrister, and the eldest of four children. She was educated at Cheltenham Ladies' College and Somerville College, Oxford, where she read history. Her first publication was a modern European history textbook, *A Century of Revolution*, in 1922. She followed this with a novel in 1923, *The Ladies of Lyndon*, but her next book, *The Constant Nymph*, a story of bourgeois society and bohemian living, loosely based on the aesthetic circles surrounding the painter Augustus John, was to become *the* bestseller of the 1920s. In 1925 she married David Davies, a successful barrister, and they lived in London.

Margaret Kennedy was also a literary biographer, critic, screenwriter and dramatist. Several of her plays were produced in London, and fourteen more novels were published before she died, in 1967, after four decades of highly praised and prizewinning fiction.

Virago published *The Constant Nymph* in 1983.

from

The Constant Nymph

'How soon can we be married?'

He would marry her and he would always be kind to her. That was the best he could do. What was she laughing at?

'I'll marry you,' she said, 'whenever you like. Lewis . . . tell the truth . . . it had only just occurred to you, hadn't it?'

'Oh, no,' he declared untruthfully. 'But I ought to have mentioned it earlier. Florence! As soon as we possibly can.'

He took her hand and kissed it. His boats were burned.

Once outside in the sunlight and traffic he could hardly make out how it had happened. The thing was absurd, unforeseen and unreasonable. But irrevocable now, and, on the whole, very pleasant. He was betrothed. Also he was very thirsty and was on the point of suggesting that they should go and have a drink somewhere when it occurred to him that she probably took tea at this hour. With a first conscious effort at adapting himself to the demands of a new life he took her to the restaurant where they had lunched and ordered coffee.

'Have some cake,' he urged. 'Have one of those pink cakes.'

He was so nervously eager to offer her the right thing that she laughed. She was sure that he had never fed a young lady with pink cakes before, and indeed he never had. Their coffee came, and she took off her gloves and poured it out, sitting opposite him, smiling her happy, tranquil smile at him across the table. He gave her back a glance which he felt to be very domestic and husbandlike. He felt as if he had been married already for quite a long time; as if his old, untamed existence was so long ago as to be almost legend. But a little bit of the legend was still alive, as he soon discovered, when he caught the eye of Minna Gertz, who was drinking with some students in the corner by the door. Minna was an old flame of his, the daughter of an innkeeper at Erfurt. Two years ago, when she served in her father's house, Lewis had been used to spend many pleasant hours in her company. Now she had migrated to the town and wore very fine hats and long boots buttoned up to her knees. She remembered him quite well though, because he had given her a pair of garnet earrings, and because he generally was remembered by people who had come across him, sometimes kindly, sometimes not. Minna was kind to everyone, but she despised him a little for being so poor. Seeing him now in the company of so beautiful, so obviously well born a lady, she opened her eyes very wide indeed and grinned at him expansively behind the lady's back. He nodded an amiable greeting. Florence turned round to see what he was smiling at, and looked a little surprised. He explained:

'That's Minna Gertz. Her father keeps an inn between Erfurt and Weissau. I've stayed there.'

Florence bent upon Minna that serene, interested scrutiny which she accorded to every new thing, observing her predecessor as if she had been a piece of architecture or an Alpine plant. She had the clear impersonal vision which is the fruit of an unshaken sense of security. Untouched, as yet, by any of life's betrayals, she could observe the world around her with a detachment impossible to her young cousins. They, with senses quickened to danger, would demand, of every strange thing, if it could hurt them and whether they wanted it.

She did not form any very favourable opinion of Minna, and thought she should have stayed in her father's inn. But she said:

'It's a pity they are giving up the peasant dress; it suits their build. That girl in Tyrolese dress must have looked comely, but in that hat you see all the coarseness of the peasant type without its rustic charm. But I suppose, to her, it's progress of a sort.'

Lewis said that he supposed so. He did not feel equal to discussing Minna's progress. He was busy proving to himself that marriage with Florence would not greatly derange his life. He did not want much; he could live quite contentedly anywhere. To make certain of this he announced that they would live in England when they were married, because it was a part of the world which he had formerly avoided.

'If you like,' she said. 'Your . . . people live in England, don't they?'

'My . . . Oh, yes!' he agreed, looking startled.

'In London you said?'

'Yes.'

'I don't want to bother you to tell me, if it's difficult. And nothing can make the slightest difference. But it's better for a wife to know, don't you think?'

'Know what?'

'What sort of people her husband belongs to. I haven't the vaguest idea about yours, Lewis, and you know all about mine.'

'My family are very disagreeable.'

'Yes?'

'That's all.'

'What do they consist of?'

'I've a father and a sister. My father was a school inspector. Now he's a Member of Parliament. And he writes books. Two a year. Little text books and outlines of things for schools and working men who want to educate themselves. Science and English literature and our Empire and those things.'

'Oh! Can he . . . is he . . . any relation to Sir Felix Dodd?'

'He is Sir Felix Dodd.'

'W—what?'

'He is Sir Felix Dodd.'

She was petrified with astonishment and could only sit gaping at him.

'Know him?' he asked pleasantly.

'My father knows him.'

'I'm sorry for your father then.'

She knew that Charles hated Sir Felix Dodd; he was always abusing him. They sat on many boards together, for the school inspector MP was a power in the educational world. Charles had dubbed him Fulsome Felix and avoided him as far as possible.

'Good heavens, Lewis!' she stammered, 'I can't . . . I never . . . how very strange! I never knew Sir Felix had a son, at least . . .'

She remembered now that she had heard of a son who was a terrible scamp, and must not be mentioned in the presence of anybody connected with the Dodds. What nonsense people talked!

'I mean I never knew his son was you.'

'Why should you?'

'Oh, it's the sort of thing one ought to know. You see, I'd heard your Symphony; but somehow I'd never connected . . .'

'It's natural. They don't boast of me, I imagine.'

'But . . . but . . . I know your sister then, by sight, anyhow. Millicent, isn't she? She was at college with me; but not my year. She sings, doesn't she? Gives ballad recitals?'

'She may. She always fancied her voice.'

'And then she married . . . oh, who? . . . Somebody in the Foreign Office . . . Simnel Gregory . . . Oh, Lewis! How extraordinary this is! I never thought . . .'

Lewis, for his peace of mind, did not grasp the full significance of it. It did not seem to him very important that Florence already knew all about his people. He said impatiently that he had quite lost touch with them and she wisely let the subject drop. Later on she would make him tell her what the trouble had been. And then, when they returned to England, she would smooth it all out. They must be brought to forgive him, whatever he had done.

For herself this news was a great blessing. She would not after all be forced to scandalise her family. She was radiant, as they set off for the station, feeling that life had been very good to her.

'I'd have married him,' she thought, 'if his father had been the hangman; but this does make a difference . . .'

1925

Ellen Glasgow

————

Ellen Glasgow was born in 1873, in Richmond, Virginia, where she lived for most of her life. A delicate child, the eighth of ten children, she educated herself by reading widely, writers like Darwin, Schopenhauer and Nietzsche, in her father's collection of books. (He was manager of one of the largest foundry and munitions works in the South.) A life of ill health, increasing deafness and domestic difficulty did not stop Glasgow writing. Her first novel, *The Descendant*, came out in 1902; she wrote ten more books – novels, short fiction and autobiography – and was awarded honorary degrees from four universities. She died in 1945.

Virago published *Barren Ground* in 1986.

from

Barren Ground

The big pine was like greenish bronze against the October sky. . .
A statue in Central Park had brought it back to her, the pine and
the ruined graveyard and the autumn sunlight raking the meadows. It
was a fortnight since she had come to New York, and in that fortnight
she felt that she had turned into stone. Her shoes were worn thin; her
feet throbbed and ached from walking on hard pavements. There
were times, especially toward evening, when the soles of her feet were
edged with fire, and the pain brought stinging tears to her eyes. Yet
she walked on grimly because it was easier to walk than to wait. Up
Fifth Avenue; down one of the cross streets to the Park, which was, she
thought, merely an imitation of the country; back again to Sixth
Avenue; and up Sixth Avenue until she drifted again over the Park
and into the prison-like streets that ran toward the river. Occasionally
she glanced up to read the name of a street; but the signs told her
nothing. Fifth Avenue she had learned by name, and Broadway, and
the dirty street where she rented a hall room, for fifty cents a day, over
a cheap restaurant. Yesterday, she had asked for work on the other
side of the city; but nobody wanted help in a store, and her obstinate
pride insisted that she would rather starve than take a place as a
servant. Twice she had waited in the restaurant beneath her room;
but the dirt and the close smells had nauseated her, and by the end of
the second day she had been too sick to stand on her feet. After that
the waitress whose place she had taken had returned, and the woman
in charge had not wanted her any longer. 'You'd better get used to
smells before you try to make a living in the city,' she had said dis-
agreeably. The advice was sound, as Dorinda knew, and she had no

just cause for resentment. Yet there were moments when it seemed to her that New York would live in her recollection not as a place but as an odour.

All day she walked from one stony street to another, stopping to rest now and then on a bench in one of the squares, where she would sit motionless for hours, watching the sparrows. Her food, usually a tough roll and a sausage of dubious tenderness, she bought at the cheapest place she could find and carried, wrapped in newspaper, to the bench where she rested. Her only hope, she felt, lay in the dogged instinct which told her that when things got as bad as they could, they were obliged, if they changed at all, to change for the better. There was no self-pity in her thoughts. The unflinching Presbyterian in her blood steeled her against sentimentality. She would meet life standing and she would meet it with her eyes open; but she knew that the old buoyant courage, the flowing outward of the spirit, was over for ever.

What surprised her, when she was not too tired to think of it, was that the ever-present sense of sin, which made the female mind in mid-Victorian literature resemble a page of the more depressing theology, was entirely absent from her reflections. She was sorry about the blue dress; she felt remorse because of the cow her mother might have had; but everything else that had happened was embraced in the elastic doctrine of predestination. It had to be, she felt, and no matter how hard she had struggled she could not have prevented it.

At night, worn out with fatigue, she would go back to the room over the restaurant. The brakeman on the train had given her the address, and he had put her in the street car that brought her to the door in Sixth Avenue. Here also the smells of beer and of the cooking below stairs had attacked her like nausea. The paper on the walls was torn and stained; all the trash in the room had been swept under the bed; and when she started to wash her hands at the rickety washstand in one corner, she had found a dead cockroach in the pitcher. Turning to the narrow window, she had dropped into a chair and stared down on the crawling throng in the street. Disgust, which was more irksome than pain, had rushed over her. After all the fuss that had been made over it, she had asked in bitter derision, was this Life?

[. . .]

At first the noises and the strange faces had confused her. Then it occurred to her that there might be temporary solace in the crowd, that she might lose herself in the street and drift on wherever the throng carried her. Her self-confidence returned when she found how easy it was to pursue her individual life, to retain her secret identity, in the midst of the city. She discovered presently that when nothing matters the problem of existence becomes amazingly simple. Fear, which had been perversely associated with happiness, faded from her mind when despair entered it. From several unpleasant episodes she had learned to be on the watch and to repulse advances that were disagreeable; but at such moments her courage proved to be as vast as her wretchedness. Once an elderly woman in deep mourning approached her while she sat on a bench in the Park, and inquired solicitously if she needed employment. In the beginning the stranger had appeared helpful; but a little conversation revealed that, in spite of her mourning garb, she was in search of a daughter of joy. After this several men had followed Dorinda on different occasions. 'Do I look like that kind?' she had asked herself bitterly. But in each separate instance, when she glanced round at her pursuer, he had vanished. In a city where joy may be had for a price, there are few who turn and follow the footsteps of tragedy. Yes, she could take care of herself. Poverty might prove to be a match for her strength, but as far as men were concerned, she decided that she had taken their measure and was no longer afraid of them.

A surface car clanged threateningly in her ears, and stepping back on the corner, she looked uncertainly over the block in front of her. While she hesitated there, a man who had passed turned and stared at her, arrested by the fresh colour in the face under the old felt hat. Her cheeks were thinner; there were violet half-moons under her eyes; but her eyes appeared by contrast larger and more radiantly blue. The suffering of the last two weeks, fatigue, hunger, and unhappiness had refined her features and imparted a luminous delicacy to her skin.

Threading the traffic to the opposite pavement, she turned aimlessly, without purpose and without conjecture, into one of the gloomy streets. It was quieter here, and after the clamour and dirt of Sixth Avenue, the quiet was soothing. Longer shadows stretched over the grey pavement, and the rows of dingy houses, broken now and then by the battered front of an inconspicuous shop, reminded her fantastically of acres of broomsedge. When she had walked several blocks she found that the character of the street changed slightly, and it occurred to her, as she glanced indifferently round, that by an accident she had drifted into the only old-fashioned neighbourhood in New York. Or were there others and had she been unable to find them? She had stopped, without observing it, in front of what had once been a flower garden, and had become, in its forlorn and neglected condition, a refuge for friendless statues and outcast objects of stone. For a few minutes the strangeness of the scene attracted her. Then, as the pain in her feet mounted upward to her knees, she moved on again and paused to look at a collection of battered mahogany furniture, which had overflowed from a shop to the pavement. 'I wonder what they'll do with that old stuff,' she thought idly. 'Some of it is good, too. There's a wardrobe exactly like the one great-grandfather left.'

She was looking at the mahogany wardrobe, when the door of the shop widened into a crack, and a grey and white cat, with a pleasant face, squeezed herself through and came out to watch the sparrows in the street.

'She is the image of Flossie,' thought Dorinda. Her eyes smarted with tears, and stooping over, she stroked the cat's arching back, while she remembered that her mother would be busy at this hour getting supper.

'Anybody can see you like cats,' said a voice behind her; and turning her head, she saw that a stout middle-aged woman, wearing a black knitted shawl over a white shirtwaist, was standing in the midst of the old furniture. Like her cat she had a friendly face and wide-awake eyes beneath sleek grey and white hair.

'She is just like one we had at home,' Dorinda answered, with her ingenuous smile.

'You don't live in New York, then?' remarked the woman, while she glanced charitably at the girl's faded tan ulster.

'No, I came from the country two weeks ago. I want to find something to do.'

The woman folded her shawl tightly over her bosom and shook her head. 'Well, it's hard to get work these days. There are so many walking the streets in search of it. The city is a bad place to be when you are out of work.'

Dorinda's heart trembled and sank. 'I thought there was always plenty to do in the city.'

'You did? Well, whoever told you that never tried it, I guess.'

1926

Sylvia Townsend Warner

———

Sylvia Townsend Warner was born in Harrow, north London, in 1893. She was educated privately, studied music, and spent a decade co-editing the ten-volume compilation *Tudor Church Music*. In the First World War she was a munitions worker. In 1925 she published a collection of poetry and the following year her first novel, *Lolly Willowes*, whose heroine passes from a dulled spinster's life into the realisation that 'nothing is impraticable for a single, middle-aged woman with an income of her own', not even witchcraft and conversations with the devil himself (the only man who'll really listen). Two more novels, *Mr Fortune's Maggot* and *The True Heart*, confirmed her early reputation as a remarkable original.

She was a member of the Executive Committee of the Association of Writers for Intellectual Liberty and, having joined the Communist Party and worked for the Red Cross in the Spanish Civil War, was a representative for the Congress of Madrid in 1937. She lived most of her adult life in quiet and passionate unorthodoxy in rural Dorset with her lover, the poet Valentine Ackland; she translated Proust, published seven novels, four volumes of poetry, several volumes of short stories (the *New Yorker* published more than 140 of her stories over forty years) and a highly acclaimed biography of T. H. White. She died in 1978.

Virago published *Lolly Willowes* in 1993.

from

Lolly Willowes

'Tell me about yourself.'

'Tell me first what *you* think,' he answered.

'I think' – she began cautiously (while he hid his cards it would not do to show all hers) – 'I think you are a kind of black knight, wandering about and succouring decayed gentlewomen.'

'There are warlocks too, remember.'

'I can't take warlocks so seriously, not as a class. It is we witches who count. We have more need of you. Women have such vivid imaginations, and lead such dull lives. Their pleasure in life is so soon over; they are so dependent upon others, and their dependence so soon becomes a nuisance. Do you understand?'

He was silent. She continued, slowly, knitting her brows in the effort to make clear to herself and him the thought that was in her mind:

'It's like this. When I think of witches, I seem to see all over England, all over Europe, women living and growing old, as common as blackberries, and as unregarded. I see them, wives and sisters of respectable men, chapel members, and blacksmiths, and small farmers, and Puritans. In places like Bedfordshire, the sort of country one sees from the train. You know. Well, there they were, there they are, child-rearing, house-keeping, hanging washed dishcloths on currant bushes; and for diversion each other's silly conversation, and listening to men talking together in the way that men talk and women listen. Quite different to the way women talk, and men listen, if they listen at all. And all the time being thrust further down into dullness when the one thing all women hate is to be thought dull. And on Sundays they

put on plain stuff gowns and starched white coverings on their heads
and necks – the Puritan ones did – and walked across the fields to
chapel, and listened to the sermon. Sin and Grace, and God and
the—' (she stopped herself just in time), 'and St Paul. All men's
things, like politics, or mathematics. Nothing for them except subjection and plaiting their hair. And on the way back they listened to
more talk. Talk about the sermon, or war, or cock-fighting; and when
they got back, there were the potatoes to be cooked for dinner. It
sounds very petty to complain about, but I tell you, that sort of thing
settles down on one like a fine dust, and by and by the dust is age, settling down. Settling down! You never die, do you? No doubt that's far
worse, but there is a dreadful kind of dreary immortality about being
settled down on by one day after another. And they think how they
were young once, and they see new young women, just like what they
were, and yet as surprising as if it had never happened before, like
trees in spring. But they are like trees towards the end of summer,
heavy and dusty, and nobody finds their leaves surprising, or notices
them till they fall off. If they could be passive and unnoticed, it would-
n't matter. But they must be active, and still not noticed. Doing,
doing, doing, till mere habit scolds at them like a housewife, and
rouses them up – when they might sit in their doorways and think – to
be doing still!'

She paused, out of breath. She had never made such a long speech
in the whole of her life, nor spoken with such passion. She scarcely
knew what she had said, and felt giddy and unaccustomed, as though
she had been thrown into the air and had suddenly begun to fly.

The Devil was silent, and looked thoughtfully at the ground. He
seemed to be rather touched by all this. She continued, for she feared
that if she did not go on talking she would grow ashamed at having
said so much.

'Is it true that you can poke the fire with a stick of dynamite in perfect safety? I used to take my nieces to scientific lectures, and I believe
I heard it then. Anyhow, even if it isn't true of dynamite, it's true of
women. But they know they are dynamite, and long for the concus-
sion that may justify them. Some may get religion, then they're all
right, I expect. But for the others, for so many, what can there be but
witchcraft? That strikes them real. Even if other people still find them
quite safe and usual, and go on poking with them, they know in their
hearts how dangerous, how incalculable, how extraordinary they are.
Even if they never do anything with their witchcraft, they know it's
there – ready! Respectable countrywomen keep their grave-clothes in

a corner of the chest of drawers, hidden away, and when they want a little comfort they go and look at them, and think that once more, at any rate, they will be worth dressing with care. But the witch keeps her cloak of darkness, her dress embroidered with signs and planets; that's better worth looking at. And think, Satan, what a compliment you pay her, pursuing her soul, lying in wait for it, following it through all its windings, crafty and patient and secret like a gentleman out killing tigers. Her soul – when no one else would give a look at her body even! And they are all so accustomed, so sure of her! They say: "Dear Lolly! What shall we give her for her birthday this year? Perhaps a hot-water bottle. Or what about a nice black lace scarf? Or a new workbox? Her old one is nearly worn out." But you say: "Come here, my bird! I will give you the dangerous black knight to stretch your wings in, and poisonous berries to feed on, and a nest made of bones and thorns, perched high up in danger where no one can climb to it." That's why we become witches: to show our scorn of pretending life's a safe business, to satisfy our passion for adventure. It's not malice, or wickedness – well, perhaps it *is* wickedness, for most women love that – but certainly not malice, not wanting to plague cattle and make horrid children spout up pins and – what is it? – "blight the genial bed". Of course, given the power, one may go in for that sort of thing, either in self-defence, or just out of playfulness. But it's a poor twopenny housewifely kind of witchcraft, black magic is, and white magic is no better. One doesn't become a witch to run round being harmful, or to run round being helpful either, a district visitor on a broomstick. It's to escape all that – to have a life of one's own, not an existence doled out to you by others, charitable refuse of their thoughts, so many ounces of stale bread of life a day, the workhouse dietary is scientifically calculated to support life. As for the witches who can only express themselves by pins and bed-blighting, they have been warped into that shape by the dismal lives they've led.'

1927

H.D.

———

Hilda Doolittle was born in Bethlehem, Pennsylvania, in 1886. She met Ezra Pound, a student of her father's, when she was fifteen, and was briefly engaged to him. Her studies at Bryn Mawr College were never completed; she toured Europe instead with her friend Frances Gregg (immortalised in the novel *Her*, which H.D. wrote in 1927 but which wasn't published until 1981). H.D. settled in London, married the writer Richard Aldington, co-edited *The Egoist* with T. S. Eliot when Aldington went to France in the First World War, and was one of Pound's self-styled Imagist group; her poems had been appearing in little magazines since 1913. Her most tenacious partnership, though, was with the heiress and writer Bryher (Winifred Ellerman), who supported H.D., adopted her daughter Perdita, funded and worked with her on the avant-garde film periodical *Close-Up*, and travelled with her through Europe until they settled in Switzerland. H.D.'s novels, all courageously experimental, include *Palimpsest* (1926) and *Bid Me to Live* (1960); one of the great modernist writers, she published eleven volumes of poetry, and an account of her analysis with Freud in 1933–4. She died in 1961.

Virago published *Her* in 1984.

from

Her

Minnie met Her by the steps. Minnie said, 'You stopped at the post office,' flung out like a sort of challenge. Minnie continued, 'Are there any letters?' Her fumbled with the lot, trying not to have to obliterate the memory of an eclipse of the sun by a huge bee (under a magnifying glass) by having to look at Minnie.

A huge bee lifted Her on translucent wings, flung straight upward, her legs either side of the stiff propeller-whirr of the wings, hung down into space. Her saw trees fly past her, trees darting downward, herself static. Trees showed clear in outline, but darker, all one colour, colour of dark cedars. Translucence of beewing veiled the terror of trees' protoplasmic function. Her rode toward a new realization . . . 'No, no letters,' not lifting her face to Minnie.

Opposite in the shadow of the porch, she sensed fragrance, tendrils of honeysuckle blossom, café-au-lait she knew and wax-white like checkerberries. She opened her eyes. At her feet, heliotrope . . . Minnie was there waiting for the letters. A face would loom at her, freckles magnified across a drawn pale countenance. She would hate Minnie and lifting her eyes to meet those, round, well-set but drained of any colour, Her would force, 'Oh Minnie . . . what a *lovely* dress you've got on.' Minnie must be flattered, compliment must fly and click and turn heels and bend gallantly. It was obvious that Minnie too was lonely though in an opposite direction. 'I think Minnie, there's no letter.'

Jock bounded off in the direction of the toolhouse, leapt ecstatically, came back. Her pushed off Jock. Minnie must never see that other people or other people's dogs liked Her. It was inevitable occasion, 'Nobody loves me.' Minnie had married Bertrand Gart. My brother Bertrand Gart. Hermione hid her brother in her gesture, braced, apologetic, by the porch step. I won't depend on Gart for greatness. Minnie was like some fraction to which everything had to be reduced. Minnie's very presence depreciated the house front, steps, the symmetrical recumbent jade pillars of low carefully clipped terrace. Minnie had on black stockings, white shoes, semitransparent sprigged organdie. Don't let her see I see her ruffles are set crooked. Straighten shoulders, don't let Minnie see how terribly black stockings with soiled white shoes upset me. 'What is that . . . spray thing I mean in your new organdie?' Ringed, washed-out blue eyes, Minnie and her eternal headaches. Escape, escape Minnie. 'But there are' (more business) 'letters.' Hermione handed Minnie Bertrand Gart's letters affecting not to know that Minnie wanted the whole lot, was waiting for the whole lot, had just said, 'I'll take the lot to father.'

Words that had not (in Philadelphia) been invented, beat about them: Oedipus complex, inferiority complex, claustrophobia. Words beat and sizzled and a word bent backward like a saw in a sawmill reversed, turned inward, to work horrible destruction. The word 'father' as Minnie spoke it, reversed itself inward, tore at the inner lining of the thing called Her Gart. It tore her inner being so that she stood stiff, alert, trying in some undefined and ineffectual manner to be 'fair'. What was it Minnie did to her, reversing machinery so that a simple word 'father' wrought such untoward havoc?

'Father' went with a river, a leap out from a boat, a forest where oaks obligingly dropped cups and saucers, acorns and their scattered woodhusks. Cups and saucers set upright on a flat stone while the wood was ringed with frail lavender, the low leafless Quaker-ladies or as some called them, bluets. 'Father' was a run forward, a plunge backward; that thing had now no visible embodiment. Nevertheless to hear Minnie say 'father' was a two-edged theft. It stole from Her a presence that left her (no one else had) alone and that again stole from her a presence: the thing that would have had that other hound, twin hounds, fleet-footed, the half of herself that was forever missing. If her father was also the father to . . . this thing, then the half of her, that twin-self sister would be forever blighted. Hermione knew she was fantastically over-wrought, bending down closer, then hiding her face to explain, 'Jock only likes me as I take him to get letters.'

Jock sometimes carried a newspaper . . . but Hermione could not trust him not to drop the letters. She tried to concentrate on Jock . . . remembering how Minnie had said 'father'. It was still incredible to

Hermione, though she tried to fend off odd superstition, that she and Minnie should call the same person 'father'. Hiding her face against the homely ginger of Jock's soft wool, she tried to dissemble: 'Minnie, I *will* take him to the lake creek, he needs a whole day bathing.' Minnie would not answer. There was no use thinking that she would ever answer. Minnie was there, a barometer that showed always glowering weather. Her eyes were the colour of mauve blotting paper that has faded almost white and is smudged with inkmarks. The inkmarks must be because Minnie had a headache, rings under Minnie's woebegone, sad eyes. It was incredible how a creature of Minnie's disposition could take it out of everyone. She set for them all a standard, 'At our Aunt Lydia's.' Aunt Lydia had never even deigned to call on Minnie, perhaps there was no Lydia . . . silver boxes late for a wedding, don't prove anything.

It was an incredible thing. Minnie made her feel eight, nine with a page of those fractions which all have to be resolved to something different because one of them is of a different common . . . something. Denominator. Even the least thought of add, subtract made Her feel blurred, she could not ever again casually deal with fractions in composite values. Minnie however was, she knew it, the one fraction that reduced them all, as family, to that level.

1928

Virginia Woolf

———

Virginia Woolf was born Adeline Virginia Stephen in 1882. While her brothers were sent to public school, she devoured her father's library and educated herself. Her mother died in 1895, precipitating the first in a series of physical and mental breakdowns for Woolf. In 1905 she began writing criticism for the *Times Literary Supplement*; by now she and her brothers and sister lived in Gordon Square, Bloomsbury, and friends' gatherings at the house became what is now known as the Bloomsbury Group. In 1912 she married one of the regular visitors, Leonard Woolf.

She started her first novel, *The Voyage Out*, in her late twenties; it was published in 1915 and, as Woolf began what would be the transformation of the English novel, was followed by book after ground-breaking book, all published by the Woolfs' own Hogarth Press – which also published Mansfield's *Prelude* (1918) and Eliot's *Poems* (1919) and *The Waste Land* (1922). *Orlando*, Woolf's lightest, most playful novel, was her biggest commercial success; a spoof of English literature, English sexuality and English history, and a love-gift to the writer and aristocrat Vita Sackville-West.

Although Woolf was an unparalleled novelist, diarist, polemic essayist and critic, her literary reputation suffered for decades after her death by drowning in 1941, and her work would still be undervalued today, had feminist criticism not given her back her proper place as one of the twentieth-century greats.

Virago published *Orlando* in 1992

from

Orlando

And as she drove, we may seize the opportunity, since the land-scape was of a simple English kind which needs no description, to draw the reader's attention more particularly than we could at the moment to one or two remarks which have slipped in here and there in the course of the narrative. For example, it may have been observed that Orlando hid her manuscripts when interrupted. Next, that she looked long and intently in the glass; and now, as she drove to London, one might notice her starting and suppressing a cry when the horses galloped faster than she liked. Her modesty as to her writing, her vanity as to her person, her fears for her safety all seems to hint that what was said a short time ago about there being no change in Orlando the man and Orlando the woman, was ceasing to be altogether true. She was becoming a little more modest, as women are, of her brains, and a little more vain, as women are, of her person. Certain susceptibilities were asserting themselves, and others were diminishing. The change of clothes had, some philosophers will say, much to do with it. Vain trifles as they seem, clothes have, they say, more important offices than merely to keep us warm. They change our view of the world and the world's view of us. For example, when Captain Bartolus saw Orlando's skirt, he had an awning stretched for her immediately, pressed her to take another slice of beef, and invited her to go ashore with him in the long-boat. These compliments would certainly not have been paid her had her skirts, instead of flowing, been cut tight to her legs in the fashion of breeches. And when we are paid compliments, it behoves us to make some return. Orlando curtseyed; she complied; she flattered the good man's humours as she would not have done had his neat breeches been a woman's skirts, and his braided coat a woman's satin bodice. Thus, there is much to support the view that it is clothes that wear us and not we them; we may make them take the mould of arm or breast, but they mould our hearts, our brains, our tongues to their liking. So, having now worn skirts for a considerable time, a certain change was visible in Orlando, which is to be found if the reader will look at plate 5, even in her face. If we compare the picture of Orlando as a man with that of Orlando as a woman we shall see that though both are undoubtedly one and the same person, there are certain changes. The man has his hand free to seize his sword, the woman must use hers to keep the satins from slipping from her shoulders. The man looks the world full in the face, as if it were made for his uses and fashioned to his liking. The woman takes a sidelong glance at it, full of subtlety, even of suspicion. Had they both worn the same clothes, it is possible that their outlook might have been the same.

That is the view of some philosophers and wise ones, but on the whole, we incline to another. The difference between the sexes is, happily, one of great profundity. Clothes are but a symbol of something hid deep beneath. It was a change in Orlando herself that dictated her choice of a woman's dress and of a woman's sex. And perhaps in this she was only expressing rather more openly than usual – openness indeed was the soul of her nature – something that happens to most people without being thus plainly expressed. For here again, we come to a dilemma. Different though the sexes are, they intermix. In every human being a vacillation from one sex to the other takes place, and often it is only the clothes that keep the male or female likeness, while underneath the sex is the very opposite of what it is above. Of the complications and confusions which thus result everyone has had experience; but here we leave the general question and note only the odd effect it had in the particular case of Orlando herself.

For it was this mixture in her of man and woman, one being uppermost and then the other, that often gave her conduct an unexpected turn. The curious of her own sex would argue, for example, if Orlando was a woman, how did she never take more than ten minutes to dress? And were not her clothes chosen rather at random, and sometimes worn rather shabby? And then they would say, still, she has none of the formality of a man, or a man's love of power. She is excessively tender-hearted. She could not endure to see a donkey beaten or a kitten drowned. Yet again, they noted, she detested household matters, was up at dawn and out among the fields in summer before the sun had risen. No farmer knew more about the crops than she did. She could drink with the best and liked games of hazard. She rode well and drove six horses at a gallop over London Bridge. Yet again, though bold and active as a man, it was remarked that the sight of another in danger brought on the most womanly palpitations. She would burst into tears on slight provocation. She was unversed in geography, found mathematics intolerable, and held some caprices which are more common among women than men, as for instance that to travel south is to travel downhill. Whether, then, Orlando was most man or woman, it is difficult to say and cannot now be decided. For her coach was now rattling on the cobbles. She had reached her home in the city. The steps were being let down; the iron gates were being opened. She was entering her father's house at Blackfriars, which though fashion was fast deserting that end of the town, was still a pleasant, roomy mansion, with gardens running down to the river, and a pleasant grove of nut trees to walk in.

1929

Nella Larsen

———

Nella Larsen was born in the early 1890s in Chicago to a Danish mother and a West Indian father who died when she was small; she was brought up by a white stepfather. She studied at a white private school, became a nurse after college, then a librarian. She married Elmer Samuel Imes, a black university scientist, in 1919. In 1926 she published some pseudonymous stories; her first novel, the prize-winning *Quicksand*, was published in 1928; her second, *Passing* (the term for successfully pretending to be white), came out in 1929 and won great acclaim for Larsen as well as a Guggenheim award (Larsen was the first black woman to receive such an award for fiction) to write about black experience in both Europe and the USA. But this and other projects were left unfinished after Larsen was charged with plagiarising a short story of Sheila Kaye-Smith's in 1930 – a charge later proven unfounded. She never recovered sufficiently from the scandal to write anything else. In the same year she divorced Imes, and she lived on alimony until 1941, when she went back to nursing. She died in 1964, her literary achievement practically forgotten.

from

Passing

The tea-things had been placed on a low table at Clare's side. She gave them her attention now, pouring the rich amber fluid from the tall glass pitcher into stately slim glasses, which she handed to her guests, and then offered them lemon or cream and tiny sandwiches or cakes.

After taking up her own glass she informed them: 'No, I have no boys and I don't think I'll ever have any. I'm afraid. I nearly died of terror the whole nine months before Margery was born for fear that she might be dark. Thank goodness, she turned out all right. But I'll never risk it again. Never! The strain is simply too — too hellish.'

Gertrude Martin nodded in complete comprehension.

This time it was Irene who said nothing.

'You don't have to tell me!' Gertrude said fervently. 'I know what it is all right. Maybe you don't think I wasn't scared to death too. Fred said I was silly, and so did his mother. But, of course, they thought it was just a notion I'd gotten into my head and they blamed it on my condition. They don't know like we do, how it might go way back, and turn out dark no matter what colour the father and mother are.'

Perspiration stood out on her forehead. Her narrow eyes rolled first in Clare's, then in Irene's direction. As she talked she waved her heavy hands about.

'No,' she went on, 'no more for me either. Not even a girl. It's awful the way it skips generations and then pops out. Why, he actually said he didn't care what colour it turned out, if I would only stop worrying about it. But, of course, nobody wants a dark child.' Her voice was earnest and she took for granted that her audience was in entire agreement with her.

Irene, whose head had gone up with a quick little jerk, now said in a voice of whose even tones she was proud: 'One of my boys is dark.'

Gertrude jumped as if she had been shot at. Her eyes goggled. Her mouth flew open. She tried to speak, but could not immediately get the words out. Finally she managed to stammer: 'Oh! And your husband, is he – is he – er – dark, too?'

Irene, who was struggling with a flood of feelings, resentment, anger, and contempt, was, however, still able to answer as coolly as if she had not that sense of not belonging to and of despising the company in which she found herself drinking iced tea from tall amber glasses on that hot August afternoon. Her husband, she informed them quietly, couldn't exactly 'pass'.

At that reply Clare turned on Irene her seductive caressing smile and remarked a little scoffingly: 'I do think that coloured people – we – are too silly about some things. After all, the thing's not important to Irene or hundreds of others. Not awfully, even to you, Gertrude. It's only deserters like me who have to be afraid of freaks of the nature. As my inestimable dad used to say, "Everything must be paid for." Now, please one of you tell me what ever happened to Claude Jones. You know, the tall, lanky specimen who used to wear that comical little moustache that the girls used to laugh at so. Like a thin streak of soot. The moustache, I mean.'

At that Gertrude shrieked with laughter. 'Claude Jones!' and launched into the story of how he was no longer a Negro or a Christian but had become a Jew.

'A Jew!' Clare exclaimed.

'Yes, a Jew. A black Jew, he calls himself. He won't eat ham and goes to the synagogue on Saturday. He's got a beard now as well as a moustache. You'd die laughing if you saw him. He's really too funny for words. Fred says he's crazy and I guess he is. Oh, he's a scream all right, a regular scream!' And she shrieked again.

Clare's laugh tinkled out. 'It certainly sounds funny enough. Still, it's his own business. If he gets along better by turning—'

At that, Irene, who was still laughing her unhappy don't-care feeling of rightness, broke in, saying bitingly: 'It evidently doesn't occur to either you or Gertrude that he might possibly be sincere in changing his religion. Surely everyone doesn't do everything for gain.'

Clare Kendry had no need to search for the full meaning of that utterance. She reddened slightly and retorted seriously: 'Yes, I admit that might be possible – his being sincere, I mean. It just didn't happen to occur to me, that's all. I'm surprised,' and the seriousness changed to mockery, 'that you should have expected it to. Or did you really?'

'You don't, I'm sure, imagine that that is a question that I can answer,' Irene told her. 'Not here and now.'

Gertrude's face expressed complete bewilderment. However, seeing that little smiles had come out on the faces of the two other women and not recognising them for the smiles of mutual reservations which they were, she smiled too.

Clare began to talk, steering carefully away from anything that might lead towards race or other thorny subjects. It was the most brilliant exhibition of conversational weight-lifting that Irene had ever seen. Her words swept over them in charming well-modulated streams. Her laughs tinkled and pealed. Her little stories sparkled.

Irene contributed a bare 'Yes' or 'No' here and there, Gertrude, a 'You don't say!' less frequently.

For a while the illusion of general conversation was nearly perfect. Irene felt her resentment changing gradually to a silent, somewhat grudging admiration.

Clare talked on, her voice, her gestures, colouring all she said of wartime in France, of after-the-wartime in Germany, of the excitement at the time of the general strike in England, of dressmakers' openings in Paris, of the new gaiety of Budapest.

But it couldn't last, this verbal feat. Gertrude shifted in her seat and fell to fidgeting with her fingers. Irene, bored at last by all this repetition of the selfsame things that she had read all too often in papers, magazines, and books, set down her glass and collected her bag and handkerchief. She was smoothing out the tan fingers of her gloves preparatory to putting them on when she heard the sound of the outer door being opened and saw Clare spring up with an expression of relief saying: 'How lovely! Here's Jack at exactly the right minute. You can't go now, 'Rene dear.'

John Bellew came into the room. The first thing that Irene noticed about him was that he was not the man that she had seen with Clare Kendry on the Drayton roof. This man, Clare's husband, was a tallish person, broadly made. His age she guessed to be somewhere between thirty-five and forty. His hair was dark brown and waving, and he had a soft mouth, somewhat womanish, set in an unhealthy-looking dough-coloured face. His steel-grey opaque eyes were very much alive, moving ceaselessly between thick bluish lids. But there was, Irene decided, nothing unusual about him, unless it was an impression of latent physical power.

'Hello, Nig,' was his greeting to Clare.

Gertrude who had started slightly, settled back and looked covertly towards Irene, who had caught her lip between her teeth and sat gazing at husband and wife. It was hard to believe that even Clare Kendry would permit this ridiculing of her race by an outsider, though he chanced to be her husband. So he knew, then, that Clare was a Negro? From her talk the other day Irene had understood that he didn't. But how rude, how positively insulting, for him to address her in that way in the presence of guests!

In Clare's eyes, as she presented her husband, was a queer gleam, a jeer, it might be. Irene couldn't define it.

The mechanical professions that attend an introduction over, she inquired: 'Did you hear what Jack called me?'

'Yes,' Gertrude answered, laughing with a dutiful eagerness.

Irene didn't speak. Her gaze remained level on Clare's smiling face.

The black eyes fluttered down. 'Tell them, dear, why you call me that.'

The man chuckled, crinkling up his eyes, not, Irene was compelled to acknowledge, unpleasantly. He explained: 'Well, you see, it's like this. When we were first married, she was white as – as – well as white as a lily. But I declare she's gettin' darker and darker. I tell her if she don't look out, she'll wake up one of these days and find she's turned into a nigger.'

He roared with laughter. Clare's ringing bell-like laugh joined his. Gertrude after another uneasy shift in her seat added her shrill one. Irene, who had been sitting with lips tightly compressed, cried out: 'That's good!' and gave way to gales of laughter. She laughed and laughed and laughed. Tears ran down her cheeks. Her sides ached. Her throat hurt. She laughed on and on and on, long after the others had subsided. Until, catching sight of Clare's face, the need for a more quiet enjoyment of this priceless joke, and for caution, struck her. At once she stopped.

Clare handed her husband his tea and laid her hand on his arm with an affectionate little gesture. Speaking with confidence as well as with amusement, she said: 'My goodness, Jack! What difference would it make if, after all these years, you were to find out that I was one or two per cent coloured?'

Bellew put out his hand in a repudiating fling, definite and final.

'Oh, no, Nig,' he declared, 'nothing like that with me. I know you're
no nigger, so it's all right. You can get as black as you please as far as
I'm concerned, since I know you're no nigger. I draw the line at that.
No niggers in my family. Never have been and never will be.'

Irene's lips trembled almost uncontrollably, but she made a desperate effort to fight back her disastrous desire to laugh again, and
succeeded. Carefully selecting a cigarette from the lacquered box on
the tea-table before her, she turned an oblique look on Clare and
encountered her peculiar eyes fixed on her with an expression so
dark and deep and unfathomable that she had for a short moment
the sensation of gazing into the eyes of some creature utterly strange
and apart. A faint sense of danger brushed her, like the breath of a
cold fog. Absurd, her reason told her, as she accepted Bellew's prof-
fered light for her cigarette. Another glance at Clare showed her
smiling. So, as one always ready to oblige, was Gertrude.

An on-looker, Irene reflected, would have thought it a most con-
genial tea-party, all smiles and jokes and hilarious laughter. She said
humorously: 'So you dislike Negroes, Mr Bellew?' But her amusement was at her thought, rather than her words.

John Bellew gave a short denying laugh. 'You got me wrong there,
Mrs Redfield. Nothing like that at all. I don't dislike them, I hate
them. And so does Nig, for all she's trying to turn into one. She
wouldn't have a nigger maid around her for love nor money. Not
that I'd want her to. They give me the creeps. The black scrimy devils.'

This wasn't funny. Had Bellew, Irene inquired, ever known any
Negroes? The defensive tone of her voice brought another start from
the uncomfortable Gertrude, and, for all her appearance of serenity,
a quick apprehensive look from Clare.

Bellew answered: 'Thank the Lord, no! And never expect to! But I
know people who've known them, better than they know their black
selves. And I read in the papers about them. Always robbing and
killing people. And,' he added darkly, 'worse.'

From Gertrude's direction came a queer little suppressed sound, a
snort or a giggle. Irene couldn't tell which. There was a brief silence,
during which she feared that her self-control was about to prove too
frail a bridge to support her mounting anger and indignation. She
had a leaping desire to shout at the man beside her: 'And you're sitting here surrounded by three black devils, drinking tea.'

The impulse passed, obliterated by her consciousness of the danger
in which such rashness would involve Clare, who remarked with a
gentle reprovingness: 'Jack dear, I'm sure 'Rene doesn't care to hear

all about your pet aversions. Nor Gertrude either. Maybe they read the papers too, you know.' She smiled on him, and her smile seemed to transform him, to soften and mellow him, as the rays of the sun does a fruit.

'All right, Nig, old girl. I'm sorry,' he apologised. Reaching over, he playfully touched his wife's pale hands, then turned back to Irene. 'Didn't mean to bore you, Mrs Redfield. Hope you'll excuse me,' he said sheepishly. 'Clare tells me you're living in New York. Great city, New York. The city of the future.'

1930s

1930

Vita Sackville-West

————

Vita Sackville-West was born at Knole in Kent in 1892, the only child of Lionel, Baron Sackville. She grew up loving Knole, and, because she was a girl, unable to inherit it (this was one of the inspirations behind Virginia Woolf's 'biography' of Sackville-West, *Orlando*, in which Woolf symbolically gifts her the house). A dashing, handsome figure, she had written eight novels by the time she was eighteen (one in French). At school in London she met Violet Trefusis, with whom she'd later have a long love affair; in 1913 she married Harold Nicolson, and together they bought Sissinghurst Castle in Kent, where they created their famous garden.

A dramatist and poet as well as a novelist – she valued her poetry above her other writings, and won the Hawthornden Prize for her 1926 poem *The Land* – she was also a writer of gardening books and newspaper columns, a book reviewer, travel writer, biographer, translator and broadcaster; amazingly prolific, and a person of great versatility in matters of both heart and art. She died in 1962.

Virago published *The Edwardians* in 1983.

from

The Edwardians

After dinner, primed by his mother's discreet signals, he moved round to talk to the Italian ambassador. He rather liked old Potini, a crank on the subject of the English character. Sebastian, depressed now and disgusted – for he suffered acutely from his moods – would have welcomed any argument, and knew he would get entertainment from old Potini, who was always bursting with things he wanted to say. Among the ruins of the dinner-table, Sebastian drew a chair up beside him, holding a glass of port under the light, and old Potini began at once, rubbing his cigar between his fingers: 'Ah, you young man! you fortunate young man! home from Oxford, I suppose? Yes, Oxford, that strange university where you young men live in segregation; a town of masculine citizens.' The ambassador's English was faultless, if a trifle elaborate; the only thing which betrayed him was the rolling of his r's. 'Now such a thing, my dear duke,' he said, drawing his chair a little nearer to Sebastian and talking confidentially, 'would be unthinkable in Italy. Or, indeed, in any Latin country. The English have no interest in women – in Woman, that is to say. What do you care about a pretty ankle? You think a lot about the fetlocks of your polo ponies, but when you look at a woman you rarely look below her face. Oh, I assure you. You yourself are nineteen – twenty? And what part do women play in your life? What do you do in the evenings at Oxford? You sit with your friends, hugging your knees and smoking your pipe, and you talk about – what? Sport, politics. Woman might not exist; she is Bad Form. An evening in London now and then, I daresay,' – and his chuckle made Sebastian feel as though the ambassador had given him a dig in the ribs, – 'then back to this male life among a thousand other young men, as though nothing had happened. Yes, you are a strange race, a secret race, ashamed of being natural. Now in Italy, at your age. . .' The ambassador's words threw Sebastian into an ill humour; he was stung, disturbed; he was ashamed of his virginity. People were not very real to him, and women least real of all. Little did he foresee, as he sat scowling at his wine, the adventure that was about to befall him. He wondered only how soon he might interrupt Potini, and suggest joining the ladies upstairs.

'Nothing ever happens,' said Sebastian violently; 'day after day goes by, and it is always the same.'

'Happenings go in series,' said Lady Roehampton, 'nothing happens, as you say; and then several things happen in a quick, odd succession. It is as though life had been gathering strength over a long period for an effort. Notice that for yourself. It is no good my telling you. One never believes other people's experience, and one is only very gradually convinced by one's own. Oh, my dear Sebastian,' she said – and she ceased to quote Mrs Cheyne and spoke for once in all sincerity, remembering a young lover who had died – 'think of all the people who have died too young to have learnt their own wisdom.'

They were walking in the garden after dinner, up and down the long path that ran parallel with the house. From the windows of the house streamed yellow light, and the sounds of music. Overhead, the sky was black and starry, and the trees of the garden were massed darkly against the faintly lingering light of the horizon. The summer air was warm and scented. Sebastian had forced her to come out; still disturbed by the veiled sneers of Potini, he had felt it necessary to make a determined gesture, and in this company of strangely artificial standards he could think of nothing more drastic than to deprive his mother's bridge-tables of Lady Roehampton's presence. He smiled inwardly and ironically at the inadequacy of his caprice; it had created so much annoyance, an annoyance, he felt, which in other company would be reserved for something of real emotional importance; yet it was an annoyance discreetly controlled, with the perfect manners of those well-bred people. Lady Roehampton herself had alone displayed graciousness; she had smiled on the boy who, suddenly masterful, demanded her society. She had risen with a great billowing of blue taffeta skirts – a graceful, warm uprising of her beauty, conscious that many eyes were curiously and speculatively turned towards her. Sebastian was intensely aware of her quality as she strolled beside him; her quality of a beautiful woman exquisitely finished, with a perfect grasp on life, untroubled, shrewd, mature, secret, betraying her real self to none. Compared with her, he felt vague and incapable of coming to terms with life. Yet he felt he could talk to her. She was charming, dangerous; he could talk to her. The knowledge that she was wholly unworthy of his confidence added a spice of pleasurable pain to the humiliation of giving himself away. For Sebastian liked to pour vinegar into his own wounds.

1931

Naomi Mitchison

Naomi Mitchison was born in Edinburgh in 1897, daughter of the philosopher and physiologist John Scott Haldane and the active suffragist Louisa Kathleen Trotter. Both she and her brother (J. B. S. Haldane the biologist) went to the Dragon School, Oxford, Naomi as one of only two girls at the school. She studied at St Anne's, Oxford, until she became a nurse in the First World War. In 1916 she married Dick Mitchison, later a Labour MP; throughout her life she combined literature with politics. She visited the Soviet Union in the 1930s, and helped establish the first birth-control clinic in London.

Her early fiction (she used to write sitting on the Underground, going round and round on the Circle Line) was historical, beginning with *The Conquered* in 1923; an exploration of the contemporary from the perspective of the far past. *The Corn King and the Spring Queen*, her study of the individual's relation to the masses, is set in the first and second centuries BC. She was astonishingly prolific; a novelist, a short-story writer, poet, dramatist, autobiographer and essayist. Later fiction was often post-apocalyptic science fiction; all her work is characterised by lightness, a sense of the pioneering mind, an intelligence of voice and an unwavering optimism. In the fifties, Naomi Mitchison became tribal mother to the Bakgatla people of Botswana. Even in her nineties she was still writing fiction: 'I just can't stop,' she wrote. She died in 1999.

Virago published *The Corn King and the Spring Queen* in 1983.

from

The Corn King and the Spring Queen

The snow began to melt. The earth began to show, ready to wake up. Several small things happened to Erif Der. She would not perhaps have paid much attention to them any other year, but now she did, her dreams got full of them. Her pony mare died suddenly and so did the magpie which Philylla had given her and which she had kept indoors and warm by the fire and fed with her own hands. She caught a bad cold, and then her nose bled in the middle of a feast. Half the stock fish in the store seemed to have got wet, and went bad. Klint had spots and cried. She lost various things. She dropped and broke one of the pots for sowing flax seed in her Spring-field. She had to get another made. The first one cracked in the kiln and the second one was a little crooked, but she dared not say so or the potter would swear it had been straight when it left him, and people would talk still more. The time for Plowing Eve came nearer and Tarrik grew excited again and happy, but a long way from her. He came into her room in the red and yellow coats he wore about that time, and his eyes were bright and he did not seem to be able to understand why she should be anxious and unhappy. It was as though he were only aware of the part of her which corresponded with the mood that was on him now. He played with Klint, tossed him and rolled him and felt about in his mouth for teeth, laughed at the little hard gums biting on his fingers, and the baby knew and held up his arms and tried to roll over towards Tarrik when he saw him coming. But he seemed a little frightened of his mother now; some-time he would cry suddenly and turn his face away. Erif said gaily that it was teeth, but she did not think so. She was very abrupt with him, suddenly snatching him up and then as suddenly handing him back at arm's length to the nurses.

Plowing Eve came. The people of Marob gathered at the fallow field and the jars of drink went round. The shouting began. Noon came, and the ring parted to let through the Corn King and the Spring Queen. Erif felt them watching her, heard a curious, alarming quality in the shouting, shivered and whitened as she went through, forced herself on against sickening fear. She brushed against a plowing mark and heard a little gasp as it wavered, was suddenly afraid she was not really settled in the middle of the field, at last dropped her head over her wrists and tried to breathe calmly and wait and cease to be herself.

But she could not do it. Her senses could not keep still and let her be. She heard the grunting and plodding of the oxen as the plow started. The wind blew smells towards her, the crowd and its drink, then after a time the opened earth. Her odd dress fidgeted her; she wanted to move; her hands were bitterly cold. Her eyeballs shifted under their lids. And then she began to hear the Corn King talking about the plowing and she knew she would have to answer. And suddenly she also knew that it was not merely the reluctance of a difficult spring which she felt. The spring was not in her at all. She had lost touch with Marob and Marob's spring. She was not the Spring Queen!

Ah then, then, pretend! Act it until it becomes real. With a great effort she raised her head to answer. It would not be impossibly difficult. Yes, the answers were coming into her mind. She heard the people calling to her urgently from all round: 'Spring Queen, be kind, be kind!' She loved them; they were her people; she would not hurt Marob! She would go through with Plowing Eve and force the spring to come.

She went on answering to Tarrik's plowing talk. It seemed to be all right. Yes, it was going to be! Why be anxious? She was strong, she was well. She was not pregnant. She had a baby at home and a splendid husband here on the field; it was all right. The spring would come, the earth would be young again and covered with flowers. Every year Marob grew young again. Trees that had been old in dull and tattered leaves grew young again. Fields that had been rough and stubbly as an old woman's face grew fresh and young again. Salt, sad marshes grew young again and made men glad of them. The islands of the secret road would make men glad with their greenness and youngness.

Yes, yes, that was good and that would always happen, but she, Erif Der, she could never turn again and grow younger, no more be a

young maiden moving consciously among glad looks! She was growing older every year – every Plowing Eve she was a year older – and
soon she would be too old to make any man glad, not any lover, not
her own Tarrik. Oh unfair, oh cruel spring to come young and young
and again young while women grow old! Oh spring, luring men from
their own women, making them see their women old and used against
the young green! She heard her voice in an answer to Tarrik, and it
was angry and hard. She knew the people of Marob would be hurt by
it, would think it meant a cold and late season. She could not help it.
She heard the farmers shouting at her, eagerly, violently: 'Spring
Queen, be kind!' And suddenly she remembered Murr, who had not
had kindness from her but had died and would not see any spring
again.

But now the plow was very near. She tried to force her voice to
kindness and gladness, raised her head, thought she was not old yet,
thought Berris would come back this year. She wondered if the people
of Marob were at all satisfied. Ah, now the plow was turning inward.
She must run between the horns of the oxen. One moment she stood,
waiting for Tarrik to give her courage. She saw in his eyes that he did
not know her. They were not Tarrik and Erif; he was the Corn King
and she – she should be the Spring Queen. She sprang between the
oxen and leapt the plowshare and did not stumble, nor even cry out
or turn pale with the pain of her arm that had been grazed by one of
the horns.

The thick, surging crowd swept inwards at her. Oh dear Marob, if
only she could be part of Marob again, their Spring Queen, oh lost
love! She shut her eyes, swaying, wrestling with herself to come and
join them. She heard them hammering together the planks of the
booth. Surely there was, after all, nothing wrong? She was the Spring
Queen, who else could she be? Every one knew she was the Spring
Queen wearing the Spring Queen's clothes! She was bringing them
their spring, she was quite, quite certain that it would come, that the
corn would grow as well as ever. She had done nothing to hurt the seasons! No, she was not anxious, she was not thinking about harvest or
anything that had happened! Yes, she was smiling now! She opened
her eyes to their loud singing and the prickling of the thrown corn-
ears. That singing answered back to her smile, growing louder and
gladder. The pipes and drums thudded up from behind the voices.
She was going to do the dance well for them!

The Corn King and the Spring Queen went up on to the booth and
began the dance. She had only to follow with her body what Tarrik led

in. She watched him. She was the gentleness of the spring. He was the strength of the corn. The corn that had been asleep all winter, but now was growing, was rising. Then suddenly a terrible thing leapt into her mind, and buzzed round and round there. Who was the risen corn? The Corn King of to-day was the Corn Man at harvest, and the Corn man was Harn Der. The risen corn was Harn Der. She was dancing again with Harn Der. She had killed him and he had risen, and now she could not kill him again, he had got out of his own body, he had risen into another body, into the Corn King's body. He was looking at her through the Corn King's eyes. She fought the image, she tried to tear it out, she looked for help to Tarrik, her lover. It was not Tarrik any longer! From all round the pipes and drums hemmed her in, crushed the two dancers spinning together in one wild, inevitable rhythm. The climax of the dance was coming again. Erif Der saw with horror and terror her own dead father leap at her. She knew with an immediate grip of the moment and what it brought, that when she had fallen ready for him, it was Harn Der who would sweep aside the Corn King's rags and show himself, Harn Der who would plunge down on her, Harn Der who was the image of God and Man and her possessor and master! Her knees, her body, on the point of bending, giving to the fall, the final yielding of spring, stiffened and shook. She flung up her arms against Harn Der and the thing she must not take from him, screamed with all her might against the rhythm, and jumped clean out of it, off the booth, into the furrow ankle-deep, turned her head to see if he was following her and yelled in panic again and rushed into the crowd that parted all about her.

She ran like a hare, screaming and doubling like a hare, across the fallow field. The crowd scattered screaming too, as though her touch would be death.

1932

Mae West

———

Mae West was born in 1893 in Brooklyn. By the age of fifteen she was a vaudeville actress, having been on the stage since the age of five. In 1926 she wrote, produced, directed and starred in *Sex*, a Broadway smash, which resulted in her being jailed for obscenity. The following year her next play, *Drag*, was banned on Broadway as too licentious, its subject matter – homosexuality – too indecent. But her 1928 play *Diamond Lil* (from which came both the 1933 film and the 1932 novelisation *She Done Him Wrong*) was a huge hit, and led to her signing with Paramount and instigating the movie legend, the combination of pantomime-grotesque humour, risqué bravado and sheer sexiness that made sailors name an inflatable lifejacket after her chest. A unique performer, a mistress of the *double entendre* and a superb writer, West had several film successes before her popularity waned in the forties (after she starred in the first film she hadn't herself scripted). She appeared again in *Myra Breckenridge* in 1970, and died ten years later in 1980.

Virago published *She Done Him Wrong* in 1995.

from

She Done Him Wrong

Lil was made uneasy by Juarez's impetuous advances in the cab. She saw plainly enough that he was burning with a passion almost beyond his control, and she did not want him to explode in the public highway.

She knew he was desperately in love with her. She had seen the beginnings of it when in the first few nights after his arrival he had sat among the tables at Gus's with Rita. In the way he looked at her while she was entertaining the late crowds she had seen that his eyes followed her every move with rapt attention and something of desire.

The manner in which he had followed her during the past week, and now his open proclamations of adoration, left no room for doubt as to the height of which his desire for her had mounted.

He did interest her even at the first meeting with him. His polish, his refinement, combined with the knowledge that he was the most distinguished toreador in Rio, alone led her to speculate upon his abilities as a lover. A champion in the bull arena, she wondered if he could conduct himself equally well within more limited confines. It was only for the reason that she did not wish to chance any trouble with Gus that she had kept Juarez at a distance this long.

Today, the fierce protestations of love that Pablo Juarez poured out to her, and his anguish when she appeared to be sending him away from her, struck a responsive fire within her. She came to the abrupt conclusion that now or never was the golden opportunity to test the quality of a Spaniard's love.

She had been faithful to Gus since she had taken up with him. But Lil believed in destiny. She felt that if it was not so intended, Fate would not have thrown Juarez into her path, particularly at a time when Gus's brand of loving had begun to pall. And who was Lil to go against the dictates of destiny?

The powerful Gus Jordan was a good man physically, but he lacked finesse. To Lil, love was as much a fine art as sculpture or music and the body was a sensitive instrument that rendered wonderful symphonies of exquisite rapture when played upon by a master of sexual counterpoint. Gus was as one who picks out a melody with an uncertain finger.

Chick Clark had been really quite remarkable as a lover. Lil often thought about him. What Chick had lacked in technique he had made up for by imagination. And he had really loved her with every fibre of his body and soul.

These thoughts occurred to Lil before she instructed Mike to drive them to Elizabeth Street. She asked herself what possible harm there could be in making the love-sick Juarez happy for a brief hour or two. She told herself that she had nothing to lose morally, and physically – well, you never missed a slice off a cut loaf. And besides, she would learn to her satisfaction and perhaps great pleasure, once and for all, whether or not these Spanish guys were really the lovers they were cracked up to be, or if their reputations were just founded on the hot dreams of silly virgins who read mushy novels. Lil liked to keep straight on her geography.

[. . .]

They located the janitor, and he came up from his hole in the basement. Richer by a coin Lil passed to him, he wiped the tobacco-juice from the corner of his mouth with the back of his hand and agreed to let them in.

They followed him into the hall, which was dark and smelt of wine-dregs from the shop on the first floor. The janitor stood aside to let Lil pass, but she instructed him to show the way.

He mounted the stairs, Lil followed, and Juarez brought up the rear. He was biting his lower lip till it almost bled. Inside of him was a raging volcano of tempestuous desire. The swaying movement of Lil's well-turned hips and the rhythm of her thighs ascending the stairs on a level with his eyes almost drove him mad. It was all he could do to beat down the terrific temptation to seize her then and there and disclose all her charms to his longing eyes. The rustle of Lil's taffeta skirt, the divine fragrance of the scent she was wearing, together with an odour of warm, pulsating flesh, had Juarez in a frenzy.

Suddenly the janitor had unlocked a door and was showing them into a room, which was bright with sunshine streaming through the window that looked out upon the street.

The janitor went out. Lil stepped at once to the window and drew the shade. Before she could even turn round she felt herself in Juarez's arms. He held her in a fierce, vice-like embrace and his hot lips were pressed to the nape of her neck. She turned as his arms relaxed their tension and met his lips with her own warm, sensuous ones.

Gus Jordan became a pale ghost in the back of Lil's mind. The present moment was an all-consuming flame. She felt herself swept from her feet, and presently the world became a place of exploding stars and bursting suns. Every nerve throbbed with a pleasure that was a refinement of pain. And then suddenly the soul hung suspended in sublimity.

And then – back to earth. The walls, the windows, the chairs, the bed, returned to entity.

Juarez could hardly believe his good fortune. Diamond Lil, the beautiful, the much-sought-after, had been his. And there she lay, watching him through slumbrous lids, a half-smile lazily curving her lovely lips.

Lil, on her part, was thinking that the youngest toreador in Rio was more than a champion. He was an artist, and she regretted that she had waited this long to find it out.

This more or less swift and impromptu affair merely whetted her sensual appetite.

Juarez seized her hand and rained kisses upon it.

'My adorable one! My beautiful! I am mad weeth happiness! You have been generous! You have been excr-r-ruciatingly kind to Pablo! Believe me, you have given me all that I would gladly die for. Nevair have I known a woman like you! Nevair have I known such love! You are marvellous! You are wonderful! You are divine!'

'You're not so bad yourself.' Lil smiled at him.

1933

Antonia White

———

Antonia White (née Botting) was born in London in 1899. Expelled from the Convent of the Sacred Heart, Roehampton, after writing a romantic novel, she was educated at St Paul's Girls' School and the Academy of Dramatic Art. She worked briefly as an actress, a copy-writer, a teacher and a journalist before turning to writing. During the Second World War she worked for the BBC and for the Foreign Office.

Her novels are all autobiographical. *Frost in May* explores her convent-school experiences; *The Lost Traveller* (1950), *The Sugar House* (1952) and *Beyond the Glass* (1954) form a trilogy around the character of Clara Batchelor. Antonia White also published a collection of short stories, a play, a memoir, two books about her cats, and *The Hound and the Falcon* (1966), a collection of letters exploring her reconversion to Catholicism as an adult. She also translated many French writers, including Colette. Subject to periods of mental illness throughout her life, she married twice and died in 1980.

Frost in May was the first book to be published in the Virago Modern Classics series in 1978.

from

Frost in May

The great day came at last. Every time she woke up during the night before, which was often, Nanda said, as she had been told to do:

'Even in the night have I desired thee, Lord. Come, Lord Jesus, come.'

Everything she put on that morning was new and white. A white prayer-book and a mother-of-pearl rosary, a gift from Reverend Mother, lay beside her new veil, and the stiff wreath of white cotton roses that every First Communicant wore. They walked into the chapel two by two, pacing slowly up the aisle like twelve brides, to the sound of soft, lacy music. In front of the altar were twelve prie-dieu covered with white muslin and flowers, with a tall candle burning in front of each. At little stools at the side knelt the children from the Poor School, who were also making their First Communion. They had no candles, and their cotton frocks looked shabby.

Nanda tried to fix her attention on the mass, but she could not. She felt light-headed and empty, unable to pray or even to think. She stole a look at Léonie, whose pale, bent face was stiff and absorbed. She tried not to be conscious of the smell of Joan Appleyard's newly-washed hair above the lilies and the incense. Theresa Leighton's head was thrown back; she had closed her prayer-book and was gazing at the altar with a rapt, avid look, her mouth a little open. Nanda was horrified at her own detachment, she tried hard to concentrate on the great moment ahead of her, but her mind was blank. In a trance she heard the bell ring for the *Domine non sum dignus*, and heard the rustle as the others got up to go to the altar rails. In terror, she

thought: 'I haven't made a proper preparation. I've been distracted
the whole time, to-day of all days. Dare I go up with them?' But almost
without knowing, her body had moved with the rest, and she was
kneeling at the rails with the others, holding the embroidered cloth
under her chin. Under her almost closed eyelids, she could see the
pattern of the altar carpet, and the thin, round hosts, like honesty
leaves, in the ciborium. The priest was opposite her now; she raised
her head and shut her eyes tight. She felt the wafer touch her tongue
and waited for some extraordinary revelation, for death even. But
she felt nothing.

Back at her prie-dieu, she kept her head bowed like the others.
Above the noise in her ears she could hear the choir singing softly and
dreamily:

> *'Ad quem diu suspiravi,*
> *Jesu tandem habeo.'*

Over and over she told herself frantically:

'This is the greatest moment of my life. Our Lord Himself is actually present, in the flesh, inside my body. Why am I so numb and
stupid? Why can't I think of anything to say?' She was relieved when
the quarter of an hour's thanksgiving was over. As they filed out of the
chapel she looked at the faces of the other eleven, to see if they felt as
she did. But every face was gay or recollected or content. Léonie's
expression was grave and courteous; in spite of her stiff white dress
and wreath, she seemed like a young soldier fresh from an audience
with the king. She thought of Polish nobles who stand with drawn
swords during the Credo, and wished she could be as much of the
blood of this ancient faith as Léonie and Theresa. With all her efforts,
all her devotion, there was something wrong with her. Perhaps a con-
vert could never ring quite true. Perhaps real Catholics were right
always to mistrust and despise them a little. For weeks she had been
preparing herself, laying stick on stick and coal on coal, and now, at
the supreme moment, she had not caught fire. Her First Communion
had been a failure.

There was an impressive breakfast laid out for the First
Communicants in the big parlour, with crisp new rolls, butter patted
into swan-like shapes and a huge, bridal-looking cake. Against the
walls stood twelve small tables laden with presents. Nanda's looked
rather bare and dismal, for it only held a missal, a new rosary and a
copy of the poems of Francis Thompson. She had no Catholic

relatives to load her with gold medals, crucifixes, coloured statues, alabaster plaques and Imitations of Christ bound in voluptuous Russian leather. She had received quite a good number of holy pictures however, including one from Hilary O'Byrne, as handsome as a Christmas card, inscribed: 'To dear Nanda, on the happiest day of her life, from Hilary E. de M.'

The First Communicants, reacting after their two days of silent retreat, chattered like starlings. Reverend Mother looked in, with her glasses positively twinkling with benevolence, and even condescended to examine everybody's presents and to exclaim politely over them. But after a few minutes, she put up her hand for silence.

'My very dear children,' she said, 'it is quite right and proper for you all to be gay and happy on this day of days. But not too much noise, remember. I would like you all to be quiet and recollect yourselves for just three minutes, while I tell you a little story . . . a true one that happened this very morning. I am going to tell you this because it shows what a true Catholic's spirit should be all through life . . . that nothing is more pleasing to God than suffering bravely borne for our Lord's sake. I expect you noticed that there were some children from the Poor School making their First Communion with you this morning. You must remember that they do not come from good homes like you; they are often quite pathetically ignorant. Well, one of the nuns was helping them to put on their veils and their wreaths, and one little girl called Molly had great difficulty with hers. So Mother Poitier fastened it on with a big safety-pin, but, as you know, she does not see very well, and she unfortunately put the pin right through Molly's ear. The poor little girl was in great pain, but she thought it was part of the ceremony, and she never uttered a word of complaint. She thought of the terrible suffering of Our Lord in wearing His crown of thorns and bore it for His sake. I am sure Molly received a very wonderful grace at her First Communion and I should like to think that anyone here had such beautiful, unselfish devotion as that. She might have gone about all day with that pin through her ear, if she had not fainted just now at breakfast. Now, talk away again, children, and be as happy as you can all day long. But even in your happiness, never forget that a good Christian is always ready to take up his cross and deny himself and unite himself to the passion of Our Blessed Lord.'

1934

Molly Keane
(M. J. Farrell)

Molly Keane (née Mary Nesta Skrine) was born into 'a rather serious Hunting and Fishing and Church-going family' in Ballyrankin, County Kildare, in 1905. She began writing fiction at seventeen and her first published novel appeared in 1928. Under the pseudonym M. J. Farrell she published ten novels and several plays (with John Perry) between 1928 and 1952. She claimed that a pseudonym was necessary because writing novels was a dubious pursuit in the circles within which she moved. Following a devastating review of her last play and the sudden death of her husband Robert Keane (whom she had married in 1938), she stopped writing for many years. In 1981, however, she published (this time under her own name) the highly acclaimed *Good Behaviour*, followed by two further novels. She died in 1996.

Devoted Ladies moves between Anglo-Irish country life and fashionable art deco London society of the thirties. It explores the uneasy relationship between Jane and her 'devoted friend' Jessica. 'I was excited about finding out about lesbians and homosexuals,' Keane later said. 'It was new. It made a subject.'

Virago published *Devoted Ladies* in 1984.

from

Devoted Ladies

Jessica stood at the foot of Jane's bed and regarded Jane sleeping.
This was the morning after Sylvester's party and Jessica felt neither very well nor very kindly disposed towards Jane.

The sun was shining warmly into the room, lighting the limp silver curtains and silvery stripped wood and searching in a deadly and accurate way into the bunch of false lilies bought in the same shop where Sylvester had bought his. There was no height in Jane's bedroom. Everything squatted on the floor. The dressing table was about twelve inches high and the stool where Jane sat to make up her face about six inches high. Her bed seemed to be made up really on the floor itself. It had oval ends, had cost the earth and was, as a matter of fact, exceedingly comfortable. A mass of small stools squatted about here and there. There were also quantities of bottles of scent in boxes of black and silver cubistic designs and shapes. Jane used buckets of scent in a year. She did everything with it except drink it. Well, she always said she didn't drink it, but she may quite likely have quaffed off an odd nip in a tooth glass. It was the sort of thing she would do and keep quiet about. There was a time when Jane filled her room with toys – wide-skirted dolls, sad dogs, rude monkeys, but Jessica had stopped that, no more vulgar playthings now, and indeed Jane did not much mind. As an affectation her toys had been rather a nuisance. And took up too much room. How she had once played her toy game for Sylvester's benefit! But not one of his heroines had gone all elfin and girlish over a teddy bear in consequence – not one. It was hard work getting into Sylvester's books, but Jane meant to do it some day or other.

Still Jessica stood and regarded the sleeping Jane. Jessica's dark hair was cut with a charming severity. If her dark face had been less heavy and turbulent in expression Jessica would almost have succeeded in looking as hard and boyish as she hoped she looked. But this plan of hers had been spoilt by God in the beginning, for He had given her a positive bosom and massive thighs. She was a heavy-minded woman too, without much gaiety of spirit. It was typical of her to break china and bite baths in moments of stress, so did she grind her teeth into life and with as little satisfaction to herself.

Now she felt evilly disposed towards Jane lying there with a lead-coloured cosmetic peeling off her face like half-dry cement. The bandage on her head reminded Jessica of last night's affray. Jane had behaved really monstrously last night. Stupidly drunk she'd been, not a bit amusing.

Jessica folded her dressing-gown severely about her and knotted its belt. She had bought it from her tailor in Savile Row. Red silk with white spots and a scarf to match – this for the concealment of the hirsute virility of the male. Then she shook Jane's bed until Jane woke up. Her yawns widened the cracks in the cement on her face. She looked very ill and unattractive.

'How awful you look, darling,' Jessica said as soon as she thought Jane was wide enough awake to be annoyed by what she said. 'Do you feel terrible, or do you only look like that?'

'Oh, Jessica,' Jane moaned, 'fix me a brandy and soda. I feel *horrible.*'

'Oh, God! Don't let's have any of your sickening after-the-party reactions,' Jessica stormed. 'You were beastly drunk last night and you're not sober yet. Can't you *say* so and leave it *alone.* Don't mess at a thing.'

'I'll say I feel very sick,' Jane said weakly, '. . . sea-sick . . .' Oh, how terrible she would say she felt. A pain in her head and sick in every nerve. If Jessica didn't stop pretty soon she would be sick too, though more from spite than necessity. What Jane required was some one to Mother her. Some one to Fix her a brandy and soda and a Cachet Faivre. Some one to draw the curtains and shut out every chink of light – rather than opening them to the unkind sun. Some one to pad about and pull up the eiderdown and pat a girl on the back – a 'there-there' atmosphere in fact was what she required, instead of Jessica going on anyhow. And wearing a dressing-gown like that – she'd get herself talked about soon. Jane roused herself from her queasy lethargy to tell Jessica this.

'My God! You are filthy—' Jessica became really pale with anger. 'Is nothing clean to you – absolutely nothing? I mean, there are some things in life sharp and clean still; must you have your dirty joke about them – *must* you?' She turned away from Jane's bed with deliberate disgust. 'I'm going out to buy some moss roses,' she bit her words in rather than spoke them out.

'*Darling*, don't leave me. I'm sorry. You know you were horrible to me—' But Jessica had gone and Jane was left alone, which she hated.

Why buy moss roses, anyhow? They were wickedly expensive and smelt of turpentine. Why not buy Madam Butterfly if you wanted a bunch of roses? Then you had a bunch of roses that looked well, real well. Jane did not mind expense provided she got what she wanted – or what some one else had wanted first, but had not been able to afford – for her money. But she was just beginning to feel a little restive over Jessica's way of expending vast sums on undecorative and short-lived bunches of flowers when yellow carnations would last twice the length of time; or on odd and ugly pieces of china which she was more liable to smash in one of her temperamental storms. Woolworth china would have done as well for that.

Had Jessica but guessed it Jane was, after six months of it, on the edge of wondering what, anyhow, she still saw for herself in this diffi-cult and passionate friendship beyond the fact that she paid and Jessica talked. However, this was no moment in which to ask herself such awkward questions with such obvious answers. Jane subsided once more into torpor beneath the bedclothes, breathing a half-conscious sigh of relief as she heard Jessica bang the door of the flat on her departure.

1935

Ann Bridge

Ann Bridge was the nom de plume of Lady Mary Ann O'Malley (née Sanders). She was born in Hertfordshire in 1891 into a large and wealthy family. In 1913 she married Owen O'Malley, a diplomat who was later knighted, and they had three children. The family set up home in Bridge End, a Surrey farm, which would later provide her Foreign Office-approved pseudonym. Her husband's career, however, took her to many parts of the world – including China (the setting for her first two novels) and Morocco (where the first of her Julia Probyn spy stories begins). O'Malley was forced to resign after allegations of currency speculation and his wife's novels provided much-needed money for the family. She published twenty-six works in all, including several chosen by the Book Society and the American Literary Guild.

She died in 1974.

Illyrian Spring was published by Virago in 1990.

from

Illyrian Spring

Lady Kilmichael, though she did not realise it, was beginning (rather late in the day) to feel the pressure of one of the more peculiar aspects of English life – the moral and intellectual subordination of women to their husbands. This phenomenon is of course not universal, but it is common enough to strike the observant Continental or American with amazement. And the attempt to define logically the causes from which it springs almost always ends in failure, because the English are not a logical people, and most of their profoundest instincts elude definition, as a very intelligent Dutchman has recently discovered. We may tell the observant American that it is due to our Teutonic ancestry, and that he will find the same thing in Germany; we may suggest that it originated with Puritanism and takes its Oriental colour from the traditions of the Old Testament; sociologists may point out that it is mainly a middle-class phenomenon, little exhibited in poorer households, where the daily work of her hands makes the labourer's wife queen in a small kingdom; feminists will seek to prove that it is due entirely to lack of female education and the economic subjection of women. Much or all of this may well be true; men have long been better educated than women, and their work, at least in the professional classes, tended to widen the intellectual gulf between them and their women-kind; while before legislation removed some of the gravest of married women's economic disabilities, they were in a singularly helpless position – the wife whose husband was allowed by law to take her income, her jewels and even her children, and hand them over to a rival, had some reason to feel rather subordinate.

But all this is too heavy, too definite, too pronounced; much of it no longer fits. A married woman's property is now secure to her; females receive a fair education, vote, have careers. The women of England no longer march from the altar to the womb with the words 'And to obey' sounding continually in their hearts, and the phrase 'your Father knows best' for ever on their lips. Queen Victoria is not only dead, but, as an ideal of domestic life, dethroned. And yet, tenuous, elusive, but tenacious, this tradition of inferiority persists – subtly imposed by the husbands; tacitly and often unconsciously acquiesced in by the wives. Their views, somehow, are worth less than men's; the moral initiative has passed from them; in some strange way – whether consciously or not – they are subordinate.

Now this subjection was tiresome and fatiguing enough while it was subjection to one person only, the husband; but for Lady Kilmichael's generation it had suddenly become subjection to their children as well, and when it reached that stage it became insupportable. What was really moving Grace Kilmichael, as she sat in her little white state-room, was a dawning consciousness of her need to think and act as an independent creature, along her own lines, though she did not as yet clearly envisage it. But it was a vague conviction of where the trouble lay, and of the urgency of her need to deal with it in herself and by herself, which made her lock her despatch-case so firmly on Walter's letter, and decide not to return to England, and not to answer it.

Linnet's letter, however, she would, she must answer. But not, if possible, from Trieste. Perhaps she could do something about that. Putting on her hat again, she went to the saloon to get some coffee. In the passage she encountered one of the white-uniformed officers; with conspicuous gallantry and a brilliant display of teeth he asked if he could help her in any way? (Lady Kilmichael's clothes and figure, and a curious rather appealing youthfulness about her expression, were very apt to produce this effect on strange men.) In her halting but rather pretty Italian she said that perhaps he could – would it be possible to get letters posted, not in Trieste but in Venice? But most easily, he told her, studying her at the same time with evident curiosity as to what this charming creature had to conceal – the letters could be taken back to Venice and posted there. So Lady Kilmichael drank her coffee with a freer mind, and then went back to her state-room and wrote to her Mother ('Dearest Mother') and then to Linnet ('My darling child'). But she told neither of them where she was going, nor did she give any hint of a return either to London or to Antibes. And to Walter she did not write at all.

1936

Rosamond Lehmann

———

Born in 1901, Rosamond Lehmann grew up in a Buckinghamshire literary family and studied modern languages at Girton College,
Cambridge. Her first, best-selling novel, *Dusty Answer*, the story of a
young girl's sexual awakening, was published in 1927 and attracted
great controversy, particularly for its lesbian theme. The three novels
that followed, *A Note in Music* (1930), *Invitation to the Waltz* (1932) and
The Weather in the Streets, continue to explore taboo questions of female
psychology and sexuality. No moral judgements are made as
Lehmann's fragmentary, often stream-of-consciousness style keeps her
close to her passionate and obsessed characters.

Lehmann married twice and had a long friendship with the poet C.
Day Lewis. After the death of her daughter in 1958, she became
increasingly preoccupied with questions about mysticism and spiritual-
ity that had first been touched upon in *The Ballad and the Source* (1944).
She published three further novels, a collection of short fiction and a
memoir. Lehmann was created a CBE in 1982 and died in 1990.

Virago published *The Weather in the Streets* in 1981.

from

The Weather in the Streets

'Stay where you are, Mrs Craig,' he said softly. 'There now. Quite comfy? That's right. Don't worry. All over. Wasn't too bad, was it, eh?'

'No, thank you.'

He put a cushion under her head, threw a light rug over her. She lay flat on the hard surgical couch and closed her eyes. Several tears ran down her face and dried there.

'Relax, Mrs Craig.'

'Yes.' She smiled blindly, obedient, behaving meekly, a good patient. He slipped a hot-water bottle under the rug, close in to her side.

'Thank you.' I'm cold – funny in this weather – glad of it.

He moved about softly, busy with something the other side of the room, his natty back turned to her. She opened her eyes. In spite of the September afternoon sun the room was in twilight. The buff blinds were lowered; and besides this, curtains of wine-coloured net across the windows diffused a lurid murkiness. From where she lay she could see an arm-chair upholstered in purple brocade, a black-and-gold lacquered screen half-concealing a two-tiered surgical wheeled table; his big desk with papers on it, one or two silver-framed photographs. There was a smell of antiseptics.

Presently he came back.

'All right, Mrs Craig?'

'Yes, thank you.' She smiled up at him faintly, meekly. His face loomed over her, broad and bland. The high-winged old-world collar carried on the motif of his pointed prominent ears.

My deliverer. Your victim, here I lie. . . 'Bit shaky still, though.'

He went away, came back with a glass.

'Drink this.'

She drank. It was sal volatile.

'I might be sick.'

He placed an enamel kidney bowl beside her chin; and soon she was sick.

'Tt-tt-tt. . .' Sympathetically he removed the bowl. 'Poor dear. You won't be troubled with this much longer.'

She sat up, swung her legs slowly over the side of the couch, did up her stockings, combed her hair.

'I'll tell my man to get you a taxi.' He touched the bell.

'I don't like your man.' Black eyes with a cast, memorising her face in one sharp furtive glance, taciturn, noiselessly showing her up. 'He frightens me.'

He glanced at her as if he thought she might be wandering; laughed.

'Why? He's quite harmless. A most trustworthy chap. Been with me for years.'

'I expect he's all right.' She sighed. 'I don't like his face.'

'We can't all be attractive young women,' he said casually.

There seemed to her to be a dreadful intimacy between them: sexual, without desire: conspirators, bound together in reluctant inevitable loyalty. She bent down to look at the photographs on the desk: a rather good-looking woman in evening dress, with a pre-war plait of hair round her head; two children, girl and boy, grinning, in party socks and pumps.

'Those are my two,' he said, picking up the photographs.

'They look very nice.' The sights those kids must have grinned at. . .

'Jolly little pair.' He scanned them with an indulgent eye. 'That was taken some years ago. The boy's just gone to Harrow.' He can afford, of course, to give them an expensive education. 'That's my wife. . .'

'Charming. . .' Does she know where the dough comes from?

He picked up an enlarged snapshot: a man in waders, with a tweed hat, holding up a dead salmon.

'Recognise that?' he said rather coyly. 'Me. . . That was in 1928. Biggest I ever landed, he was: thirty-pounder. Game old boy, too: gave me the tussle of my life. Played him for four hours. Between you and me I thought I'd pass out before he did.' Simple pride and pleasure warmed his voice. He put down the snapshot, sighed: not sinister at all, rather wistful; playing salmon more to his taste than performing abortions. 'Fishing's a grand sport,' he said. 'Ever do any?'

'Not often,' she said regretfully. 'I don't often get the chance.'

She opened her bag, extracted the envelope and gave it to him.

'Oh, thanks, thanks very much.' He whisked it into a drawer.

'When will it begin?'

'Oh – some time within the next twelve hours.'

'I see.'

'Good-bye, Mrs Craig.' He shook hands. 'Best of luck on your travels.'

'Thank you so much. Good-bye.'

They stood and looked at each other. Never to meet again, please God.

'I should trot home now and go straight to bed with a book. Something cheerful. There's nothing to worry about. If you *should* want to ring me up, you can. But you understand – no messages. . . You quite understand?'

'I quite understand. I won't ring up.'

He put an arm lightly across her shoulders and led her to the door. On the other side of it, in the dark hall, waited the manservant. He opened the front door for her, and there in the quiet sunny street waited the ordinary taxi.

1937

Zora Neale Hurston

Zora Neale Hurston was born in 1891 in Eatonville, Florida – the first incorporated, self-governing black town in America, where her father, a Baptist preacher, was elected mayor three times. In 1918 she became a student at Howard College and began to write. She moved to New York in 1925 and earned a scholarship to study anthropology with Franz Boas and Ruth Benedict at Barnard College. (She was the only black student.) After graduating in 1928 she spent four years studying folklore in the South and the Caribbean; she collected her findings in two books, *Mules and Men* (1935) and *Tell My Horse* (1939). Her first novel, *Jonah's Gourd Vine*, was published in 1934, followed by *Their Eyes Were Watching God* (1937) and *Seraph on the Sewanee* (1948). Her autobiography of life among what she wryly termed the 'niggerati', *Dust Tracks on a Road*, was published in 1942. Acclaimed as a bright star in the Harlem Renaissance, Hurston fell out of favour in the forties and died in poverty in 1960. Partly thanks to the efforts of Alice Walker, Hurston's work was rediscovered in the seventies and enjoys a high reputation today.

Virago published *Their Eyes Were Watching God* in 1986.

from

Their Eyes Were Watching God

Janie saw her life like a great tree in leaf with the things suffered, things enjoyed, things done and undone. Dawn and doom was in the branches.

'Ah know exactly what Ah got to tell yuh, but it's hard to know where to start at.

'Ah ain't never seen mah papa. And Ah didn't know 'im if Ah did. Mah mama neither. She was gone from round dere long before Ah wuz big enough tuh know. Mah grandma raised me. Mah grandma and de white folks she worked wid. She had a house out in de backyard and dat's where Ah wuz born. They was quality white folks up dere in West Florida. Named Washburn. She had four gran'chillun on de place and all of us played together and dat's how come Ah never called mah Grandma nothin' but Nanny, 'cause dat's what everybody on de place called her. Nanny used to ketch us in our devilment and lick every youngun on de place and Mis' Washburn did de same. Ah reckon dey never hit us ah lick amiss 'cause dem three boys and us two girls wuz pretty aggravatin', Ah speck.

'Ah was wid dem white chillun so much till Ah didn't know Ah wuzn't white till Ah was round six years old. Wouldn't have found it out then, but a man come long takin' pictures and without askin' anybody, Selby, dat was de oldest boy, he told him to take us. Round a week later de man brought de picture for Mis' Washburn to see and pay him which she did, then give us all a good lickin'.

'So when we looked at de picture and everybody got pointed out there wasn't nobody left except a real dark little girl with long hair standing by Eleanor. Dat's where Ah wuz s'posed to be, but Ah couldn't recognize dat dark chile as me. So Ah ast, "where is me? Ah don't see me."

'Everybody laughed, even Mr Washburn. Miss Nellie, de Mama of de chillun who come back home after her husband dead, she pointed to de dark one and said, "Dat's you, Alphabet, don't you know yo' ownself?"

'Dey all useter call me Alphabet 'cause so many people had done named me different names. Ah looked at de picture a long time and seen it was mah dress and mah hair so Ah said:

'"Aw, aw! Ah'm colored!"

'Den dey all laughed real hard. But before Ah seen de picture Ah thought Ah wuz just like de rest.

'Us lived dere havin' fun till de chillun at school got to teasin' me 'bout livin' in de white folks back-yard. Dere wuz uh knotty-head gal name Mayrella dat useter git mad every time she look at me. Mis' Washburn useter dress me up in all de clothes her gran'chillun didn't need no mo' which still wuz better'n whut de rest uh de colored chillun had. And then she useter put hair ribbon on mah head fuh me tuh wear. Dat useter rile Mayrella uh lot. So she would pick at me all de time and put some others up tuh do de same. They'd push me 'way from de ring plays and make out they couldn't play wid nobody dat lived on premises. Den they'd tell me not to be takin' on over mah looks 'cause they mama told 'em 'bout de hound dawgs huntin' mah papa all night long. 'Bout Mr Washburn and de sheriff puttin' de bloodhounds on de trail tuh ketch mah papa for whut he done tuh mah mama. Dey didn't tell about how he wuz seen tryin' tuh git in touch wid mah mama later on so he could marry her. Naw, dey didn't talk dat part of it atall. Dey made it sound real bad so as tuh crumple mah feathers. None of 'em didn't even remember whut his name wuz, but dey all knowed de bloodhound part by heart. Nanny didn't love tuh see me wid mah head hung down, so she figgered it would be mo' better fuh me if us had uh house. She got de land and everything and then Mis' Washburn helped out uh whole heap wid things.'

Pheoby's hungry listening helped Janie to tell her story. So she went on thinking back to her young years and explaining them to her friend in soft, easy phrases while all around the house, the night time put on flesh and blackness.

She thought awhile and decided that her conscious life had commenced at Nanny's gate. On a late afternoon Nanny had called her to come inside the house because she had spied Janie letting Johnny Taylor kiss her over the gatepost.

It was a spring afternoon in West Florida. Janie had spent most of the day under a blossoming pear tree in the back-yard. She had been spending every minute that she could steal from her chores under that tree for the last three days. That was to say, ever since the first tiny bloom had opened. It had called her to come and gaze on a mystery. From barren brown stems to glistening leaf-buds; from the leaf-buds to snowy virginity of bloom. It stirred her tremendously. How? Why? It was like a flute song forgotten in another existence and remembered again. What? How? Why? This singing she heard that had nothing to do with her ears. The rose of the world was breathing out smell. It followed her through all her waking moments and caressed her in her sleep. It connected itself with other vaguely felt matters that had struck her outside observation and buried themselves in her flesh. Now they emerged and quested about her consciousness.

She was stretched on her back beneath the pear tree soaking in the alto chant of the visiting bees, the gold of the sun and the panting breath of the breeze when the inaudible voice of it all came to her. She saw a dust-bearing bee sink into the sanctum of a bloom; the thousand sister-calyxes arch to meet the love embrace and the ecstatic shiver of the tree from root to tiniest branch creaming in every blossom and frothing with delight. So this was a marriage! She had been summoned to behold a revelation. Then Janie felt a pain remorseless sweet that left her limp and languid.

After a while she got up from where she was and went over the little garden field entire. She was seeking confirmation of the voice and vision, and everywhere she found and acknowledged answers. A personal answer for all other creations except herself. She felt an answer seeking her, but where? When? How? She found herself at the kitchen door and stumbled inside. In the air of the room were flies tumbling and singing, marrying and giving in marriage. When she reached the narrow hallway she was reminded that her grandmother was home with a sick headache. She was lying across the bed asleep so Janie tipped on out of the front door. Oh to be a pear tree – *any* tree in bloom! With kissing bees singing of the beginning of the world! She was sixteen. She had glossy leaves and bursting buds and she wanted to struggle with life but it seemed to elude her. Where were the singing bees for her? Nothing on the place nor in her grandma's house answered her. She searched as much of the world as she could from the top of the front steps and then went on down to the front gate and leaned over to gaze up and down the road. Looking, waiting, breathing short with impatience. Waiting for the world to be made.

Through pollinated air she saw a glorious being coming up the road. In her former blindness she had known him as shiftless Johnny Taylor, tall and lean. That was before the golden dust of pollen had beglamored his rags and her eyes.

In the last stages of Nanny's sleep, she dreamed of voices. Voices far-off but persistent, and gradually coming nearer. Janie's voice. Janie talking in whispery snatches with a male voice she couldn't quite place. That brought her wide awake. She bolted upright and peered out of the window and saw Johnny Taylor lacerating her Janie with a kiss.

'Janie!'

The old woman's voice was so lacking in command and reproof, so full of crumbling dissolution, – that Janie half believed that Nanny had not seen her. So she extended herself outside of her dream and went inside of the house. That was the end of her childhood.

1938

Stevie Smith

Stevie Smith was born ('a cynical babe') in Hull in 1902. Named Florence Margaret, she was nicknamed Stevie after the jockey Steve Donohue because she was short. At the age of three she moved to London, where she remained all her life, living in Palmer's Green with her sister and 'Lion Aunt'. When in 1935 she tried to publish her poetry, she was told to 'go away and write a novel'. *Novel on Yellow Paper, or Work It Out for Yourself* (the title refers to the paper on which she wrote while working as a secretary for a publishing firm) was published in 1936. It was followed in 1937 by her first collection of poetry, *A Good Time Was Had by All*. Smith went on to publish another ten poetry collections, the best known of which is *Not Waving but Drowning* (1957). Two further novels also followed: *Over the Frontier* (1938) and *The Holiday* (1949). All are narrated by the irrepressibly digressive Pompey Casmilus.

Smith died in 1971. A collection of her essays, stories, letters and a radio play, *Me Again*, was published in 1981.

Virago published *Over the Frontier* in 1980.

from

Over the Frontier

My darling friend Harriet is giving a party.

I am lying now on the divan in her flat, lying back on the cushions, glancing through the shadows and the flickering firelight at the faces of the friends and the friends of the friends of Harriet. It is very restful, really for once we are not talking so much. Reggie holds my hand in a quiet trance. He is lying beside me on the divan. It is very quiet.

I am now feeling so sad and quiet with the thoughts that go helter-pelter through my mind. They are making me so tired. I am so wishing for a moment that they were not there, do you know, that the mind of Pompey was an empty and as spick and span as a new washed saucepan.

Do you ever have the thought, gentle Reader, the thought to have an empty mind, to be like the clam that sits upon the mud in the sunlight, without the burden of this voracious consciousness that goes to eating up everything it sees and hears to make up a thought about it?

You must be receptive to your own thoughts, said I to the great established and polished man of letters that sat having lunch with me one fine day, after a couple of bottles of Liebfraumilch. This man was certainly a silent man in the beginning, not one word, not one single word to ease a situation that was becoming rather acutely painful, these long silences that beget longer silences, till it is like you would burst.

But presently, getting into the second bottle of Liebfraumilch, and, Here's to us, old chap, we began to find we were both of us having a lot of brilliant and unusual things to say, and these brilliant remarks (it was a pity there was no one there to make a book out of them) got to coming out at the same moment. So with no offence, no offence in the world, there we were both of us talking together, and going at it like we would never stop.

So here it was I came out with this clever idea that if you are going to write, and then why certainly you must go on writing, and above all you must be receptive to your own thoughts.

But now I feel that you must be very careful about this clever idea, or you will go to opening a door that never never will it be shut again. And all these ideas that have by this time got so upstage and unruly, they will come rushing in at you from the outside-of. And heaven must help you in that last situation, for all else is all up with you then, and you will have put yourself under a tyranny that will make Hitler look like the lady-companion that advertises in the *Church Times* for her keep, her bed-oh, with five shillings a week pocket-money, Catholic Privileges and Indoor Sanitation.

Well now, is it not sad? Why now certainly this Pompey is becoming very sad-case and dippy, for see now I am crying, yes the tears are coming out plop and rolling down my cheeks, to think of these thoughts that have so many behind them, coming rolling in with the long rolling surges of the Pacific Ocean up against the Australian coastline; with so many thoughts, crested and predatory, coming rolling up alongside, and behind them out to sea a whole ocean of thoughts to come rolling and slithering up the beach of consciousness. Oh there will perhaps not be time for all the thoughts, all that great wilderness of thought, coming rolling up from the deep deep sea.

So with Reggie lying beside me on the divan, suddenly I sit up and turn away from him, and look round the room of Harriet's flat, to think about the room and keep my thoughts from the thoughts.

First of all I must think about the Lion Vase that is no longer upon the mantelshelf. When Harriet gives one of her lovely parties, she takes down the Lion Vase that stands on her mantel overshelf, this Lion Vase that she brought with her from her house in Athens, smuggling it out of Greece with great adroitness, this registered ancient Lion Vase that is more than two thousand years old, she takes it down, and puts it safely away behind the fabric curtains of the alcove. And there the Lion Vase sits in shrouded safety. But to-night Harriet's party is not so wild that Lion Vase might fear for his great age, that has brought him down from ancient times to be a registered memorial and a prohibited export.

This animal, this lion, (I will describe for you), he is walking round the base of the vase. He has puffed out the pads of his paws. With great precision he places them upon the ground. He turns his head making a delicate *moue*; he is in a quiet mood you would say, he is walking there quietly, a little abstracted, in the jungle evening perhaps. He is a serious animal in middle life. Only his tail is a little wild. This tail is very vivid, very tense with an upward rake and twist that has a suggestion of something that is wicked. Looking at that lion I should say now at once, Beware of the quiet lion with the rogue tail walking quietly in the jungle evening. Be careful not to cross the path of this serious middle-aged lion, that is turning his head, that has this funny look upon his lion face.

Beautiful Lion Vase, sombre and ferocious lion, so set in upon himself, so quiet and aloof. And quiet horse of my earlier picture-gallery excursion, set in again in quietness upon a sombre ferocity. Ah, the animals *are* so quiet. There is no fuss up there, no fret and fume for guilt and delinquency, no mind sickness and a thought upon death.

Reggie puts his arm around me, I think he is getting rather bored.

1939

Jan Struther

———

Jan Struther was born Joyce Anstruther in 1901. During the thirties she published poetry (for children and adults) and essays in magazines such as *Punch*. When asked by *The Times* to write a column about 'an ordinary sort of woman who leads an ordinary sort of life – rather like yourself', she created Mrs Miniver in 1937. Her collected articles were published in 1939, shortly after the outbreak of war. The book proved an enormous success, both in Britain (Churchill declared it had done more for the Allies than a flotilla of battleships) and in America (where Roosevelt claimed it had hastened the US entry into the war). Mrs Miniver's popularity was given a further boost by the hugely successful 1942 film staring Greer Garson and Walter Pidgeon.

In 1923 she married Anthony Graham and had three children – to her chagrin, fans of *Mrs Miniver* confused her family with that of her fictional heroine. The couple divorced after the war, but in 1948 remarried. Struther died in New York in 1953.

Virago published *Mrs Miniver* in 1989.

from

Mrs Miniver

They went away nearly every week-end, either to Starlings or to other people's houses, but about once a month they made a point of staying in London. On Saturday afternoon they would drive down to see Vin at school, and on Sunday the two younger children would take it in turns to choose a treat. This time it was Toby's turn, and he chose Hampstead Heath because he wanted to sail his boat on the pond. Judy wasn't particularly keen on boats, but her favourite doll Christabel had a new spring coat and she was quite glad of a chance to take her out in it.

It was a clear, clean, nonchalant kind of day, with a billowy south wind. The scene round the pond, as they burst upon it suddenly up the hill, would have made an admirable opening for a ballet – a kind of English *Petrouchka* or *Beau Danube*. The blue pond, the white sails, the children in their Sunday clothes, the strolling grown-ups, the gambolling dogs, the ice-cream men (hatched out prematurely by the unseasonable heat) tinkling slowly round on their box-tricycles – it all had an air of having been rehearsed up to a perfection of spontaneity. The choreography was excellent, the décor charming; it remained to be seen whether any theme would develop.

When they got out of the car Toby discovered that he had left the key of his motor-boat at home. It was much too late to go back, of course: there was nothing to be done except wait and see how he would take it. One never knew, when setting out to comfort Toby, whether to prepare first aid for a pinprick or a broken heart. He was not yet old enough to be able to grade his own misfortunes: it is one of the maturer accomplishments. Fortunately he was in a philosophical mood. He just said: 'Oh, well, we can watch the others,' and trotted off to the pond with Clem, his feet beating crotchets against his father's minims.

Mrs Miniver found a deck-chair and sat down in the sun. Judy walked about, carrying Christabel rather ostentatiously so that people could see her new coat. It was really magnificent – pale yellow tweed with a brown velvet collar and brown buttons. Watching her, Mrs Miniver wondered whether the modern unbreakable dolls, which lasted for years, were more, or less, precious to their owners than the old china ones, whose expectation of life had been a matter of months. The old ones had had the agonising charm of transience: the modern ones held the promise of a reliable and enduring companionship – you could make plans for their future, think out their next winter's wardrobe. But it was a silly problem, after all. For love is no actuary: and a new-born baby was probably neither more, nor less, treasured three hundred years ago than it is now, in spite of all our statistics about infant mortality.

The sun was getting quite hot. From where she sat Mrs Miniver could see two street orators setting up their flimsy platforms and angling for an audience. Judging by their clothes and general demeanour she guessed that the one on the right was Left-wing and the one on the left Right-wing: but she was too far away to read the wording on their notice boards, and when they began to speak nothing reached her except a confused gabble, like a mix-up of stations on the wireless. Seeing Clem and Toby leave the pond and walk over towards the speakers, she collected Judy and joined them. As soon as she got near she found that her guess had been wrong: the right-hand speaker was extreme Right and the left extreme Left. But how many of their audience, she wondered, would have noticed if they had got up behind the wrong placards by mistake?

It was hard to take in the sense of what the speakers were saying, so confusing was the double clamour. But one thing was certain, that the fabric of both speeches was shot through and through with the steely tinsel of war. 'To combat the forces of tyranny . . .' one of them ranted. 'To crush down the menace of revolution . . .' mouthed the other just as glibly. 'Is any sacrifice too great . . . ?' 'Which of us would not willingly lay down . . . ?'

And now, from somewhere behind them, came the sound of a third voice, so shrill, reedy and raucous that it made itself heard even through the babel nearer at hand. It seemed only half human, and for a moment Mrs Miniver had a sense of nightmare; but as soon as she realised what it was she grabbed Clem by the arm. 'Come on!' she said. 'There's a Punch and Judy!' Clem's face lit up. He hoisted Toby on to his shoulder and they all four edged their way out of the crowd.

The rest of the morning was pure bliss. For over an hour they stood, absorbed, while the immortal melodrama unfolded itself before their eyes. The proscenium was shabby, the properties crude, the puppets battered almost featureless by the years of savage slapstick they had undergone: but the performance was superb. The baby yelled and was flung out of the window; Judy scolded and was bludgeoned to death; the beadle, the doctor, and the hangman tried to turn to perform their professional duties and were outrageously thwarted; Punch, cunning, violent and unscrupulous, with no virtues whatever except humour and vitality, came out triumphant in the end. And all the children, their faces upturned in the sun like a bed of pink daisies, laughed and clapped and shouted with delight.

'So what?' said Mrs Miniver at the end, to Clem.

'So nothing,' said Clem, shrugging his shoulders. 'It's great art, that's all. Come on, I'm hungry.'

1940s

1940

Martha Gellhorn

———

Martha Gellhorn was born in St Louis in 1908. After studying at Bryn Mawr for a year, she went to Paris as a reporter for the *New Republic* and the *Hearst Times Union*. There, she later said, she became 'involved in Europe's politics the way a tadpole is involved in a pond'. In 1934 she returned to America and in 1936 published *The Trouble I've Seen*, a highly acclaimed volume of four novellas exploring the effects of the Depression. She served as a war correspondent in, among other places, Spain, Finland, France and Germany, Vietnam and Israel, and described many of her experiences in her fiction as well as her non-fiction. *A Stricken Field* explores the powerlessness of an idealistic American journalist in Czechoslovakia after the Munich Pact. In the afterword to the 1986 reprint, Gellhorn says she wrote the book to 'show what history is like for people who have no choice except to live through it or die from it'.

In all, Gellhorn published five novels, two collections of stories and four of novellas, as well as numerous volumes of reportage – *The Face of War* (1959; fourth edition 1998) is an essential selection of the war writing, while *The View from the Ground* (1998) collects the best peace-time pieces. Gellhorn was married twice, for five years to Ernest Hemingway (about which she wrote *Travels with Myself and Another* 1978) and for ten years to Thomas Matthews.

In the last years of her life, Gellhorn lived in Wales. Thanks mainly to *Granta* magazine, which commissioned new work, she found herself acclaimed by a new generation of readers before she died in 1998.

A Stricken Field was published by Virago in 1986.

from

A Stricken Field

The distant woods waved like high ferns under a rain-dark sky. In every hollow, a small lake gleamed black as the sky was, and smooth. The fields stretched between the curves of the land, evenly laid out in potatoes and sugar beets. The earth was clodded and rich and carefully furrowed. Peasants worked in the fields, bending in that slow uncomfortable way, straight down and sideways, to weed and tend the low green plants. The villages all looked new, the pale colour of cement, and as you came to them you saw, rising over the house-tops and the neighbouring hills, the square practical towers of their churches.

They had passed the last line of defence north of Prague, a heavy barrier made of steel spools wound with barbed wire, each spool about five feet high. The spools lay in an unbroken black spiky line over the fields, but they had been cut to leave the highway open. The Germans had the first line of fortifications, that improved model of the Maginot which stretched along the Bohemian frontier, and the second line of defence, which was a crafty use in depth of strong points: concealed machine gun posts made of reinforced concrete and looking closeup like round black warts on the earth, deep concrete trenches dominating heights, artillery emplacements so hidden that all you would ever see was the quick emerging and recoiling gun barrel.

Having seen, in the past two years, how fortified positions could resist, Mary Douglas thought now, it wouldn't have been so easy for the Germans to get all that, if they'd had to fight for it; and she guessed some of the awful in-eating bitterness of the Czechs, who knew just how hard it would have been.

Now on an empty stretch of road, they passed soldiers, in twos and threes, with unbuttoned coats and dusty shoes and dusty faces, walking aimlessly from town to town. They did not raise their heads as the car passed, and walked with the shame and the weariness of a retreat.

The driver asked her if she wanted to stop, when they came to Slany, and she said no, we'll go on to the frontier. The driver honked and slowed the car to avoid two children, both blond and plump, who were walking one behind the other as confidently as if they were walking across the fields. They jumped back and stared at the car with frightened faces. Mary looked at them out of the back window and thought what an enchanting pair they made, with their round fluffy yellow heads and round cheeks, and the soiled pinafore of the girl, the little boy's stockings falling down. She thought their mother must be quite foolish with pride at having produced two such children. (Karel said to Elsi, 'Well, hold my hand then. I was looking, I saw it coming.')

The refugees no longer moved in the daytime, crowding and clogging the roads as far as you could see. Now they passed the frontier at night. It was like war now, the frontier was closed and dangerous; flight was forbidden, those who were caught on the other side of the barbed wire were prisoners and must escape like prisoners. To go home to your own country and your own people was a crime, and they waited for night. But here there were stragglers, moving farther inland, having found that the villages nearest to the frontier were full and food was scarce and there was no work or hope of work. They walked south, looking for a home again.

The land was open here and bare and the people looked bent and small under the sky, and they walked as if they were pushing against a current, their bodies bending and straining forward. First there was a man pulling a two-wheeled cart, and beside him walked his woman and behind, painfully, their eyes on the cart, keeping up with it, trying not to be lost and left behind, came the old people, the man walking with a stick, the woman shading her eyes, her face soft and folded with age, but gaunt with weariness. The cart was piled high with mattresses and blankets, the pots tied on behind clinked cheerfully. The younger woman opened her worn black leather purse and took out a large piece of dry bread. She did not stop walking. She carved off a strip of the bread with a clasp knife and handed it to the man. He shook his head; he could not pull the cart with one hand, they must keep walking.

Farther on was a woman carrying a suitcase on her head; her children walked beside her, the youngest holding onto the blowing edge of her apron for support, the others stumbling and thirsty-looking and incurious. The faces were all hard and staring ahead; the eyes saw only the long white cement road.

(They knew now that you would have to go a great distance from home to be safe; but was there work ahead, or a house to live in? Where they came from the land was all taken up, always had been, from father to son as long as anyone could remember. Everyone had the same house too, there were no empty houses for strangers in their village.)

Then they passed six people, resting by the side of the road, their bodies cramped even as they sat, as if they were too tired and stiff ever to move or lie easily again. They carried nothing except small bundles wrapped in brown paper or cloth. One of them looked at his worn-out shoes.

The road went on, a wide flat concrete strip, climbing a hill past a clump of trees and a white farmhouse, and curved and lost itself beyond. There was nothing wrong with the road, there was no sign up, there was nothing to tell you: but the road was condemned. The country had come to an end.

'What is it?' Mary asked the chauffeur.

'That is Germany now,' he said and pointed ahead.

'I don't understand.'

He looked at her. 'Nobody does. But if we drive on, after a while we will meet the German soldiers.'

'But isn't there a frontier post or something, how do you know where you are?'

'Sometimes there is. Not here. I will turn off on this side road.'

They drove over a dirt road, bumping in the ruts. Deep ditches lined it, and cultivated fields. Then up ahead, they saw a group of people standing in the road.

'What are they doing?' Mary asked. 'What is happening here?'

'They are looking,' the chauffeur said.

He stopped the car behind the people and she walked to join them. There were about twenty of them, some seemed to be peasants from the neighbourhood, in their work clothes, but there were city people too. No one talked. They stood in the road and stared at a piece of barbed wire that was pegged into the ground over the road and cut short on either side.

'That's the frontier,' the chauffeur explained.

She looked at it with absolute unbelief. You did not simply peg up fifty feet of barbed wire and proclaim a new rule; you did not drive people from their homes or jail them or shoot them, confiscate property and deny their language and the old forms of life, and then lay down fifty feet of barbed wire to prove it. The people beside her were looking at the barbed wire with the same shocked, unbelieving faces. Why here? Why not farther ahead or farther behind? The land on the other side belonged to the land on this side; it had the same shape. The fields had been planted by one man, and now he had sown in two countries. Oh, no, she told herself, I don't believe it. Why don't we lift the pegs ourselves and move the silly frontier backwards into that newly stolen piece of Germany?

Then she saw the soldier. He had been leaning against a tree, on his side of the wire, green-clad and silent, and she had not seen him. He was dark, good-looking, and very young. Twenty, she thought. The Czechs watched him, not saying anything, not moving, their faces blank and polite. The boy shouldered his rifle and began to do sentry-go but it was too embarrassing, and he leaned on his rifle and tried to stare the Czechs down. But the Czechs were not insolent or afraid, they were only amazed that men could do what these men had done. Underneath, behind the expressions he had learned from his masters and heroes, the soldier's face was ashamed and shy and uneasy. He knew that this was no way for the conquering German army to seem or behave, and he overlaid his face with an arrogant, boastful smile. He stood there, shaping his mouth into a smile that became a sneer, and the Czechs examined him quietly. The silence was too much for him and he called out, 'Why don't you come on over here then?' like a small boy, bullying.

No one answered. Mary Douglas stared at him, fascinated like the others, unbelieving. But he was true, he stood six feet in his field-grey uniform, with his square steel helmet and heavy boots and his rifle; he was part of the army that had overrun the land, and behind him lay Czechoslovakia, that piece fitting into this piece reasonably, as the shape of the land demanded, but now it was called Germany and he was on guard.

'Come on over here,' he said again, to no one in particular, laughing to give himself confidence.

A peasant who had been near the wire, looking at the crazily divided fields, sighed to himself, with unhurried contempt.

'Ah, the fool,' he said, not loud, not for the soldier or anyone, but just speaking his thoughts, 'the poor stupid young fool.'

The soldier flushed with anger and said, 'Come over here and say that.'

The peasant answered him, 'With a rifle you are very brave. You are all very brave with a rifle. We have none now. Do you want me to say it again?'

Mary Douglas wondered whether the soldier would shoot. No one would punish him; he would simply have protected the honour of the Fatherland and shot down an enemy of the Reich. He might even get a promotion; and surely the Czech government was in no position to raise a fuss because one old peasant was shot by a German soldier in the line of duty. They all waited, the old man waiting too, perfectly ready, but keeping his contempt, and keeping it very surely and proudly, as a man who is used to making up his mind. The people watched the soldier with unwavering, not hating, but cool, and mocking eyes.

A woman said, in the silence, 'He does what he is ordered. He cannot know what he does and he is not allowed to know. Leave him.'

The peasants and the city people turned slowly and started walking back along the dirt road towards the highway. The soldier looked after them, with hate in his eyes now, because they had shamed him. If there were three of them they would start shooting, Mary thought, but it is too risky for one alone. And she thought, his own father is probably someone like the old peasant, a poor man, a farmer or a worker. And the land is exactly the same, on the other side of the barbed wire.

1941

Kate O'Brien

Kate O'Brien was born in Limerick (the Mellick of her novels) in 1897, one of the nine children of a prosperous horse dealer. After her mother died when she was five, she was sent to Laurel Hill Convent, where she spent the next twelve years and which forms the backdrop to *The Land of Spices*. In 1916 she went to University College, Dublin, and after graduating, travelled in America before spending a year as a governess in Bilbao, Spain. After working briefly for the *Manchester Guardian*, she moved to London, where she taught in a convent school. In 1923 O'Brien married (although the marriage lasted only a few months), and during the 1930s she lived in Spain with a woman friend. They were forced to leave in 1937, however, because of their Republican sympathies. After the war, O'Brien returned to Ireland, settling in County Galloway, but eventually she returned to England, where she lived for nine years before her death in 1974.

O'Brien's first play, *Distinguished Villa*, was produced in 1926, and was followed by articles, stories, more plays and, from 1931, nine novels, many chronicling the Irish bourgeois society of her youth. These were a great success, although *The Land of Spices* and *Mary Lavelle* (1936) were banned in Ireland for their supposed immorality. (The former offended because of a single 'repulsive' sentence, included in this pivotal passage.) Other works draw on a Spanish background, including her most popular work, *That Lady* (1946), which is set in the time of Philip II, and was made into a successful film starring Olivia De Havilland.

The Land of Spices was reissued by Virago in 1988.

from

The Land of Spices

Helen was not sure that she was quite truthful in saying to her father that she did not want a nun's life – but at least such untruth as she suspected was directed as much to deceive herself as him. For she was sometimes afraid of her own erratic, moody understanding of the rightness of the religious life, visitations of which she turned from with emphasis again and again. And she was glad of what she had always known without his own brief expression of it – her father's horror of such a vocation for her. In sympathy with him, and in proud desire to be the daughter he desired and saw in her, she shared his horror, and felt safeguarded by his reliance on her, and his apparent need of her. Besides, instructed by him, steeped in his poets, she believed in human love, and felt in her English blood the rightness of compromise in the English mystics. And if love had somehow failed her father and mother, perhaps her love, and the development of her life on his principles of goodness, perhaps above all one day, her children would make up to him for whatever had gone wrong in a life which should have known completion in itself.

So, vaguely, she argued herself away from the threat of vocation. But perhaps her soul always knew that these arguments were beside the point, and that the issue was quite simple – that it lay between him and the only thing that measured up to him in her mind – the religious ideal. But all her *feelings* gave victory to him – and the other thing remained only an intellectual temptation, a shadow moving stealthily about her brain. And she was not afraid of it; it would pass, as her need and love of him could not. So it followed she would not be a nun, and when she said she did not want that life, she had spoken truly.

It was strange, after thirty-three years in religion, to lie in the dark
in her cell and recall each foolish *nuance* of that adolescent flight
towards life and her father, and away from God. Sharply indeed her
course had been reversed. But perfection, or the sight of it, is nevertheless not to be won, as a child might know, by the clamour of
egoism, the display of wounds, the reactions of vanity. It seemed
indeed that spiritual victory can only be gained by those who have
never lost it, who set out for purity already pure-intentioned. It was
hardly fair to make the difficult thing impossibly difficult. 'The land
of spices, something understood.' She remembered her mother smiling over that line one day not long before her death, and saying that
whereas to her the image was odd and surprising, 'yet your father
accepts it with his whole imagination – only, at the same time, he
happens to have no real use for it. Isn't that ironic?'

Helen had been puzzled.

'All I mean, darling,' her mother went on, 'is that religious understanding is really a gift, like a singing voice – and can be wasted.'

Life among nuns had clarified this observation, and had made her
ponder, sometimes amusedly, sometimes in sad longing, the poet's line.

Far off on the Grand Staircase a clock struck one. At half-past four
the community rising bell would ring, as usual; and Sœur Antoine
would knock on her door and call out: '*Loué soit Jésu,*' and she would
answer, as all these years, from childhood at *Place des Ormes*: '*Béni soit
le Seigneur à jamais.*' And another day, the first day of *Quarant' Ore*,
would have begun.

But she could not seek sleep.

She struck a match and lighted a candle at her bedside. She felt
that she must pray. She rose and put her black chapel cloak about her
and knelt at her *prie-dieu*. She considered the Crucifix on the wall
above her, and sought with her whole will to find the formal pattern
of meditation.

But the past would not lie still.

And suddenly its last scene, the last scene of youth, of innocence,
filled the austere dim cell.

It was June and brilliant weather. Helen's last term as a boarder at
Place des Ormes. At the end of July she was going to Italy with her
father and they would not return until mid-October, when his autumn
classes, and her university studies, began. This brilliant prospect dis-
sipated much of the sentimental melancholy she felt at giving up her
schoolgirl life at *Sainte Famille*, yet she savoured the last term with
particular affection.

One Saturday evening many of the girls who lived in Brussels had gone home for the week-end, and there was a pleasant sense of indolence through the convent. Helen, after having played some tennis, amused herself by helping *Mère Alphonsine* to arrange the flowers for the chapel. The next day was the Sunday within the Octave of *Corpus Christi* and *Mère Alphonsine* was dissatisfied with the colours of the roses Sœur Josèphe had sent in from the garden. She wanted more red ones, she said, and Sœur Josèphe said she couldn't have what wasn't there, and that she was never satisfied.

Helen said that unless *Marie-Jeanne* had taken them all to Malines that day, whither she had gone for her nephew's First Communion, there were red roses in the garden at *Rue Saint Isidore*. *Mère Alphonsine* commanded her to go and fetch them.

She went very happily, as she was, hatless and in tennis shoes. Glad of the sun and the lovely evening, and the chance of a word with Daddy, if he was at home.

The gate squeaked and let her in unwillingly, as usual. She never rang the front-door bell, even when *Marie-Jeanne* was at home to hear it; she always went straight through the garden to the ever-open kitchen door.

Her father's study was at the back of the house, above the kitchen. It had a long, wide balcony of wrought iron which ran full across the wall and ended in an iron staircase to the garden. This balcony made a pleasant, deep shade over the flagged space by the kitchen door, where *Marie-Jeanne* often sat to prepare vegetables, or to have a sleep. Traffic was free up and down these stairs; and Henry Archer was not formal about access to his study, even when he was working, even when he was having a silent and solitary mood.

Helen glanced in at the empty kitchen, scratched the cat behind the ears, and hoped that *Marie-Jeanne* wasn't getting too drunk at Malines. Then she ran up the iron stairs and along the balcony to the open window of her father's study.

She looked into the room.

Two people were there. But neither saw her; neither felt her shadow as it froze across the sun.

She turned and descended the stairs. She left the garden and went on down the curve of *Rue Saint Isidore*.

She had no objective and no knowledge of what she was doing. She did not see external things. She saw *Etienne* and her father, in the embrace of love.

1942

Jane Bowles

Jane Bowles (née Auer) is, as the poet John Ashbery put it, 'a writer's writer's writer'. She published only one novel, *Two Serious Ladies* (when she was twenty-five), some short stories collected as *Everything is Nice* and a play, yet her reputation goes from strength to strength. Truman Capote described her as 'a modern legend'.

She was born in 1917 in New York, married Paul Bowles in 1938 and soon the couple began a nomadic existence, living in, among other places, Central America and Sri Lanka, before settling in Tangiers in 1947. Jane Bowles suffered a cerebral haemorrhage in 1957 and wrote very little after that. She died in Malaga in 1973.

Two Serious Ladies was published by Virago in 1979.

from

Two Serious Ladies

As a grown woman Miss Goering was no better liked than she had been as a child. She was now living in her home outside New York, with her companion, Miss Gamelon.

Three months ago Miss Goering had been sitting in the parlour, looking out at the leafless trees, when her maid announced a caller.

'Is it a gentleman or a lady?' Miss Goering asked.

'A lady.'

'Show her in immediately,' said Miss Goering.

The maid returned followed by the caller. Miss Goering rose from her seat. 'How do you do?' she said. 'I don't believe I've ever laid eyes on you before this moment, but please sit down.'

The lady visitor was small and stocky and appeared to be in her late thirties or early forties. She wore dark, unfashionable clothing and, but for her large grey eyes, her face might on all occasions have passed unnoticed.

'I'm your governess's cousin,' she said to Miss Goering. 'She was with you for many years. Do you remember her?'

'I do,' said Miss Goering.

'Well, my name is Lucie Gamelon. My cousin used to talk about you and about your sister Sophie all the time. I've been meaning to call on you for years now, but one thing and another always got in the way. But then, we never know it to fail.'

Miss Gamelon reddened. She had not yet been relieved of her hat and coat.

'You have a lovely home,' she said. 'I guess you know it and appreciate it a lot.'

By this time Miss Goering was filled with curiosity concerning Miss Gamelon. 'What's your business in life?' she asked her.

'Not very much, I'm afraid. I've been typing manuscripts for famous authors all my life, but there doesn't seem to be much demand for authors any more unless maybe they are doing their own typing.'

Miss Goering, who was busy thinking, said nothing.

Miss Gamelon looked around helplessly.

'Do you stay here the greater portion of the time or do you travel mostly?' she asked Miss Goering unexpectedly.

'I never thought of travelling,' said Miss Goering. 'I don't require travel.'

'Coming from the family you come from,' said Miss Gamelon, 'I guess you were born full of knowledge about everything. You wouldn't need to travel. I had opportunity to travel two or three times with my authors. They were willing to pay all my expenses and my full salary besides, but I never did go except once, and that was to Canada.'

'You don't like to travel,' said Miss Goering, staring at her.

'It doesn't agree with me. I tried it that once. My stomach was upset and I had nervous headaches all the time. That was enough. I had my warning.'

'I understand perfectly,' said Miss Goering.

'I always believe,' continued Miss Gamelon, 'that you get your warning. Some people don't heed their warnings. That's when they come into conflict. I think that anything you feel strange or nervous about, you weren't cut out to do.'

'Go on,' said Miss Goering.

'Well, I know, for instance, that I wasn't cut out to be an aviator. I've always had dreams of crashing down to the earth. There are quite a few things that I won't do, even if I am thought of as a stubborn mule. I won't cross a big body of water, for instance. I could have everything I wanted if I would just cross the ocean and go over to England, but I never will.'

'Well,' said Miss Goering, 'let's have some tea and some sandwiches.'

Miss Gamelon ate voraciously and complimented Miss Goering on her good food.

'I like good things to eat,' she said; 'I don't have so much good food any more. I did when I was working for the authors.'

When they had finished tea, Miss Gamelon took leave of her hostess.

'I've had a very sociable time,' she said. 'I would like to stay longer, but tonight I have promised a niece of mine that I would watch over her children for her. She is going to attend a ball.'

'You must be very depressed with the idea,' said Miss Goering.

'Yes, you're right,' Miss Gamelon replied.

'Do return soon,' said Miss Goering.

The following afternoon the maid announced to Miss Goering that she had a caller. 'It's the same lady that called here yesterday,' said the maid.

'Well, well,' thought Miss Goering, 'that's good.'

'How are you feeling today?' Miss Gamelon asked her, coming into the room. She spoke very naturally, not appearing to find it strange that she was returning so soon after her first visit. 'I was thinking about you all last night,' she said. 'It's a funny thing. I always thought I should meet you. My cousin used to tell me how queer you were. I think, though, that you can make friends more quickly with queer people. Or you don't make friends with them at all – one way or the other. Many of my authors were very queer. In that way I've had an advantage of association that most people don't have. I know something about what I call real honest-to-God maniacs, too.'

Miss Goering invited Miss Gamelon to dine with her. She found her soothing and agreeable to be with. Miss Gamelon was very much impressed with the fact that Miss Goering was so nervous. Just as they were about to sit down, Miss Goering said that she couldn't face eating in the dining-room and she asked the servant to lay the table in the parlour instead. She spent a great deal of time switching the lights off and on.

'I know how you feel,' Miss Gamelon said to her.

'I don't particularly enjoy it,' said Miss Goering, 'but I expect in the future to be under control.'

Over wine at dinner Miss Gamelon told Miss Goering that it was only correct that she should be thus. 'What do you expect, dear,' she said, 'coming from the kind of family you come from? You're all tuned high, all of you. You've got to allow yourself things that other people haven't any right to allow themselves.'

Miss Goering began to feel a little tipsy. She looked dreamily at Miss Gamelon, who was eating her second helping of chicken cooked in wine. There was a little spot of grease in the corner of her mouth.

'I love to drink,' said Miss Gamelon, 'but there isn't much point to it when you have to work. It's fine enough when you have plenty of leisure time. I have a lot of leisure time now.'

'Have you a guardian angel?' asked Miss Goering.

'Well, I have a dead aunt, maybe that's what you mean; she might be watching over me.'

'That is not what I mean – I mean something quite different.'

'Well, of course . . .' said Miss Gamelon.

'A guardian angel comes when you are very young, and gives you special dispensation.'

'From what?'

'From the world. Yours might be luck; mine is money. Most people have a guardian angel; that's why they move slowly.'

'That's an imaginative way of talking about guardian angels. I guess my guardian angel is what I told you about heeding my warnings. I think maybe she could warn me about both of us. In that way I could keep you out of trouble. Of course, with your consent,' she added, looking a little confused.

Miss Goering had a definite feeling at that moment that Miss Gamelon was not in the least a nice woman, but she refused to face this because she got too much enjoyment from the sensation of being nursed and pampered. She told herself that it would do no harm for a little while.

'Miss Gamelon,' said Miss Goering, 'I think it would be a very fine idea if you were to make this your home – for the time being, at least. I don't think you have any pressing business that would oblige you to remain elsewhere, have you?'

'No, I haven't any business,' said Miss Gamelon. 'I don't see why I couldn't stay here – I'd have to get my things at my sister's house. Outside of that I don't know of anything else.'

1943

Eudora Welty

Eudora Welty, born in 1909 in Jackson, Mississippi (where she still lives), is one of the finest American writers of the twentieth century. She is the author of five novels, including *Delta Wedding* (1946) and *The Optimist's Daughter* (1972), but the heart of her achievement lies in her short fiction. *The Wide Net*, in which 'First Love' appeared, was the second of four volumes; a *Collected Stories* was published in 1980.

During the Depression Welty worked as a writer and photographer for the Works Progress Administration (the result was published as *One Time, One Place* in 1971); and the precise, framed nature of her tales has much in common with the quality of her photography. She also draws on a strong Southern storytelling tradition, and it is perhaps this that most informs 'First Love' (the opening of which is included here). She has said that what she most strives for in her writing is to 'enter the mind, heart, and skin of a human being who is not myself'. Welty discusses the aesthetics of storytelling, particularly focusing on its reliance on a sense of place, most fully in a deeply illuminating collection of essays, *The Eye of the Story* (1978).

Collected Stories was published by Virago in 1998.

from

'First Love'

Whatever happened, it happened in extraordinary times, in a season of dreams, and in Natchez it was the bitterest winter of them all. The north wind struck one January night in 1807 with an insistent penetration, as if it followed the settlers down by their own course, screaming down the river bends to drive them further still. Afterwards there was the strange drugged fall of snow. When the sun rose the air broke into a thousand prisms as close as the flash-and-turn of gulls' wings. For a long time afterwards it was so clear that in the evening the little companion-star to Sirius could be seen plainly in the heavens by travellers who took their way by night, and Venus shone in the daytime in all its course through the new transparency of the sky.

The Mississippi shuddered and lifted from its bed, reaching like a somnambulist driven to go in new places; the ice stretched far out over the waves. Flatboats and rafts continued to float downstream, but with unsignalling passengers submissive and huddled, mere bundles of sticks; bets were laid on shore as to whether they were alive or dead, but it was impossible to prove it either way.

The coated moss hung in blue and shining garlands over the trees along the changed streets in the morning. The town of little galleries was all laden roofs and silence. In the fastness of Natchez it began to seem then that the whole world, like itself, must be in a transfiguration. The only clamour came from the animals that suffered in their stalls, or from the wildcats that howled in closer rings each night from the frozen cane. The Indians could be heard from greater distances and in greater numbers than had been guessed, sending up placating but proud messages to the sun in continual ceremonies of dancing.

The red percussion of their fires could be seen night and day by those waiting in the dark trance of the frozen town. Men were caught by the cold, they dropped in its snare-like silence. Bands of travellers moved close together, with intenser caution, through the glassy tunnels of the Trace, for all proportion went away, and they followed one another like insects going at dawn through the heavy grass. Natchez people turned silently to look when a solitary man that no one had ever seen before was found and carried in through the streets, frozen the way he had crouched in a hollow tree, grey and huddled like a squirrel, with a little bundle of goods clasped to him.

Joel Mayes, a deaf boy twelve years old, saw the man brought in and knew it was a dead man, but his eyes were for something else, something wonderful. He saw the breaths coming out of people's mouths, and his dark face, losing just now a little of its softness, showed its secret desire. It was marvellous to him when the infinite designs of speech became visible in formations on the air, and he watched with awe that changed to tenderness whenever people met and passed in the road with an exchange of words. He walked alone, slowly through the silence, with the sturdy and yet dreamlike walk of the orphan, and let his own breath out through his lips, pushed it into the air, and whatever word it was it took the shape of a tower. He was as pleased as if he had had a little conversation with someone. At the end of the street, where he turned into the Inn, he always bent his head and walked faster, as if all frivolity were done, for he was boot-boy there.

He had come to Natchez some time in the summer. That was through great worlds of leaves, and the whole journey from Virginia had been to him a kind of childhood wandering in oblivion. He had remained to himself: always to himself at first, and afterwards too – with the company of Old Man McCaleb, who took him along when his parents vanished in the forest, were cut off from him, and in spite of his last backward look, dropped behind. Arms bent on destination dragged him forward through the sharp bushes, and leaves came towards his face which he finally put his hands out to stop. Now that he was a boot-boy, he had thought little, frugally, almost stonily, of that long time . . . until lately Old Man McCaleb had reappeared at the Inn, bound for no telling where, his tangled beard like the beards of old men in dreams; and in the act of cleaning his boots, which were uncommonly heavy and burdensome with mud, Joel came upon a little part of the old adventure, for there it was, dark and crusted . . . came back to it, and went over it again. . .

He rubbed, and remembered the day after his parents had left
him, the day when it was necessary to hide from the Indians. Old Man
McCaleb, his stern face lighting in the most unexpected way, had
herded them, the whole party alike, into the dense cane brake, deep
down off the Trace – the densest part, where it grew as thick and
locked as some kind of wild teeth. There they crouched, and each one
of them, man, woman, and child, had looked at all the others from a
hiding place that seemed the least safe of all, watching in an eager
wild instinct for any movement or betrayal. Crouched by his bush, Joel
had cried; all his understanding would desert him suddenly and
because he could not hear he could not see or touch or find a familiar thing in the world. He wept, the Old Man McCaleb first felled the
excited dog with the blunt end of his axe, and then he turned a fierce
face toward him and lifted the blade in the air, in a kind of ecstasy of
protecting the silence they were keeping. Joel had made a sound. . .
He gasped and put his mouth quicker than thought against the earth.
He took the leaves in his mouth. . . In that long time of lying motionless with the men and women in the cane brake he had learned what
silence meant to other people. Through the danger he had felt
acutely, even with horror, the nearness of his companions, a speech-
less embrace of which he had had no warning, a powerful, crushing
unity. The Indians had then gone by, followed by an old woman – in
solemn, single file, careless of the inflaming arrows they carried in
their quivers, dangling in their hands a few strings of catfish. They
passed in the length of the old woman's yawn. Then one by one
McCaleb's charges had to rise up and come out of the hiding place.
There was little talking together, but a kind of shame and shuffling. As
soon as the party reached Natchez, their little cluster dissolved completely. The old man had given each of them one long, rather forlorn
look for a farewell, and had gone away, no less preoccupied than he
had ever been. To the man who had saved his life Joel lifted the
gentle, almost indifferent face of the child who has asked for nothing.
Now he remembered the white gulls flying across the sky behind the
old man's head.

Joel had been deposited at the Inn, and there was nowhere else for
him to go, for it stood there and marked the foot of the long Trace,
with the river back of it. So he remained. It was a noncommittal
arrangement: he never paid them anything for his keep, and they
never paid him anything for his work. Yet time passed, and he became
a little part of the place where it passed over him. A small private
room became his own; it was on the ground floor behind the saloon,

a dark little room paved with stones with its ceiling rafters curved not higher than a man's head. There was a fireplace and one window, which opened on the courtyard filled always with the tremor of horses. He curled up every night on a highbacked bench, when the weather turned cold he was given a collection of old coats to sleep under, and the room was almost excessively his own, as it would have been a stray kitten's that came to the same spot every night. He began to keep his candlestick carefully polished, he set it in the centre of the puncheon table, and at night when it was lighted all the messages of love carved into it with a knife in Spanish words, with a deep Spanish gouging, came out in black relief, for anyone to read who came knowing the language.

Late at night, nearer morning, after the travellers had all certainly pulled off their boots to fall into bed, he waked by habit and passed with the candle shielded up the stairs and through the halls and rooms, and gathered up the boots. When he had brought them all down to his table he would sit and take his own time cleaning them, while the firelight would come gently across the paving stones. It seemed then that his whole life was safely alighted, in the sleep of everyone else, like a bird on a bough, and he was alone in the way he liked to be. He did not despise boots at all – he had learned boots; under his hand they stood up and took a good shape. This was not a slave's work, or a child's either. It had dignity: it was dangerous to walk about among sleeping men. More than once he had been seized and the life half shaken out of him by a man waking up in a sweat of suspicion or nightmare, but he dealt nimbly as an animal with the violence and quick frenzy of dreamers. It might seem to him that the whole world was sleeping in the lightest of trances, which the least movement would surely wake; but he only walked softly, stepping around and over, and got back to his room. Once a rattlesnake had shoved its head from a boot as he stretched out his hand; but that was not likely to happen again in a thousand years.

1944

Katherine Anne Porter

Katherine Anne Porter was born in 1890 and, after the death of her mother, was brought up in poverty by her storytelling grandmother in Indian Creek, Texas. At sixteen she ran away, was briefly married, and began working as a journalist in Chicago. From 1918 to 1921 she was involved in revolutionary politics in Mexico, about which she later wrote many stories, notably 'Flowering Judas', and *Outline of Mexican Popular Arts and Crafts* (1922). She then travelled in Europe, settling in Paris for some years in the early thirties. After returning to the USA she lived in Baton Rouge, Louisiana. Porter died in 1980.

Although she had published in magazines for some time before, Porter's first collection of stories, *Flowering Judas* (1930), came out when she was forty. Several other volumes, including *Pale Horse, Pale Rider* (1935) and *The Leaning Tower* (1944), followed and *The Collected Stories* was published to great acclaim in 1965. Her only novel, *Ship of Fools* (1962), was also a instant bestseller.

Admired for their precise and elegant style, Porter's stories frequently examine the legacy of the past and the way that it is distilled and distorted by the workings of memory.

Virago reprinted *The Collected Stories* in 1985.

from

'The Journey'

Nannie, born in slavery, was pleased to think she would not die in it. She was wounded not so much by her state of being as by the word describing it. Emancipation was a sweet word to her. It had not changed her way of living in a single particular, but she was proud of having been able to say to her mistress, 'I aim to stay wid you as long as you'll have me.' Still, Emancipation had seemed to set right a wrong that stuck in her heart like a thorn. She could not understand why God, Whom she loved, had seen fit to be so hard on a whole race because they had got a certain kind of skin. She talked it over with Miss Sophia Jane. Many times. Miss Sophia Jane was always brisk and opinionated about it: 'Nonsense! I tell you, God does not know whether a skin is black or white. He sees only souls. Don't be getting notions, Nannie – of course you're going to heaven.'

Nannie showed the rudiments of logic in a mind altogether untutored. She wondered, simply and without resentment, whether God, Who had been so cruel to black people on earth, might not continue His severity in the next world. Miss Sophia Jane took pleasure in reassuring her; as if she, who had been responsible for Nannie, body and soul in this life, might also be her sponsor before the judgment seat.

Miss Sophia Jane had taken upon herself all the responsibilities of her tangled world, half white, half black, mingling steadily and the confusion growing ever deeper. There were so many young men about the place, always, younger brothers-in-law, first cousins, second cousins, nephews. They came visiting and they stayed, and there was no accounting for them nor any way of controlling their quietly head-strong habits. She learned early to keep silent and give no sign of uneasiness, but whenever a child was born in the Negro quarters, pink, wormlike, she held her breath for three days, she told her eldest grand-daughter, years later, to see whether the newly born would turn black after the proper interval . . . It was a strain that told on her, and ended by giving her a deeply grounded contempt for men. She could not help it, she despised men. She despised them and was ruled by them. Her husband threw away her dowry and her property in wild investments in strange territories: Louisiana, Texas; and without protest she watched him play away her substance like a gambler. She felt that she could have managed her affairs profitably. But her natural activities lay elsewhere, it was the business of a man to make all decisions and dispose of all financial matters. Yet when she got the reins in her hands, her sons could persuade her to this and that enterprise or investment; against her will and judgment she accepted their advice, and among them they managed to break up once more the stronghold she had built for the future of her family. They got from her their own start in life, came back for fresh help when they needed it, and were divided against each other. She saw it as her natural duty to provide for her household, after her husband had fought stubbornly through the War, along with every other man of military age in the connection; had been wounded, had lingered helpless, and had died of his wound long after the great fervour and excitement had faded in hopeless defeat, when to be a man wounded and ruined in the War was merely to have proved oneself, perhaps, more heroic than wise. Left so, she drew her family together and set out for Louisiana, where her husband, with her money, had bought a sugar refinery. There was going to be a fortune in sugar, he said; not in raising the raw material, but in manufacturing it. He had schemes in his head for operating cotton gins, flour mills, refineries. Had he lived . . . but he did not live, and Sophia Jane had hardly repaired the house she bought and got the orchard planted when she saw that, in her hands, the sugar refinery was going to be a failure.

She sold out at a loss, and went on to Texas, where her husband had bought cheaply, some years before, a large tract of fertile black land in an almost unsettled part of the country. She had with her nine children, the youngest about two, the eldest about seventeen years old; Nannie and her three sons, Uncle Jimbilly, and two other Negroes, all in good health, full of hope and greatly desiring to live. Her husband's ghost persisted in her, she was bitterly outraged by his death almost as if he had wilfully deserted her. She mourned for him at first with dry eyes, angrily. Twenty years later, seeing after a long absence the eldest son of her favourite daughter, who had died early, she recognised the very features and look of the husband of her youth, and she wept.

During the terrible second year in Texas two of her younger sons, Harry and Robert, suddenly ran away. They chose good weather for it, in mid-May, and they were almost seven miles from home when a neighbouring farmer saw them, wondered and asked questions, and ended by persuading them into his gig, and so brought them back.

Miss Sophia Jane went through the dreary ritual of discipline she thought appropriate to the occasion. She whipped them with her riding whip. Then she made them kneel down with her while she prayed for them, asking God to help them mend their ways and not be undutiful to their mother; her duty performed, she broke down and wept with her arms around them. They had endured their punishment stoically, because it would have been disgraceful to cry when a woman hit them, and besides, she did not hit very hard; they had knelt with her in a shamefaced gloom, because religious feeling was a female mystery which embarrassed them, but when they saw her tears they burst into loud bellows of repentance. They were only nine and eleven years old. She said in a voice of mourning, so despairing it frightened them: 'Why did you run away from me? What do you think I brought you here for?' as if they were grown men who could realise how terrible the situation was. All the answer they could make, as they wept too, was that they had wanted to go back to Louisiana to eat sugar cane. They had been thinking about sugar cane all winter . . . Their mother was stunned. She had built a house large enough to shelter them all, of hand-sawed lumber dragged by ox-cart for forty miles, she had got the fields fenced in and the crops planted, she had, she believed, fed and clothed her children; and now she realised they were hungry. These two had worked like men; she felt their growing bones through their thin flesh, and remembered how mercilessly she had driven them, as she had driven herself, as she had driven the Negroes and the horses, because there was no choice in the matter. They must labour beyond their strength or perish. Sitting there with her arms around them, she felt her heart break in her breast. She had thought it was a silly phrase. It happened to her. It was not that she was incapable of feeling afterward, for in a way she was more emotional, more quick, but griefs never again lasted with her so long as they had before. This day was the beginning of her spoiling her children and being afraid of them. She said to them after a long dazed silence, when they began to grow restless under her arms: 'We'll grow fine ribbon cane here. The soil is perfect for it. We'll have all the sugar we want. But we must be patient.'

1945

Elizabeth Hardwick

Born in Lexington, Kentucky, in 1916, Elizabeth Hardwick graduated from the University of Kentucky in 1939. She moved to New York to continue her studies at Columbia University and taught briefly at Barnard College. From 1949 to 1972 she was married to the poet Robert Lowell, with whom she had a daughter in 1957.

The author of three novels, *The Ghostly Lover* (1945), *The Simple Truth* (1955) and *Sleepless Nights* (1979), Hardwick is also much admired for her critical writing – much of which focuses on women's writing. In 1963 she co-founded the *New York Review of Books* and remains an advisory editor.

Virago published *The Ghostly Lover*, with a new Afterword by Hardwick, in 1986.

from

The Ghostly Lover

Marian Coleman was aware that someone was watching her from the side porch of the house beyond the garden. She had seen the man's blond head and his body swaying in the swing. She saw him turn the pages of the book which he held in his hand and she thought, he isn't reading now. He's looking over here. In a spot partially concealed by a short row of bushes, she stretched out and faced the summer sun. With her eyes closed she was able to forget, somewhat, the man in the house beyond and to concentrate upon the visit of her parents.

It had been two years since Marian had seen her mother and father. Now that they were returning, they had no reality. They were like remote ancestors, those raw-boned ghosts whose sins fill you with mystery and dread and whose virtues are an obscure challenge. If there were anything wrong with the parents, if they had shamefully altered in any way, she and the rest of the family would be made to feel the blight. Like the primitive's fear of the anger of a revered bat, she was apprehensive about the elusive parents.

A door slammed in the house beyond and she opened her eyes, being careful not to turn too quickly at the sound. The man was still in the swing. He had put the book aside and was lighting a cigarette. Someone inside the house spoke to him and she could hear him answer. Before she turned away, she was certain that he had seen her look at him and that he was smiling.

[. . .]

She heard him leave the porch swing and descend the few steps into the yard. He paused, rocking back and forth on his heels, and absent-mindedly stared at the sun falling on the dark green tree leaves. Marian watched the way he moved. He was slightly swivel-hipped, big-framed and graceful. He picked up a little grey stone and threw it into the air. Then he turned toward her and she knew he was looking at the tips of her toes and the top of her hair, the parts of her body not concealed by the bush. Walking slowly, and with a half-smile already on his face, he crossed from his yard into hers. As she had known he would, he stopped before her and looked down into her startled eyes. His skin was fair and she noticed that his eyes looked reddish-yellow in the sunlight. His lips were parted, but he did not speak. Every muscle in her body felt wooden and mute and she thought, with those lightning calculations one makes in front of a pos-sible foe, I will be childish and quiet. Feeling that she could not move quickly enough, she retreated fiercely into childhood and her face met his with a frightened, protective embarrassment. She could feel a strain in her back from the position in which she was sitting, and yet she could not move.

He had on white trousers and a shirt striped with blue. It was open at the collar. At the base of his throat she could see the dry, blond hairs. Because she was looking up at him, his eyes seemed rather gaily out of focus.

'Sun bathing?' he said.

She nodded and he sat down beside her on the ground.

She reached out for a weed and drew the stem through her fingers. The sun was as clear and white as ice now, and the faint perfume of lilacs blew steadily through the air. In the distance the church bells rang out the time. The illuminated quiet of early afternoon lay over the street. Sometimes the steamy sound of a truck moving over the smooth road could be heard. A bird suddenly stepped in the shadows of the trees.

'You look a little bit like your mother, if I remember her,' Bruce said. 'Maybe it's the eyes with the nice smooth eyebrows. And a little bit like your father. The mouth, I think.'

'Your name is Bruce,' she said. He nodded and closed his eyes against the sun. She looked squarely at his face. It was relaxed and had fallen into its purest shape. The face was like that of a baby who had grown into full manhood with a beard and lines, but still retained the child's lack of pain and indecision. It was a face of the present, a startling face that seemed to have reached some ultimate static stage. It was remotely arrogant and cruel. She looked at her dress and saw that it was wrinkled, unfit to meet his close-eyed gaze which was as engrossed, quick and discerning as the face of a buyer inspecting a warehouse of goods.

He opened his eyes and laughed. She smiled back to him, without knowing why he had laughed. She thought, rather uneasily, that the laughter of adults was always very different from the laughter of children. The former indicated a recognition of the familiar, but in children it came from the shock of the new. She had the feeling that he had been through this moment before.

'Ted isn't in town?' he asked.

'My father?' she whispered.

He paused and stretched out his arms. His face was hot and red, and his cheek bones stood out like parched ridges in a rock. He started to speak again and his voice was loud, a market place voice, assured and casual. 'I met him several times. Fishing I think it was. Not that he was doing much fishing. . . I don't know what he was doing at the lake, unless . . .'

Marian threw away the bruised weed she had picked up. 'That must have been a long time ago,' she said coldly. He looked at her amazed, and almost pleased, she thought. Did he know that she had stopped him because she wanted so much to hear about her father that the actuality frightened her? There was too much objectivity in his voice and she wondered if he too knew her parents were grotesque in the way they remained warring lovers. The last time she had been with them she had felt this strangely youthful tension. They had never relaxed, never accepted the triumph or defeat, which it was she did not know, of marriage. They were still sparring in that sensuous valley of courtship.

'At the lake,' she said. 'You say it was the lake?' Her eyes were fast upon his face, because she hoped that he might, without saying anything upsetting, give her some clue to her parents. She was only sixteen and she feared her inexperience might make her judge them wrongly. She was looking at him as she had often looked at the parents of her friends. Every 'dear' and 'darling', every automatic evening kiss made her start, because it was important that she know exactly what older people felt and meant. She observed every flickering eye, every hand placement, and listened for sudden lowerings of the voice. And then she compared them with the glances, sighs, and weighted exchanges she had seen in her own parents. Sometimes she was filled with envy for her friends with the solid, chattering families; but at other times she hated them and their faces seemed greedy. She felt that they were paltry in their ravenously explored familiarity.

When Bruce did not answer she said, 'I suppose it will be much hotter later on,' as if she had been thinking about the weather for a long time.

'You don't really want to talk about your father,' he said gaily. 'That's rather admirable and shows an amazing intelligence. Most of us spend too damned much time talking and thinking about our families.'

He turned on his side now and looked at her. She could see in his eyes that the time had come for the final and complete examination of every feature, the weighing of every fault, like turning a naked body on a slave block. He seemed to say, This is what it means for me to be male and you female. This and no more. She lifted her face to him and it was as servile as a eunuch's, until he turned away from her and seemed to settle down within himself because he had found her satisfactory.

Bruce's hand lay palm flat on the grass and she noticed the wide, flexible fingers and the reddish skin pulled tightly over the knuckles. She felt that whatever he had seen in her in that one glance was the beginning and end of all he would ever see. It was as if some hardening mould had fallen over her. There would be no room for alteration.

'How old are you?' he said suddenly.

His voice frightened her, and she did not answer. Her thinking and reacting seemed to come from a tight, airless space between the skin and bone of her forehead. He threw her into heavy half-consciousness, like the minutes before sleep. After a moment, she merely said, 'Oh?' questioningly, as if she had not understood.

He chuckled indifferently. 'Well, anyway, you're damned young. Damned young.'

1946

Ann Petry

———

Ann Petry was born in Old Saybrook, Connecticut, in 1908, into one of two black families in the small New England town. After working for some years in the family pharmacy, she married and moved to New York in 1938. She became a journalist for the Harlem newspapers, the *Amsterdam News* and then the *People's Voice*, and was also a member of the American Negro Theater. After studying creative writing at Columbia University, she published her first stories in the mid-forties. Her first, and most acclaimed, novel, *The Street*, came out in 1946. Petry went on to write two further novels, *Country Places* (1947) and *The Narrows* (1951), as well as volumes of poetry, stories and children's fiction.

Virago published *The Street* in 1986.

from

The Street

There was always a crowd in front of the Junto Bar and Grill on 116th Street. For in winter the street was cold. The wind blew the snow into great drifts that stayed along the kerb for weeks, gradually blackening with soot until it was no longer recognisable as snow, but appeared to be some dark eruption from the street itself.

As one cold day followed swiftly on the heels of another, the surface of the frozen piles became encrusted with bags of garbage, old shoes, newspapers, corset lacings. The frozen debris and the icy wind made the street a desolate place in winter and the people found a certain measure of escape from it by standing in front of the Junto where the light streaming from the windows and the music from its gramophone created an oasis of warmth.

In summer the street was hot and dusty, for no trees shaded it, and the sun beat straight down on the concrete pavement and the brick buildings. The inside of the houses fairly steamed; the dark passages were like ovens. Even the railings on the high steep stairways were warm to the touch.

As the thermometer crawled higher and higher, the people who lived on the street moved outdoors because the inside of the buildings was unbearable. The grown-ups lounging in chairs in front of the houses, the half-naked children playing along the kerb, transformed the street into an outdoor living room. And because the people took to sleeping on rooftops and fire escapes and park benches, the street also became a great outdoor bedroom.

The same people who found warmth by standing in front of the Junto in winter continued to stand there in summer. In fact, the number of people in front of the Junto increased in summer, for the whirr of its electric fans and the sound of ice clinking in tall glasses reached out to the street and created an illusion of coolness.

Thus, in winter and in summer people stood in front of the Junto from the time its doors opened early in the morning until they were firmly shut behind the last drunk the following morning.

The men who didn't work at all – the ones who never had and never would – stood in front of it in the morning. As the day slid toward afternoon, they were joined by tipsters, men who worked at night in factories and warehouses. And at night the pavement spilled over with the men who ran elevators and cleaned buildings and swept out subways.

All of them – the idle ones and the ones tired from their day's labour – found surcease and refreshment either inside or outside the Junto's doors. It served as social club and meeting place. By standing outside it a man could pick up all the day's news: the baseball scores, the number that came out, the latest neighbourhood gossip. Those who were interested in women could get an accurate evaluation of the girls who switched past in short tight skirts. A drinking man who was dead broke knew that if he stood there long enough a friend with funds would stroll by and offer to buy him a drink. And a man who was lonely and not interested in drinking or in women could absorb some of the warmth and laughter that seeped out to the street from the long bar.

The inside of the Junto was also crowded, too, because the white bartenders in their immaculate coats greeted the customers graciously. Their courteous friendliness was a heart-warming thing that helped rebuild egos battered and bruised during the course of the day's work.

The Junto represented something entirely different to the women on the street and what it meant to them depended in large measure on their age. Old women plodding past scowled ferociously and jerked the heavy shopping bags they carried until the stalks of celery and the mustard greens within seemed to tremble with rage at the sight of the Junto's doors. Some of the old women paused to mutter their hatred of it, to shake their fists in a sudden access of passion against it, and the men standing on the pavement moved closer to each other, forming a protective island with their shoulders, talking louder, laughing harder so as to shut out the sound and the sight of the old women.

Young women coming home from work – dirty, tired, depressed –

looked forward to the moment when they would change their clothes and head towards the gracious spaciousness of the Junto. They dressed hurriedly in their small dark bedrooms, so impatient for the soft lights and the music and the fun that awaited them that they fumbled in their haste.

For the young women had an urgent hunger for companionship and the Junto offered men of all sizes and descriptions: sleek, well-dressed men who earned their living as tipsters; even better-dressed and better-looking men who earned a fatter living supplying women to an eager market; huge, grimy longshoremen who were given to sudden bursts of generosity; Pullman porters in on overnight runs from Washington, Chicago, Boston; and around the first of the month the sailors and soldiers flush with crisp pay-day money.

On the other hand, some of the young women went to the Junto only because they were hungry for the sight and sound of other young people and because the creeping silence that could be heard under the blaring radios, under the drunken quarrels in the bedrooms, was no longer bearable.

Lutie Johnson was one of these. For she wasn't going to the Junto to pick up a man or to quench a consuming, constant thirst. She was going there so that she could for a moment capture the illusion of having some of the things that she lacked.

As she hurried toward the Junto, she acknowledged the fact that she couldn't afford a glass of beer there. It would be cheaper to buy a bottle at the delicatessen and take it home and drink it if beer was what she wanted. The beer was incidental and unimportant. It was the other things that the Junto offered that she sought: the sound of laughter, the hum of talk, the sight of people and brilliant lights, the sparkle of the big mirror, the rhythmic music from the gramophone.

Once inside, she hesitated, trying to decide whether she should stand at the crowded bar or sit alone at one of the small tables in the centre of the room or in one of the booths at the side. She turned abruptly to the long bar, thinking that she needed people around her tonight, even all these people who were jammed against each other at the bar.

They were here for the same reason that she was – because they couldn't bear to spend an evening alone in some small dark room; because they couldn't bear to look what they could see of the future smack in the face while listening to radios or trying to read an evening paper.

'Beer, please,' she said to the bartender.

There were rows of bottles on the shelves on each side of the big mirror behind the bar. They were reflected in the mirror, and looking at the reflection Lutie saw that they were magnified in size, shining so that they had the appearance of being filled with liquid, molten gold.

She examined herself and the people standing at the bar to see what changes the mirror wrought in them. There was a pleasant gaiety and charm about all of them. She found that she herself looked young, very young and happy in the mirror.

Her eyes wandered over the whole room. It sparkled in the mirror. The people had a kind of buoyancy about them. All except Old Man Junto, who was sitting alone at the table near the back.

She looked at him again and again, for his reflection in the mirror fascinated her. Somehow even at this distance his squat figure managed to dominate the whole room. It was, she decided, due to the bulk of his shoulders which were completely out of proportion to the rest of him.

Whenever she had been in here, he had been sitting at that same table, his hand cupped behind his ear as though he were listening to the sound of the cash register; sitting there alone watching everything – the customers, the bartenders, the waiters. For the barest fraction of a second, his eyes met hers in the mirror and then he looked away.

Then she forgot about him, for the gramophone in the far corner of the room started playing 'Swing It, Sister'. She hummed as she listened to it, not really aware that she was humming or why, knowing only that she felt free here where there was so much space.

The big mirror in front of her made the Junto an enormous room. It pushed the walls back and back into space. It reflected the lights from the ceiling and the concealed lighting that glowed in the corners of the room. It added a rosy radiance to the men and women standing at the bar; it pushed the world of other people's kitchen sinks back where it belonged and destroyed the existence of dirty streets and small shadowed rooms.

She finished the beer in one long gulp. Its pleasant bitter taste was still in her mouth when the bartender handed her a bill for the drink.

'I'll have another one,' she said softly.

No matter what it cost them, people had to come to places like the Junto, she thought. They had to replace the haunting silences of rented rooms and little flats with the murmur of voices, the sound of laughter; they had to empty two or three small glasses of liquid gold so they could believe in themselves again.

She frowned. Two beers and the films for Bub and the budget she had planned so carefully was ruined. If she did this very often, there wouldn't be much point in having a budget – for she couldn't budget what she didn't have.

For a brief moment she tried to look into the future. She still couldn't see anything – couldn't see anything at all but 116th Street and a job that paid barely enough for food and rent and a handful of clothes. Year after year like that. She tried to recapture the feeling of self-confidence she had had earlier in the evening, but it refused to return, for she rebelled at the thought of day after day of work and night after night caged in that flat that no amount of scrubbing would ever get really clean.

She moved the beer glass on the bar. It left a wet ring and she moved it again in an effort to superimpose the rings on each other. It was warm in the Junto, the lights were soft, and the music coming from the gramophone was sweet. She listened intently to the record. It was 'Darlin',' and when the voice on the record stopped she started singing: 'There's no sun, Darlin'. There's no fun, Darlin'.'

The men and women crowded at the bar stopped drinking to look at her. Her voice had a thin thread of sadness running through it that made the song important, that made it tell a story that wasn't in the words – a story of despair, of loneliness, of frustration. It was a story that all of them knew by heart and had always known because they had learned it soon after they were born and would go on adding to it until the day they died.

Just before the record ended, her voice stopped on a note so low and so long sustained that it was impossible to tell where it left off. There was a moment's silence around the bar, and then glasses were raised, the bartenders started counting change, and opening long-necked bottles, conversations were resumed.

The bartender handed her another bill. She picked it up mechanically and then placed it on top of the first one, held both of them loosely in her hand. That made two glasses and she'd better go before she weakened and bought another one. She put her gloves on slowly, transferring the bills from one hand to the other, wanting to linger here in this big high-ceilinged room where there were no shadowed silences, no dark corners; thinking that she should have made the beer last a long time by careful sipping instead of the greedy gulping that had made it disappear so quickly.

A man's hand closed over hers, gently extracted the two slips. 'Let me take 'em,' said a voice in her ear.

1947

Mollie Panter-Downes

Born in London in 1906, Mollie Panter-Downes grew up in Sussex. She married in 1929 and after travelling for several years she and her husband settled on the Surrey–Sussex border, where she remained until her death in 1997.

In addition to several works of non-fiction, Panter-Downes wrote five novels, the last of which was *One Fine Day*. Her first novel, *The Shoreless Sea*, was published when she was just seventeen and within a year went into eight editions. Nevertheless *One Fine Day* was the only one of her novels which Panter-Downes later felt any attachment to; it was, she said, 'her only novel'.

In 1939 Panter-Downes became the London correspondent to *The New Yorker* magazine, writing to America of the way that ordinary people lived their day-to-day life through the Blitz. Two collections of her 'Letters from London' were published (in 1940 and 1972) and had some of the same influence as Jan Struther's *Mrs Miniver*.

One Fine Day was serialised in the *Atlantic Monthly* and published in book form in 1947. A compelling evocation of post-war England, it was originally entitled 'The Vanished House', the significance of which becomes apparent in the following extract.

from

One Fine Day

She went slowly back into the dining-room. The debris of breakfast things looked cold, awful, as though they were the mummified remains of some meal eaten a thousand years ago. But she sat down among them and poured out a last cup of tea. Ah, how good! Now, said the house to Laura, we are alone together. Now I am yours again. The yellow roses in the bowl shed half a rose in a sudden soft, fat slump on the polished wood, a board creaked on the stairs, distant pipes chirped. She knew all her houses's little voices, as she had never done in the old days when there had been more people under her roof. Then there had been nothing but cheerful noises all day long. In the kitchen, caps and aprons shrieked with sudden merriment over their bread-and-cheese elevenses. The butcher's young man came whistling to the back door, on his shoulder a clean white enamel tray, reposing on it a leg of lamb which looked as though someone had just powdered it, and eight red-and-white cutlets, tiny and perfect as though they were doll's house viands attached by glue. Good morning, madam, he would say, touching his forehead pleasantly if he saw Laura. Oh, madam! called the voices, Are you there, madam? The telephone bell was always ringing through those petrified remembered summers. A popular young couple, the Marshalls. Voices of people who were now dead cried Laura! over the wires from flower-filled, book-lined rooms in London that were now dust, the exposed tints of their freakish walls fading and streaking lividly in sun and rain. Chandler followed the butcher round to the kitchen, carrying a trug basket which he had arranged like a Dutch painting with crisp veined lettuce heads, sweet corn, white beans, and aubergine. He had enjoyed trying something new, outlandish vegetables unknown to Wealding. Oh, madam! called the voices. From the nursery, Nannie's wireless supplied a constant dreamy accompaniment of masculine sopranos and feminine tenors dealing with Junes and moons and you-hoo-hoo-de-do. Nannie's voice was heard, as Laura paused on the nursery landing, chanting, Prick it and bake it and mark it with Vee, and Victoria chirping imitatively, Bake it and mark it with *Wee*. Other children came to tea, leaning shyly against starched apron fronts secured by enormous safety-pins. The garden echoed with laughter and infant howls, checked and appeased in slices of iced cake. Guests arrived every week-end, turning up at cocktail time with dogs and little leather cases, an armful of magazines, grapes for Laura, chocolate drops for Victoria, who would be viewed, damp and delicious from the bath, in a fleecy blue dressing-gown with a pink rabbit on the pocket. They had never been alone.

What had happened? Where had they gone? The pretty, hospitable house seemed to have disappeared like a dream back into the genie's bottle, leaving only the cold hillside. Laura sat alone, the silence settled with the dust on the empty rooms, and the caps and aprons rustled their way – whither? Into factories, people said, where they would learn to assemble the bright and shoddy as they had learnt to pack the capsules of splintered destruction. It was funny to think that Ethel and Violet, who had spent their days setting things in a precise pattern, plumping the sofa cushion, straightening the little mat under the finger-bowl, drawing curtains against the wild stalking darkness, had learnt to pack the capsule of hideous muddled death. They would never come back into the tame house again. Everyone said so. Like young horses intoxicated with the feel of their freedom, Ethel and Violet had disappeared squealing into the big bright world where there were no bells to run your legs off, where you knew where you were, where you could go to the flicks regular, and where you worked to the sound of dance music pouring out continuously, sweet and thick and insipid as condensed milk dripping through a hole in a tin.

Meanwhile, here they were awkwardly saddled with a house which, all those pleasant years, had really been supported and nourished by squawks over bread-and-cheese elevenses, by the sound of Chandler's boots on the paths, by the smell of ironing and toast from the nursery. The support, the nourishment, had been removed. Now, on this summer morning, when doors and windows stood open, it was possible to hear the house slowly giving up, loosening its hold, gently accepting shabbiness and defeat. Nature seemed to realise its discomfiture. Birds hopped boldly through the front door, evidently meditating a lodging; Laura's dusting hardly discouraged the bold machinations of the spiders. As she sat drinking her tea, a yellow butterfly came in and settled on the faded plum-and-white pattern of the curtains as though it could no longer plainly distinguish between outside and in. It fluttered its wings comfortably, and the other half of the rose quietly, fatly fell, bearing down with it a shocked head of golden stamens.

1948

Dodie Smith

Dodie (Dorothy Gladys) Smith, born in 1896, was brought up in Manchester and London. After studying at RADA, she attempted a career as an actress but soon turned to playwriting, using the pseudonym C. L. Anthony. *Autumn Crocus* made her reputation in 1931 and was made into a film starring Ivor Novello in 1934. By the outbreak of the Second World War, she had written five further plays and was at the pinnacle of her success with *Dear Octopus* (1938), which was described as 'the family play of the decade'.

Smith left England for the USA in 1939 with her future husband (and manager) Alec Beesley, a conscientious objector, and her Dalmatian dog Pongo. Pongo later provided the inspiration for the book for which she is best known, *A Hundred and One Dalmatians* (1956), filmed by Walt Disney in 1961. (A sequel, *The Starlight Barking*, was published in 1967.)

While Smith was writing screenplays in Hollywood, her nostalgia for England found an outlet in *I Capture the Castle*, the story of an eccentric and impoverished family in the 1930s. Smith's close friend Christopher Isherwood described it as a book one could 'live inside', and generations of readers have concurred. Smith was especially pleased when Ralph Vaughan Williams chose it as his 1949 'book of the year'.

In 1954 Smith returned to England, where she continued to write until her death in 1990. Four volumes of autobiography were published between 1974 and 1985; a fifth volume was unfinished at the time of her death.

I Capture the Castle was published by Virago in 1996.

from

I Capture the Castle

I write this sitting in the kitchen sink. That is, my feet are in it; the rest of me is on the draining-board, which I have padded with our dog's blanket and the tea-cosy. I can't say that I am really comfortable, and there is a depressing smell of carbolic soap, but this is the only part of the kitchen where there is any daylight left. And I have found that sitting in a place where you have never sat before can be inspiring – I wrote my very best poem while sitting on the hen-house. Though even that isn't a very good poem. I have decided my poetry is so bad that I mustn't write any more of it.

Drips from the roof are plopping into the water-butt by the back door. The view through the windows above the sink is excessively drear. Beyond the dank garden in the courtyard are the ruined walls on the edge of the moat. Beyond the moat, the boggy ploughed fields stretch to the leaden sky. I tell myself that all the rain we have had lately is good for nature, and that at any moment spring will surge on us. I try to see leaves on the trees and the court-yard filled with sunlight. Unfortunately, the more my mind's eye sees green and gold, the more drained of all colour does the twilight seem.

It is comforting to look away from the windows and towards the kitchen fire, near which my sister Rose is ironing – though she obviously can't see properly, and it will be a pity if she scorches her only nightgown. (I have two, but one is minus its behind.) Rose looks particularly fetching by firelight because she is a pinkish person; her skin has a pink glow and her hair is pinkish gold, very light and feathery. Although I am rather used to her I know she is a beauty. She is nearly twenty-one and very bitter with life. I am seventeen, look younger, feel older. I am no beauty but have a neatish face.

I have just remarked to Rose that our situation is really rather romantic – two girls in this strange and lonely house. She replied that she saw nothing romantic about being shut up in a crumbling ruin surrounded by a sea of mud. I must admit that our home is an unreasonable place to live in. Yet I love it. The house itself was built in the time of Charles II, but it was grafted on to a fourteenth-century castle that had been damaged by Cromwell. The whole of our east wall was part of the castle; there are two round towers in it. The gate-house is intact and a stretch of the old walls at their full height joins it to the house. And Belmotte Tower, all that remains of an even older castle, still stands on its mound close by. But I won't attempt to describe our peculiar home fully until I can see more time ahead of me than I do now.

I am writing this journal partly to practise my newly acquired speed-writing and partly to teach myself how to write a novel – I intend to capture all our characters and put in conversations. It ought to be good for my style to dash along without much thought, as up to now my stories have been very stiff and self-conscious. The only time father obliged me by reading one of them, he said I combined stateliness with a desperate effort to be funny. He told me to relax and let the words flow out of me.

I wish I knew of a way to make words flow out of father. Years and years ago, he wrote a very unusual book called *Jacob Wrestling*, a mix-ture of fiction, philosophy and poetry. It had a great success, particularly in America, where he made a lot of money by lecturing on it, and he seemed likely to become a very important writer indeed. But he stopped writing. Mother believed this was due to something that happened when I was about five.

We were living in a small house by the sea at the time. Father had just joined us after his second American lecture tour. One after-noon when we were having tea in the garden, he had the misfortune to lose his temper with mother very noisily just as he was about to cut a piece of cake. He brandished the cake-knife at her so menac-ingly that an officious neighbour jumped the garden fence to intervene and got himself knocked down. Father explained in court that killing a woman with our silver cake-knife would be a long, weary business entailing sawing her to death; and he was completely exonerated of any intention of slaying mother. The whole case seems to have been quite ludicrous, with everyone but the neighbour being very funny. But father made the mistake of being funnier than the judge and, as there was no doubt whatever that he had seriously damaged the neighbour, he was sent to prison for three months.

When he came out he was as nice a man as ever – nicer, because his temper was so much better. Apart from that, he didn't seem to me to be changed at all. But Rose remembers that he had already begun to get unsociable – it was then that he took a forty years' lease of the castle, which is an admirable place to be unsociable in. Once we were settled here he was supposed to begin a new book. But time went on without anything happening and at last we realised that he had given up even trying to write – for years now, he has refused to discuss the possibility. Most of his life is spent in the gate-house room, which is icy cold in winter as there is no fireplace; he just huddles over an oil-stove. As far as we know, he does nothing but read detective novels from the village library. Miss Marcy, the librarian and schoolmistress, brings them to him. She admires him greatly and says 'the iron has entered into his soul'.

Personally, I can't see how the iron could get very far into a man's soul during only three months in jail – anyway, not if the man had as much vitality as father had; and he seemed to have plenty of it left when they let him out. But it has gone now; and his unsociability has grown almost into a disease – I often think he would prefer not even to meet his own household. All his natural gaiety has vanished. At times he puts on a false cheerfulness that embarrasses me, but usually he is either morose or irritable – I think I should prefer it if he lost his temper as he used to. Oh, poor father, he really is very pathetic. But he might at least do a little work in the garden. I am aware that this isn't a fair portrait of him. I must capture him later.

Mother died eight years ago, from perfectly natural causes. I think she must have been a shadowy person, because I have only the vaguest memory of her and I have an excellent memory for most things. (I can remember the cake-knife incident perfectly – I hit the fallen neighbour with my little wooden spade. Father always said this got him an extra month.)

Three years ago (or is it four? I know father's one spasm of socia-bility was in 1931) a stepmother was presented to us. We *were* surprised. She is a famous artist's model who claims to have been christened Topaz – even if this is true there is no law to make a woman stick to a name like that. She is very beautiful, with masses of hair so fair that it is almost white, and a quite extraordinary pallor. She uses no make-up, not even powder. There are two paintings of her in the Tate Gallery: one by Macmorris, called 'Topaz in Jade', in which she wears a magnificent jade necklace; and one by H. J. Allardy which shows her nude on an old horsehair-covered sofa that she says was very prickly. This is called 'Composition'; but as Allardy has painted her even paler than she is, 'Decomposition' would suit it better.

Actually, there is nothing unhealthy about Topaz's pallor; it simply makes her look as if she belonged to some new race. She has a very deep voice – that is, she puts one on; it is part of an arty pose, which includes painting and lute-playing. But her kindness is perfectly genuine and so is her cooking. I am very, very fond of her – it is nice to have written that just as she appears on the kitchen stairs. She is wearing her ancient orange tea-gown. Her pale, straight hair is flowing down her back to her waist. She paused on the top step and said: 'Ah, girls . . .' with three velvety inflections on each word.

Now she is sitting on the steel trivet, raking the fire. The pink light makes her look more ordinary, but very pretty. She is twenty-nine and had two husbands before father (she will never tell us very much about them), but she still looks extraordinarily young. Perhaps that is because her expression is so blank.

The kitchen looks very beautiful now. The firelight glows steadily through the bars and through the round hole in the top of the range where the lid has been left off. It turns the whitewashed walls rosy; even the dark beams in the roof are a dusky gold. The highest beam is over thirty feet from the ground. Rose and Topaz are two tiny figures in a great glowing cave.

Now Rose is sitting on the fender, waiting for her iron to heat. She is staring at Topaz with a discontented expression. I can often tell what Rose is thinking and I would take a bet that she is envying the orange tea-gown and hating her own skimpy old blouse and skirt. Poor Rose hates most things she has and envies most things she hasn't. I really am just as discontented, but I don't seem to notice it so much. I feel quite unreasonably happy this minute, watching them both; knowing I can go and join them in the warmth, yet staying here in the cold.

Oh, dear, there has just been a slight scene! Rose asked Topaz to go to London and earn some money. Topaz replied that she didn't think it was worth while, because it costs so much to live there. It is true that she can never save more than will buy us a few presents – she is very generous.

'And two of the men I sit for are abroad,' she went on, 'and I don't like working for Macmorris.'

'Why not?' asked Rose. 'He pays better than the others, doesn't he?'

'So he ought, considering how rich he is,' said Topaz. 'But I dislike sitting for him because he only paints my head. Your father says that the men who paint me nude paint my body and think of their job, but that Macmorris paints my head and thinks of my body. And it's perfectly true. I've had more trouble with him than I should care to let your father know.'

Rose said: 'I should have thought it was worth while to have a little trouble in order to earn some real money.'

'Then *you* have the trouble, dear,' said Topaz.

This must have been very annoying to Rose, considering that she never has the slightest chance of that sort of trouble. She suddenly flung back her head dramatically and said:

'I'm perfectly willing to. It may interest you both to know that for some time now I've been considering selling myself. If necessary, I shall go on the streets.'

I told her she couldn't go on the streets in the depths of Suffolk.

'But if Topaz will kindly lend me the fare to London and give me a few hints—'

Topaz said she had never been on the streets and rather regretted it, 'because one must sink to the depths in order to rise to the heights,' which is the kind of Topazism it requires much affection to tolerate.

'And anyway,' she told Rose, 'you're the last girl to lead a hard-working, immoral life. If you're really taken with the idea of selling yourself, you'd better choose a wealthy man and marry him respectably.'

This idea has, of course, occurred to Rose, but she has always hoped that the man would be handsome, romantic and lovable into the bargain. I suppose it was her sheer despair of ever meeting any marriageable men at all, even hideous, poverty-stricken ones, that made her suddenly burst into tears. As she only cries about once a year I really ought to have gone over and comforted her, but I wanted to set it all down here. I begin to see that writers are liable to become callous.

1949

Olivia

———

Olivia was the pseudonym for Dorothy Strachey, born in London, one of ten children, in 1866. (Her younger brother was Lytton Strachey, and Olivia was a sister who died in infancy.) At the age of sixteen Dorothy was sent to school at Fontainebleau, near Paris, and it is her experiences there that form the basis of *Olivia*.

Dorothy Strachey taught in London before marrying the French painter Simon Bussy in 1903. They lived in the south of France and had one daughter. In 1918 she met André Gide and became his main English translator and a good friend. She published *Olivia* in 1949 and the following year *Fifty Nursery Rhymes, with a Commentary on English Usage for French Students*.

Olivia was filmed in 1950, by the French director Jacqueline Audry, with Simone Simon in the title role, and soon achieved cult status.

Dorothy Bussy died in 1960 shortly after the death of her daughter.

Virago published *Olivia* in 1987.

from

Olivia

Then there was a more passive, a more languorous state, when I seemed to myself dissolving, when I let myself go, as I phrased it to myself, when I felt as though I were floating luxuriously down a warm, gentle river, every muscle relaxed, every portion of me open to receive each softest caress of air and water, down, down, towards some unknown, delicious sea. My indefinite desire was like some pervading, unlocalised ache for my whole being. If I could only know, thought I, where it lies, what it is. In my heart? In my brain? In my body? But no, all I felt was that I desired something. Sometimes I thought it was to be loved in return. But that seemed to me so entirely impossible that it was really and truly unimaginable. I could not imagine *how* she could love me. *Like* me, be fond of me, as a child, as a pupil, yes, of course. But that had nothing to do with what I felt. And so I made myself another dream. It was a man I loved as I loved her, and then he would take me in his arms . . . and kiss me . . . I should feel his lips on my cheeks, on my eyelids, on my—No, no, no, that way lay madness. All this was different – hopeless. Hopeless! A dreadful word, but with a kind of tonic in it. I would hug it to my heart. Yes, hopeless. It was that that gave my passion dignity, that made it worthy of respect. No other love, no love of man and woman could ever be as disinterested as mine. It was I alone who loved – it was I alone whose love was an impossible fantasy.

And yet she sometimes showered me with marvellous kindnesses. Often when she was reading aloud to me in the library, she would drop her hand into mine and let me hold it. Once when I had a cold, she visited me in my room, petted me, brought me delicacies from the table, told me stories that made me laugh, left me cheerful and contented. It was during my convalescence from that little indisposition that she put her head into my room one evening and said:

'I'm going out to dinner in Paris, but I'll look in on you when I get back and see how you are and say good-night to you.' Her good-night was gay and tender and the next day I was well.

A fortnight later she went out to dinner again. The last train from Paris reached the station at about half-past eleven and she used to be up at the house a little before twelve. How could I help keeping awake that night, half expecting her, listening for her? She had to pass my door to go to her room. Perhaps, perhaps she would come in again. Ah, straining ears and beating heart! But why was she so long? What could she be doing? Again and again I lit my candle and looked at my watch. Can she have passed the door without my having heard her? Impossible! At last, at last, the step came sounding down the long passage. Nearer, nearer. Would it stop? Would it go on? It stopped. A breathless pause. Would the handle turn? It turned. She came in in the dim light of the unshuttered room and stood beside my bed:

'I've brought you a sweet, you greedy little thing,' she said and pulled it out of her bag.

Oh yes, I was greedy, but not for sweets. Her hands were my possession. I covered them with kisses.

'There, there, Olivia,' she said. 'You're too passionate, my child.'

Her lips brushed my forehead and she was gone.

1950s

1950

Barbara Comyns

___

Born in Warwickshire in 1909 (or 1912?), Barbara Bayley began writing at the age of ten and was the author of eight novels. Her
best-known works are *The Skin Chairs* (1962) and *The Vet's Daughter*
(1959), which was adapted by Sandy Wilson into a musical called *The
Clapham Wonder*.

Our Spoons Came from Woolworths draws on her first marriage to an
impoverished London artist. In 1945 she married Richard Carr-
Comyns and lived for eighteen years in Spain (which forms the basis
of her 1960 novel *Out of the Red into the Blue*). Barbara Comyns died in
1992.

Virago published *Our Spoons Came from Woolworths* in 1983.

from

Our Spoons Came from Woolworths

Sophia Fairclough was my new name and quite soon I became used to it and to being called 'Mrs' and wearing a wedding-ring. Already, after a few weeks' married life, my saucepans had burnt marks on them. I had hoped to keep them always shiny, because I had a stupid feeling that as long as I could keep them like new my marriage would stay the same, but in spite of the saucepans we were quite happy. Sometimes I worried about money a little because my weekly two pounds did not go very far, but we had some cheques in one of the dresser drawers, and whenever we ran out of money we asked my sister Ann to cash one. She earned enough to have a banking account and was a real bachelor girl with a flat. She was two years older than I and rather efficient at her job on a woman's weekly. She collected material for a page 'Ways of wasting not more than five shillings' and all the articles on the page had captions underneath like this: 'This dainty little butter-dish made of leather costs but 2/11' or 'Wouldn't the kiddies just love this jolly little squeaking mouse – a bargain at 4/9'. They gave her the things she wrote about quite often, so her flat was full of gadgets, and she had a box under her bed simply stiff with things to give people for Christmas.

Before our marriage Charles used to paint and draw me quite a lot, but now we were living together I had to pose in every imaginable position. In the middle of washing the supper things, Charles would say 'Don't move', and I would have to keep quite still, with my hands in the water, until he finished drawing me, or I might be preparing the supper and everything would get all held up. He painted me in the bath once and I have never been so clean before or since.

Sometimes when I woke in the morning, there would be Charles painting me asleep. That was the most comfortable way to be painted, but it made me late for work. When I was out during the day he liked to paint still lives. He would arrange a group on a cushion – a melon, a banana and some carrots and perhaps a kipper or an egg, but the kitten, Matthew, would eat the fish in the night and play football with the fruit and Charles would be most upset, although he was rather batty about the kitten usually; he was called Matthew after the church we were married in, he was grey and dainty. Most morning Charles would walk with me to Chalk Farm station and Matthew would follow about halfway and wait for Charles until he returned, and they would be company for each other during the day. Charles stayed at home painting most of the day; he did the shopping, too. Sometimes he went to commercial studios in search of work, but nothing ever came of it; not that he really expected anything, this was the time of the Great Depression or Slump, but there were still a few cheques in the drawer.

On Saturday afternoon I had a holiday and we would give the flat a great clean and shop, and on Sunday we went for long walks on the Heath or read and were lazy by the gas fire. In the evening Ann or other friends came to supper.

At first everything I cooked tasted very strongly of soap, I can't think why, but soon I became quite a good cook. During the week I was so hungry when I returned home I couldn't attempt anything that took a long time, but I used to experiment in the weekend. Quite often James came to dinner and we would discuss cooking. He was a very good cook and could even make bread. One evening I returned to find the windows streaming with steam and the most awful smell of burnt frying. Even the cat had run away. I walked through a haze to the kitchen to find Charles trying to curry eggs from Mrs Beeton's cookery book. He had been at it since four o'clock and he was just burning his third lot of eggs, but we ate them.

It was a long time before the smell of burnt curry left the flat.

One Saturday, after we had been married about two months, we thought we would skip the housework, so Charles met me and we had lunch in Charlotte Street and then went to the Tate. We returned home with masses of postcards in time for tea. I glanced through the windows of the flat as we passed on our way to the side door. To my surprise the room was full of people. Charles said, 'It must be Mummy, I can hear her voice.' He was quite right. There was Eva surrounded by the same relations she had brought with her the night before the wedding. My first thought was, 'Well, they can't unmarry us now.' Then I remembered the flat was all dusty and uncleaned. My heart sank right down to my rather holey shoes. If only I had known they were coming and had polished the floor and had everything grand and tidy. I had thought it too good to be true that Eva had ignored us all this time, although I believe she sometimes wrote pained letters to Charles.

Charles went in first and I followed feeling pretty scared. Eva kissed Charles and then me, so I knew it was meant to be a friendly visit. I couldn't help feeling glad I'd smudged her lipstick when she kissed me, I knew she would feel pretty mad when she arrived home, and saw her face. I started muttering about the place being untidy and that I would have made a cake if I'd known they were coming, but she said it did not matter as she had imagined it much worse, but she had had to hunt everywhere for the teaspoons. I could imagine her going through the dresser drawers, looking at all my shabby clothes and holding them up for her relations to see.

She said she admired the flat very much, but thought the hard chairs rather uncomfortable and she couldn't understand how we could sleep on such a small divan and why didn't we have a charwoman. Then Edmund, the husband of Stiff-black-hat, said he was sure Eva would be able to give me some useful hints on economical housekeeping. As Eva was quite famous for her extravagance in dress and home, I was rather interested to hear what she would have to say. She cleared her throat once or twice, and said something about poor people should eat a lot of herrings, as they were most nutritious, also she had heard poor people ate heaps of sheeps' heads and she went on to ask if I ever cooked them. I said I would rather be dead than cook or eat a sheep's head; I'd seen them in butchers' shops with awful eyes and bits of wool sticking to their skulls. After that helpful hints for the poor were forgotten, because Charles told her about our visit to Paul. She was most interested, because she wanted to know how he was situated for money, because she needed her allowance increasing. Charles and I both assured her he was living in the most abject poverty and his house was understaffed and his car just falling to bits, so she began to worry in case her allowance was cut.

Then Edmund started asking Charles about his prospects. Had he a job in view? Had he sold any paintings? Had he any prospects at all? So Charles had to pretend things were much better than they were, and he talked very brightly and rather unconvincingly about his future. As a matter of fact Edmund had business troubles of his own;

I couldn't help wishing Charles would ask him a few questions about his financial position.

At last Stiff-black-hat, who had not spoken all this time, said it was time to go and dress for dinner. Eva was staying with them for the night. All this time she had been sitting on the unpaid-for divan, looking around with cold blue eyes, her thin white lips tightly pressed together. I had no relations with the exception of a sister and brother. They had all died for one reason or another, but I felt Charles had enough for us both.

There was a great searching about the room for Eva's belongings. Then the kitten was found asleep on her coat and there had to be a great brushing to get the hairs off, but at last they left and it felt as if there had been a great wind which had suddenly ceased.

After this first visit Eva and I had a kind of truce; she continued to criticise and talk at me, but as she did the same to everyone she knew, even Charles, I couldn't object too much. Although most of Charles's relations came from Wiltshire they used to come to London very frequently. They all talked and asked questions about our financial position and took the line of 'I hope you are looking after dear Charles properly', or 'What a lucky girl you are to have married into our family.' In those days I was too timid to say much, but I used to resent it all the more and sometimes, after they left, I would be nervy and resentful with Charles. Also they would keep suggesting impractical ways we could earn extra money. They sent cuttings from the *Daily Mail* about how I could make sweets or gloves at home and make a fortune, or complicated rackets for Charles to sell note-cases to our friends on commission. As none of our friends had any notes, he wouldn't have done very well from it.

Except when his relations came fussing around Charles was quite happy just painting away, and as long as I earned two pounds a week and there were a few cheques in the drawer he hadn't a care in the world. He was very loving and gentle with me. One day we went to the sea for the day with James and a huge wave knocked me down when we were bathing. He was dreadfully distressed and kept asking if I was all right. I liked him to be concerned for me, because it was a very long time since anyone had been. I'd been living alone in bed-sitting-rooms since I was seventeen and it had been rather a hard life and lonely sometimes, too.

1951

Carson McCullers

———

Born Lula Carson Smith in Columbus, Georgia, in 1917, McCullers moved to New York in 1934 to study music at Juilliard and creative writing at Columbia University. She published her first story, 'Wunderkind', when she was only nineteen. Her highly acclaimed first novel, *The Heart is a Lonely Hunter*, came out six years later. Several others quickly followed: *Reflections in a Golden Eye* (1941), *The Member of the Wedding* (1946), *The Ballad of the Sad Café* (1951) and *Clock without Hands* (1961).

In 1937 she married Reeves McCullers and the couple had a chaotic, drunken life together, frequently parting and reuniting, partly because McCullers 'demanded, craved, a reciprocal love relationship with a woman'. They divorced in 1941 and remarried in 1945 after he was wounded during the war. During a separation in 1948, she attempted suicide, but she refused to take part in a double suicide he proposed before killing himself in 1953.

McCullers was plagued by poor health all her life. She was fifty when she died. A collection of essays, stories and poems, *The Mortgaged Heart* (1971), was published posthumously.

from

The Ballad of the Sad Café

It must have been arranged in some manner beforehand. For just at the stroke of seven Miss Amelia showed herself at the head of the stairs. At the same instant Marvin Macy appeared in front of the café and the crowd made way for him silently. They walked towards each other with no haste, their fists already gripped, and their eyes like the eyes of dreamers. Miss Amelia had changed her red dress for her old overalls, and they were rolled up to the knees. She was barefooted and she had an iron strengthband around her right wrist. Marvin Macy had also rolled his trouser legs – he was naked to the waist and heavily greased; he wore the heavy shoes that had been issued him when he left the penitentiary. Stumpy MacPhail stepped forward from the crowd and slapped their hip pockets with the palm of his right hand to make sure there would be no sudden knives. Then they were alone in the cleared centre of the bright café.

There was no signal, but they both struck out simultaneously. Both blows landed on the chin, so that the heads of Miss Amelia and Marvin Macy bobbed back and they were left a little groggy. For a few seconds after the first blows they merely shuffled their feet around on the bare floor, experimenting with various positions, and making mock fists. Then, like wildcats, they were suddenly on each other. There was the sound of knocks, panting, and thumpings on the floor. They were so fast that it was hard to take in what was going on – but once Miss Amelia was hurled backward so that she staggered and almost fell, and another time Marvin Macy caught a knock on the shoulder that spun him round like a top. So the fight went on in this wild violent way with no sign of weakening on either side.

During a struggle like this, when the enemies are as quick and strong as these two, it is worth while to turn from the confusion of the fight itself and observe the spectators. The people had flattened back as close as possible against the walls. Stumpy MacPhail was in a corner, crouched over and with his fists tight in sympathy, making strange noises. Poor Merlie Ryan had his mouth so wide open that a fly buzzed into it, and was swallowed before Merlie realised what had happened. And Cousin Lymon – he was worth watching. The hunchback still stood on the counter, so that he was raised up above everyone else in the café. He had his hands on his hips, his big head thrust forward, and his little legs bent so that the knees jutted outwards. The excitement had made him break out in a rash, and his pale mouth shivered.

Perhaps it was half an hour before the course of the fight shifted. Hundreds of blows had been exchanged, and there was still a deadlock. Then suddenly Marvin Macy managed to catch hold of Miss Amelia's left arm and pinion it behind her back. She struggled and got a grasp around his waist; the real fight was now begun. Wrestling is the natural way of fighting in this county – as boxing is too quick and requires much thinking and concentration. And now that Miss Amelia and Marvin were locked in a hold together the crowd came out of its daze and pressed in closer. For a while the fighters grappled muscle to muscle, their hipbones braced against each other. Backward and forward, from side to side, they swayed in this way. Marvin Macy still had not sweated, but Miss Amelia's overalls were drenched and so much sweat had trickled down her legs that she left wet footprints on the floor. Now the test had come, and in these moments of terrible effort, it was Miss Amelia who was the stronger. Marvin Macy was greased and slippery, tricky to grasp, but she was stronger. Gradually she bent him over backward, and inch by inch she forced him to the floor. It was a terrible thing to watch and their deep hoarse breaths were the only sound in the café. At last she had him down, and straddled; her strong big hands were on his throat.

But at that instant, just as the fight was won, a cry sounded in the café that caused a shrill bright shiver to run down the spine. And what took place has been a mystery ever since. The whole town was there to testify what happened, but there were those who doubted their own eyesight. For the counter on which Cousin Lymon stood was at least twelve feet from the fighters in the centre of the café. Yet at the instant Miss Amelia grasped the throat of Marvin Macy the hunchback sprang forward and sailed through the air as though he had grown hawk wings. He landed on the broad back of Miss Amelia and clutched at her neck with his clawed little fingers.

The rest is confusion. Miss Amelia was beaten before the crowd could come to their senses. Because of the hunchback the fight was won by Marvin Macy, and at the end Miss Amelia lay sprawled on the floor, her arms flung outward and motionless. Marvin Macy stood over her, his face somewhat pop-eyed, but smiling his old half-mouthed smile. And the hunchback, he had suddenly disappeared. Perhaps he was frightened about what he had done, or maybe he was so delighted that he wanted to glory with himself alone – at any rate he slipped out of the café and crawled under the back steps. Someone poured water on Miss Amelia, and after a time she got up slowly and dragged herself into her office. Through the open door the crowd could see her sitting at her desk, her head in the crook of her arm, and she was sobbing with the last of her grating, winded breath. Once she gathered her right fist together and knocked it three times on the top of her office desk, then her hand opened feebly and lay palm upward and still. Stumpy MacPhail stepped forward and closed the door.

The crowd was quiet, and one by one the people left the café. Mules were waked up and untied, automobiles cranked, and the three boys from Society City roamed off down the road on foot. This was not a fight to hash over and talk about afterwards; people went home and pulled the covers up over their heads. The town was dark, except for the premises of Miss Amelia, but every room was lighted there the whole night long.

Marvin Macy and the hunchback must have left the town an hour or so before daylight. And before they went away this is what they did:

They unlocked the private cabinet of curios and took everything in it.

They broke the mechanical piano.

They carved terrible words on the café tables.

They found the watch that opened in the back to show a picture of a waterfall and took that also.

They poured a gallon of sorghum syrup all over the kitchen floor and smashed the jars of preserves.

They went out in the swamp and completely wrecked the still, ruining the big new condenser and the cooler, and setting fire to the shack itself.

They fixed a dish of Miss Amelia's favourite food, grits with sausage, seasoned it with enough poison to kill off the county, and placed this dish temptingly on the café counter.

They did everything ruinous they could think of without actually breaking into the office where Miss Amelia stayed the night. Then they went off together, the two of them.

That was how Miss Amelia was left alone in the town.

1952

Isabel Bolton

———

Mary Britton Miller was born in New York in 1883. She published her first novel, *In the Days of Youth* (1943), and several volumes of poetry (for adults and children) under her own name. In her sixties she began writing novels under the pseudonym Isabel Bolton. *Do I Wake or Sleep* appeared in 1946, *The Christmas Tree* in 1949 and *Many Mansions* in 1952. Highly regarded by such critics as Diana Trilling and Edmund White, these novels nevertheless fell out of print until they were published under the title *New York Mosaic* in 1997.

In 1966 Mary Britton Miller published a memoir, *Under Gemini*, about the childhood death by drowning of her identical twin sister, and the following year, at the age of eighty-four, she wrote her final novel, *The Whirligig of Time*. She died in 1979.

Virago published the first British edition of *New York Mosaic* in 1998.

from

Many Mansions

The life of the aged was a constant manoeuvring to appease and assuage the poor decrepit body. Why, most of the time she was nothing more than a nurse attending to its every need. As for the greater part of the nights one's position was positively disreputable – all alone and clothed in ugly withering flesh – fully conscious of the ugliness, the ignominy – having to wait upon oneself with such menial devotion – Here now, if you think you've got to get up mind you don't fall, put on the slippers, don't trip on the rug. There now, apply the lotions carefully, they'll ease the pain; that's it, rub them in thoroughly. Now get back to bed before you're chilled. Here, take the shawl, wrap it round your shoulders. Turn on the electric heater. It won't be long before you're off to sleep. Try not to fret and for heaven's sake don't indulge in self-pity. This is the portion of the old – having to lie here filled with cramps and rheums and agues – so aged and ugly with your teeth in water in the tumbler by your bed and your white hair streaming on the pillow and the old mind filled with scattered thoughts and memories, flying here, flying there, like bats in a cracked old belfry – haunted by fears, visited by macabre dreams.

Dear me, dear me, she thought, looking through the gloom into the lighted offices, if she could meet death upon her own terms how often she would choose to die. How beautiful to have floated away upon that tide of reverence. It was one's ignorance of just how and where death might come to take one off that made it hard to contemplate. There were all the grisly speculations.

Would she have a stroke followed by a helpless dotage? Would she die of some grave heart condition long drawn out? She might be run over any day by a taxi or a truck. She might slip on the sidewalk and break a leg or a femur. She could hear the clanging bells, the siren of the ambulance that gave her right of way, bearing her off amid the city traffic to the nearest hospital. She could see the doctors and the nurses going through their paces – everything efficient, ordered, utterly inhuman – all the nightmare apparatus attendant on keeping the breath of life in her another day – who knew? Maybe another week; maybe a month or two longer – the oxygen tanks and the transfusions, the injections – penicillin and the sulfa drugs – Heaven knew what! And would there be sufficient funds she wondered to pay for all this nonsense – keeping the breath of life in one old woman more than prepared to give up the fight? Expenses mounted to the skies. Nurses were worth their weight in gold. And as for private rooms in hospitals! All these extravagances. Dear me, dear me. Could she imagine herself in an Old Ladies Home – in a hospital ward?

She worried woefully about her finances. Eating into her principal like a rat eating into the cheese, the only capital that remained to her those few government bonds. However, she'd figured it all out very carefully. She could live to be ninety – selling out a bond when necessary and keeping something for emergencies. Was it possible that she'd live to be ninety?

1953

Tillie Olsen

———

Tillie Lerner was born in Nebraska in 1913 of Russian immigrant parents. Politically active from an early age, she joined the Young Communist League and was jailed in 1932 for handing out leaflets to packing-house workers. At nineteen she began her first novel – a chapter of which was published in *Partisan Review* and which was finally published as *Yonnondio: From the Thirties* (the title comes from an Indian word meaning 'lament for the lost') in 1974. 'Public libraries were my college,' she later said.

From 1936 she lived with Jack Olsen, whom she married in 1943. She had four daughters and did not write again until the 1950s, when she published four short stories, 'I Stand Here Ironing', 'Hey Sailor, What Ship?', 'O Yes', and 'Tell Me a Riddle', which won the O. Henry Prize and gave its name to her acclaimed 1961 story collection. In 1965 she published *Silences*, which combines the personal memoir of Olsen's own struggle to write with a historical account of the social pressures which more generally thwart women's and men's writing and publishing. The book provided an important impetus to feminist publishing, and in 1972 Olsen wrote an introduction to the American Feminist Press's first reprint, Rebecca Harding Davis's *Life in the Iron Mills* (1861).

Virago reprinted *Tell Me a Riddle* in 1980.

from

'I Stand Here Ironing'

I stand here ironing, and what you asked me moves tormented back and forth with the iron.

'I wish you would manage the time to come in and talk with me about your daughter. I'm sure you can help me understand her. She's a youngster who needs help and whom I'm deeply interested in helping.'

'Who needs help. . .' Even if I came, what good would it do? You think because I am her mother I have a key, or that in some way you could use me as a key? She has lived for nineteen years. There is all that life that has happened outside of me, beyond me.

And when is there time to remember, to sift, to weigh, to estimate, to total? I will start and there will be an interruption and I will have to gather it all together again. Or I will become engulfed with all I did or did not do, with what should have been and what cannot be helped.

She was a beautiful baby. The first and only one of our five that was beautiful at birth. You do not guess how new and uneasy her tenancy in her now-loveliness. You did not know her all those years she was thought homely, or see her poring over her baby pictures, making me tell her over and over how beautiful she had been – and would be, I would tell her – and was now, to the seeing eye. But the seeing eyes were few or non-existent. Including mine.

I nursed her. They feel that's important nowadays. I nursed all the children, but with her, with all the fierce rigidity of first motherhood, I did like the books then said. Though her cries battered me to trembling and my breasts ached with swollenness, I waited till the clock decreed.

Why do I put that first? I do not even know if it matters, or if it explains anything.

She was a beautiful baby. She blew shining bubbles of sound. She loved motion, loved light, loved colour and music and textures. She would lie on the floor in her blue overalls patting the surface so hard in ecstasy her hands and feet would blur. She was a miracle to me, but when she was eight months old I had to leave her daytimes with the woman downstairs to whom she was no miracle at all, for I worked or looked for work and for Emily's father, who 'could no longer endure' (he wrote in his good-bye note) 'sharing want with us'.

I was nineteen. It was the pre-relief, pre-WPA world of the depression. I would start running as soon as I got off the streetcar, running up the stairs, the place smelling sour, and awake or asleep to startle awake, when she saw me she would break into a clogged weeping that could not be comforted, a weeping I can yet hear.

After a while I found a job hashing at night so I could be with her days, and it was better. But it came to where I had to bring her to his family and leave her.

It took a long time to raise the money for her fare back. Then she got chicken pox and I had to wait longer. When she finally came, I hardly knew her, walking quick and nervous like her father, looking like her father, thin, and dressed in a shoddy red that yellowed her skin and glared at the pock marks. All the baby loveliness gone.

She was two. Old enough for nursery school they said, and I did not know then what I know now – the fatigue of the long day, and the lacerations of group life in the kinds of nurseries that are only parking places for children.

Except that it would have made no difference if I had known. It was the only place there was. It was the only way we could be together, the only way I could hold a job.

And even without knowing, I knew. I knew the teacher that was evil because all these years it has curdled into my memory, the little boy hunched in the corner, her rasp, 'why aren't you outside, because Alvin hits you? that's no reason, go out, scaredy.' I knew Emily hated it even if she did not clutch and implore 'don't go Mommy' like the other children, mornings.

She always had a reason why we should stay home. Momma, you look sick. Momma, I feel sick. Momma, the teachers aren't there today, they're sick. Momma, we can't go, there was a fire there last night. Momma, it's a holiday today, no school, they told me.

But never a direct protest, never rebellion. I think of our others in their three-, four-year-oldness – the explosions, the tempers, the denunciations, the demands – and I feel suddenly ill. I put the iron down. What in me demanded that goodness in her? And what was the cost, the cost to her of such goodness?

The old man living in the back once said in his gentle way: 'You should smile at Emily more when you look at her.' What *was* in my face when I looked at her? I loved her. There were all the acts of love.

1954

Elizabeth Jenkins

Elizabeth Jenkins was born in 1905 and grew up in Herefordshire. Educated at Newnham College, Cambridge, where she studied English and history, she later described herself as 'gauche, prim, covered with ink, and wrapped up in work'. She became a teacher and was senior English mistress at King Alfred's School, Hampstead from 1924 to 1939, writing in her spare time. During the war she worked for the civil service; afterwards, she returned to writing full-time.

Jenkins's first novel, *Virginia Water*, was published in 1930; twelve more followed, including *Harriet* (1934), an engrossing account of a Victorian murder case which won the Femina Vie Heureuse Prize, and in 1992, after a twenty-year gap, *A Silent Joy*. She is also well known as a biographer, having published lives of, among others, Jane Austen, Henry Fielding and Lady Caroline Lamb. Jenkins was awarded an OBE in 1981.

The Tortoise and the Hare was reissued by Virago in 1983.

from

The Tortoise and the Hare

That summer of two years before was the beginning of the new era in their lives that succeeded the war. Evelyn had been on war service till 1945; the years immediately following his release, in which he had no sooner picked up his practice than he found it develop with great rapidity, opened the most hard-driven period of his career. At the same time, life became progressively easier for Imogen. The return of Miss Malpas to their household after absence on war work, being able to employ a gardener once again, and to have groceries sent home by the shops instead of lugging them back in a heavy basket that had to be set down many times on the way, and above all the mere fact of Evelyn's being at home again, though in London for the middle of the week and irritable and preoccupied when in the house, all this brought back an almost forgotten ease and calmness. It seemed an irony of Fate that her own existence should afford leisure and self-possession once again just as the pace and strain of Evelyn's was increasing to an extent that was alarming, and causing him to settle down to domestic life on an iron ration of patience and self-control. The sense that something she had been longing and waiting for had slipped her grasp just as it had come within her reach, haunted her sometimes with an unnameable premonition of dread. No longer an idol, no longer young enough to have allowances made for her, she now had to devote herself to the task of making Evelyn's domestic background so smooth that it never aroused his unfavourable attention. This required just that efficient management of detail which she found difficult. Her anxiety was acute but only a small part of it was caused by a fear of his displeasure. She had an ardent sympathy for him over the hardness of his professional life. She had only once seen him come out of court after an important case. He had come down the steps of the Central Criminal Court, looking as she had never seen or imagined him to look, pale and sweating with exhaustion. Though she was to meet him there by his arrangement, though he had gained a verdict for his client, she could not go forward to speak to him. She stood at the side of the flight of steps, watching him walk down them and get into a taxi, oblivious of her absence. Everything about him looked unfamiliar. It was dreadful to her to understand as she afterwards did, that the condition in which her husband then was, at half-past four, did not mean that he stopped work. It meant only that when he got back to his chambers his clerk gave him half a pint of milk with a tablespoonful of brandy in it. When he had drunk this slowly and come to himself, he began to work on the case in which he would appear next morning. Some men carried on this existence with a carelessness and imperturbability which meant that nothing used up their nervous energy except the work itself. These were not men of magnetism, of histrionic ability and commanding physique. They were rather small men, spare and dry, witty and immune. Evelyn Gresham was of the opposite type, of formidable presence, severe but vulnerable.

Imogen felt that to love him now was the natural consequence of having loved him before, for now all the qualities were developed in him which had been foreshadowed then. His face now showed in the most distinct form characteristics of which it had once borne hints, then made unnoticeable by the handsomeness of youth. Now his face was plain to read, like a bold landscape revealed in the strong light of day. There was in it a strange contradiction between the regular mould of the features and something turbulent suggested by the jutting brows and a gleam, fugitive but startling in the clear, piercing eyes. Imogen thought that Wordsworth's sonnet about the boy whose character was influenced by the sight and sound of streams might have been written about Evelyn, who had, in fact, spent many holidays in the northern dales and loved to watch:

> *The sullen reservoirs whence their bold brood*
> *Pure as the morning, fretful, boisterous, keen,*
> *Poured down the hills, a choral multitude.*

The cast of his mind suggested that it had been influenced by some clear, forceful, passionate element. He, too, might have said:

Maturer fancy owes to their rough noise
Impetuous thoughts that brook not servile chains.

There was never a doubt in her mind that to meet his demands was the most absorbing and the most valuable end to which her energies could be used. She tried hard to foresee what should be done and to carry out his requests; but she never acquired that unthinking grasp of practical matters that creates confidence. Evelyn never felt able to omit the precaution of saying: 'Did you telephone to the garage? I suppose you did post those letters? Has that coat gone to the cleaners?' And though more often than not she could say 'Yes,' it was never without an inward shudder and the thought, suppose I had forgotten! which made the occasion almost as painful as those on which she had. She could not remember any such strain of mind before the war; perhaps in those days Evelyn still had leisure to do for himself the things that now fell to her; perhaps her shortcomings then had been merely smiled at. Certainly his rare fallings out with her in those days had been lovers' quarrels between two people on equal terms, not the irritation of a master of the house whose requirements have not been met.

Another defect in her relationship with him had never weighed on her in the early years of their marriage. Her capacity for romantic affection was so great, the happiness of being the object of his passionate love was so enchanting, that for a long time she scarcely recognised her own deficiency in the sphere of physical passion. When she did realise it she hoped always that her capacity would improve, that what was bright already would become brighter, and what was sweet, wildly and unimaginably so. She had now to face the truth that the happiness of this relationship would never improve and could from now onwards only decay. Her own content would have been complete had she not known that he wished her to feel something more. Now that their relationship was no longer romantic, this knowledge, the sense of missing something herself and being subtly belittled and condemned because she did so, began to have a slow but fatal effect upon her happiness.

'It's an art, I suppose,' he had said carelessly. 'Some people have it.' The faint, unconscious note of contempt she thought she detected made her long wildly not only to be dead, but never to have been born. The tears flooded her eyes and welled down over her cheeks. Evelyn sighed, and caressed her kindly, absently.

1955

Ivy Compton-Burnett

Ivy Compton-Burnett was born in Pinner, Middlesex, in 1884 and educated at home and at Royal Holloway Women's College,London. She
acted as governess to her younger siblings and after the death of her
mother, in 1911, took over the running of the family household. Her
closest brother died while she was a student, another died in the First
World War, and in 1918 her two youngest sisters inexplicably committed suicide together. Compton-Burnett suffered a long mental
breakdown in the early twenties.

In 1911 Compton-Burnett published her first novel, *Dolores*, but it
has little in common with the novels she began to write after her illness. (Indeed she later forcefully rejected it as mere juvenilia.)
Including *Pastors and Masters* (1925) and the posthumously published
The Last and the First (1969), she published twenty-five further novels.
Most of them explore the tyrannies of Edwardian family life and concentrate on dialogue; she described her work as constituting
'something between a novel and a play'.

From 1919 Compton-Burnett lived with the historian Margaret
Jourdain, who died in 1951. Compton-Burnett, who was made a CBE
in 1951, a Dame in 1967 and a Companion of Honour in 1968, died in
1969.

Virago reprinted *The Mighty and Their Fall* in 1994.

from

The Mighty and Their Fall

'Can you hear me, Mother?' said Ninian.

'Yes, of course. I am not dead.'

'We hope you are not going to die.'

'That might go without saying.'

'You know it does,' said Hugo.

'It did not,' said Selina, wearily.

'Do you want to say anything, Mother?'

'No, I don't want a deathbed scene. When it is acted, it means nothing. And why should I consider my last moments? The others have done more for me.'

'And it is so terrible of them to be the last,' murmured Hugo.

'All of them count to us,' said Ninian. 'We need not tell you how much.'

'We need not call up memories. I cannot carry them with me.'

'You will leave them with us,' said Hugo.

'Well, I have been as good to you as you have to me. And better to the son who has left me.'

'We have nothing to regret,' said Ninian.

'He will find enough when I cannot know about it. And it will do nothing for either of us.'

'The word need not exist between you and me.'

'If I die, you will find some reason for it. But it will pass.'

'You don't sound as if you are going to die,' said Hugo.

'No,' said Selina, almost smiling. 'And I can see the nurse agrees. She feels I am not fit for a higher life; and I would choose the lower one. And she thinks I should be afraid to die.'

'And you are afraid of nothing,' said her son.

'I don't feel I am going to meet my Maker. And if I were, I should not fear him. He has not earned the feeling. I almost think he ought to fear me.'

'I think he must,' murmured Hugo. 'She seems so much her usual self.'

'It may be coming back,' said Selina. 'The doctor is not sure.'

'He has not said anything to you?'

'How can he, when there is nothing to say? And when he sees I know it.'

'Would you like to see the children?' said Ninian. 'I mean it might make a change for you.'

'I know what you might have meant. You should take more care. I know all I want to about them. It might hardly be a suitable moment to know the whole.'

'They need not know – we need not tell them you are ill.'

'They would not mind. It could only mean I might die.'

'You know how they would feel about that.'

'I believe I do. And I can't explain it,' said Selina, almost petulantly.

'They feel your bark is worse than your bite.'

'That is an empty saying. Only bark has a place in life. There is no opportunity to bite. I have wished there was.'

'They know you would not have used it.'

'I am going to sleep,' said Selina, and closed her eyes.

1956

Brigid Brophy

Brigid Brophy was born in London in 1929. She studied classics at
Oxford University but was expelled for unspecified reasons. (Later she
spoke frankly of her bisexuality.) In 1954 she married the art historian
Michael Levey, director of the National Gallery, with whom she had a
daughter.

In 1953 she published a collection of short stories, *The Crown
Princess*, and a novel, *Hackenfeller's Ape*, which considers *Homo sapiens* as a
species like any other and argues strongly against vivisection. (She
later became vice-president of the Anti-Vivisection Society). In the
novels that followed she explored sexuality in all its forms, a theme
which also informs her numerous critical works – notably studies of
Aubrey Beardsley and Ronald Firbank.

With Maureen Duffy she organised a pop-art exhibition in 1969
and the Writers' Action Group, which worked to produce the Public
Lending Act in 1979. Brophy was diagnosed with multiple sclerosis in
1984 and died in 1995.

Virago published *The King of a Rainy Country*, with a new Afterword
by Brophy, in 1990.

from

The King of a Rainy Country

The memory was quite sharp, but distant. It was like a small photograph in which, if I tried to enlarge it, the detail blurred outwards into nothing. The four of us were there in the sunlight, miniature figures in school blazers: myself a short, compact child, with a fringe of dark hair across my forehead, large eyes and a tiny, very white-skinned nose; my satellite, Gill, a still smaller girl, monkey-like in her way of moving and her sense of humour; Annette, tall, thin, unsuitably named, colourless in hair, face and personality, who accompanied Cynthia everywhere; and Cynthia herself.

I had a special place on the bank above the tennis courts, which ran along the sun-struck wall of the main building. As I lay there in the grass, my gaze would descend the wall, slip round the gothic windows, slide down the paint-thick drainpipe; it would outline the statelier lower windows, peering for a moment into the hall inside; then down, over the last few feet of grainy brick; across the path, which was bumpy with flints; up, like a sparrow's hop, on to the grass verge; proceed for a foot or two level, until the lawn took its sudden roll down the bank – then my gaze would plunge too, would roll too, until it fetched up short and expanded away without interest over the kempt, flat tennis courts.

This process I could not communicate to anyone, not even to Gill who lay comically, tossing her head, by my side. It was my method of apprehending everything. Relationships, the fact of Latin words, my appreciation of the warm early afternoon – I took them all in as if they had been shapes. I did not think or feel my thoughts: I travelled them. Without a defending layer of words, I was at the mercy of every fact. Facts and events, the warmth itself, lapped me like waves lapping a helpless body on the shore; and the feelings which from time to time plunged up about me were quite involuntary.

The afternoon stirred, split and became brilliant. The mist was shattered from the tennis courts: only a few strands lay low, like superstition, about the bushes at the edge. Like strips of tinsel, the mist ornamented the day, reminding me, in its prettiness, of the idea of fairies; it seemed to have degenerated from something once powerful and still malevolent, its danger pagan, disquieting but alluring.

A few strangers arrived. A girl panicked and ran, calling, across the lawns.

For an interval nothing had begun. I knew this was the last day of term, but it meant nothing to me. I could not remember the beginning of summer, nor of the summer term, and could not imagine their end: July lapped me immortally on either side. The approach of the school fête, which had taken up so much of Cynthia's and Annette's time, had not troubled me. The fête was organised by their form, the form above ours. Gill and I had been told we should have to play some part in it next year, but we had taken no notice.

Presently the grounds were full. Strange voices shouted; familiar ones were raised to solicit custom. A crowd moved to the swimming bath where there was a display: splashes and inarticulate names lay on the air above the bath, half trapped by the surrounding walls. The dismantled courts were trodden from stall to stall; and at one stall, in front of a screen labelled Garden Produce, stood Annette, with another girl I paid no attention to, and Cynthia.

My gaze crossed Cynthia's forehead; it descended her nose; then, moving methodically outwards in each direction in turn, it traced her thin mouth. It was a face where the flesh seemed pared away. Planes, spines and the declivities my gaze lingered in almost with agony, were all as bare as an archaic statue or the blanched breast-bone of a bird.

Her gestures were leanly angular. Talking to Annette, her hands inside her blazer pockets flat against her hips, drawing the clothes taut across her back, she would slightly and not unintentionally overbalance; and the angles made by her elbows would sharpen suddenly. As she served a customer, her head would plunge, sideways and down, while she searched the stall: or she would disappear behind it, leaving her hand stretched fine against the wooden screen. Each gesture created, for me, a shape of poignancy; I would move in the grass, drawing breath, as if a glance had been deflected or a subject impetuously changed.

The grounds were warm, now, with people as well as sun; and the air, vibrating in the July afternoon, was alive with opportunity. Gill urged me to go and explore. She was excited by the mystery of the occasion: the possibility of meeting somebody's parents; perhaps of being rude to them, or even, in this atmosphere of licence and no time for revenge, to one of the staff. However, I lay still, pinned where I was by the sight of Cynthia. Out of temper, Gill stayed with me.

Then Cynthia moved. Leaving their stall to the third girl, she and Annette wandered away over the lawn into the people. I followed them. Gill followed me; but she made a show of independence by stopping on her own at various stalls.

Cynthia stopped at the lemonade booth. I waited, separated from her by only one or two people, knowing she was aware of my presence.

A raucous noise sounded behind me. I turned. Gill was holding up a klaxon horn.

'Where did you get that?'

'White elephant stall.'

'Give it me.' I took it and approached Cynthia. She asked:

'What's that?'

Instead of saying a klaxon horn, I sounded the answer on it: short-long, short-long.

Cynthia giggled.

I made the horn imitate her, in a phrase of squeaks.

Over the rim of her lemonade Cynthia giggled again, even as she said: 'It's a revolting noise. How can you be so *young*?'

I made the horn grunt.

She handed her lemonade to Annette and began to droop with laughter. I had not myself thought the horn so funny as that. I began to dread a punishment that might follow my receiving kudos undeserved: either there was some vacuity in Cynthia or I did not understand quite what she was laughing at. I found myself precipitated, out of my uneasiness, into daring. 'Cynthia, will you walk round the grounds with me?'

'Silly, I've got my stall to look after.'

'O, of course. I didn't mean now,' I said disingenuously.

'When did you mean?'

'At break. Or in the dinner hour.'

'You *are* funny,' Cynthia said, turning away. 'I suppose you mean next term.'

I caught at her. 'All right then. Next term. Every day of next term.'

'I couldn't possibly say now.' She put her arm through Annette's. 'We must get back to our stall.'

As they went, Gill touched my shoulder. 'Can I have my klaxon back?'

I gave it her.

'Come and look around the fête,' she said. I followed, unwilling and half embarrassed, as she ran from stall to stall sounding her horn in each stallholder's face. 'Shall I honk one of the staff?' 'If you like.' She waylaid the English mistress, who smiled and brushed her aside. The whole enterprise, indeed everything connected with Gill, had for me a curious prosaicness. As soon as I could I led her back to my place on the bank. Cynthia and Annette had disappeared.

I stood in disorientated misery, like a child missing its mother in a public place. Although I knew what was going on, I failed to recognise it: I wondered what all these strange people were doing. The blue, the green, the bright summer frocks, were all violent enough in colour but not vivid, like a painting that had not succeeded in representing light.

Annette came along the path. I ran to her and asked where Cynthia was.

'Gone.'

'Where?'

'To catch her train. She has special permission to go early, you know.'

'I didn't know.'

'I've been helping her get her things in the cloakroom. She left you a message. She says we will walk around the grounds with you next term.'

'O.'

Annette began to walk towards the Vegetable Produce stall. 'Tell me something about Cynthia,' I said.

'What do you want to know?'

I could think of nothing to ask. 'She has special permission?'

'Yes. A lot of girls have in our form. Haven't they in yours?'

'O yes. Several.'

I no longer watched the stall; I did not even follow my course down the side of the building. Stretched out on the grass bank I laid my head on the ground between my arms, letting the diminishing sun beat the back of my neck while I cherished the afterglow. I rehearsed my conversation with Cynthia, and even my conversation with

Annette, which I could remember more coherently. I blushed for the errors I had made. I tried to summon Cynthia's face and found that Annette's, much clearer, obtruded. From time to time Gill poked her hand, her smiling face or her klaxon horn over the wall of my arms, and I drew closer into myself to preserve my happiness from her.

The warmth dropped out of the day. I sat up; Gill was glad, but I paid no attention to her. Up against the rhododendrons a little mist was collecting like re-formed battalions. The sunlight was still at its splendour, but there were hints of cold, of dark, like a crack developing on the surface of the afternoon.

I realised the sentence of next year, which I had precipitately agreed to; I recognised it meant an interval of eight weeks before my excitement would be taken up. I was being kept waiting by another person's deliberate wish. The autumn must advance, fighting its way up the hill; slowly the summer must yield ground, slipping down the damp slope, sliding anyhow, turning back the blades of the grass in its reluctance to descend into the dangers, the dark, the swirling ground-level winds, the dry, smothering drifts of leaves. I knew I could keep my excitement waiting. With an adult patience I contemplated the dangers not only of this particular descent but of the descent of a whole lifetime. Now I had realised time, I surrendered totally to Cynthia; in her conviction that I would wait she had shown me the immensity of her confidence. Yet for the same reason I had less to surrender; my plunge down any slope would be, from now on, less involuntary.

1957

Elizabeth Taylor

———

Elizabeth Coles was born in Reading in 1912 and in 1924 married John Taylor. The couple settled in a small village in Buckinghamshire, and had two children. Elizabeth Taylor died in 1975.

Her first novel, *At Mrs Lippincote's*, was published in 1945, and her last, posthumously, in 1976. She is also the author of four volumes of short stories and a children's book as well as ten further novels, including the best-selling *A Game of Hide and Seek* (1951). Ostensibly a novelist of village manners, Taylor subtly examines the issues of morality and mortality that lie beneath the most idyllic surfaces.

Angel, perhaps her most widely acclaimed work, tells the story of the rise and fall of Angelica Deverell, a poor Edwardian girl who becomes a best-selling romantic novelist only to find that fashions change.

Virago reprinted *Angel* in 1984.

from

Angel

To the older people in Norley, Alderhurst had once been a remote upland village where the children went in wagonettes on Sunday School treats. Its water-tower was a landmark for miles and its bluebell woods and silver birches were famous. As time went on, industry made Norley an impossible place for industrialists to live in; the Georgian residential streets were too involved in areas of working-class houses and had fallen into desuetude. By the end of the century the houses being built all over old estates, old farmlands, had reached Alderhurst. Laburnums and other suburban trees mingled with the silver birches, and hedges of spotted laurel and golden privet hid the lawns and the gravelled sweeps in front of the new houses where it was now fashionable to live.

By the time Angel and her mother went there to live, the roads had been made smooth and pavements laid. The water-tower rose above the thinned-out woods. Very few of the inhabitants felt the sadness of the place; but Mrs Deverell was one of them. In the days of the Sunday School treats she had thought it an enchanted country; she had plundered sheaves of bluebells from its woods and had loved to run shouting between the trees, with snapping twigs underfoot and brambles catching at her skirt. Her memories were all of happiness; even of the year when it had rained. She had sheltered with her coat over her head, and listened to the drops beating down from leaf to leaf. When it had stopped, a rainbow had come out behind the water-tower and the earth and air had smelled poignantly sweet.

'I never thought I would live here,' she had told Angel. But nowadays she often suffered from the lowering pain of believing herself happy when she was not. 'Who *could* be miserable in such a place?' she asked; yet, on misty October evenings or on Sundays, when the church bells began, sensations she had never known before came over her.

'It's your age,' Lottie told her. 'Madam's been the same. Pecks at her food, they say, and keeps sighing, and the tears always ready for the turning on.'

'Yes, that's how it is,' she agreed.

She sometimes felt better when she went back to see her friends in Volunteer Street; but it was a long way to go, Angel discouraged the visits, and her friends seemed to have changed. Either they put out their best china and thought twice before they said anything, or they were defiantly informal – 'You'll have to take us as you find us' – and would persist in making remarks like 'I don't suppose you ever have bloaters up at Alderhurst' or 'Pardon the apron, but there's no ser- vants here to polish the grate.' In each case, they were watching her for signs of grandeur or condescension. She fell into little traps they laid and then they were able to report to the neighbours. 'It hasn't taken *her* long to start putting on side.' She had to be especially care- ful to recognise everyone she met, and walked up the street with an expression of anxiety which was misinterpreted as disdain.

The name 'Deverell Family Grocer' stayed for a long time over the shop, and she was pleased that it should, although Angel frowned with annoyance when she heard of it. Then one day the faded name was scraped and burnt away, and on her next visit to Volunteer Street, she saw that 'Cubbage's Stores' was painted there instead. She felt an unaccountable panic and dismay at the sight of this and at the strange idea of other people and furniture in those familiar rooms. 'Very nice folk,' she was told. '*She's* so friendly. Always the same. And such lovely kiddies.' Mrs Deverell felt slighted and wounded; going home she was so preoccupied that she passed the wife of the landlord of The Volunteer without seeing her. 'I wouldn't expect Alderhurst people to speak to a publican's wife,' the woman told everyone in the saloon bar. 'Even though it was our Gran who laid her husband out when he died.' All of their kindnesses were remembered and brooded over; any past kindness Mrs Deverell had done – and they were many – only served to underline the change which had come over her.

At a time of her life when she needed the security of familiar things, these were put beyond her reach. It seemed to her that she had wasted her years acquiring a skill which in the end was to be of no use to her; her weather-eye for a good drying day; her careful ear for judging the gentle singing sound of meat roasting in the oven; her touch for the freshness of bacon; and how, by smelling a cake, she could tell if it were baked: arts, which had taken so long to perfect, fell now into disuse. She would never again, she grieved, gather up a great fragrant line of washing in her arms to carry indoors. One day when they had first come to Alderhurst, she had passed through the courtyard where sheets were hanging out: she had taken them in her hands and, finding them just at the right stage of drying, had begun to unpeg them. They were looped all about her shoulders when Angel caught her. 'Please leave work to the people who should do it,' she had said. 'You will only give offence.' She tried hard not to give offence; but it was difficult. The smell of ironing being done or the sound of eggs being whisked set up a restlessness which she could scarcely control.

The relationship of mother and daughter seemed to have been reversed, and Angel, now in her early twenties, was the authoritative one; since girlhood she had been taking on one responsibility after another, until she had left her mother with nothing to perplex her but how to while away the hours when the servants were busy and her daughter was at work. Fretfully, she would wander about the house, bored, but afraid to interrupt; she was like an intimidated child.

Angel worked incessantly, locked in the room she had chosen for a study. When she had finished a book, she would pause with exhaustion and wonder if she could not rest for a while, travel, spend some of the vast amount of money she had earned. For a day or two, she would relapse into the indolence of her childhood and sit inert in her chair with the cat on her lap, for hour after hour. The idea of the holiday faded: there was no one to go with her, except her mother whose chatter vexed her; and she was afraid that while she rested she might be forgotten. The publication of some other woman's novel would send her scurrying back to her study: men writers did not affect her so strongly.

1958

Elaine Dundy

Elaine Dundy was born on Long Island and educated in various schools and colleges in New York, California and Virginia. She then studied acting at the Dramatic Workshop, and spent a year acting in Paris. In 1951 she went to London, where she met and married the critic Kenneth Tynan. She wrote two further novels and two plays before returning to America in 1964, after her divorce. There she continued to write plays, which she also produced, as well as, increasingly, non-fiction. She has written numerous biographies, including *Elvis and Gladys* (1985). Elaine Dundy now lives in Los Angeles. Virago will shortly publish her autobiography, *Life Itself*.

The Dud Avocado was reissued by Virago in 1993.

from

The Dud Avocado

It was a hot, peaceful, optimistic sort of day in September. It was around eleven in the morning, I remember, and I was drifting down the Boulevard Saint Michel, thoughts rising in my head like little puffs of smoke, when suddenly a voice bellowed into my ear: 'Sally Jay Gorce! What the hell? Well, for Christ's sake, can this really be our own little Sally Jay Gorce?' I felt a hand ruffling my hair and I swung around, furious at being so rudely awakened.

Who should be standing there in front of me, in what I immediately spotted as the Left Bank uniform of the day, dark wool shirt and a pair of old Army suntans, but my old friend Larry Keevil. He was staring down at me with some alarm.

I said hello to him and added that he had frightened me, to cover any bad-tempered expression that might have been lingering on my face, but he just kept on staring dumbly at me.

'What *have* you been up to since . . . since . . . when the hell *was* it that I last saw you?' he asked finally.

Curiously enough I remembered exactly.

'It was just a week after I got here. The middle of June.'

He kept on looking at me, or rather he kept on looking over me in that surprised way, and then he shook his head and said, 'Christ, Gorce, can it only be three short months?' Then he grinned. 'You've really flung yourself into this, haven't you?'

In a way it was exactly what I had been thinking, too, and I was on the point of saying, 'Into what?', very innocently, you know, so that he could tell me how different I was, how much I'd changed and so forth, but all at once something stopped me. I knew I would have died rather than hear his reply.

So instead I said, 'Ah well, don't we all?' which was my stock phrase when I couldn't think of anything else to say. There was a pause and then he asked me how I was and I said fine how was *he*, and he said fine, and I asked him what he was doing, and he said it would take too long to tell.

It was then we both noticed we were standing right across the street from the Café Dupont, the one near the Sorbonne.

'Shall we have a quick drink?' I heard him ask, needlessly, for I was already halfway across the street in that direction.

The café was very crowded and the only place we could find was on the very edge of the pavement. We just managed to squeeze under the shade of the shade of the awning. A waiter came and took our order. Larry leant back into the hum and buzz and brouhaha and smiled lazily. Suddenly, without quite knowing why, I found I was very glad to have run into him. And this was odd, because two Americans re-encountering each other after a certain time in a foreign land are supposed to clamber up their nearest lamp-posts and wait tremblingly for it all to blow over. Especially me. I'd made a vow when I got over here never to *speak* to anyone I'd ever known before. Yet here we were, two Americans who hadn't really seen each other for years: here was someone from 'home' who knew me *when*, if you like, and, instead of shambling back into the bushes like a startled rhino, I was absolutely thrilled at the whole idea.

'I like it here, don't you?' said Larry, indicating the café with a turn of his head.

I had to admit I'd never been there before.

He smiled quizzically. 'You should come more often,' he said. 'It's practically the only non-tourist trap to survive on the Left Bank. It's *real*,' he added.

Real, I thought . . . whatever that meant. I looked at the Sorbonne students surging around us, the tables fairly rocking under their pounding fists and thumping elbows. The whole vast panoramic carpet seemed to be woven out of old boots, checkered wool and wild, fuzzy hair. I don't suppose there is anything on earth to compare with a French student café in the late morning. You couldn't possibly reproduce the same numbers, noise, and intensity anywhere else without producing a riot as well. It really was the most colourful café I'd ever been in. As a matter of fact, the most *coloured* too; there was an especially large number of Sinhalese, Arab, and African students, along with those from every other country.

I suppose Larry's 'reality' in this case was based on the café's internationality. But perhaps all cafés near a leading university have that authentic international atmosphere. At the table closest to us sat an ordinary-looking young girl with lank yellow hair and a grey-haired bespectacled middle-aged man. They had been conversing fiercely but quietly for some time now in a language I was not even able to *identify*.

All at once I knew that I liked this place, too.

Jammed in on all sides, with the goodish Tower of Babel working itself up to a frenzy around me, I felt safe and anonymous and, most of all, thankful we were going to be spared those devastating and shattering revelations one was always being treated to at the more English-speaking cafés like the Flore.

And, as I said, I was very glad to have run into Larry.

We talked a little about the various cafés and he explained carefully to me which were the tourist traps and which weren't. Glancing down at my Pernod, I discovered to my astonishment that I'd already finished it. Time was whizzing past.

I felt terribly excited.

'White smoke,' said Larry clicking his tongue disapprovingly at my second Pernod. His hand twirled around the stem of his own virtuous glass of St Raphael. 'You keep that up,' he said, tapping my glass, 'and it'll blow your head off – which may be a good thing at that. Why pink?' he asked, studying my new coiffure carefully. 'Why not green?'

As a matter of fact I'd had my hair dyed a marvellous shade of pale red so popular with Parisian tarts that season. It was the first direct remark he made about the New Me and it was hardly encouraging.

Slowly his eyes left my hair and travelled downwards. This time he really took in my outfit and then that Look that I'm always encountering; that special one composed in equal parts of amusement, astonishment, and horror came over his face.

I am not a moron and I can generally guess what causes this look. The trouble is, it's always something different.

I squirmed uncomfortably, feeling his eyes bearing down on my bare shoulders and breasts.

'What the hell are you doing in the middle of the morning with an *evening* dress on?' he asked me finally.

'Sorry about that,' I said quickly, 'but it's all I've got to wear. My laundry hasn't come back yet.'

He nodded, fascinated.

'I thought if I wore this red leather belt with it people wouldn't actually notice. Especially since it's such a warm day. I mean these teintureries make it so difficult for you to get your laundry to them in the first place, don't they, closing up like that from noon till three? I mean, my gosh, it's the only time I'm up and around over here – don't you think?'

'Oh sure, *sure*,' said Larry, and murmured 'Jesus' under his breath. Then he smiled forgivingly. 'Ah well, you're young, you're new, you'll learn, Gorce.' A wise nod of the head. 'I know your type all right.'

'My type?' I wondered. 'My type of what?'

'Of tourist, of course.'

I gasped and then smiled cunningly to myself. Tourist indeed! Ho-ho! That was the last thing I could be called – did he but know.

'Tell me about this,' I said. 'You seem to have tourists on the brain.'

He crossed his legs and pulled out of his shirt-pocket a crumbled pack of cigarettes as du pays as possible – sort of Gauloises Nothings – offered one to me, took one himself, lit them both, and then settled back with pleasure. This was obviously one of his favourite subjects.

'Basically,' he began, 'the tourist can be divided into two categories. The Organised – the Disorganised. Under the Organised you find two distinct types: first, the Eager-Beaver-Culture-Vulture with the list ten yards long, who *just* manages to get it all crossed off before she collapses of aesthetic indigestion each night and has to be carried back to her hotel; and second, the cool suave Sophisticate who comes gliding over gracefully, calmly, and indifferently. But don't be fooled by the indifference. This babe is determined to maintain her incorruptible standards of cleanliness and efficiency if the entire staff of her hotel dies trying. She belongs to the take-your-own-toilet-paper set. Stuffs her suitcases full of nylon, Kleenex, soapflakes, and DDT bombs. Immediately learns the rules of the country. (I mean what time the shops open and close, and how much to tip the waiter.) Can pack for a week-end in a small jewel-case and a large handbag and still have enough room for her own soap and washrag. Finds the hairdresser who speaks English, the restaurant who knows how she likes her steak, and the first foreign word she makes absolutely sure of pronouncing correctly is the one for drugstore. After that she's all set and the world is her ash-tray. If she's got enough money she's got no trouble at all. On the whole, I rather like her.'

So far so good, I told myself. They neither one had the slightest, smallest, remotest connexion with me. Then a thought caught me sharply.

'And the Disorganised?' I asked rather nervously.

'The Disorganised?' He considered me carefully for a moment, narrowing his eyes.

'Your cigarette's gone out,' he said finally. 'You have to *smoke* this kind, you know, they won't smoke themselves.' He lit it for me again and blew out the match without once taking his eyes off my décolletage, which was slipping quite badly. I gave it a tug and he resumed the discourse.

'Yes. The Disorganised. They get split into two groups as well. First of all the Sly One. The idea is to see Europe casually, you know, sort of vaguely, out of the corner of the eye. All Baedekers and Michelins and museum catalogues immediately discarded as too boring and too corny. Who wants to see a pile of old stones anyway? The general "feel" of the country is what she's after. It's even a struggle to get her to look at a map of the city she's in so she'll know where the hell she is, and actually it's a useless one since this type is constitutionally incapable of reading a map and has no sense of direction to begin with. But, as I say, she's the sly one – the 'Oh, look, that's the Louvre over there, isn't it? I think I'll drop in for a second. I'm rather hot. We'd better get out of the sun anyway . . .' or 'Tuileries did you say? That sure strikes a bell. Aren't those flowers pretty over there? Now haven't I heard something about it in connexion with the – what was it – French Revolution? Oh, yes, *of course* that's it. Thank you, hon.'"

I laughed – a jolly laugh – to show I was with him.

'The funny thing,' he continued, 'is, scratch the sly one and out comes the *real* fanatic, and what begins with "Gosh, I can never remember whether Romanesque was *before* or *after* Gothic" leads to secret pamphlet-readings and stained-glass studyings, and ends up in wild aesthetic discussions of the relative values of the two towers at Chartres. Then all restraint is thrown to the wind and anything really *old* enough is greeted with animal cries of anguish at its beauty. In the final stage small discriminating lists appear about her person – but they only contain, you may be damn sure, the good, the pure, and the truly worthwhile.'

Larry paused, took a small, discriminating sip of his St Raphael, and puffed happily away at his cigarette.

I swallowed the last of my Pernod, folded my arms seductively on the sticky table, and took a long pull on my own French cigarette. It had gone out, of course. I hid it from Larry but he hadn't noticed. He was lost in reverie.

Blushingly I recalled a night not so long before when I had suddenly fallen in love with the Place de Furstenberg in the moonlight. I

had actually – Oh Lord – had *actually* kissed one of the stones at the
fountain, I remembered, flung my shoes off, and executed a crazy
drunken dance.

The September sun was blazing down on us and the second
Pernod was beginning to have a pleasant soporific effect on me. A
couple of street arabs came up and listlessly began to try selling us
silver jewellery and rugs. After a while they drifted away. I began studying Larry closely. The mat of auburn hair curling to his skull, the
grey-green eyes now so blank and far away, the delicate scar running
down the pale skin of his forehead, the well-shaped nose covered
with a faint spray of freckles, and his large mouth so gently curved, all
contributed to give his face, especially in repose, a look of sappy sweetness that was sharply at odds with – and yet at the same time
enhanced – his tough, wise-guy manner. Maybe because I had been
out very late the night before and was not able to put up my usual
resistance, but it seemed to me, sitting there with the sound of his
voice dying in my ears, that I could fall in love with him.

And then, as unexpected as a hidden step, I felt myself actually
stumble and *fall*. And there it was, I *was* in love with him! As simple as
that.

1959

Paule Marshall

Paule Marshall (née Burke), whose parents emigrated from Barbados during the First World War, was born in Brooklyn, New York, in 1929. Growing up during the Depression, she claims that she learned how to tell stories in the 'wordshop' of her mother's kitchen.

Marshall was educated at Hunter and Brooklyn colleges and then in the early fifties went to work as the only woman staff writer on *Our World Magazine*. Her first novel, *Brown Girl, Brownstones*, is a richly textured work exploring the complexities of assimilation and racism, materialism and idealism, in the context of the story of a young girl's relationship with her mother and coming of age. It forms a trilogy with *The Chosen Place, the Timeless People* (1969) and *Praisesong for the Widow* (1983). Marshall has also published several collections of short stories, including *Soul Clap Hands and Sing* (1961) and *Merle, a Novella and Other Stories* (1983), and a further novel, *Daughters* (1991).

Virago published *Brown Girl, Brownstones* in 1982.

from

Brown Girl, Brownstones

'Hello,' she said and swung into the small sitting room behind Margaret.

The woman there must have carefully arranged her smile before Selina had entered. While she had been dancing down the hall perhaps or finishing her punch with Rachel, the woman's mouth, eyes, the muscles under her pale powdered skin must have been shaping that courteous, curious and appraising smile. Months, years later, Selina was to remember it, since it became the one vivid memory of the evening, and to wonder why it had not unsettled her even then. Whenever she remembered it – all down the long years to her death – she was to start helplessly, and every white face would be suspect for that moment. But now, with her mind reeling from the dance and slightly blurred from the punch she did not even notice it.

'This is Selina, Mother,' Margaret said and the woman rose from a wing chair under a tall lamp and briskly crossed the room, her pale hand extended. Her figure in a modish dress was still shapely, her carefully applied make-up disguised her worn skin and the pull of the years at her nose and mouth. Under her greying blond hair her features were pure, her lacklustre blue eyes almost colourless. Something fretful, disturbed, lay behind their surface and rove in a restless shadow over her face.

She took Selina's hand between hers, patting it, and Selina could *feel* her whiteness – it was in the very texture of her skin. A faint uneasiness stirred and was forgotten as the woman led her to the wing chair and said effusively, 'Well, my dear, how does it feel to be the star of the show?'

Selina fell back in the chair and, laughing, gestured upward. 'A little like the real ones. Very high up. Out of this world almost.'

The woman's laugh joined hers. 'What was it you danced again?'

Margaret called from the doorway, 'The birth-to-death cycle, Mother, and I had . . .'

'I know, dear. A catharsis.' Irritation flitted across her pale exterior, but when she turned back to Selina she was smiling. 'I should think you're much too young to know anything about birth or death.'

'I don't. I had to rely on my imagination.'

The smile stiffened and the woman studied her openly, sharply, then asked, 'And how was my Margaret?'

Thinking of Rachel's description of Margaret she said, too enthusiastically, 'Very good. The entire chorus was good.'

'Yes . . . I keep telling her she'll never get out of the chorus if she doesn't lose some weight.' She touched her own narrow hips. 'But still it's good for her. All girls want to dance or act or write at some stage. I fancied myself a great tragedienne after I played Lady Macbeth my freshman year . . .'

For a long time she talked of this, perched on the edge of a chair near Selina, her white textured hands meshed on her lap, her pale eyes under the finely arched eyebrows bright with a smile. Selina turned the empty punch glass in her hands, listening politely but impatient to leave, while Margaret stood near the door, outside their circle.

Still the woman talked, but after a while the brightness left her eyes and from behind their pale screen she regarded Selina with an intense interest and irritation. Her lively voice became preoccupied. Other words loomed behind it and finally she could no longer resist them and asked abruptly, 'Where do you live, dear, uptown?'

'No, Brooklyn.'

'Oh? Have you lived there long?'

'I was born there.'

'How nice,' and her hair gleamed palely as she nodded. 'Not your parents, I don't suppose.'

'No.' Despite the encouraging smile, Selina added nothing more. She was vaguely annoyed. It was all like an inquisition somehow, where she was the accused, imprisoned in the wing chair under the glaring lamp, the woman the inquisitor and Margaret the heavy, dull-faced guard at the door.

Suddenly the woman leaned forward and rested her hand on Selina's knee. 'Are they from the South, dear?'

It was not the question which offended her, but the woman's manner – pleasant, interested, yet charged with exasperation. It was her warm smile, which was cold at its source – above all, the consoling hand on her knee, which was indecent. Selina sensed being pitted against her in a contest of strength. If she answered unwisely the woman would gain the advantage.

She muttered evasively, 'No, they're not.'

The woman bent close, surprised, and the dry sting of her perfume was another indignity. 'No . . . ? Where then?'

'The West Indies.'

The woman sat back, triumphant. 'Ah, I thought so. We once had a girl who did our cleaning who was from there . . .' She caught herself and smiled apologetically. 'Oh, she wasn't a girl, of course. We just call them that. It's a terrible habit . . . Anyway, I always told my husband there was something different about her – about Negroes from the West Indies in general . . . I don't know what, but I can always spot it. When you came in tonight, for instance . . .'

Her voice might have been a draft which had seeped under the closed windows and chilled the room. Frightened now, as well as annoyed, Selina gazed across to Margaret, who stood in a stolid heap at the door, her eyes lowered.

The woman's eyes followed Selina's and she called, 'Can you remember Ettie, dear? She used to call you Princess Margaret because you looked so much like the real princess then.'

'A little,' the girl murmured. 'She was very nice, Selina.' Margaret gave Selina a fleeting glance.

'She was wonderful,' her mother cried effusively, 'I've never been able to get another girl as efficient or as reliable as Ettie. When she cleaned, the house was spotless. Margaret, remember what your father used to do when she cleaned?'

'Yes . . .' It was a strained whisper after a long pause. 'He'd . . . he'd take off his shoes in the doorway – just like in a Japanese house . . .' Her pained glance fled Selina's. 'She was just like one of the family, Selina.'

'She was!' Her mother carried this to a higher pitch. 'We were all crazy about her. Margaret was always giving her things for her little girl. She was so ambitious for her son, I remember. She wanted him to be a dentist. He was very bright, it seems.'

Her voice, flurrying like a cold wind, snuffed out the last small flame of Selina's happiness. She started to rise, and the woman's hand, like a swift, deadly, little animal, pounced on her knee, restraining her, and the brisk voice raced on, 'We were heartbroken when she took ill. I even went to the hospital to see her. She was so honest too. I could leave my purse – anything – lying around and never worry. She was just that kind of person. You don't find help like that every day, you know. Some of them are . . . well . . .' And here she brought her powdered face with its aging skin close to Selina's, the hand fluttered apologetically, '. . . just impossible!' It was a confidential whisper. 'Oh, it's not their fault, of course, poor things! You can't help your colour. It's just a lack of the proper training and education. I have to keep telling some of my friends that. Oh, I'm a real fighter when I get started! I wish they were here tonight to meet you. You . . . well, dear . . . you don't even act coloured. I mean, you speak so well and have such poise. And it's just wonderful how you've taken your race's natural talent for dancing and music and developed it. Your race needs more smart young people like you. Ettie used to say the same thing. We used to have these long discussions on the race problem and she always agreed with me. It was so amusing to hear her say things in that delightful West Indian accent . . .'

Held down by her hand, drowning in the deluge of her voice, Selina felt a coldness ring her heart. She tried to signal the woman that she had had enough, but her hand failed her. Why couldn't the woman *see*, she wondered – even as she drowned – that she was simply a girl of twenty with a slender body and slight breasts and no power with words, who loved spring and then the sere leaves falling and dim, old houses, who had tried, foolishly perhaps, to reach beyond herself? But when she looked up and saw her reflection in those pale eyes, she knew that the woman saw one thing above all else. Those eyes were a well-lighted mirror in which, for the first time, Selina truly saw – with a sharp and shattering clarity – the full meaning of her black skin.

1960s

1960

Flannery O'Connor

———

Mary Flannery O'Connor was born in Savannah, Georgia, in 1925. Her family moved to Milledgeville when her father was diagnosed with lupus erythematosus, a rare and incurable genetic blood disease. After gaining a BA from Georgia State College for Women, she studied writing at the University of Iowa. Her first novel, *Wise Blood*, was published in 1952, the year in which O'Connor learned that she too was suffering from lupus. She moved back to Georgia, where she lived with her mother on the family dairy farm and raised many birds, particularly peacocks. She was thirty-nine when she died.

Wise Blood was followed by a collection of short stories, *A Good Man Is Hard to Find* (1955), and a novel, *The Violent Bear It Away* (1960). After her death a further collection of stories, *Everything That Rises Must Converge* (1965), was published. Her essays are collected in *Mystery and Manners* (1969).

O'Connor was brought up a Roman Catholic in the deeply Protestant South and much of her fiction is concerned with what she called 'the action of grace in territory held largely by the devil'. Her stories may begin with the specifics of social satire, but they inevitably end in sacramental vision.

from

'The Comforts of Home'

Thomas withdrew to the side of the window and with his head between the wall and the curtain he looked down on the driveway where the car had stopped. His mother and the little slut were getting out of it. His mother emerged slowly, stolid and awkward, and then the little slut's long slightly bowed legs slid out, the dress pulled above the knees. With a shriek of laughter she ran to meet the dog, who bounded, overjoyed, shaking with pleasure, to welcome her. Rage gathered throughout Thomas's large frame with a silent ominous intensity, like a mob assembling.

It was now up to him to pack a suitcase, go to the hotel, and stay there until the house should be cleared.

He did not know where a suitcase was, he disliked to pack, he needed his books, his typewriter was not portable, he was used to an electric blanket, he could not bear to eat in restaurants. His mother, with her daredevil charity, was about to wreck the peace of the house.

The back door slammed and the girl's laugh shot up from the kitchen, through the back hall, up the stairwell and into his room, making for him like a bolt of electricity. He jumped to the side and stood glaring about him. His words of the morning had been unequivocal: 'If you bring that girl back into this house, I leave. You can choose – her or me.'

She had made her choice. An intense pain gripped his throat. It was the first time in his thirty-five years . . . He felt a sudden burning moisture behind his eyes. Then he steadied himself, overcome by rage. On the contrary: she had not made any choice. She was counting on his attachment to his electric blanket. She would have to be shown.

The girl's laughter rang upward a second time and Thomas winced. He saw again her look of the night before. She had invaded his room. He had waked to find his door open and her in it. There was enough light from the hall to make her visible as she turned toward him. The face was like a comedienne's in a musical comedy – a pointed chin, wide apple cheeks and feline empty eyes. He had sprung out of his bed and snatched a straight chair and then he had backed her out the door, holding the chair in front of him like an animal trainer driving out a dangerous cat. He had driven her silently down the hall, pausing when he reached it to beat on his mother's door. The girl, with a gasp, turned and fled into the guest room.

In a moment his mother had opened her door and peered out apprehensively. Her face, greasy with whatever she put on it at night, was framed in pink rubber curlers. She looked down the hall where the girl had disappeared. Thomas stood before her, the chair still lifted in front of him as if he were about to quell another beast. 'She tried to get in my room,' he hissed, pushing in. 'I woke up and she was trying to get in my room.' He closed the door behind him and his voice rose in outrage. 'I won't put up with this! I won't put up with it another day!'

His mother, backed by him to her bed, sat down on the edge of it. She had a heavy body on which sat a thin, mysteriously gaunt and incongruous head.

'I'm telling you for the last time,' Thomas said, 'I won't put up with this another day.' There was an observable tendency in all of her actions. This was, with the best intentions in the world, to make a mockery of virtue, to pursue it with such a mindless intensity that everyone involved was made a fool of and virtue itself became ridiculous. 'Not another day,' he repeated.

His mother shook her head emphatically, her eyes still on the door.

Thomas put the chair on the floor in front of her and sat down on it. He leaned forward as if he were about to explain something to a defective child.

'That's just another way she's unfortunate,' his mother said. 'So awful, so awful. She told me the name of it but I forget what it is but it's something she can't help. Something she was born with. Thomas,' she said and put her hand to her jaw, 'suppose it were you?'

Exasperation blocked his windpipe. 'Can't I make you see,' he croaked, 'that if she can't help herself you can't help her?'

His mother's eyes, intimate but untouchable, were the blue of great distances after sunset. 'Nimpermaniac,' she murmured.

'Nymphomaniac,' he said fiercely. 'She doesn't need to supply you with any fancy names. She's a moral moron. That's all you need to know. Born without the moral faculty – like somebody else would be born without a kidney or a leg. Do you understand?'

'I keep thinking it might be you,' she said, her hand still on her jaw. 'If it were you, how do you think I'd feel if nobody took you in? What if you were a nimpermaniac and not a brilliant smart person and you did what you couldn't help and . . .'

Thomas felt a deep unbearable loathing for himself as if he were turning slowly into the girl.

'What did she have on?' she asked abruptly, her eyes narrowing.

'Nothing!' he roared. 'Now will you get her out of here!'

'How can I turn her out in the cold?' she said. 'This morning she was threatening to kill herself again.'

'Send her back to jail,' Thomas said.

'I would not send *you* back to jail, Thomas,' she said.

He got up and snatched the chair and fled the room while he was still able to control himself.

Thomas loved his mother. He loved her because it was his nature to do so, but there were times when he could not endure her love for him. There were times when it became nothing but pure idiot mystery and he sensed about him forces, invisible currents entirely out of his control. She proceeded always from the tritest of considerations – it was the *nice thing to do* – into the most foolhardy engagements with the devil, whom, of course, she never recognised.

1961

Attia Hosain

Attia Hosain was born in 1913 in Lucknow in northern India into a traditional feudal (*Taluqdari*) family. She was educated at home in Arabic, Persian and Urdu, and at Western-style schools. In the 1930s she was greatly influenced by the emerging nationalism of the Indian National Congress and the Progressive Writers' Association and began to write fiction as well as journalism. When, in 1947, Indian independence was accompanied by the creation of Pakistan as a separate Muslim state, however, Hosain decided to move to London with her husband and two children. In London she remained involved in journalism and published a collection of short stories, *Phoenix Fled*, in 1951.

Sunlight on a Broken Column (1961), a complex and intricate novel, is set in pre-Independence India and negotiates between the literary traditions of English and Persian literature to create a style and a structure that are very much its own. Attia Hosain died in 1998.

Virago published *Sunlight on a Broken Column* in 1988.

from

Sunlight on a Broken Column

I felt I lived in two worlds; an observer in an outside world, and solitary in my own – except when I was with the friends I had made at College. Then the blurred, confusing double image came near to being one.

Nita Chatterji was the strongest character among my friends. She was short, plump and always in a hurry as if she were tripping on the heels of time. Her large eyes seemed to bulge as if strained, and her mouth closed impatiently over wide, strong teeth. Her hair was thick and waved darkly away from her pale face, to a carelessly looped 'bun'. It was very beautiful, but she deliberately neglected it because of a puritanical obsession against feminine vanity. 'When I go to prison I will cut it off,' she would say.

'Are you planning to go to prison?'

'Of course not. I'm not a sentimental fool. But if I do all the things I plan to do, the British will have to put me in prison sooner or later. And I'll try to make it later. I'm not like that stupid cousin of mine who tried to shoot some pompous official and was nearly hanged for his pains. Children in politics, that is what terrorists are, heroic but misguided. To fight British imperialism we have to be organised and disciplined, and use the kind of weapons that will not misfire.'

She used to say to me when I accused her of being presumptuously self-confident, 'The trouble with you is you walk round and round in circles because you have no sense of direction. You sway and bend backwards thinking you are flexible and being fair, but you really are unsure.'

Nita and I attended the same English classes and became friends, though we quarrelled constantly.

Shortly after we met she asked me, 'What are you going to do after you leave College?'

'I don't really know.'

'How typical of your class! You think a degree is a piece of jewellery, an additional ornament to be listed in your dowry.'

'Rubbish! I believe my education will make me a better human being.'

'I'm afraid I cannot afford such abstract ideals. My education has to help me to earn my living, so I have to make a definite plan. You are all the same, you have money to wrap round you like cotton wool against life. Nadira, with her opium eaters' religion, you with your lotus eaters' humanity. But I like you, because you are fundamentally honest, though everything in your background tends to manufacture hypocrites.'

'I wonder why I like you though you talk to me as you do.'

'*Because* I talk as I do. I take out the sting from what your conscience whispers to you, by saying it loudly. Then you are so busy defending yourself you need do nothing. Your ancestors probably had court jesters to serve much the same purpose.'

When Nadira argued with Nita she defended her religious beliefs with greater conviction than I defended my class because she had no doubts. Her visions of the greatness of the Islamic world in the past was blurred for me by its decadence in the present.

Nadira was the daughter of my aunt's friend Begum Waheed. Like her mother her strongest belief was that Muslims had to defend their heritage.

Nadira's family were comparative newcomers to our city; they had come from the neighbouring province of the Punjab only twenty years ago. Her father was a doctor, known to be clever but said to be so grasping that, before starting his treatment, one had to decide between dying of bankruptcy or the disease.

After he had become successful they moved from their small house in a socially inferior part of the city, to a large house on the Mall. Begum Waheed came out of purdah, began to call herself 'Begum', and sent Nadira to a Convent.

Nadira and I quarrelled frequently about her political beliefs which were tied up with her religious fervour, but we shared other interests – books and music and poetry.

It was our wish to understand Western music that led to our friendship with Joan Davis who led the College orchestra.

Joan's mother was a widow, a matron at the Medical College. Joan had been awarded a scholarship and was very conscientious, simple and generous. She intended being a doctor.

Her home was small and unpretentious. Whenever I visited her and saw her with her mother, I felt a sense of deprivation. Their love and understanding were real, and not only a need and desire; their worlds were not separated by an age of ideas.

When Joan joined our group she had to stand alone in defence of her convictions, because she passionately believed in the rightness and the greatness of the British Empire. When Nita talked of her ambition to join actively in the struggle for freedom Joan said quite sincerely:

'I believe in the English not only because I am an Anglo-Indian but because they have brought peace and justice and unity.'

'They have built roads and schools and hospitals,' mocked Nita. 'They have done good for the sake of doing good and for love of us, and any incidental exploitation is really for our benefit. In any case, how can one be loyal to aliens?'

'The Muslims were aliens,' began Joan.

'They settled down here,' I reminded her.

'They can go back to where they came from if they think they're aliens,' said Nita.

'There speaks the Hindu,' Nadira cut in angrily. 'Scratch deep, and what is hidden under your progressive ideas? The same communalism of which you accuse me.'

When this point was reached in any argument we were all glad to be drawn away from it. God was a safer subject for discussion than His religions.

I said lightly, 'It's the P. & O. that is losing you the Empire, Joan. The faster their ships, the easier it is to go back "Home" and we never get to know our benevolent English patrons.'

Joan's weakness in arguments came from the very quality that gave her personal strength. She did not hate as we did. She did not hate Indians as we hated the British; she merely considered them a race apart. Yet she did not identify herself with the English.

'I am an Anglo-Indian and nothing can make it otherwise. My grandfather came here from England; we still talk of England as home, we have more in common with the English than with Indians, but we still remain just Anglo-Indians. It makes one feel like those riders who canter round the ring of a circus, balanced on two horses, except that those horses are trained to keep in step, and their riders are respected.'

Joan neutralised in me the remembered venom of Sylvia Tucker. Her friendship blunted the sharp points of prejudice. I could not make Sylvia the excuse for hatred when Joan provided a reason for respect.

Our small group of friends was completed by Romana. She was unlike us in every possible way, uninterested in our arguments and amused by our quarrels because she questioned nothing.

Romana was related to Nadira and that is how we came to know her. Her family had migrated to a small Muslim state where her father was a minor official, but powerful because he had relations and friends in every branch of the State's administration. Also, he had flattered his way into becoming the ruler's favourite.

Romana had many tales to tell. She told us of the treasure-house in the heart of a hill whose secret approach through a maze was known only to its hereditary guardians, giant Negroes, bearing on their cheeks strange, secret, branded signs. She told us of the necklace that had belonged to a concubine who had been walled alive many centuries ago by a jealous ruler; its giant central ruby was said to drip blood on the anniversary of her death, and the pearls dripped with salty tears. She told of the kidnappings of beautiful women and of the disappearance of inconvenient husbands.

Not even Nita invested her stories with social significance. Romana looked too much part of a fairy tale. She was like an ivory miniature, delicately carved. Her beauty was not disturbing, it gave a sense of diffused pleasure. It was like the warmth of the sun on a winter's day.

The five of us spent as much time together as possible. When we were not arguing we were dissecting and questioning life, with the fear and the courage, the doubts and the certainty of inexperienced, questioning youth. Our world was bounded by our books, and the voices that spoke to us through them were of great men, profound thinkers, philosophers and poets.

I used to forget that the world was in reality very different, and the voices that controlled it had once been those of Baba Jan, Aunt Abida, Ustaniji, and now belonged to Uncle Hamid, Aunt Saira, and their friends. Always I lived in two worlds, and I grew to resent the 'real' world.

1962

Dorothy Baker

Dorothy Dodds was born in Missoula, Montana, in 1907. After attending Whittier College, she graduated from the University of California at Los Angeles in 1929. There she met Howard Baker, also a writer, and the couple married in Paris in 1930. On returning to America, she taught high-school French and Spanish in Oakland, before taking her MA in French at UCLA in 1934.

Baker's first novel, *Young Man with a Horn* (1938), was inspired by the music of Bix Beiderbecke and filmed in 1950 from her screenplay. She followed it with *Trio* (1943) which she and her husband dramatised in 1944, although a campaign by local Protestant clergymen, upset by its lesbian theme, forced it to close after only a few months. She published two further novels, *Our Gifted Son* (1948) and her most successful work, *Cassandra at the Wedding* (1962), the story of the deep and damaging psychological ties between twin sisters. In 1957 she collaborated with her husband on a television play, *The Ninth Day*. After suffering from cancer for many years, Dorothy Baker died in 1968.

Virago published *Cassandra at the Wedding* in 1982.

from

Cassandra at the Wedding

I got my thumbnail under the tape and released one side of the lid and folded it back. Inside there was a sea of white tissue paper, systematically crumpled around the edges, and with a pretty pink sales slip on top. I picked up the slip, folded it and pushed it down along the edge of the box, out of sight, because I didn't want anybody's opinion of the dress to be influenced by what it cost. Then I broke a seal and unfolded the paper. The dress lay there quietly and unobtrusively white against the white paper, but with extreme elegance and style. Easily the best dress I'd had since the seventh grade.

I think I was expecting Judith to whistle and granny to chirp, but neither one of them made any sound at all; so I took hold of the shoulders and lifted it out of the box and told them it was the kind of dress that doesn't give the best account of itself lying in a box. Or hanging on a hanger, for that matter. The way it fits is the thing. And the way it's made.

'This back pleat, for instance,' I said. I turned it over and showed granny the beautiful tailor's tracks that held the pleat at the top and the bottom, and granny looked and didn't say a thing.

'Pure silk,' I said, 'feel the weight of it. It crunches.'

I was beginning to feel like a saleswoman making a hard sale to an unconvinced customer. Two unconvinced customers. And when I looked away from the dress I saw them looking at each other in a way that was hard to interpret. It was as if they were sharing a private joke. And they were, of course, but I had no idea what it was. All I could tell was that something was wrong with either me or my choice.

'It's obvious enough you don't like it,' I said, and Jude sat there looking first at the dress and then at gran with this puzzled and puzzling look on her face, a sort of combination of astonishment and dismay.

'I didn't say I didn't like it,' she said in a rather low, unemphatic voice. 'I'm crazy about it. I was crazy about it before I ever saw yours.'

She stopped and sat there looking somehow baffled, and then looked at gran and said: 'Go ahead, Granny, you tell her.'

Granny didn't look baffled. I hadn't seen her look so excited in years.

'Oh Cassie, this is rich,' she said, 'after all these years of you two refusing to dress alike.'

I stopped breathing, and then started again. By rich, our grandmother usually means side-splittingly amusing. She says it where other people say this will kill you, and I got the idea clearly enough, what I'd done wrong, and where my gross error lay, without letting myself consciously believe it. I let everything get vague, the dress, the voice, the voices, and I sat there sullen in my tied-together tank suit and considered the part chance plays in a life, or two lives, and how little control can be brought to it. I also thought about brandy.

'Let's leave God out of this,' I heard Jude say, and I sat up straighter and asked her what she'd been talking about.

'Where've you been?' Jude said, and I told her here, but not listening, and then she told me that granny had been saying it all went to prove that God had meant us to dress alike all the time. How else after twenty-four years of carefully avoiding any duplication in clothes could we have come up with the same dress, in two separate cities, all independently? And for the same occasion.

Granny was sitting at the foot of my bed now, across from Jude, looking truly triumphant. And vindicated.

'Goodness knows *I* always wanted to dress you alike, and I never could understand what Jane had against it. Or Jim either.'

'I believe,' I said, quite stiffly and slowly, so that she'd listen, 'they were concerned to have us become individuals, each of us in our own right, and not be confused in ourselves, nor confusing to other people.'

'That's right,' Judith said, like an amen.

'Oh I've heard them explain it a hundred times,' gran said, and she sighed. 'I used to bring you the dearest outfits, everything alike right down to the little socks and panties, and every time I'd do it they'd make me send them right back.'

She sighed again, and I felt a light twinge in an old war wound. I could still remember having to say goodbye to some very pretty presents, and crying with Jude after they'd been sent back.

We looked at each other now while granny went on with variations on her theme – ending where it began, with how rich it was for us to have chosen, separately, the very same wedding dresses.

And there she went too far. Mine was not a wedding dress. It was only a dress I'd bought to wear to somebody's wedding. It might have been all right for *me* to call it my wedding dress because I'd have let the irony show through good and thick, but it wasn't that way with gran saying it. It sounded indecent, and the room began to feel much too small and full of tissue paper.

'Let's have a look at yours,' I said to Jude. 'Maybe they aren't so much alike as you think.'

'Don't be silly,' she said.

'Let's see it.'

She got up and slid her closet door open and brought out the dress on its hanger. Dead ringer. Identical signature. Size ten. White silk. Feel the weight of it, the intolerable crushing weight. I looked away from it and what did I see? The other one, fallen across the box on my bed. The one I'd been thinking of as mine – the one that was going to contrast so signally in its elegant simplicity with the kind of thing a bride is stuck to wear, including I hoped, the fluty corsage, the white prayer book and the fingertip veil.

I looked back at Judith holding the white flag on the hanger and it came to me that if ever there were a time when it would seem right and natural to start smoking again after an abstinence of two and a half years, it would be now.

But I couldn't get up.

Granny kept up a stream of talk, saying in quite a few new ways what she'd already said in quite a few too many ways before – that it was an amazing coincidence, wasn't it amazing? And yet, in another way of looking at it, not amazing at all; it only went to show that our dear well-meaning parents, for all their enlightenment and all their theories, had simply always pushed us in the wrong direction.

I gave her a sharp look which I think she must have construed as loyalty to our parents, because she stopped talking. And when she did, the quiet became more obtrusive than any amount of talking. There was Judith in her bikini hanging onto the hanger and me in my tank suit sitting in all the tissue paper, and our grandmother, between us, so fragile and so pretty, and none of us saying a word.

Then I decided not to start smoking again, to speak up instead from where I sat, and say something that came to me.

'You're the one that made the mistake,' I said, 'not me.'

Judith looked down at me with the clear bland face she gets when she's waiting for more. So I gave her more.

'That's no dress for a bride, don't you know that? I'm sorry, but it just isn't.'

I waited until I saw gran open her mouth to say something and then I went ahead.

'It's too God-damned simple.'

I looked at gran and saw what I expected to see – the look of shock and hurt she always gets when she hears any profanity. It was a look I've seen her turn on Jane a hundred times, as if she could not believe her ears.

'Don't you know the bride is supposed to be gussied up?'

'Who says?' Jude said.

'I say,' I said. 'It's a rule. Nobody ever gets married in anything decent. You wear something you wouldn't be caught dead in any-place else but your own wedding. And you never wear it again. You pack it away to show your dumb kids.'

I waited just long enough to make the contrast have a chance.

'It's a very different matter with me. I bought this dress – or rather charged it to dear granny – with the idea that I'd wear it again. Frequently.'

'Me too,' Jude said with a show of spirit I didn't care much for.

'But where?' I said. 'Where'll *you* ever go?'

It was lame, I knew, and overdone, but it was the best I could do at the time, and the whole place was suddenly so choked with tissue paper that I had to get out and away.

I folded the dress – the one lying beside me – in a way that could just barely not be called wadding it up, and then I crammed the paper in on top of it and got the lid approximately back in place and shoved the box under the bed and went out into the hall and closed the door after me.

1963

Nell Dunn

Nell Dunn was born in London in 1936, the daughter of Sir Philip Gordon Dunn, second Baronet Bathurst, and grew up on the family estate in Wiltshire. She attended convent school but dropped out to go to London to study art history. In an attempt to become a 'refugee' from her own background, in the early sixties Dunn moved from fashionable Chelsea to working-class Battersea, where she set the vivid stories that were first published in the *New Statesman* and later as *Up the Junction*. The stories feature a recurrent set of characters (Rube, Annie, Sylvie and the narrator), yet each also stands alone.

Dunn's first novel, *Poor Cow* (1967), was a bestseller and was successfully filmed by Ken Loach in the same year. Since the sixties, Dunn has continued to publish plays, including the hit comedy *Steaming* (1981), and novels, notably *My Silver Shoes* (1996), which is a continuation of *Poor Cow*.

Virago published *Up the Junction* in 1988.

'Bang on the Common'

The little slum house was locked and in darkness. A voice came out of the night: 'Are you looking fer Winny?'

'Oh, hello, Annie.'

'Oh, it's you, Rube.'

The three of us stood under the dim gas-light. 'She bought a big place out at Wimbledon bang on the Common. As it happens I'm just going to phone her up. A flash tart in a big motor came down looking for her today – said if I'd find Winny and get her done for ten she'd give me a couple of quid for meself.'

'Who's it for, you or her?'

'A mate in work.'

'Come off it, Rube. I won't blacken yer character.'

'Oh, all right. It's me, Annie. I think I'm up the spout. I can't seem to sit still. I can't stay in for nothing. I've got to be movin' around the whole time. I can't eat nothing. Directly I start to eat I feel full.'

'Sounds like yer in the club all right.'

'I can't have it done. I might get an air-bubble in me inside and die. I walked out on me job today, I'm all on edge. I'd run away but I've nowhere to run to.'

'You'd best have it done. You're only a kid, she'd do it for five quid.'

'I said to the doctor, "I've bin going with a fella and you know how it happens." "Yes," he says.'

'You'd best go up to Winny's and have done with it. I *could* get you some quinine. I took some once. There was a loud ringing in me ears and a violent pain in me stomach, it lifted me into another world –

but it didn't do no good. This Barry, he gets it from the chemist. Tells him he's got a mate just back from Africa with a touch of the malaria, then he sells the tablets ten bob each to the girls.'

Rube was cheerful now the first move had been made. 'Will you phone her for me, Annie?'

'Yeah. When do yer want to go?'

'Tomorrer. When me mum's in the kitchen I have to take a deep breath and hold me stomach in and run past, then when I get out into the scullery I let it out. She said to me today, "You got ulcers in yer mouth? Your stomach must be upset" and she gave me one of her looks.'

The next evening we took a bus up to Wimbledon. A long street with rows of red-brick villas. The three of us traipse along the road.

'I thought it was bang on the Common, Annie.'

'Well, it's near enough.' She stopped at a corner house with a hardware store in front. 'So she's got a shop and all.'

'Yeah, it's her sideline.' We went in.

'Hello, darling. Hello, love.' Winny was about forty-five. She wore a red dress above her knees showing her varicose-vein legs, ankle socks and gym shoes.

'I had that Harry here again last night. He didn't go till six this morning. I made him sleep in the bath. He's bringing me fifty gal's of paint tomorrer – free sample. "Well," I says to him, "you've had my free sample, now what about yours?"' She had delicate arms and huge bony hands with long red fingers which she waved around.

'Well, what have we here, Annie?'

'I've come, I've come . . .' said Rube, nervous.

'I know why you've come – there's only one reason good-looking girls come to see Winny. Here, Annie, pop across the off-licence and get me a quarter-bottle whisky.' She gave her a ten-shilling note and Rube and I were left alone with Winny.

'How far are you gone, love?'

'About three months.'

Winny poked Rube in the stomach. 'Oh, then you've only got a small problem in there.'

'You see I can't keep it . . .' Rube began.

'Don't try and explain, love. How can you ever explain anything? It's the most bloody impossible thing in the world. How much money have you got?'

'Four pounds.'

'Give it over. You don't look more than seventeen.'

'I'm eighteen next month.'

'Come on upstairs, then your friend can wait for you down here.'

But that wasn't the last time Rube and I trailed up to Wimbledon. She had to go seven times before anything happened. Often we'd go into the kitchen and Winny would be sitting on some man's knee. As Rube said, 'She wouldn't care if you was watching her – teasin' em, sloppin' over em.' Winny didn't eat anything all day. She was always on the bottle.

Later I'd cart Rube home weak-kneed and trembling on the bus. 'Terry came down for me last night – the first time in six weeks. He said, "Don't you go up there no more, I don't want no kid of mine to go down the drain." But Sylvie said, "Now she's started she's gotta keep on or it'll be born a monster." So Terry walks out, but not before he shouted so half the street can hear: "Anyway she was nothing but a cheap thrill".'

We rode past the park. The water lilies are opening red mouths. The birds hop in the flower garden and the crazy music streams from the fairground.

'When she does the syringe you feel a sort of weakening pain shoot up in yer . . .'

It was about six on a Sunday morning. There was a banging on my door. I looked out of the window and saw Johnny Macarthy below. I knew it must be serious because Johnny deserted from the army fifteen years ago and hadn't been outside his own house since in case they caught up with him – so far they hadn't.

I let him in out of the dark mist, 'It's Rube. She's ever so bad. I want to phone up Winny.'

Johnny phoned Winny. It rang a long time and when she finally answered it she said she couldn't come.

I went back over with Johnny. Rube was lying back against her mum's knees, a green eiderdown covering her, white and heaving.

'Let me get the doctor.'

'No, they might try and save the baby. I don't want no kids from that gink – we've enough kids in this house as it is without no more.'

'I told her, didn't I, to keep away from him? said her mum.

A few hours later Rube started to shriek. Her jet-black hair stuck to her face and tiny rivulets of blue rinse coursed down her white cheeks. She was semi-delirious.

The smell of Sunday dinner cooking floated up the stairs. Rube bent up tight with pain.

'It's lucky I ain't got me health and strength no more else I'd do him, do him right up I would,' said her mum. Sylvie came in. 'I'll hold her now, Mum, if you want to go and have yer dinner. Ray says he'd hit him sky-high if it wasn't that he might get nicked for it.'

The voice of Johnny sailed up from the kitchen: 'He'd better watch it from me, too – I shan't always be stayin' in, will I?'

Rube shrieked again.

'Let me ring the doctor.'

'Oh, all right then.'

In the kitchen everyone was eating. The Light was full on. Ben E. King sang:

> Oh yes, she said, yes,
> And she opened her arms.
> Oh yes, she said, yes and
> She closed her eyes.

When I came back from the ringing, Rube was shrieking, a long, high, animal shriek. The baby was born alive, five months old. It moved, it breathed, its heart beat.

Rube lay back, white and relieved, across the bed. Sylvie and her mum lifted the eiderdown and peered at the tiny baby still joined by the cord. 'You can see it breathing, look!'

Rube smiled. 'It's nothing – I've had a look meself.'

'I reckon she had some pluck going seven times,' said her mum.

Finally the ambulance arrived. They took Rube away, but they left behind the baby, which had now grown cold. Later Sylvie took him, wrapped in the *Daily Mirror*, and threw him down the toilet.

1964

Anaïs Nin

———

Anaïs Nin was born in the Paris suburb of Neuilly in 1903. After her parents' separation in 1914 she moved to New York with her mother and brothers. On the boat on the way there she began the journal which she was to continue all her life, and which many claim contains her best work. Nin returned to Paris when she was twenty with her husband Hugh Guiler.

Nin's first book was a study of the novelist D. H. Lawrence and through this she met another Lawrence fan, Henry Miller, with whom she began a passionate affair. Nin continued to write – her journals, a prose-poem, *House of Incest* (1936), and her first novel, *Winter of Artifice* (1939). Nin also studied with the psychoanalyst Otto Rank and practised briefly herself. Her work remained deeply focused on the workings of the psyche. *Collages*, for example, explores the fantasies of a woman artist called Renate.

At the outbreak of the Second World War, Nin returned to America where she published, among other works, the five novels (1946–61) that constitute her *roman fleuve*, *Cities of the Interior*. She began to publish her diaries (in many volumes) in 1966. Nin died in Los Angeles in 1977; shortly afterwards, *Delta of Venus*, a collection of erotic writing which she had written to make money in the 1940s, became an international bestseller.

Virago published *Collages* in 1993.

from

Collages

In the small towns of California the occasional absence of inhabitants, or animation, can give the place the air of a still life painting.
Thus it appeared for a moment in the eyes of a woman standing in the
centre of an empty lot. No cars passed, no light shone, no one walked,
no windows blinked, no dogs barked, no children crossed the street.

The place had a soft name: Downey. It suggested the sensation of
downy hairs on downy skins. But Downey was not like its name. It was
symmetrical, tidy, monotonous. One house could not be distinguished from another, and gaping open garages exposed what was
once concealed in attics; broken bicycles, old newspapers, old trunks,
empty bottles.

The woman who was standing in the empty lot had blurred her
feminine contours in slacks, and a big loose sweater. But her blonde
hair was round and puffed like the hair of a doll.

She stood motionless and became, for a moment, part of the still
life until a station wagon arrived and friends waved at her as they
slowed down in front of her. She ran swiftly towards them and helped
them open the back of the car and unload paintings and easels which
they all carried to the empty lot.

Then the woman in slacks became intensely active, placing and
turning the paintings at an angle where the sunlight would illumine
rather than consume them.

The paintings were all in sharp contrast to the attenuated colours
of Downey. Deep nocturnal blues and greens and purples, all the
velvet tones of the night.

Cars began to stop and people came to look.

One visitor said: 'These trees have no shadows.'

Another visitor said: 'The faces have no wrinkles. They do not look real.'

The crowd that had gathered was the same one who came to the empty lot at Christmas to buy Christmas trees, or in the summer to buy strawberries from the Japanese gardeners.

'I have never seen a sea like this,' said another spectator.

The woman in slacks laughed and said: 'A painting should take you to a place you have never seen before. You don't always want to look at the same tree, the same sea, the same face every day, do you?'

But that was exactly what the inhabitants of Downey wanted to do. They did not want to uproot themselves. They were looking for duplicates of Downey, a portrait of their grandmother, and of their children.

The painter laughed. They liked her laughter. They ventured to buy a few of the smaller paintings, as if in diminutive sizes they might not be so dangerous or change the climate of their living-room.

'I'm helping you to tell your house apart from your neighbours,' said the painter.

There was no wind. Between visitors the painter and her friends sat on stools and smoked and talked among themselves. But one capricious, solitary puff of wind lifed a strand of blonde hair away from the painter's face and revealed a strand of dark hair under the mesh of the wig. But no one noticed or commented on it.

The light grew dim. The painter and her friends packed the remaining paintings and drove away.

Back at her house by the sea, the painter stacked her paintings against the wall. She went into her bedroom. When she came out again the wig was gone, her long black hair fell over her shoulders, and she wore a Mexican cotton dress in all the soft colours of a rainbow.

It was Renate. The blonde wig lay on the bed, with the slacks and the big sweater. And now she also had to make the paintings look like her own art work again, which meant restituting to them the phantasmagorical figures of her night dreams. The plain landscapes, the plain seascapes, the plain figures were all transformed to what they were before the Downey exhibit. The figures undulated, became bells, the bells rang over the ocean, the trees waved in cadences, the sinuosities of the clouds were like the scarves of Arab or Hindu women, veiling the storms. Animals never seen before, descendants of the unicorn, offered their heads to be cajoled. The vegetative patience of flowers was depicted like a group of twittering nuns, and it was the animals who had the eyes of crystal gazers while people's eyes seemed made of stalactites. Explosions of the myth, garrulous streets, debauched winds, oracular moods of the sands, stasis of the rocks, attrition of stones, acerose of leaves, excrescence of hours, sibylline women with a faculty for osmosis, adolescence like cactus, the corrugations of age, the ulcerations of love, people seeking to live two with one heart, inseparable twins.

She restored to the empty landscapes all the mythological figures of her dreams, thinking of Rousseau's words in answer to the question: 'Why did you paint a couch in the middle of the jungle?' And he had said: 'Because one has a right to paint one's dreams.'

1965

Rosa Guy

———

Rosa Cuthbert was born in Trinidad in 1925 and moved to New York in 1932. In 1941 she married Warner Guy. While raising her son, she worked in a garment factory before joining the American Negro Theater. She began writing stories and plays as a student at New York University. *Bird at My Window* was Guy's first novel.

A co-founder of the Harlem Writers' Guild, Guy is the author of ten novels in all, including *A Measure of Time* (1983) and *My Love, My Love* (1985), as well as several highly regarded works for children.

Virago published *Bird at My Window* in 1989.

from

Bird at My Window

Mumma was afraid about everything, not only for herself but for them. She refused to let them go out of the neighbourhood, setting their limits between 116th Street and 125th Street. She wouldn't go downtown shopping, afraid to tangle with the white folks, buying instead at the higher-priced stores of 125th Street, saying that what she put out in money, she made up in peace of mind.

Willie Earl listened to everything she said, nodded his head and went about his own way of doing things. But once when someone saw him past 116th Street and Mumma got after him, he pleaded and cried, argued and got excited, angry and then repentant, saying that he was not a baby to be confined to a ten-block limit. He carried on in such a way that Mumma, tired and worn, unable to endure such persistence, gave in, extending his boundaries to most of Harlem.

Faith and Wade listened to everything Mumma had to say, never questioned her, never went past the limits she set for them, except for that one time when Wade went with Willie Earl. That one time was enough and he never did it again.

After Big Willie died, Willie Earl had taken to hustling shoe shines to help Mumma out. And one morning, after months of listening and ignoring Wade's pleas, Willie agreed to make Wade a shoe-shine box and take him along.

Mumma helped them dress, kissed them, sending them on their way. He was proud as anything to be going out with his big brother. Willie was six years older and tall for his age. Folks said he was just like Papa. But Wade, ever since he could remember, clung to the idea that he was the one like his father, and the idea of bringing home money and throwing it in Mumma's lap casually the way Papa used to, saying, 'Here, Evelyn, see what you can do with this,' pleased him.

Willie walked him right past 116 Street to 110th. It was the first time he had been that far from home, but before he could get used to the excitement, Willie Earl had grabbed his arm and was pulling him into the subway. 'Listen, Wade,' he whispered as though Mumma might have been right behind them. 'I'm going to take you where we can make a lot of money, but if you tell, I'm going to knock the hell outa you and I ain't never going to take you with me again.' That was always Willie Earl. Nothing but a bag of secrets.

Willie Earl waited until the train rushed into the station and had almost closed its doors before pushing Wade under the turnstile, dragging him across the platform, shoving him through the closing door, and wiggling in after him. They were off, making it to 'Willie's' corner in a place that Willie called 'wop-town', and all the while they were riding, Willie Earl kept giving instructions: 'Keep your eyes peeled for the kids on the block. Never set up when you see a kid around. If he ain't seen you, hide until he passes. If he catches one glimpse of you, we can just call it a day, understand? Cause if you see one, you'll see a dozen.'

Wade nodded to every instruction. He didn't understand anything, but he was puzzled more than a little at Willie's running battle with Mumma for a 110th Street limit, when the whole city was already his stomping ground. That was the way with Willie Earl, he had a natural knack of fighting over a little bone to hide a whole *side* of meat he had stored up somewhere.

Willie's corner was near a broken-down tenement on the Lower East Side, where people came and went as if it was a train station. Fine cars stopped here and well-dressed men flashing big diamond rings jumped out to disappear into the interior of the broken-down house, coming out in a very few minutes to drive away. But many, seeing a shoe-shine box, decided on a shine. The boys started making money right away, for these men didn't mind paying twenty-five cents or fifty cents, and sometimes as much as a dollar for a five-cent shine. Of course, Willie made the big tips because he knew how to shine. He could have made even more, except that he had to stop every few minutes to give Wade pointers, and even to finish some of the shoes Wade started. But he still made money, and Wade did too.

It was because of Wade taking so long to finish one pair of shoes that they got caught. Willie looked up in the middle of a shine, saw one of the neighbourhood kids and said under his breath, 'Psst, chicky Wade, let's cut.' He gave the shoe he had been working on a lick and a promise, then he was ready. Wade, stuck with too much of the thick liquid over his customer's shoe, was afraid to stop, and by the time Willie Earl had run to the corner to look around, come back and grabbed his arm, pulling him away from the unfinished shoe, they were surrounded.

'Hey,' one big boy, the leader, called. 'Don't you know we don't let no spooks around here? How you get out of nigger town?' That was the first instant when Wade realised that he had not seen one black face since they started. The very thought made him shake inside.

Slick Willie Earl wasted no words, he just kept looking around for a way out, holding on to Wade's arm, because he knew he could talk his way out of anything with Mumma, except leaving his little brother in another part of town. Willie Earl tried to inch toward the corner, but they were locked in. The leader was a boy much older than Willie Earl; and the youngest, much older than Wade, who was hardly rid of his baby fat.

The kids called them black sons-of-bitches and dirty niggers and coons. Told them that they would show them what they did to dirty bastards when they caught them where they didn't belong. Willie Earl never wasted a breath, he just kept looking around and thinking.

Wade later heard Willie Earl often say, 'When you know all you can do is talk, start working your mouth so that nobody gets in a word. But when talking ain't gon' do it, save your breath and use your head.' That was what he was doing then, because when the leader of the group took a long switchblade knife and started playing with it, touching the blade as though he saw it already disappearing into their guts, Willie's hand left Wade's arm and before anyone knew what was happening, he had brought the shoe-shine box down on the boy's head. The crack of bones sounded in the air and at the same time, Wade felt himself flying, his feet not even touching the ground.

The surprise attack upset the white boys, giving Willie and Wade a good head start. They had almost reached the subway when two of the bigger ones caught up with them – and the fight was on.

A policeman broke it up and took them down the steps into the station, paid their fares and said, 'Look, this part of town ain't no place for you little niggers. Stay uptown where you belong because the next time I catch you guys around here, I'll run you in myself.'

Wade remembered looking at this giant of a man with his big pistol bulging at his hip, and promised himself and Mumma on the spot that he would never go around where white folks were again. He had never been so afraid, not before, not since.

1966

Christina Stead

———

Christina Stead was born in Sydney, Australia in 1902, and trained as a teacher before leaving for Europe in 1928. After spending time in Paris, London and Spain, she moved to the USA at the outbreak of the Second World War with her husband William Blake. She worked for a time for MGM in Hollywood and then taught writing at New York University.

Stead's first book *The Salzburg Tales*, a modern *Decameron*, was published in 1934. This was followed by eleven novels, among which the most acclaimed today are *The Man Who Loved Children* (1940) and *For Love Alone* (1944). In 1947 Stead returned to England, and in 1974 to Australia. She died in 1983.

Cotter's England tells the story of Nellie Cook (née Cotter) who leaves behind her Tyneside roots to pursue life as a socialist journalist in postwar London. When Nellie's husband finds a job abroad, she accuses him of abandoning his country and his principles.

Virago published *Cotter's England* in 1980.

from

Cotters' England

'Mr George Cook, late of the working class,' said Nellie. 'Aye, he's a typical old socialist, trying to be glorious at the expense of the workers. I despise you, George Cook: the back of me hand to you. Did you struggle your way up from the docks of Tyneside for this pitiful glass of brandy?'

'I did,' cried George. 'A worker's a figment to you, Nellie; it's a schoolgirl dream. It's a vague, dirty, hungering man, weak and a failure: someone for you to mother and maunder over. You're just a plain Fleet Street sobsister.'

'That's a bloody lie, you bastard,' cried Nellie, springing up, 'I won't sit at the table with you; you're on the way over to the other side.'

George bellowed with laughter. 'But you sit at table with every ex-IRA sellout, who'll hand you a dishful of workman romance. Ah, the British sods, the murderers of the Irish people: what can ye do? Ye must write tripe to fill your unworthy belly and ye must write the tripe they want, the poor beggarly Sassenachs living on king and country, for they know no better. I'm no traitor, I'm just an Englishman who wants to represent his country abroad. In the old days it was the young lords and the promising young scholars and now it's the worker from Blaydon way.'

'Why, Nellie, must we shoot the bolts on our own jail-door? He's right. The rich still go abroad: it's only the poor that stay. It's a class law,' said Bob, looking pinpoints at Nellie through her pebbles.

'Ah, don't flatter the sod,' cried Nellie: 'ye can't give him enough: he'll be hungry for more, whatever ye say. It's a fine figure, the self-elected Atlas holding up England abroad. It's not for the wine then you're going? It's for your principles, ye sod? It's a damn disgrace. Deserting your country for the sake of a meal.'

'Why doesn't my country offer me a square meal?' said George angrily. 'I'm a big man, I'm not a half-starved sparrow. I've worked all my life: I've fought for my class. It's a rule in demonstrations that after you've got in some good hits, you step aside or get off to some other area, you don't waste yourself: you keep yourself so you're there next time.'

'I'd a damned sight rather waste myself than make a show of myself as a runaway.' But Nellie couldn't find words bad enough to characterise this excuse.

Bob said it was a time when not only individuals but masses of people were driven from their countries or sought refuge for their own sakes in other countries: there seemed to be no end to it, then.

But Nellie repeated that George was hauling down the flag, betraying his class and turning his back on his life of struggle.

'If all Englishmen had stayed home, true to their dear sod,' George said with irony, 'I should like to know where the Empire would have come from, that's kept us in sugar and tea? We don't grow it ourselves, that I know of.'

'You're avoiding the personal point with your grand comparisons,' said Nellie.

'And you're trying to drag everything down to the personal plane like you,' shouted George. George was angry. 'And you're helping them. You're helping your lords and masters by talking a lot of frill about patriotism. Whose country is it? Whose pound sterling is it? Whose indebtedness is it? Whose empire is it? Whose revenues are they? Am I going to lose my eyes and hair and get to be like your Uncle Sime, old scrap nobody wants, and everyone spits on, to save their England? Or to save Cotters' England?'

'What do you mean by Cotters' England?' she cried out. 'What's wrong with my England?'

'The England of the depressed that starved you all to wraiths, gave Eliza TB, sent your sister into the Home, got your old mother into bed with malnutrition, and is trying it on with me, too, getting at my health. I never had an ache or pain in my life: I beat their England. I lived through the unemployment, the starvation, the war, I knocked out a few bloody eyes and I got me fists skinned a few times, that's all I ever got: and now I'm going to live for my country. You stay here and die in it. Don't you want to change it? Or is it only the beer-soaked sawdust of bohemia you love? The dirt and sweat of the tear-stained bachelor's bedroom; Bridgehead in all its glory? You don't know what you're fighting for. To change Cotters' England. Wasn't that what drove you on? Or just ragged rebellion?'

1967

Angela Carter

Angela Carter was born in Eastbourne, Sussex, in 1940. She worked as a journalist before reading English at Bristol University. From 1976 to 1978 she taught creative writing at Sheffield University, and later, 1980–81, was visiting professor of creative writing at Brown University in the USA. She lived in Japan, the USA and Australia but for most of her life in London, a city she riotously critiqued in her last novel, *Wise Children* (1991).

Her first novel, *Shadow Dance*, was published in 1965, followed by *The Magic Toyshop*, which won the John Llewellyn Rhys Prize, heralding the start of a spectacular and ground-breaking career: seven more novels, three volumes of short stories, several film scripts, radio plays, a vast amount of journalism and theatre work. She died in 1992.

The Magic Toyshop was published by Virago in 1981.

from

The Magic Toyshop

The summer she was fifteen, Melanie discovered she was made of flesh and blood. O, my America, my new found land. She embarked on a tranced voyage, exploring the whole of herself, clambering her own mountain ranges, penetrating the moist richness of her secret valleys, a physiological Cortez, da Gama or Mungo Park. For hours she stared at herself, naked, in the mirror of her wardrobe; she would follow with her finger the elegant structure of her rib-cage, where the heart fluttered under the flesh like a bird under a blanket, and she would draw down the long line from breast-bone to navel (which was a mysterious cavern or grotto), and she would rasp her palms against her bud-wing shoulderblades. And then she would writhe about, clasping herself, laughing, sometimes doing cartwheels and handstands out of sheer exhilaration at the supple surprise of herself now she was no longer a little girl.

She also posed in attitudes, holding things. Pre-Raphaelite, she combed out her long, black hair to stream straight down from a centre parting and thoughtfully regarded herself as she held a tiger-lily from the garden under her chin, her knees pressed close together. A la Toulouse Lautrec, she dragged her hair sluttishly across her face and sat down in a chair with her legs apart and a bowl of water and a towel at her feet. She always felt particularly wicked when she posed for Lautrec, although she made up fantasies in which she lived in his time (she had been a chorus girl or a model and fed a sparrow with crumbs from her Paris attic window). In these fantasies, she helped him and loved him because she was sorry for him, since he was a dwarf and a genius.

She was too thin for a Titian or a Renoir but she contrived a pale, smug Cranach Venus with a bit of net curtain wound round her head and the necklace of cultured pearls they gave her when she was confirmed at her throat. After she read *Lady Chatterley's Lover*, she secretly picked forget-me-nots and stuck them in her pubic hair.

Further, she used the net curtain as raw material for a series of nightgowns suitable for her wedding night which she designed upon herself. She gift-wrapped herself for a phantom bridegroom taking a shower and cleaning his teeth in an extra-dimensional bathroom-of-the-future in honeymoon Cannes. Or Venice. Or Miami Beach. She conjured him so intensely to leap the spacetime barrier between them that she could almost feel his breath on her cheek and his voice husking 'darling'.

In readiness for him, she revealed a long, marbly white leg up to the thigh (forgetting the fantasy in sudden absorption in the mirrored play of muscle as she flexed her leg again and again); then, pulling the net tight, she examined the swathed shape of her small, hard breasts. Their size disappointed her but she supposed they would do.

All this went on behind a locked door in her pastel, innocent bedroom, with Edward Bear (swollen stomach concealing striped pyjamas) beadily regarding her from the pillow and *Lorna Doone* splayed out face down in the dust under the bed. This is what Melanie did the summer she was fifteen, besides helping with the washing-up and watching her little sister to see she did not kill herself at play in the garden.

Mrs Rundle thought Melanie was studying in her room. She said Melanie ought to get out more into the fresh air and would grow peaked. Melanie said she got plenty of fresh air when she ran errands for Mrs Rundle and, besides, she studied with her window open. Mrs Rundle was content when she heard this and said no more.

Mrs Rundle was fat, old and ugly and had never, in fact, been married. She adopted the married form by deed poll on her fiftieth birthday as her present to herself. She thought 'Mrs' gave a woman a touch of personal dignity as she grew older. Besides, she had always wanted to be married. In old age, memory and imagination merge; Mrs Rundle's mental demarcations were already beginning to blur. She would sit, sometimes, in her warm fireside chair, at the private time when the children were all in bed, dreamily inventing the habits and behaviour of the husband she had never enjoyed until his very face formed wispily in the steam from her bed-time cup of tea and she greeted him familiarly.

She had hairy moles and immense false teeth. She spoke with an old-world, never-never land stateliness, like a duchess in a Whitehall farce. She was the housekeeper. She had brought her cat with her; she was very much at home. She looked after Melanie, Jonathon and Victoria while Mummy and Daddy were in America. Mummy was keeping Daddy company. Daddy was on a lecture tour.

'A lecher tour!' crowed Victoria, who was five, beating her spoon upon the table.

'Eat up your bread pudding, dear,' said Mrs Rundle. They ate a lot of bread pudding under Mrs Rundle's régime. She did bread pudding plain and fancy, with or without currants or sultanas or both; and she performed a number of variations on the basic bread-pudding recipe, utilising marmalade, dates, figs, blackcurrant jam and stewed apples. She showed extraordinary virtuosity. Sometimes they had it cold, for tea.

Melanie grew to fear the bread pudding. She was afraid that if she ate too much of it she would grow fat and nobody would ever love her and she would die virgin.

1968

Joyce Carol Oates

Joyce Carol Oates was born in 1938 in Millersport, New York, and was educated at Syracuse University. She graduated first in her class in 1960, and in 1961 completed an MA in English at the University of Wisconsin. She later gave up work on a PhD to write full-time, and started on a career in which to date she has written nearly a hundred books – poetry, short stories, novels, cultural commentary, literary criticism and drama. She said in 1972 that she has 'a laughably Balzacian ambition to get the whole world into a book'; the scope of her vision makes her one of the finest contemporary commentators on American culture, particularly on the harsh, unsentimental side of the American dream. She is the Roger S. Berlind Distinguished Professor at Princeton University.

Expensive People was reissued by Virago in 1998.

from

Expensive People

I was a child murderer.

I don't mean child-murderer, though that's an idea. I mean child murderer, that is, a murderer who happens to be a child, or a child who happens to be a murderer. You can take your choice. When Aristotle notes that man is a rational animal one strains forward, cupping his ear, to hear which of those words is emphasised – *rational* animal, rational *animal*? Which am I? *Child* murderer, child *murderer*? It took me years to start writing this memoir, but now that I'm started, now that those ugly words are typed out, I could keep on typing forever. A kind of quiet, blubbering hysteria has set in. You would be surprised, normal as you are, to learn how many years, how many months, and how many awful minutes it has taken me just to type that first line, which you read in less than a second: I was a child murderer.

You think it's easy?

Let me explain the second line. Child-murderer is an 'idea'. I am writing this memoir in a rented room, ignoble enough and smelling of garbage, and outside in the street children are playing. Normal, like you and everyone who chances upon these sweaty words of mine, the children are making noise. Normal people always make noise. So it crosses my desperate, corrupt, cobwebbed mind, my flabby, cringing mind, that those noises could be silenced in the way I once silenced someone else. Already you are struggling and tugging with your distaste, eh? You're tempted to glance at the back of this book to see if the last chapter is a prison scene and a priest visits me and I either stoically refuse him or embrace his knees manfully. Yes, you are thinking of doing that. So I might as well tell you that my memoir will not end in any such convenient way; it isn't well rounded or hemmed in by fate in the shape of novelistic architecture. It certainly isn't well planned. It has no conclusion but just dribbles off, in much the same way it begins. This is life. My memoir is not a confession and it is not fiction to make money; it is simply . . . I am not sure what it is. Until I write it all out I won't even know what I think about it.

Look at my hands tremble! I am not well. I weigh two hundred and fifty pounds and I am not well, and if I told you how old I am you would turn away with a look of revulsion. How old am I? Did I stop growing on that day when 'it' happened, note the shrewd passivity of that phrase, as if I hadn't made 'it' happen myself, or did I maybe freeze into what I was, and outside of that shell layers and layers of fat began to form? Writing this is such hard work that I have to stop and wipe myself with a large handkerchief. I sweat all over. And those children outside my window! I think they are unkillable anyway. Life keeps on, getting noisier and noisier as I get quieter and quieter, and all these normal, noisy, healthy people around me keep pressing in, mouths full of laughing teeth and biceps charmingly bulging. At the second in which the slick lining of my stomach finally bursts, some creature next door will turn her radio from Bill Sharpe's 'Weather Round-Up' to Guy Prince's 'Top-ten Jamboree'.

This memoir is a hatchet to slash through my own heavy flesh and through the flesh of anyone else who happens to get in the way.

One thing I want to do, my readers, is to minimise the tension between writer and reader. Yes, there is tension. You think I am trying to put something over on you, but that isn't true. It isn't true. I am honest and dogged and eventually the truth will be told; it will just take time because I want to make sure everything gets in. I realise my sentences are slack and flabby and composed of too many small words – I'll see if I can't fix that. And you are impatient because I can't seem to get started telling this story in any normal way (I don't mean to be ironic so much, irony is an unpleasant character trait), and you would like to know, whimsically enough, whether I am in a mental institution now or crazy in some less official setting, whether I am repentant (a tongueless monk, maybe), whether much gore will be splattered throughout these pages, many violent encounters between male and female, and whether after these extravaganzas I am justly punished. Just punishment after illicit extravaganzas is usually served up for the benefit of the reader, who feels better. But, you see, this is not fiction. This is life. My problem is that I don't know what I am doing. I lived all this mess but I don't know what it is. I don't even know what I mean by 'it'. I have a story to tell, yes, and no one else could tell it but me, but if I tell it now and not next year it will come out one way, and if I could have forced my fat, heaving body to begin this a year ago, it would have been a different story then. And it's possible that I'm lying without knowing it. Or telling the truth in some weird, symbolic way without knowing it, so only a few psychoanalytic literary critics (there are no more than three thousand) will have access to the truth, what 'it' is.

So there is tension, all right, because I couldn't begin the story by stating: *One morning in January a yellow Cadillac pulled up to a curb.* And I couldn't begin the story by stating: *He was an only child.* (Both these statements are quite sensible, by the way, though I could never talk about myself in the third person.)

And I couldn't begin the story by stating: *Elwood Everett met and wed Natashya Romanov when he was thirty-two and she was nineteen.* (Those are my parents! It took me some time to type out their names.)

And I couldn't begin the story with this pathetic flourish: *The closet door opened suddenly and there he stood, naked. He stared in at me and I stared out at him.* (And that also will come to pass, though I hadn't intended to mention it so soon.)

All these devices are fine and I offer them to any amateur writer who wants them, but for me they don't work because . . . I'm not sure why. It must be because the story I have to tell is my life, synonymous with my life, and no life begins anywhere. If you have to begin your life with a sentence, better make it a brave summing up and not anything coy: *I was a child murderer.*

My readers, don't fret, don't nibble at your nails: indeed I was punished. Indeed I am being punished. My misery is proof of God's existence – yes, I'll offer that to you as a special bonus! It will do your souls good to read of my suffering. You'll want to know when my crime took place, and where. And what do I look like, this fat degenerate, dripping sweat over his manuscript, and how the hell old am I anyway, and whom did I kill, and why, and what sense does it make?

1969

Mary Benson

Mary Benson was born in Pretoria, South Africa in 1919. She says she had the 'normal prejudiced attitudes of white South Africans' until she read Alan Paton's *Cry, the Beloved Country* in 1948. She has since studied, lobbied, written and lectured about her country, testifying before the United Nations on apartheid and human rights between 1963 and 1970. While reporting on political trials she was put under house arrest and banned from all writing. She left South Africa in 1966.

She has written historical and political works, radio drama and the novel *At the Still Point*. She lives in London.

At the Still Point was reissued by Virago in 1988.

from

At the Still Point

In Auschwitz, Sonderkommando No. 12 were the only Jews who fought back against their torturers, against the murderers of all the previous Sonderkommandos. By fighting back they *used* their deaths. No waste. 853 deaths that meant something. Useful deaths. Against how many millions that were meaningless? The lemmings. The millions who went like lemmings to be gassed. Why? Because '*Business as usual*' was their mentality. (Nyiszli paperback)

'The persecution of the Jews was aggravated, slow step by slow step, when no violent fighting back occurred.' (Bettelheim)

Must not happen again! Jewish acceptance of degradation maybe gave the SS the idea Jews would go meekly to the gas chambers.

Resignation is peculiar to our race, that creature, that Jewish doctor, Nyiszli, says. No No No!

The torturer needs to create guilt in the prisoner. Jews willing. The guilty tribe?

From what experience did our forefathers pray: 'Thou hast chosen us from all peoples, Thou hast loved us and taken pleasure in us'? From what dark well of self-deceiving did we accept that we were 'chosen', thence that our guilt was the heavier?

How many innocents walked naked into the gas chambers, comforting themselves with: 'We have committed abomination, we have gone astray.' My God, religion corrupts! Innocence corrupts!

We scapegoats bring upon us anti-Semitism by our very abjectness.

Israel is not the answer, but to find self-respect wherever we may be. To insist, but not assert. To say No!

Ghastly story that man told at that awful party, of the Jew who owned a big hardware store who said to him, 'Isn't it the most wonderful thing, the local golf club *invited* me to apply for membership?' And this man replied, 'No, you've earned it. Through your humanity.' And telling me how the Jew had tears in his eyes!

Ghastly party. Why do I go? Always the same.

It is for the Sonderkommando that I must act. How they inspire! It is unthinkable that they should not have existed. This world would be out of the question, utterly intolerable, had there only been the SS and creatures like Nyiszli . . . Jesus! when they drove, with guns and dogs, 'a living chain' of naked men and women – and children, dear God – into the great ditches filled with fire. Five to six thousand a day. And Nyiszli says he agrees with Mengele: after the pyres the crematorium is 'a place where one could live in a pretty decent way'.

Why do I often feel like a cur, anticipating being kicked?

Today is March 21. Sharpeville Day. And it is Bach's birthday. Sharpeville . . . Jesus! that photograph of them still laughing as they are shot in the back, shot dead . . . after they have made their protests against the pass laws. Men and women and children. 'Have mercy upon me, my bones are consumed.' ''Tis your hour now, ye dread powers of darkness.' St. Matthew Passion says it all.

How to be efficient? I'm such a muddle. Not good enough to mean well. Even passion is not enough. Discipline!

Sorel wanted the ashes stirred to make flames leap. To be alive, only alive, alive unto the end. (Pasternak) That's my desire. Because I'm *not* alive. Is suffering proof of life? How can you measure suffering unless you've experienced bliss?

To see people happy. That is beautiful. That young couple watching the squirrels in the Gardens. How I want people to be happy, to feel for each other.

Johannesburg. Staying with Helen, horrid experience – walking from Parkview bus after sunset, African tried to grab my bag and I felt something sharp prod my spine, thought – this is it! – when people suddenly came out of a gate and he just vanished. Nightmare thought – tsotsis kill and cripple more and more thousands in townships. Will the struggle ultimately be between anarchistic black gangsters and white neo-Nazis?

Today I was waiting for the bus in town, a barefoot shriveled kid was begging, hands cupped together in customary manner. I gave something to him and got on bus. As we drove off saw two hefty men get hold of him, cursing and hitting him with their fists and no one protesting and I unable to move as we speeded away. More dreadful than wild beasts. What is to be done . . .

Camus: 'If we are to fail, it is better in any case to have stood on the side of those who choose life than on the side of those who are destroying.' And – 'We think we are dying of grief and yet life wins out.' We must do what is necessary 'so that life for all will again be possible with all'.

Aim of rebellion is to transform. How to rebel without becoming destructive? *The* question: how to cease to be victims without becoming executioners?

Self-respect. To the rebel this matters more than life.

Freedom. Justice. How I've accepted these without thought and only now see them to be clichéd slogans. A balance between them, the only reasonable aspiration?

Mystic virtue of 'the people' – can there be virtue simply in being oppressed, poor? Can it be true that 'victims' quickly become a bore? Surely not.

Mother would say, 'You should find yourself a nice boy, then you could make a nice home.' Poor Mother. She would despair if she knew! As if I was not awkward enough before. People are daring, generous, to embark on relationships. I wear armour. Yet marriage can be so beautiful. Alan and Jill just after the twins born – the family made a full circle. But hard for a woman, the man's passion for his work. I would be jealous, would want to be in his work as well as in his home. Is that greedy? Possessive? Besides, look how Jill is no longer political!

Louis Trichardt case: white farmer who beat black labourer to death. The 'labourer'? Twelve years old, weight a hundred pounds. The farmer, sentenced to five years. 2,000 neighbouring farmers promptly petition for his release, express distress at the suffering *his* family must endure if he is jailed!

'If today Negroes in Africa march against the guns of a police that defends apartheid – even if hundreds of them will be shot down and tens of thousands

rounded up in concentration camps – their march, their fight will sooner or later assure them of a chance of liberty and equality.' (Bettelheim, Foreword, page 12)

Danger collective. Responsibility individual. We must use what tools we have – what tools we are – we can not, must not, sit by in apathy. Indifference equals support of Verwoerd and Vorster. Apathy led to the Nazis' gas chambers. To be indifferent is to condone. Worse! It is to collaborate. What is the moral distinction between the doctor who cut up his fellow Jews, who dissected two-year-old twins, *knowing* they'd been killed specially, knowing knowing KNOWING, and Hitler and the SS who ordered the experiments? Where draw the line between Jews here who gave a gold medal to the Prime Minister, and the farmer who beats a labourer to death? Between Verwoerd and the English-speaking businessmen who whitewash apartheid? Business as usual!

At long last – to act! Against cruelty, against injustice, against Master Race bigotry. Knowing there will be no harm to any human being. To act! Fear, yet – what? Exaltation? The putting away of self-consideration. Becoming part of all those others.

The sole object of revolution is the abolition of senseless suffering. Do all revolutions inevitably increase suffering at first?

Dostoievsky's *The Possessed* – is this what we resemble?

Alas, *here* what are we? Show-offs? Yet where else find *action*?

1970s

1970

Louise Meriwether

———

Louise Meriwether was born in 1923 in Haverstraw, New York. She studied for a BA in English at New York University and received an MA in journalism from UCLA in 1965. She went to work as a free-lance writer, a faculty member at Sarah Lawrence College, New York, and as black story analyst at Universal Studios. In the early sixties she began to publish sketches of important African-American figures; her short stories were published later that decade. *Daddy Was a Number Runner* was published in 1970 and her second novel, *Fragments of the Ark*, was published in 1994. In the twenty-four years between them, Meriwether often favoured political activism over writing time, most famously founding the Black Anti-Defamation Association to prevent the filming of William Styron's controversial novel *The Confessions of Nat Turner*. She has also written extensively for children, working against what she sees as 'the deliberate omission of Blacks from American history'. She lives in the Bronx, New York.

Daddy Was a Number Runner was first published in the UK by Virago in 1997.

from

Daddy Was a Number Runner

'All I'm trying to do is hit a big one again,' Daddy said. 'Those two-cent hits of yours ain't gonna make it. Nine thirty-six almost played today and I had two dollars on it. Lord, how I prayed that last figure would be a six and out pops another damned nine. We almost had us twelve hundred dollars, baby. That's all I'm trying to do. Hit us a big one.'

'We can't wait until you hit a big one,' Mother said, her voice cracking. She took a big breath and spoke quickly as if she had memorised the words. 'I went to the relief place yesterday and put in an application. The social worker will be here Monday to talk to you.'

Daddy jumped to his feet with surprising speed. The muscles in his neck bunched up and he opened his mouth but no words came. He looked like he was strangling.

Mother winced as if the sight of him hurt her. 'Your pride won't feed these children,' she said quietly.

Oh, Lord, I thought, as Daddy raised his hand, he's going to hit her, something he'd never done before. But he snatched up my cup instead and hurled it with all his might against the wall. It exploded into bits as he roared:

'I'm a motherfucking man. Why can't you understand that?'

I whimpered, but Mother didn't move. Then Daddy was gone, the front door slamming shut behind him.

The walls of the room were falling down on me. I had to get out of there. I jumped up and ran toward the door. Sterling came out of his room, and as I stumbled down the stairs I heard him yelling at me to come back.

I didn't stop running until I reached 115th Street and only then because I was out of breath. I was surprised to discover that my face was wet with tears.

At 114th Street a street speaker, standing on top of a ladder with a small American flag stuck in one rung, was jabbering away at a small crowd in front of him. He was West Indian, black and runty, his face purple with sweat.

'God made you black and he didn't make a mistake,' the speaker shouted. 'That's what Marcus Garvey said and times haven't changed. We still need a country of our own. Black people should not be encouraged to remain in the white man's land. Do you want to be a slave forever?' He glared at the crowd which stared back at him with indifference.

I moved on. These street speakers, mostly West Indians, were crazy, I thought. Who wanted to go back to Africa? Didn't we have enough trouble right here? A mounted policeman rode up and yelled at the crowd to break it up.

The next block was jammed with Puerto Ricans babbling away in Spanish, just like it was high noon instead of midnight. It was depressing, like stepping into another world and not knowing what anybody was talking about.

I walked to 110th Street and looked across Central Park at the lights twinkling in the skyscrapers. That was another world, too, all those lights way over there and this spooky park standing between us. But what good would those lights do me anyway? I bet they didn't even allow coloured in those big buildings.

I turned around and started for home, creeping along, 'cause I didn't care if I never got there. I had been searching for him all the time, in every black and brown face, not really knowing I had been looking. Daddy, Daddy. Where are you? And when I got home, I knew he wouldn't be there either.

He wasn't.

1971

Maureen Duffy

Maureen Duffy was born in Worthing, Sussex, in 1933 and took a degree in English at King's College, London, in 1956. She was writing poetry and plays before leaving university, and after a brief spell working as a schoolteacher she published her first novel, *That's How It Was* (1962), which won her immediate acclaim. Since then she has published many novels, including *The Microcosm* (1966), *Gor Saga* (1982), *The Change* (1987), *Illuminations* (1991), *Occam's Razor* (1993) and most recently *Restitution* (1998), four books of poetry, a biography of Aphra Behn, a social history, an animal-rights handbook and several plays, including the trilogy *Rites, Solo* and *Olde Tyme*.

Love Child was published by Virago in 1994 as part of the Lesbian Landmarks series.

from

Love Child

'Perhaps we should go too,' said my mother. 'You must be tired, darling.' Slowly we climbed the hill. I said goodnight and went upstairs. On the landing I waited by the window. Very shortly my mother and Ajax appeared as faintly luminous shapes below. I heard the car start. Then I crept down the stairs into the kitchen. My father's and Renata's voices came from the other room. I closed the kitchen window but left it unfastened and then went through the front door into the cover of the night. With Gennaro's ladder about my body outside my shirt I worked quickly along my route, occasionally flicking on my torch. A little wind moved the foliage. A shape loomed suddenly but it was only a tall cactus I'd forgotten from daytime. As I climbed, my chest began its familiar choking clench so that at the honeysuckle I had to stop and gasp in the sweet air. Gerry must be still down in the bar. Was that a light behind Ajax' shutters? I counted balconies.

Avoiding the light spilling out of the hotel entrance I got to the side between the thin columns. The first time I threw up the grappling hook it fell back without touching the balcony, straight down like a tennis ball tossed for service. I managed to catch it before it clanged to the ground, paused a minute, feeling a feather tickle of damp blow over my body, and threw again, wishing for Gennaro's expertise. It caught with, to my ears, a huge clatter but although I waited, counting under my breath for two minutes, quite still, no one appeared. I'd been supremely lucky. Only the cognac had given me strength and courage to get the hook over the balcony at all I was quite sure. I tested it with a strong pull but I was sure Gennaro would have made it able to take more than his weight and I was even lighter.

I managed to haul myself up to the bottom rung and then I was up and over the top, drawing the ladder up behind me. The catch of the French door I opened with my penknife. I was inside at last.

There wasn't any reason that I could see for not putting on the light. As I'd climbed I'd been aware of a faint radiance through Ajax' shutters like a distant galaxy you haven't time to examine. When the room was lit I practised deep breathing to steady myself and as soon as my hands no longer trembled I took out the periscope and went into the bathroom.

Ajax I couldn't see at first but my mother lay quite naked on the bed in my vision. I had often seen her naked before, since my father like most Scandinavians believes in family exposure, in the natural-ness of nudity. He is quite wrong. There's nothing natural about a naked human being. Millennia ago in our civilised and artificial way we assumed clothing and our own covering moulted away. An animal is never naked. Even the pig and the elephant are hidebound, cam-ouflaged, bristled. Man wears clothes as naturally as he speaks so that as a superlatively artificial and artful act he can take them off and catch the breath with his vulnerable beauty that painters have always perceived. Flesh is made not by God but by man and enhanced by beautiful gestures and attitudes into the art of love. I can say this now; I have seen it. My mother lay on the damask quilt in the dark, like that precious stone the alchemists prized, with the soft green and yellow fire from the black tarry heart of a nugget of coal. I had seen her walking about and admired in a domestic way the flow of limbs, the polished penetrability of skin, without understanding. This was quite different. Now as if I had shaken a kaleidoscope Ajax moved into the picture so that it became unfallen Adam and Eve, Eros and Psyche. My mother lifted her arms and her lover went into them to be entwined there. I saw the strong tensing of carved marble muscles as the knee thrust to part her thighs.

1972

Penelope Gilliatt

———

Penelope Gilliatt was born in London in 1932, grew up in Northumberland and was educated at Queen's College, London, and Bennington College, USA. She was known primarily as film critic for the *New Yorker*, which she worked for from 1967, and also film and theatre critic for the *Observer*. She published novels, short stories, drama, and wrote extensively on film, publishing books about Renoir and Tati. In 1971 she wrote the award-winning screenplay for the film *Sunday, Bloody Sunday*. She died, following a long illness, in 1993.

The extract is from the title story of *Nobody's Business*, which was reissued by Virago in 1990.

from

'Nobody's Business'

A big man with a municipal face was swimming toward Edward and Emily Prendergast across the glassy Mediterranean.

'Morning!' he shouted to Sir Edward, who is a judge. A tall, skinny man, with a soft voice that sometimes strikes the court as coming from behind his left ear. He has been married to Emily for nearly forty years. Emily is a woman of obscure stylishness who gardens, carpenters, reads science fiction, bottles fruit and pickles according to Elizabethan family recipes, and writes the most popular low comedies of the century. They are done weekly on the radio in the lunch hour, and people listen to them in factories by the million.

The big man splashed up to Edward and held his hand out of the water cordially, bobbing up and down.

'How do you do?' Edward said, turning his august profile with a politeness that Emily didn't believe necessarily to be lasting.

'Long time no see,' said the big man.

'Have we met?' said Edward.

There he goes, Emily thought gaily.

'In the BBC canteen,' the big man said. 'You came to pick up your lady wife one day after a rehearsal. You won't remember. Long ago. I was the producer.'

Two striking bodies were swimming after the big man, lifting themselves rhythmically out of the water with the butterfly stroke. Magnificent tanned shoulders consecutively emerged. One pair male, one female, probably, Emily thought.

'I don't believe you know Maximilian Keller,' the big man said, making introduction gestures awkwardly a few inches above the surface of the sea, 'and Jo-Ann Sills. Maximilian is from the University of Basel and Jo-Ann is from the University of California at Los Angeles.'

'I'm the archivist who bothered you last April, and I wondered if you'd had any second thoughts,' Jo-Ann said to Edward. Her long hair spread out in the water around her.

'Second thoughts about what?' said Edward.

'About letting us have your papers for the Sir Edward Prendergast Collection and the Lady Prendergast Collection – the *Emily Firle* Collection.'

'The only papers we seem to keep are bills, and they're for the accountant,' Emily said.

'But you must have kept your manuscripts,' the beautiful girl said, and turned her head to Edward in the sea. 'Your office surely must have kept your briefs over the years.'

Emily stayed quiet, treading water and wondering where the others' breath for talking came from.

'And what about your memorabilia?' said Jo-Ann.

'*Is* there an Edward Prendergast Collection?' said Edward. '*What* Lady Prendergast Collection? What the hell are memorabilia?'

'"Emily Firle," I said,' Jo-Ann answered, in a voice of quartz.

'Don't ignore Women's Liberation,' Emily said privately to Edward.

He made one of his expostulatory noises, seldom employed but powerful, and looked at her carefully from ten feet away in the water, lifting his spectacles to the bridge of his nose and then having to peer under them because they were crusted with salt, raising his head rather merrily, like a sea lion balancing a ball on its snout. 'Are you all right?' he said, moving round so that he had his back to the others.

'Bored,' she said softly.

'What's the big man's name?' he said in his lowest voice.

'I don't know.' It was someone she had been to bed with. Long ago. Nothing. But indecent to forget. She made an effort: 'David Willoughby, I think.'

'Maximilian and Jo-Ann wrote a joint thesis about you both,' Willoughby said loudly.

Emily had turned onto her back to save her strength and was staring at the sun.

'About us?' she said, turning upright again to go on treading water.

The talk in the sea lasted for another half an hour. Maximilian said grimly that his special interest was humour, and Jo-Ann said that her topic in the thesis had been the theme of male chauvinism in Edward's published legal opinions.

'What do you think of Women's Lib?' she said to Emily.

'I should think it's quite right, probably. Is anyone else tired?'

"Probably?" I hear doubt here,' Maximilian said, raising a finger astutely out of the water.

'Shall we go in?' Emily said.

'Doubt, when you're generally so decided? Crisp? In your dialogue?' Maximilian said with disappointment.

'Doubt is the courtesy of the intellect,' Edward said, sounding irritable and throwing his voice like a cat.

'And that seems to me a very uncharacteristic thing for *you* to say,' Willoughby said firmly. He lifted his hand out of the water to smooth his hair. Emily tried to remember if she had ever known in the days of seeing him that he was such a strong swimmer, but nothing much came back.

At the same time she said, exhausted, 'Not really uncharacteristic. If it weren't that a judge has to decide a case, quite a few of Edward's legal opinions would probably end in a question mark.'

Maximilian drew out a plastic notebook from underwater with his left hand and started to make a note in it with his right, using a gadget pencil with his name on it in gold.

Emily only then took in that the others were not swimming at all but standing on the bottom, and that the reason she was worn out from treading water was that she was a good eight or twelve inches shorter than the rest. It made her laugh, and she sank. She had not had a violent case of laughing for years. She came up once and tried to get out a cry for help to the others standing there, but the laughing gripped her lungs and they thought she was fooling. She choked and spat out some seawater and then swallowed a lungful as she went into a spasm again. She sank slowly to the bottom and opened her eyes and saw the legs of the four underwater. One pair Californian legs, one pair Swiss legs, one pair forgotten legs, one pair Edward's legs. My finishing-school clothes list: One pair plimsolls, one pair best silk stockings, one Liberty bodice, amen, we give Thee most humble and hearty thanks, we Thine unworthy servants. Damn. I can remember everything. Life up to its old clichés again. I suppose it means I'm drowning. The three of them are presiding over us like a tribunal. She lost track.

Her husband, seventy-four, was the one who fished her out.

Willoughby helped. The hale and hearty young archivists stood by, worried that she might die – worried partly because of the venerable old man's fever that she shouldn't; and partly because of professional affront at the possibility of all that memorabilia going west.

1973

Ivy Litvinov

Ivy Litvinov was born in London in 1889. She attended Maida Vale High School and in 1905, aged sixteen, she contributed the first of many articles to the *Manchester Guardian*. While working at the Prudential insurance company, she published her first novel, *Growing Pains* (1913), followed by *The Questing Beast* (1914). A few weeks after the outbreak of the First World War she met and fell in love with the influential Bolshevik revolutionary Maxim Litvinov, a close associate of Lenin. They married in 1916, had two children and went to live in Moscow, where Litvinov worked as a translator and wrote a novel, *His Master's Voice* (1930). They briefly lived in Washington, DC, when her husband was appointed ambassador but, victims of a typical Stalinist purge, they returned to Moscow, where Maxim died six years later.

Ivy Litvinov stayed in Moscow, translating and working on the hybrid of fiction and autobiography she called her 'Sorterbiography'. She eventually returned to the UK and continued to write the short stories which were collected in *She Knew She Was Right* (1971). She died in 1977.

The story 'Pussy Cat, Pussy Cat, Where Have You Been?' was written in 1973 and was added posthumously to the collection when it was reissued by Virago in 1988.

from

'Pussy Cat, Pussy Cat, Where Have You Been?'

The reintroduction of a white pussy into the overwhelmingly tabby ranks of the Moscow cat population at once fulfilled and annulled Murochka's function in life. Reproduce she could not, being inherently incapable of communication with her kind, but she accepted saucers of warm milk, a share of the family dinner and a soft place to sleep as rightful dues earned by simply being a cat.

Elena Nikolaevna's life after her release was more complicated. She went back to the provincial medical institute she had graduated from and – with what painful effort and sacrifice – managed to gain a research scholarship after which, with more effort and more help, she struggled back to Moscow to a post on the staff of the Moscow Institute of Stomatology.

There she found short-lived happiness with a young colleague who died at the front, leaving her with a small daughter, an antiquated dental chair and the ageing Murochka. The daughter was away at nursery school all day and Murochka was no trouble at all, but the dental chair, imperturbably inanimate, had more profound involutions. It was both a boon and an incubus. It had helped Elena Nikolaevna through many a financial crisis – a private patient could always be counted on when need arose. On the other hand (there is always another hand), it was so cumbersome that all furniture and movement in the room were confined to a few feet from the walls. Still worse, it was a continual threat to Elena Nikolaevna's peace of mind. At any moment an ill-disposed neighbour in the communal flat might denounce her for not registering with the tax authorities. This was not very likely because everyone found it convenient to have a first-class dentist on the premises. But the craving for excitement and enforced idleness can be as effective as malice, and a certain disagreeable old woman stayed at home all day taking heart drops and poking her head out of her door every time she heard Elena Nikolaevna usher a patient through the hallway to her own room. Indeed, as often as not she answered the front door bell before Elena Nikolaevna had time to get there. But even the watchful and malevolent crone had a nephew with an impacted molar.

The chair occupied too much of Elena Nikolaevna's thoughts, and often in the watches of the night she decided to sell it. But patients, well-recommended and enjoined never to make appointments by telephone or send post-cards, were worth a ski-suit for the little Anyuta in winter, the price of a holiday by the sea in summer. So when a portly lady in an expensive fur coat murmured through the slit in the doorway, which was all that the fettered and slotted ball in its socket allowed for communication, that she came with a recom-mendation from a trusted friend, a bolt was drawn and the stranger was admitted by Elena Nikolaevna herself. Once in her own room with the door shut, Elena Nikolaevna listened with professional inter-est to a familiar tale of woe, and smiled compassionately when it ended with: 'I do hope you'll be able to help me. Dr Kaplan says you're always so careful not to give unnecessary pain.'

'I suppose all dentists are,' said Elena Nikolaevna briskly, and asked her visitor to seat herself in the chair.

With a glance of abject entreaty the patient lifted a foot in a fur-lined bootee to the step of the awful throne, only to draw it back with a little shriek at the sight of a cat curled up on the seat. A white cat with dark ears. 'Murochka!' she whispered and turned to face Elena Nikolaevna. 'Elena Nikolaevna, I knew you at once. At least I was almost sure it was you. But I saw you didn't recognise me, so I didn't say anything.' The moment her visitor had shown emotion at the sight of Murochka, Elena Nikolaevna recognised in the prosperous matron before her the odious Varvara Simyonovna, who now paled round heavily rouged lips and took a step backwards on the carpet. 'Surely you remember how I held Murochka in my blanket all the way to Moscow.'

'I remember everything,' said Elena Nikolaevna sternly. 'Get on the chair if you want me to look at your teeth. Get down, Murochka.' The old cat, offended, hoisted itself on all four paws to the arm-rest of the chair, jumped to the floor with a heavy thud and took refuge on the sofa.

From the moment of recognising Varvara Simyonovna, Elena Nikolaevna's mind had become a battle-field. She told herself that a trusty was always a trusty. She believed that nobody at her work or in the communal apartment knew she had been in a camp, and if Varvara Simyonovna chose to denounce her as a tax-evader it would come out, it would be sure to come out. Throughout the ten years since she had left the camp, Elena Nikolaevna had been struggling with this fear, and she still crossed the street to avoid being seen by the militiaman at the corner. And now fear suggested that it might be wiser to behave as if she had forgotten the past. During treatment Varvara Simyonovna would keep quiet, and the moment it was over, Elena Nikolaevna would sell the chair. 'Open your mouth a little wider, please,' she said, peering steadfastly into the inflamed gap in her enemy's gums. 'I see,' she said quietly. 'This may take three or four sittings. Can you come tomorrow at six?'

Varvara Simyonova agreed in humble, almost fawning tones. 'Why, you're a wizard!' she said. 'I hardly felt a thing.' As she picked her way out of the cluttered room, Murochka raised her head inquisitively, braced herself against the back of the sofa and stiffened her forelegs, yawning cavernously. Then she closed her teeth on the rosy grotto of her maw, the muscles of her limbs and tail relaxed, and Murochka was asleep on the sofa cushions before the front door slammed behind Varvara Simyonovna.

Years after, a colleague in the library where I worked recommended her dentist to me. 'She never hurts, she feels your pain before you do yourself, and she's wonderfully quick and conscientious. Mind you ask her to show you her cat. You never saw anything so extraordinary – pure white with tabby ears. She brought it from camp, only don't say anything about that. She thinks nobody knows, poor thing.'

1974

Margaret Laurence

Margaret Laurence was born in 1926 of Scots–Irish descent. She grew up in the small prairie town of Neepwa, Manitoba, Canada, which inspired her fictional town of Manawaka. In 1947 she graduated from United College (now Winnipeg University) and in the same year married John Laurence, a civil engineer, with whom she had two children. She travelled to Somaliland and Ghana, and in 1962 to the UK, where she wrote her Manawaka sequence: *The Stone Angel* (1964), *A Jest of God* (1966), *The Fire Dwellers* (1969), *A Bird in the House* (1970) and *The Diviners* (1974). In 1972 she was made a Companion of the Order of Canada, and in 1977 she became a Fellow of the Royal Society of Canada. She was twice given the Governor General's Award. Writer in residence for (and later Chancellor of) Trent University, Ontario, she also published children's fiction, a study of Nigerian writing and a volume of essays. She died in 1987.

The Diviners was reissued by Virago in 1989.

from

The Diviners

Morag gave up the battle to block her ears against the birds, and got up. The kitchen was cool and would remain so. The thick walls kept out the heat. She put her head outside the door. The river was still. No breeze. The trees across the river were reflected in the water so sharply you could imagine it was another world there, a tree-world in the water, willows and oak and maples, all growing there, climbed upon by river-children, and slithered finnily through by muskie and yellow perch. The day, she predicted, was going to be a scorcher.

Royland would be here in about an hour. Today was the day.

You wondered about people like the Cooper family, all those years ago. Trekking in here to take up their homestead. No roads. Bush. Hacking their way. Wagons and horses? Probably coming much of the way by river. Barges teetering and overloaded. Then the people clearing the first growth of timber. Shifting the rocks from fields, making stone walls to outline the land to be cultivated. The sheer unthinkable back-and-heart-breaking slog. Women working like horses. Also, probably pregnant most of the time. Baking bread in brick ovens, with a loaf in their own ovens. Looking after broods of children and kids. Terrible. Appalling.

Healthy life, though. No one died of lung cancer. Strong and fit, they were, tanned and competent. Pioneers oh pioneers.

But what about a burst appendix? Desperately ill kids? Fever? Women having breech births or other disorders of childbearing? The tiny cemetery on the hill contained, among other stones, the one to Simon Cooper's first wife.

> In Memory of Sarah Cooper
> Who Died In Childbirth
> June 20, 1880, Age 24.
>
> She Rests In The Lord.

Probably glad to rest anywhere, poor lady, even In The Lord. How many women went mad? Loneliness, isolation, strain, despair, over-work, fear. Out there, the bush. In here, a silent worried work-sodden man, squalling brats, an open fireplace, and would the shack catch fire this week or next? In winter, snow up to your thighs. Outdoor privy. People flopping through drifts to the barn to milk the cow. What fun. Healthy life indeed. A wonder they weren't all raving lunatics. Probably many were. It's the full of the moon, George – Mrs Cooper always howls like this at such a time – nothing to worry about – she'll be right as rain come the morning – c'mon there, Sarah, quit crouching in the corner and stop baring your fangs like that – George and me's hungry and would appreciate a spot of grub. *Onward, Christian Soldiers. Thy Way Not Mine O Lord However Dark It Be.*

The fact remained that they *had* hacked out a living here. They had survived. Like so-called Piper Gunn and the Sutherlanders further West. Was it better or worse now? Both. Both. At least *their* children did not wander to God knows where. Unknown destinies, far and probably lethal places. If any *did*, though, there were no telephones and the mail services could hardly have been very snappy. Well, then, *they* did not have to wrench up their guts and hearts etcetera and set these carefully down on paper, in order to live. Clever of them, one might say. Anyway, some of them did. Including women. Catharine Parr Traill, mid-1800s, botanist, drawing and naming wildflowers, writ-ing a guide for settlers with one hand, whilst rearing a brace of young and working like a galley slave with the other.

From the birch, a thousand useful utensils can be made.
A Few Hints On Gardening (including how to start an orchard, how to *start* it!)
How To Make: Cheap Family Cake
                Hot Tea-Cakes
                Indian-Meal Yorkshire Pudding
                Maple Vinegar
                Potted Fish
                Potash Soap

Rag Carpets
Candles
A Good Household Cheese
Cures For Ague and Dysentery

And so on. It did not bear thinking about. Morag, running her log house with admirable efficiency and a little help from the electric fridge, kettle, toaster, stove, iron, baseboard heaters, furnace, lights, not to mention the local supermarket and Ron Jewitt's friendly neighborhood taxi. Great God Almighty.

The song sparrow was tuning up in the small elm outside the window. Its song was unambiguous.

Pres-pres-pres-pres-Presbyterian!

Mrs Eula McCann from several miles away had dropped in with welcome raisin buns when Morag and Pique originally moved in, and had asked Morag if she had heard the bird which said that word. Morag, until that moment, had only heard it as a pleasant trill. Since that day, however, its message came across loud and clear.

Catharine Parr Traill, one could be quite certain, would not have been found of an early morning sitting over a fourth cup of coffee, mulling, approaching the day in gingerly fashion, trying to size it up. No. No such sloth for Catharine P.T.

Scene at the Traill Homestead, circa 1840

C.P.T. out of bed, fully awake, bare feet on the sliver-hazardous floorboards – no, take that one again. Feet on the homemade hooked rug. Breakfast cooked for the multitude. Out to feed the chickens, stopping briefly on the way back to pull fourteen armloads of weeds out of the vegetable garden and perhaps prune the odd apple tree in passing. The children's education hour, the umpteen little mites lisping enthusiastically over this enlightenment. Cleaning the house, baking two hundred loaves of delicious bread, preserving half a ton of plums, pears, cherries, etcetera. All before lunch.

Catharine Parr Traill, where are you now that we need you? Speak, oh lady of blessed memory.

Where the hell was Pique and why didn't she phone or write? If Pique were not carrying any form of identification (as was likely), how would anyone know who she was and be able to get in touch with

Morag if anything happened? Should Morag try to trace her? Pique
had been okay not too long ago. The phone message from Pique's
father had established that. But where was she now and why didn't she
simply *say*? Was this over-concern on Morag's part? No doubt. But still.
How could you stop yourself from worrying? The kid was eighteen.
Only. What had Catharine said, somewhere, about emergencies?

Morag loped over to the bookshelves which lined two walls of the
seldom-used livingroom. Found the pertinent text.

> In cases of emergency, it is folly to fold one's hands and sit down
> to bewail in abject terror. It is better to be up and doing.
> *(The Canadian Settlers' Guide*, 1855)

Morag: Thank you, Mrs Traill.
Catharine Parr Traill: That, my dear, was when we were at one time sur-
    rounded by forest fires which threatened the crops, fences, stock,
    stable, cabin, furniture and, of course, children. Your situation, if I
    may say so, can scarcely be termed comparable.
Morag: Well, uh no, I guess not. Hold on, though. *You* try having your
    only child disappear you know where, Mrs Traill. Also, with no
    strong or even feeble shoulder upon which to lean, on occasion.
    Okay, don't say it, lady. You'd go out and plant turnips, so at least
    you wouldn't starve during the winter. You'd pick blueberries or
    something. Start a jam factory. Make pemmican out of the sway-
    back which dropped dead of exhaustion on the Back Forty. Don't
    tell me. I know.

The knocking (only now noticed by Morag) at the kitchen door had
ceased and Royland had stepped inside. She knew from his step, slow
but not heavy, that it was him.

'First sign of going off your rocker, Morag, so they say.'

Embarrassed, she returned the book to its place and went back to
the kitchen.

'Don't you ever talk out loud to yourself, Royland?'

'Oh sure. It's when I start answering myself I get worried.'

Ha ha. The ancient joke.

1975

Leonora Carrington

Leonora Carrington was born in 1917, spent her childhood in a Lancashire mansion, and was educated at convent schools before going to Florence to be 'finished'. She was presented at court in 1936, after which her family gave in to her desire to paint, and she attended art school in London just as the first Surrealist exhibition came to the city. Inspired, she soon afterwards eloped with the painter Max Ernst, first to Paris and then to the south of France, where they both painted and Carrington started writing. She has continued painting and writing throughout her colourful life, as well as designing for the theatre. She now divides her time between Chicago and Mexico City.

A Seventh Horse and Other Tales was first published in the UK by Virago in 1989, and included 'A Mexican Fairy Tale'.

'A Mexican Fairy Tale'

Once there lived a boy in a place called San Juan. His name was Juan, his job was looking after pigs.

Juan never went to school, none of his family had ever been to school because where they lived there was no school.

One day when Juan took the pigs out to eat some garbage he heard somebody crying. The pigs started to behave in a funny way, because the voice was coming out of a ruin. The pigs tried to see inside the ruin, but weren't tall enough. Juan sat down to think. He thought: This voice makes me feel sad inside my stomach, it feels as if there was an iguana caught inside jumping around trying to escape. I know that this feeling is really the little voice crying in the ruin, I am afraid, the pigs are afraid. However I want to know, so I shall go to the village and see if Don Pedro will lend me his ladder so I can climb over the wall and see who is making such a sad sound.

Off he went to see Don Pedro. He said: 'Will you please lend me your ladder?'

Don Pedro said: 'No. What for?'

Juan said to himself: I had better invent something, because if I tell him about the voice he might hurt it.

So out loud he said: 'Well a long way off behind the Pyramid of the Moon there is a tall fruit tree where there are a lot of big yellow mangoes growing. These mangoes are so fat that they look like gas balloons. The juice they drip is like honey *but* they grow so high up on the tree that it would be impossible to pick them without a tall ladder.'

Don Pedro kept looking at Juan and Juan knew he was greedy and lazy so he just stood and looked at his feet. At last Don Pedro said: 'All right, you may borrow the ladder but you must bring me twelve of the fattest mangoes to sell in the market. If you do not return by the evening with the mangoes and the ladder I will thrash you so hard you will swell up as big as the mangoes and you will be *black* and *blue*. So take the ladder and come back quickly.'

Don Pedro went back into his house to have lunch and he thought: Mangoes growing up here in the mountains seems very peculiar.

So he sat down and screamed at his wife: '*Bring me little meats and tortillas. All women are fools.*'

Don Pedro's family were afraid of him. Don Pedro was terrified of his boss, somebody called Licenciado Gómez, who wore neckties and dark glasses and lived in the town and owned a black motorcar.

During this time Juan was pulling and dragging the long ladder. It was hard work. When Juan arrived at the ruin he fainted with fatigue.

All was quiet, except for the faint grunting of the pigs and the dry sound of a lizard running past.

The sun was beginning to sink when Juan woke up suddenly shouting: '*Ai.*' Something was looking down at him, something green, blue, and rusty, glittering like a big myrtle sucker. This bird carried a small bowl of water. Her voice was thin, sweet, and strange. She said: 'I am the little granddaughter of the *Great God Mother* who lives in the Pyramid of Venus and I bring you a bowl of life water because you carried the ladder so far to see me when you heard me inside your stomach. This is the right place to listen, in the Stomach.'

However Juan was terrified so he kept on shrieking: '*Ai. Ai. Ai. Ai. Mamá.*'

The bird threw the water in Juan's face. A few drops went inside his mouth. He got up feeling better and stood looking at the bird with joy and delight. He was afraid no longer.

All the while her wings moved like an electric fan, so fast that Juan could see through them. She was a bird, a girl, a wind.

The pigs had all fainted by now with utmost fright.

Juan said: 'These pigs do nothing but eat and sleep and make more pigs. Then we kill them and make them into little meats which we eat inside tortillas. Sometimes we get very sick from them, especially if they have been dead for a long time.'

'You do not understand pigs,' said the bird, whirling. 'Pigs have an angel.' Whereupon she whistled like an express train and a small cactus plant rose out of the earth and slid into the bowl which the bird had left at her feet.

She said: 'Piu, Piu, Little Šervant, cut yourself into bits and feed yourself to the pigs so they become inspired with Pig Angel.'

The cactus called Piu cut himself into little round bits with a knife so sharp and fast that it was impossible to behold.

The morsels of Piu leapt into the mouths of the unconscious pigs, whereupon the pigs disintegrated into little meats roasting in their own heat.

The smell of delicious roasting pork brought drops of saliva into Juan's mouth. Laughing like a drainpipe the bird took out a telescope and a pair of pincers, picked up the morsels of pig meat, and set them in her small bowl. 'Angels must be devoured,' she said, turning from green to blue. Lowering her voice to the dark caves under the earth she called: 'Black Mole, Black Mole, Come out and Make the Sauce because Juan is going to eat the Angel, he is hungry and has not eaten since daybreak.'

The new moon appeared.

With a heaving and steaming of the earth, Black Mole poked his starred snout out of the ground; then came flat hands and fur, sleek and clean out of so much earth.

'I am blind,' he said, 'but I wear a star from the firmament on my nose.'

Now the bird whirled so fast she turned into a rainbow and Juan saw her pour herself into the Pyramid of the Moon in a curve of all colours. He didn't care because the smell of roasting pigs made food his only desire.

Mole took out all sorts of chiles from the pouch he wore. He took two big stones and ground up the chiles and seeds into pulp, then spat on them and poured them into the bowl with the cooking pig meat.

'I am blind,' said Mole, 'but I can lead you through the labyrinth.'

The red ants then came out of the ground carrying grains of corn. Every ant wore a bracelet of green jade on each of her slim legs. A great heap of corn was soon ground up. Mole made tortillas with his flat hands.

All was ready for the feast. Even Saint John's Day had never seen anything so rich.

'Now eat,' said Mole.

Juan dipped his tortilla into the bowl and ate until he was gorged with food. 'I never had so much to eat, never,' he kept saying. His stomach looked like a swollen melon.

All the while Mole stood by saying nothing, but taking stock of all that happened with his nose.

When Juan had finished the last scrap of the fifth pig Mole began to laugh. Juan was so full of food he could not move. He could only stare at Mole and wonder what was so funny.

Mole wore a scabbard under his fur. Quickly he drew out a sharp sword and, swish and shriek, cut up Juan into small pieces just like Piu had sliced himself up to feed the pigs.

The head and hands and feet and guts of young Juan jumped about shrieking. Mole took Juan's head tenderly in his big hands and said: 'Do not be afraid, Juan, this is only a first death, and you will be alive again soon.'

Whereupon he stuck the head on the thorn of a maguey and dived into the hard ground as if it were water.

All was quiet now. The thin new moon was high above the pyramids.

María

The well was far off. María returned to the hut with a bucket of water. The water kept sloshing over the side of the bucket. Don Pedro, María's father, was shouting: 'I shall beat that hairless puppy Juanito. He stole my ladder. I know mangoes don't grow around here. I shall thrash him till he begs for mercy. I shall thrash you all. *Why isn't my dinner ready?*'

Don Pedro yelled again: 'She has not come back with the water? I shall beat her. I shall twist her neck like a chicken. You are a no-good woman, your children are no good. *I am master here. I command. I shall kill that thief.*'

María was afraid. She had stopped to listen behind a large maguey. Don Pedro was drunk. She thought: He's beating my mother. A thin yellow cat dashed past in terror. The cat is also afraid, if I go back he will beat me, perhaps he will kill me like a chicken.

Quietly María set down the pail of water and walked north towards the Pyramid of the Moon.

It was night. María was afraid, but she was more afraid of her father, Don Pedro. María tried to remember a prayer to the Virgin of Guadalupe, but every time she began *Ave Maria*, something laughed.

A puff of dust arose on the path a few metres ahead. Out of the dust walked a small dog. It was hairless, with a speckled grey skin like a hen.

The dog walked up to her and they looked at each other. There was something distinctive and dignified about the animal. María understood that the dog was an ally. She thought: This dog is an ancient.

The dog turned north, and María followed. They walked and sometimes ran till they came to the ruin and María was face to face with Juan's decapitated head.

María's heart leapt. Grief struck her and she shed a tear which was hard as a stone and fell heavily to the earth. She picked up the tear and placed it in the mouth of Juan's head.

'Speak,' said María, who was now old and full of wisdom. He spoke, saying: 'My body is strewn around like a broken necklace. Pick it up and sew it together again. My head is lonely without my hands and my feet. All these are lonely without the rest of my poor body, chopped up like meat stew.'

María picked a thorn off the top of a maguey, made thread out of the sinews of the leaf, and told the maguey: 'Pardon me for taking your needle, pardon me for threading the needle with your body, pardon me for love, pardon me for I am what I am, and I do not know what this means.'

All this time Juan's head was weeping and wailing and complaining: 'Ai, Ai, Ai. My poor self, poor me, my poor body. Hurry up, María, and sew me together. Hurry, for if the sun rises and Earth turns away from the firmament I shall never be whole again. Hurry, María, hurry. Ai, Ai, Ai.'

María was busy now and the dog kept fetching pieces of the body and she sewed them together with neat stitches. Now she sewed on the head, and the only thing lacking was the heart. María had made a little door in Juan's breast to put it inside.

'Dog, Dog, where is Juan's heart?' The heart was on top of the wall of the ruin. Juan and María set up Don Pedro's ladder and Juan started to climb, but María said: 'Stop, Juan. You cannot reach your own heart, you must let me climb up and get it. Stop.'

But Juan refused to listen and kept on climbing. Just as he was reaching out to get hold of his heart, which was still beating, a black vulture swooped out of the air, snatched the heart in its claws, and flew off towards the Pyramid of the Moon. Juan gave a shriek and fell off the ladder; however María had sewn his body together so well that he was not really hurt.

But Juan had lost his heart.

'My heart. There it was, beating alone on the wall, red and slippery. My beautiful heart. Ah me, ah me,' he cried. 'That wicked black bird has ruined me, I am lost.'

'Hush now,' said María. 'If you make so much noise the *Nagual* may hear us, with his straw wings and crystal horns. Hush, be quiet, Juan.'

The hairless dog barked twice and started to walk into a cave that had opened up like a mouth. 'The Earth is alive,' said María, 'we must feed ourselves to the Earth to find your heart. Come, follow the Esquinclé.'

They looked into the deep mouth of the Earth and were afraid. 'We will use the ladder to climb down,' said María. Far below they could hear the dog barking.

As they started to climb down the ladder into the dark earth the first pale light of dawn arose behind the Pyramid of the Sun. The dog barked. María climbed slowly down the ladder and Juan followed. Above them Earth closed her mouth with a smile. The smile is still there, a long crack in the hard clay.

Down below was a passage shaped like a long hollow man. Juan and María walked inside this body holding hands. They knew now that they could not return and must keep on walking. Juan was knocking on the door in his chest crying, 'Oh my poor lost heart, oh my stolen heart.'

His wailing ran ahead of them and disappeared. It was a message. After a while a great roar came rumbling back. They stood together, shaking. A flight of stairs with narrow slippery steps led downwards. Below they could see the Red Jaguar that lives under the pyramids. The Big Cat was frightful to behold, but there was no return. They descended the stairs trembling. The Jaguar smelled of rage. He had eaten many hearts, but this was long ago and now he wanted blood.

As they got closer, the Jaguar sharpened his claws on the rock, ready to devour the meat of two tender children.

María felt sad to die so far under the earth. She wept one more tear, which fell into Juan's open hand. It was hard and sharp. He threw it straight at the eye of the beast and it bounced off. The Jaguar was made of stone.

They walked straight up and touched it, stroking the hard red body and obsidian eyes. They laughed and sat on its back; the stone Jaguar never moved. They played until a voice called: 'María. Juan. Juan. Mari.'

A flight of hummingbirds passed, rushing towards the voice.

'The Ancestor is calling us,' said María, listening. 'We must go back to Her.'

They crawled under the belly of the stone Jaguar. Mole was standing there, tall and black, holding a silver sword in one of his big hands. In the other hand he held a rope. He bound the two children tightly together and pulled them into the presence of the Great Bird. Bird, Snake, Goddess, there She sat, all the colours of the rainbow and full of little windows with faces looking out singing the sounds of every thing alive and dead, all this like a swarming of bees, a million movements in one still body.

María and Juan stared at each other till Mole cut the rope that bound them together. They lay on the floor looking up at the Evening Star, shining through a shaft in the roof.

Mole was piling branches of scented wood on a brazier. When this was ready, the Bird Snake Mother shot a tongue of fire out of her mouth and the wood burst into flame. 'María,' called a million voices, 'jump into the fire and take Juan by the hand, he must burn with you so you both shall be one whole person. This is love.'

They jumped into the fire and ascended in smoke through the shaft in the roof to join the Evening Star. Juan-Mari, they were one whole being. They will return again to Earth, one Being called Quetzalcoatl.

Juan-Mari keep returning, so this story has no end.

1976

Nina Bawden

Nina Bawden was born in 1925 in London. She attended Somerville College, Oxford, where she received both a BA and an MA. After university, besides a prolific and prestigious writing career which spans twenty adult novels, including *Birds on a Tree*, *Family Money* and *Circles of Deceit*, and seventeen for children, including *Carrie's War* and *The Peppermint Pig*, she served for a long time as a magistrate both in her local court and in the Crown Court. Pastiche of this process forms the centre of her 1976 novel *Afternoon of a Good Woman*. Her fiction is characterised by its wry observation of the English middle classes and the popularity of her writing has made her in demand and taken her all over the world. She was awarded a CBE in 1995 and now spends her time between London and Greece.

Devil by the Sea originally appeared in a longer version in 1957 but was adapted in 1975 into a children's edition and in 1976 published in its current form. Virago reissued the novel in 1997.

from

Devil by the Sea

The first time the children saw the Devil, he was sitting next to them in the second row of deckchairs in the bandstand. He was biting his nails.

On the roof, the coloured flags cracked and streamed in the cold breeze from the sea but in the sheltered well of the bandstand it was warm and windless, the sun held the last heat of summer. Sleepy flies droned heavily over the sand scuffed on the flagstones by the children's feet. From time to time the blue sky split as an American jet plane screamed low.

The audience, this September afternoon, was made up of the very young, and the very old. The children, bright as butterflies in their summer dresses, filled the front rows of chairs; the old people huddled in rugs and scarves at the back, beyond the aisle. The local pensioners were issued with cheap season tickets by the council: wringing their last advantage from a mean world, they filled their seats at every performance.

Looking at the man sitting next to them, the children thought he must be old too, or sick. He wore a full-skirted naval bridge coat and a blue woollen muffler knotted round his neck. Beneath his cloth cap his face was thin, the cheeks so hollow that his mouth stuck forwards like a dog's mouth.

Grinning, Hilary nudged Peregrine with her elbow. She aped the man, tearing at the sides of her fingers with her teeth, rolling her eyes like a mad person. Peregrine watched her uncomfortably and then, as her acting grew wilder, he was seized by a fearful joy and laughed aloud.

The man turned and looked at them. A shadow crossed his face:

like an animal, he seemed to shrink and cringe before the mockery Hilary had made of him. She stopped biting her nails and moved her hand nervously up her cheek and across her hair, pretending she had been brushing something from her face. He continued to watch her with a steady, careful stare. She fumbled in the pocket of her cotton dress. Her voice croaked with embarrassment.

'Would you like a toffee?'

The man looked beyond her, to Peregrine. Briefly, their eyes met. Peregrine could not look away, he was transfixed. The man's eyes were dark and dull, dead eyes without any shine in them. They reflected nothing.

The man stirred and coughed. His thin cheeks filled out and the spit sprayed from his mouth. 'You're a nice little girl,' he said, and smiled. It was a gentle smile, quite at odds with his appearance. He took a toffee with long, sharp fingers and popped it quickly in his mouth as if he were afraid it would be taken from him.

Hilary said, 'Are you hungry? It must be awful to be hungry.'

She was aware that it had been unkind to make fun of him. He could not help being sick and ugly. Normally, she did not suffer unduly for her bad behaviour towards other people unless she was punished for it. Her imagination was almost entirely absorbed by her own feelings which were, on occasion, bitter and terrible, and by the wild, dramatic happenings of her private world. But now her conscience was aroused by the man's sad and derelict air. Her heart swelled with pity.

'You can have them all if you're hungry. I don't want them.'

She thrust the crumpled bag of sweets on to the man's lap. His narrow, yellow face bent towards her. Reluctantly she looked up at the muddy eyes that showed nothing, neither hope nor despair nor love nor hate.

The man clicked his tongue against his teeth. 'Are you sure you don't want them?'

She shook her head and lied, 'I don't like toffees.'

'What about your little brother?' Peregrine had withdrawn himself to another chair further along the row. He disliked embarrassing situations.

'They make his teeth wobble. He's just seven and all his teeth are falling out.'

The man edged his chair closer to Hilary's. He smelt of wet mackintoshes like the cloakroom at school. Slowly his nervous tongue crept out of his mouth and slithered along his lips.

Hilary hunched herself small in her deckchair and watched the stage. Uncle Jack, the Kiddies' Friend, was making a bunch of flowers grow in an empty can. There was only one more trick after the can and then they would have the Children's Talent Competition. It was always held on a special day, the last day of the season. The Fun Fair would remain open for a little longer but after to-morrow there would be no more shows on the pier, the deckchairs would be hidden under their tarpaulin covers, the summer would be over. *The summer I was nine, thought Hilary. It will never come again. Next summer I shall be ten and then eleven and soon I shall be old. Soon, I shall die.*

The man was leaning closer still. His smell was in her nose and throat. She felt his hand stroking her knee and squirmed away. His fingers felt cold and hard like a chicken's foot. Ashamed, she stared at the stage, trying not to cry, pretending she hadn't noticed what he was doing.

Uncle Jack came to the front of the stage and smiled at the children, his perpetual, shining smile. He had stiff, curly hair like a doll. His teeth shone and his hair shone and he wore a great ring with a winking stone on the little finger of his left hand.

'Now, children, this is what you've been waiting for, isn't it? What? I can't hear you.'

'*Yes*,' bellowed the children with scarlet faces and straining lungs.

'That's better. *That's* better.' He held up his hand for silence. 'Those of you who have tickets, come up on to the stage. Gently, now. Don't all rush at once. You might knock me over.'

There was a roar of laughter. A little girl sitting in front of Hilary stood up and skipped in front of her mother's chair. The woman creaked forward to pick up her canvas beach-bag, enormous, sun-reddened shoulders bulging out of her dress. She took out a green ticket.

'Here you are, Poppet. Now remember, stand up nice and straight and smile. . .'

Poppet took the ticket. Over her mother's shoulder she smiled triumphantly at Hilary. She was very beautiful. She had fair, polished hair that bobbed on the shoulders of her green, satin dress. Her eyes were wide and blue like china; beneath her short skirt her long, brown legs looked like a miniature chorus-girl's. The man took his hand away from Hilary's knee. His teeth tore at his nails again.

Poppet jumped up on to the front of the stage. Her skirt flew up showing white frilly knickers with lace round the legs. Hilary saw them enviously. Her own knickers were voluminous, made of the same stuff as her dress and fastened with tight elastic.

Slowly, like the tide, the children flowed on to the stage. Some of them were shy: if they were little, Uncle Jack patted them on the head, if they were big he shook hands with them in a jolly, comradely way.

Hilary sighed. Screwing round in her chair, she looked for her half-sister, Janet. She saw her, standing by the entrance to the bandstand and talking to Uncle Aubrey. Waving her hands about in an affected way, she was quite preoccupied with her conversation. Her back was to the stage.

Hilary felt her heart pump inside her like an engine. She turned to her brother and said, 'I'm going in the competition, too.'

Blithely, he refused to believe her. 'You haven't got a ticket.'

She scowled. 'I shall say I've lost it.'

'That's wicked,' he accused her. 'It's a lie. God doesn't like us to tell lies.'

Hilary saw the limpid light of Heaven shining from his eyes and hesitated. Peregrine was good: his goodness was as unquestioned as the rising sun. She knew him to be her spiritual superior and herself to be hateful and base.

She wriggled her shoulders and flung at him, 'Mind your own business.' She stood up and walked towards the stage, appalled by her own behaviour. Her legs seemed to be moving independently like someone else's legs. She could feel eyes sticking into her like hot spikes.

1977

Marilyn French

Marilyn French was born in 1929 in Brooklyn, New York. One of America's leading feminist thinkers, she studied philosophy and English at Hofstra University and has published fiction, literary criticism and polemic. She declared in 1987, in an interview in New York *Newsday*, 'I am an enemy of the order,' and her work continually questions and challenges the power imbalance between men and women. *The Women's Room* is commonly considered to be one of the most influential feminist novels of the modern period; it has sold over 4 million copies and been translated into twenty languages.

The Women's Room was published by Virago in 1997.

from

The Women's Room

Mira was hiding in the ladies' room. She called it that, even though someone had scratched out the word *ladies'* in the sign on the door, and written *women's* underneath. She called it that out of thirty-eight years of habit, and until she saw the cross-out on the door, had never thought about it. 'Ladies' room' was a euphemism, she supposed, and she disliked euphemisms on principle. However, she also detested what she called vulgarity, and had never in her life, even when handling it, uttered the word *shit*. But here she was at the age of thirty-eight huddled for safety in a toilet booth in the basement of Sever Hall, gazing at, no, studying that word and others of the same genre, scrawled on the grey enamelled door and walls.

She was perched, fully clothed, on the edge of the open toilet seat, feeling stupid and helpless, and constantly looking at her watch. It would all have been redeemed, even translated into excitement, had there been some grim-faced Walter Matthau in a trench coat, his hand in a gun-swollen pocket, or some wild-eyed Anthony Perkins in a turtleneck, his itching strangler's hands clenching and unclenching – someone glamorous and terrifying at any rate – waiting for her outside in the hall, if she had been sitting in panic searching for another way out. But of course if that were the case, there would also be a cool and desperate Cary Grant or Burt Lancaster sliding along the walls of another hallway, waiting for Walter to show himself. And that by itself, she thought mournfully, feeling somehow terribly put upon, would have been enough. If she had one of them, anyone at all, waiting for her at home, she would not be hiding in a toilet booth in the basement of Sever Hall. She would have been upstairs in a corridor with the other students, leaning against a wall with her books at her feet, or strolling past the unseeing faces. She could have transcended, knowing she had one of them at home, and could therefore move alone in a crowd. She puzzled over that paradox, but only briefly. The graffiti were too interesting.

'Down with capitalism and the fucking military-industrial complex. KILL ALL FASCIST PIGS!'

This had been answered. 'You simplify too much. New ways must be found to kill pigs: out of their death new pigs spring as armed men sprouted from the bulls' teeth planted by that mcp Jason. Pigs batten on pig blood. The way is slow and hard. We must cleanse our minds of all the old shit, we must work in silence, exile, and cunning like that mcp Joyce. We must have a revolution of sensibility.'

A third party entered the argument in purple ink:

'Stay in your cocoon. Who needs you? Those who are not with us are against us. Anyone who supports that status quo is part of the problem. THERE IS NO TIME. THE REVOLUTION IS HERE! KILL PIGS!'

Writer No. 2 was apparently fond of this booth and had returned, for the next entry was in her handwriting and in the same pen:

'Those who live by the sword die by the sword.'

Wild printing in the purple felt-tip followed this in great sprawling letters:

'FUCKING CHRISTIAN IDIOT! TAKE YOUR MAXIMS AND STUFF THEM! THERE IS ONLY POWER! POWER TO THE PEOPLE! POWER TO THE POOR! WE ARE DYING BY THE SWORD NOW!'

The last outburst ended that symposium, but there were others like it scrawled on the side walls. Almost all of them were political. There were pasted-on notices of SDS meetings, meetings of Bread and Roses, and Daughters of Bilitis. Mira withdrew her eyes from a crude drawing of female genitalia with 'Cunt is Beautiful' scratched beneath it. She presumed, at least, that it was a drawing of female genitalia, although it looked remarkably like a wide-petaled flower. She wasn't sure because she had never seen her own, that being a part of the anatomy that did not present itself directly to the vision.

She looked at her watch again: she could leave now. She stood and from force of habit turned to flush the unused toilet. On the wall behind it someone had printed great jagged letters in what looked like nail polish. The red enamel had dripped and each stroke had a thick pearl at its base. It looked as if it had been written in blood. SOME DEATHS TAKE FOREVER, it read. She drew her breath in sharply and left the booth.

It was 1968.

1978

Sara Maitland

Sara Maitland was born in 1950 in London, but moved as a child to
southwest Scotland. She was educated at St Anne's College, Oxford,
where she received her BA in English in 1971. She was a member of
the Feminist Writers' Group which produced the collective *Tales I Tell
My Mother* in 1978. In her own work she explores and questions myths;
she has written several novels and several collections of short fiction,
including *A Book of Spells* and *Arky Types* (with Michelene Wandor). She
also works as a journalist and feminist historian, lecturing on feminist
theology and contemporary literature, and has written a life of the
music-hall cross-dresser Vesta Tilley and edited *Very Heaven*, a collection of essays about 1960s culture. *Daughters of Jerusalem* won the
Somerset Maugham Award in 1979.

   Daughters of Jerusalem was reissued by Virago in 1993.

from

Daughters of Jerusalem

She pushed the balls of her thumbs into her eye-sockets, hard. Yellow streaks and whorls shot across the blue film. She pushed almost hard enough to hurt herself. She thought she might scream or faint or kill someone. After a small moment she found she had done none of these things and she leaned forward, elbows on her knees, exhausted, trying to relax. When she opened her eyes nothing had changed: the bus was still stopped at the red lights and below her a pretty girl in long skirts and a long scarf was trying to tuck both up so she could start her bike when the lights changed.

She was not going to go to work anyway. She was still afraid she might cry; and she refused to cry at work. If she went home the flat would be empty, and would stay empty for over six more hours. If she went to Nancy's, the baby, clumsy but determined, would struggle into her lap, would flop his heavy head against her and bring her his latest activity to admire. But that might be good. She could cry at Nancy's safely enough, they were well used to one another's tears now. Going to Nancy would certainly induce tears – of habit, relief and security, but that might be good. If she were going to cry there would be the best place, with Nancy tough and firm, but immensely generous.

But she did not understand, she could not understand. Another wave of misery threatened to engulf her; not just misery, but fear and a sense of shame. Which was silly. Perhaps she had deserved it anyway; perhaps she had asked for it. She looked down at her jeans rolled up to the knees, the green and yellow football socks, the fluorescent green sneakers.

'Are you wearing that lot to the clinic?' Ian had asked that morning. The bright red T-shirt with 'I am a humourless feminist' stamped black across the bosom was hidden now by her donkey-jacket, but had been part of the view that both Ian and Dr Marshall had enjoyed.

'Yes.'

'Don't let him get to you, darling.'

'I wear this lot pretty often.'

'You know what I mean.'

'Yes. I can't help it, Ian. He makes such assumptions. I see the other women there in their best coats, with their hair fresh done, as though it was a treat to get to see Mr Mighty, giver of children, the rewarder of the virtuous . . . I want him, and them, to know I'm not taken in; that I refuse to feel like that.'

'You're still dressing up for him.'

'Don't be so clever.'

He rocked her in his arms, half teasing, really tender. 'Will you ring me?'

'If there's anything to say.'

'No. Anyway . . .'

'No promises. I thought I might go over to Nancy's afterwards. Tony won't expect me back at work.'

'Look, shall I come with you? I can easily get myself covered for the morning.'

'Oh Ian, you don't have to do that. I'm a big girl now. I'm just sorry I make such a fuss every time. He is such a shit you know.'

'It's not him, it's your relationship. His position. You wouldn't like him whatever. He seemed okay the times I've met him. Considerate and pretty sensitive, you know.'

It was useless to tell Ian that it was precisely the doctor's sensitivity to *him* that made her dislike him so much. If he could be so tender of Ian's feelings, why was he so brutal to her? Or was he? What were her expectations anyway? She'd only been going to his clinic for ten months; it was not his fault if she did not get pregnant. Especially if his new line was correct. She disciplined herself against the new spasm of grief and made herself look at what the consultant had said: that she should see a psychiatrist; that the suppression of ovulation without apparent physical cause could have its roots in the rejection of the patient's own femininity.

'Look,' Dr Marshall had said, 'this is not an easy thing to face up to, and if I had not found you so forthright, so willing to cooperate in everything we have suggested so far, I might beat about the proverbial bush a little more. But I have thought a good deal about all this, especially in relation to everything you have told me about your past, your, mm, sexual connections, your, shall I say, interests. Now even you would have to admit that the overall picture presenting, your politics, your unashamed promiscuity – past, I acknowledge – is hardly one of the standard, well-integrated woman.'

She wanted to say, 'I haven't the least idea what you are talking about.' But she had a very good idea, and she sat dumbly listening.

1979

Zoë Fairbairns

Zoë Fairbairns was born in 1948 in England. She studied at the College of William and Mary in Virginia and took an MA at St Andrews University, Scotland, in 1972. She was a member of the Feminist Writers' Group, wrote regularly for magazines such as *Spare Rib* and *Everywoman* and has taught creative writing widely. Her success as one of Britain's most popular feminist authors rests largely on her debunking of literary genres – she transformed the usual landscape of science fiction, for instance, in *Benefits*, and the conventions of the family saga in *Stand We at Last* (1983) and the crime thriller in *Here Today* (1984). She has also had three other novels published. *Closing*, *Daddy's Girls* and *Other Names* and written short stories and one play. She lives in London and works part-time as a TV subtitler.

Benefits was first published by Virago in 1979, and is now published by Five Leaves Publications.

from

Benefits

It was a tall, wide structure, and it stood like a pack of chewing gum, upended in a grudging square of grass on the side of a hill. It was made of glass, grey metal and rough brown brick, and had a depressing but all-too-familiar history. It was one of the last tower blocks to be built in the sixties for London families to live in. By the time it was up, planners, builders and social workers were already losing faith in tower blocks and the families that moved in from the dirty, neighbourly streets being cleared around Collindeane's feet did so without enthusiasm.

Ninety-six flats had meant more than twice that many children; but once the older boys had staked territorial claims to the grass patch, no one young or weak got a look-in. The boys found other sources of fun: filling the lift with bricks, tying door-knockers together, calling in the fire-brigade. Windows got smashed. Families withheld rent and were evicted; or vanished overnight, leaving massive arrears and furniture that had not been paid for. Childish high spirits turned malignant. Paraffin was poured through letter boxes and lit; human shit was left on landings; bricks and planks and crockery were thrown from high windows. Soon anyone with any choice in the matter moved out of the flats, leaving behind only those with no choice. Teenage mothers who looked forty. Drunken, shuffling, unemployed men. Ragged litters of children, yelling as they slithered down the endless banisters or hung from high windows to terrorise passers-by. Old folk with multiple locks on the doors, peering out at the stray dogs that met and fought and mated in the corridors.

Disease entered the flats – pneumonia, gastroenteritis, rumours of typhoid, even a rabies scare – and the council said it would close the flats and pull them down. The local paper declared such waste inexcusable. The council promised to rehabilitate instead, and put up some swings. But before this could be done, the curtain came down on the era of affluence that had spawned and nurtured the British welfare state. The international oil crisis brought inflation that galloped through dreams, slashed welfare budgets. There was no money to rehabilitate Collindeane Tower. The council closed it, rehoused its inmates, nailed wooden planks across the doorway and tried to pretend they had never built it, indeed had not noticed it was there – one of the biggest, most embarrassing statutory nuisances on the London skyline.

Soon after, Collindeane Tower was spotted by a group of women looking for somewhere to squat and establish a feminist community. One of them chopped through the planks with her axe, and they moved in while the council averted its eyes.

Everyone who was in London in the summer of 1976 remembers the weather. The four-month heatwave brought pleasure at first, then incredulity, then resignation and unease as the curious realities of urban drought upset the jocular complacency of those who would never have believed that Londoners would pray for rain. People remember what they were doing that summer in the same way that they can pinpoint their location and activity at the time they heard about the death of President Kennedy.

From May to September, misty mornings preceded glaring debilitating days and dry airless nights. The Thames became unnavigable. Workers went on strike for better ventilation. Grass browned, trees drooped, earth subsided under foundations and buildings cracked. Commuters left jackets and cotton cardigans at home and adhered to each other in packed trains, licking ices. Umbrella sellers went out of business, shorts were worn in the staidest of offices, and members of parliament were outraged by the price of cold drinks in Oxford Street. Day followed incredible day and still the heat did not let up, still it did not rain. Once or twice a grey, brooding constipated sky rumbled and flashed and a few drops of water fell, but you could not call that rain; not when there was talk of standpipes in the streets and even Buckingham Palace (it was rumoured) had a sign up in the loo saying 'Don't pull for a pee.' It rained enough, it was true, to kill the Saturday of the Lords' Test against Australia (if it had to rain one day of the year, Londoners told each other wisely, that would be the one) but that was not enough to break the drought – an almost indecent word to be used about their city, thought Londoners, to whom drought meant sandy deserts and cracked farmland in places near the equator. In unaccustomed chats between strangers, sympathy for our own farmers (pictured each night on television running dust through their fingers and waving parched roots as if the government ought to do something about it) alternated only with contrived sighs of ecstasy: 'Isn't it glorious?'. Londoners did not really believe in farmers.

1980s

1980

Shirley Hazzard

———

Shirley Hazzard was born in Sydney, Australia, in 1931. She worked for British intelligence in Hong Kong and New Zealand, and went on to work at the United Nations in New York, employment which informed the linked short stories that make up her 1967 collection *People in Glass Houses*. Her novella *The Evening of the Holiday* appeared in 1966 and was followed in 1970 by what is perhaps her most famous novel, *The Bay of Noon*. *The Transit of Venus* became a bestseller and won the USA National Book Circles Award. She divides her time between New York and southern Italy.

The Transit of Venus was published by Virago in 1995.

from

The Transit of Venus

In the government office where Caroline Bell worked there was a young woman called Valda. That she was called Valda was to the point, for she objected to this. None of the other women there objected to being Milly, Pam, or Miranda with their appointed Mr Smedleys and Mr Renshaw-Browns. None of the other women objected, for that matter, to being girls.

By that epoch the men themselves were no longer Bates or Barkham to one another, but instant Sam or Jim. Those who had irreducibly formal names, such as Giles or Julian, even seemed to be lagging dangerously and doomed to obscurity. There was one older man in Planning who would say Mister to his subordinates – 'Mister Haynes', 'Mister Dandridge' – like the skipper of an old ship with his first mate or boatswain. But he too, among the women, permitted himself an occasional Marge or Marigold; although at home calling his charwoman Mrs Dodds.

When Caro asked, 'If they make a true friend, what will they call him?' Valda told her: 'They're hoping to put true friendship out of business.'

New, compulsory congeniality among males was at least, however, in Valda's view, a loss equally shared. Unlike the outright seizure of June or Judy.

Soon after her arrival Valda had drawn attention to herself. Her little Mr Leadbetter, the administrative officer, had come out of his hutch, ears up, holding a button, and asked if she would sew it on. This, he estimated, would not take a minute. Valda politely consented.

And, laying aside her papers, brought from a desk drawer a house-wifely pouch of needles and coloured threads. With Mr Leadbetter's jacket aswoon in her lap, she narrowed her own eye to the needle's and was soon stitching. Leadbetter stood to watch her. His shirt was striped and blue, his trousers came to his armpits, depending from canvas braces, also striped, that had long ago been made to last. It was pleasant to doff his armour and watch the handsome Valda at her humble and womanly task. When she had done, when she had wound the thread and broken it off, he was grateful.

'Thank you, Valda. I am not handy with such things. And would jab myself to pieces.' It was important to show appreciation.

To this, Valda replied, echoing his own benevolent thoughts: 'These are small things to do for one another.'

The following week Valda came into his office, where he was reading over a penultimate draft, and asked him to change her typewriter ribbon.

Mr Leadbetter stared.

She said, 'I am not handy with machines.'

He was baffled and displeased. 'Have you never needed a new ribbon before? Were you not trained to do these things?'

'It will not take a minute.'

'You had better get one of the girls to show you.' It was incomprehensible.

'They will dirty their hands.' She said, 'It is a small thing to do.'

Now he understood. He went out and got one of the other girls – the real girls – in a rage. 'Miss Fenchurch needs help with her machine.' It was the first time he had not called her Valda, but respect was accorded only from pique. The second girl looked with ingratiating timidity at him, and with terror at Valda, and at once bent to the machine as if over a cradle.

When the time came, Mr Leadbetter wrote in Valda's file that she tended to be aggressive over trifles. 'Tended' was official code for going the whole hog.

There was a small inner room like a cupboard where, morning and afternoon, these girls took turns to make the tea. A list was tacked to the wall, of all the men and their requirements: Mr Bostock weak with sugar, Mr Miles strong and plain. Valda's Leadbetter had an infusion of camomile flowers, which he bought at Jackson's in Piccadilly; these were prepared in a separate pot and required straining. Another notice cautioned against tea-leaves in the sink. The room was close and shabby. There were stains on the lino and a smell of stale biscuits. On one spattered wall the paint was peeling, from exhalations of an electric kettle.

Sometimes when Valda made tea Caro would set out cups for her on a scratched brown tray.

It was something to see the queenly and long-limbed Valda measure, with disdainful scruple, the flowers for Mr Leadbetter's special pot (which carried, tied to its handle, a little tag: 'Let stand five minutes'). To hear her reel off the directions: 'Mr Hoskins, saccharin. Mr Farquhar, squeeze of lemon.' She filled the indeterminate little room with scorn and decision, and caused a thrill of wonderful fear among the other women for the conviction that, had one of these men entered, she would not have faltered a moment in her performance.

When Valda spoke of men more generally, it was in an assumption of shared and calamitous experience. None of the other women entered on such discussions – which were not only indelicate but would have mocked their deferential dealings with Mr This or That. Furthermore, they feared that Valda, if encouraged, might say something physical.

Watching the office women file towards the exit at evening, Valda observed to Caro: 'The lowing herd wind slowly o'er the lea.'

There was another male faction in the office, of ageing young men who spoke bitterly of class divisions and of the right, or absence, of opportunity. For these, equally, Valda had no patience. 'They don't quite believe they exist, and are waiting for someone to complete the job for them, gratis.' She would set down the biscuit tin, switch off the electric kettle. 'Oh Caro, it is true that the common man is everlastingly embattled, but he has a lot of people on his side. It's the uncommon man who gets everyone's goat.'

Valda would tell Caro, 'You feel downright disloyal to your experience, when you do come across a man you could like. By then you scarcely see how you can decently make terms, it's like going over to the enemy. And then there's the waiting. Women have got to fight their way out of that dumb waiting at the end of the never-ringing telephone. The *receiver*, as our portion of it is called.' Or, slowly revolving the steeping teapot in her right hand, like an athlete warming up to cast a disc: 'There is the dressing up, the hair, the fingernails. The toes. And, after all that, you are a meal they eat while reading the newspaper. I tell you that every one of those fingers we paint is another nail in their eventual coffins.'

All this was indisputable, even brave. But was a map, from which rooms, hours, and human faces did not rise; on which there was no

412 The Virago Book of Twentieth-Century Fiction

bloom of generosity or discovery. The omissions might constitute life itself; unless the map was intended as a substitute for the journey.

These at least were the objections raised by Caroline Bell.

For her part, Valda considered Caro as a possibility lost. Caro might have done anything, but had preferred the common limbo of sexual love. Whoever said, 'When you go to women, take your whip,' was on to something deep, and deeply discouraging.

Valda would watch Caro, and think along these lines. She would think, Oh yes, let them show her their whip, or some comparable attraction.

1981

Lorna Tracy

―――――

Lorna Tracy was born in Oregon and educated in America. She has lived since 1969 in Newcastle upon Tyne, where she married the poet and critic Jon Silkin and was fiction editor of *Stand* magazine from 1969 to 1999. During this time she occasionally published short fiction in British magazines. Her most recent stories appeared in *New Writing* 5 and 6. Nowadays, as she puts it, she spends her time finishing her second collection, 'watching birds, and staying out of trouble'.

The extract is the Sixth Piece of 'The Mama Stories', taken from *Amateur Passions*, first published by Virago in 1981.

from

'The Mama Stories'

Amongst the duties assigned to Mama in her new job at the Polk Park Public Library was delivering books to house-bound persons in the town. The Misses Fellowman, a pair of able-bodied spinsters in their middle sixties, were on Mama's route. She couldn't think why. They lived not far from the library. She decided they had a taste for service. Mama made her first visit to them on a fine warm day in October.

'You must come in,' they said. It was to drink their tea and be questioned. 'Are you a Christian?'

'Yes,' said Mama for she knew she must. And in any case her parents had meant her to be.

'What do you believe?'

Oh-Oh.

'Well,' said Mama, 'I believe in doing all the good I can here in the world.' She reached for her bookbag to distract them with Literature, but they forestalled her.

'And of course you believe in God.'

'Of course.'

'And in Jesus Christ our Lord?'

Mama acted on a belated decision to be truthful. 'No,' she said, 'I'm afraid I haven't come to that yet.'

'Oh, you *must* believe that. The Bible *tells* us we must believe that. If you don't believe that you can't go to Heaven, and there are only two places you can go: Heaven and Hell. Are you prepared to die?'

Mama was twenty-seven years old and in superb health. She was an excellent defensive driver with an unblemished eleven-year record

and no automobile of her own. She was agile and alert at street cross-
ings. She kept off step ladders, never waxed her floors and rarely flew
anywhere. One of her grandfathers had been a nonagenarian. Mama
hadn't been to a funeral in her life.

'No,' she said.

'You must be prepared,' said the elder Miss Fellowman. 'You don't
know. You might die in five minutes. I'm ready to go any time.'

So was Mama. Though perhaps not so much ready to go as ready to
leave this place.

'I don't think a lot about it,' she said, standing up.

'Jesus Christ died to save us. We were born full of sin. No one is
good. We are all wicked. The love of God is the greatest love there is.
Hallelujah! First He gave us the Law. Then He was lovely enough to
give us His Son who died to save our souls.'

Her eyes, like those of her sister, were now full of tears, but she
maintained firm control of herself and the topic of conversation.

'The Bible was written by God. God inspired the men who wrote it
and every word in it is true. Hallelujah! Revelations tells us – in the
last chapter, I believe – that at the time the world comes to an end
there will be things happen which have never been before. Well – look
around you! It's happening! These children, afraid of nothing and no
one. Are you a Catholic?'

'No.'

'You know the Catholics have their own Bible. They take out and
put in anything they please. It says in Revelations that woe to anyone
who takes out or puts in anything. I was talking to a young man
recently who said he was trying to find the middle way. I told him
there was no middle way. There was Heaven and there was Hell. You
won't go to Heaven if you're not prepared, if you don't believe in
Jesus Christ our Lord. He said he knew that, but he wanted to find a
middle way. I told him to quit looking for something that didn't exist.
He said he knew I was right. If you find that wonderful love of God –
far, far greater than the love of a boy and girl, you will be happy. Not
that you aren't happy. You look happy. But you will be much happier
still. I was talking to a Catholic man just this morning. He said he
never worried about anything, ever in his life. He confessed to the
priest. I told him the priest couldn't forgive him if he had done nothing against the priest. He said the priest prayed for him. I said I don't
need anyone to pray for me. I can pray for myself because I am saved.
Hallelujah!'

Miss Fellowman was too kindly, earnest, genteel and silly for Mama to argue with, even though Mama was curious to know how, in her undoubted purity, Miss Fellowman could so confidently compare the relative ecstasies of carnal and spiritual passion. It seemed better not to ask.

'I've told you how to have salvation and if you don't choose to take it you will go to Hell, but it won't be blood on my hands. I've told you The True Way.'

It was true what she said about her hands. They *were* bloodless. Thick and white, without visible evidence of veins or arteries – the pallor interrupted here and there with brown freckles like stains.

'Now if there was a fire in your house and you saved someone's life in that fire, you'd be the happiest person in the world, wouldn't you.'

Mama got as far as the front door before she said, 'I doubt whether I'd be any happier than the person whose life had been saved.'

'Oh, you'd be the happiest person in the world. That person who you'd saved would love you all the rest of his life. That's the way it is with God.'

The door had a big pane made of lacy frosted glass showing, enclosed in broad borders of long feathery forms like crystalline fossil leaves, the noble figure of a stag, and a lacy curtain hung across it. Mama turned the knob.

'Well, I'll be getting back to the library. Thank you for the tea.'

'Polk Park used to be very aristocratic. It's not that way anymore You're new here, aren't you. Well, all kinds of foreigners have moved here now. The population's exploded. There are a lot more wealthy people now. It used to be that you had to have a dozen introductions here. You'd be introduced once and the next time they wouldn't even remember you.'

Mama pushed open the old-fashioned screen door on to the porch.

'Everybody builds ranch houses these days. I don't like the idea of having the kitchen in front and the parlour in back, do you? I think a lot of it is the ministers' fault. They don't preach that way any more. They just talk about daily topics. Oratory. Just showing how much they know. That's not doing the Lord's work.'

On the porch Mama asked the ladies whether there were any books they'd especially like to have next time. She had already started a list for them in her head. The first item on it was a nicely produced pamphlet called *Organising Fire Prevention Week in Your Community*.

'Yes, there is,' said one of the sisters. 'That new book by Norman Vincent Peale. I don't remember what it's called. You know he's the President's spiritual advisor, don't you.'

'Yes. And do *you* know that studies have recently been published indicating that in both Nazi concentration camps and Korean and Chinese war prisons those POWs who held up best under torture and brain-washing seemed to be Jehovah's Witnesses? Others who made a good showing were Communists, criminals and priests.

'Well, you see! It's those foreigners with their Popes and atheists. And that's another thing. There's a lot of Jews moving here.'

Mama plunged.

'Miss Fellowman, think: What unites this disparate lot of people? Is it not, surely, the fact that each of them has something for which he wants to live and behave in a particular way? Belief may be the key. But no one belief seems superior to any other for purposes of strong survival. From this point of view, at least, the Communist true believer is the equal of the convinced Catholic. In these studies no mention was made of Jews.'

Mama was off the porch and down the sidewalk before Miss Fellowman found her tongue again.

'Here! You've forgotten to take back our books that we've read.'

'Oh, that's all right,' Mama called from the staff car window. 'Just drop them off at the library next time you're passing by.'

1982

Pat Barker

———

Pat Barker was born in Thornaby-on-Tees in 1943. She was educated at the local grammar school and at the London School of Economics, where she studied economics, politics and history. She taught for several years, until the birth of her first child. She had already produced three 'sensitive and polite' unpublished novels when, on a writing course, Angela Carter read a story about her grandmother and advised her to write more about her past. The result was her novel *Union Street*, which was later made into the film *Stanley and Iris*, starring Robert De Niro and Meryl Streep. In 1983 she was chosen as one of the twenty best young British novelists by *The Times*. She went on to write several more novels, including the *Regeneration* trilogy about the experience of the First World War. She won the 1995 Booker Prize for *Regeneration*.

Union Street was first published by Virago in 1982.

from

Union Street

It was January now. Alice Bell spent her days in bed: it was her solution to the price of coal. Whenever she moved newspapers stirred and rustled all around her. The bed was full of them. She had read somewhere that newspapers were as good as blankets, and the house was cold.

There wasn't a lot of fat on her to keep her warm. Her thighs were folds of creased skin, hanging from the bone. Yet beside her on the bed was a black handbag with £100 inside. She had saved it out of her social security money: the 'pancrack' as she contemptuously called it. What she got was barely adequate for heating and food. To save out of it, as she was determined to do, meant hunger and cold. Though she didn't usually feel hungry: she had been depriving herself of food too long for that.

She liked the feel of the notes, especially if she was lucky enough to get a new one, though the old, crumpled ones also had their charm. But she liked best to crisp the new ones through her fingers. When she was alone she would often take them out and count them. And yet she was not in the usual sense of the word a miser. This was no meaningless accumulation of money for its own sake. She was saving up for her funeral.

As a little girl, more than seventy years ago, she had witnessed the funerals of paupers. And she still remembered the old rhyme:

> Rattle his bones
> Over the stones.
> He's only a pauper
> Whom nobody owns.

Children followed the coffins, jeering sometimes, and throwing stones. Perhaps she'd been one of them, she didn't remember. But the horror of that final rejection had stayed with her all her life. The death grant would not bury her. Inflation had made her small insurance policy useless. And there had to be a proper funeral, paid for out of her own money. Her self-respect, her dignity as a human being, required it. And so she had to save. And starve.

Her other dread was the Workhouse. As a small child on her way to school she had walked past its gates, never without a shudder. It was still in use, though they called it something different now. But to her it would always be the Workhouse: the place paupers' funerals started from.

The 'pancrack' she had to submit to: there was no choice. She was entitled to nothing else. You could get what they called a seventy pension, but the man had explained to her that it was really the same thing. Her second husband had been self-employed and too mean to pay a stamp. Every six months she received a visit from the social security people, to find out if her circumstances had changed. The humiliation of these visits, the posh voices, the questions, the eyes everywhere, only strengthened her determination to preserve her independence at all costs. To hang on to her house, to save up for her funeral, and never, never to ask them for a penny more than she was forced. She wasn't going to lie in a pauper's coffin, and she would never, while she had breath in her body, let them talk her into the Workhouse.

'Them buggers have been here again,' she would say to Iris King.

'Well, and you shouldn't let them upset you.'

'Asking bloody questions. Begrudging you every penny you get.'

'T'isn't coming out of their pockets.'

'You'd think it was, but.'

'Ah, well. You want to think: they'll be old themselves one day.'

And so Iris soothed her. And she let herself be soothed.

A stranger coming into the room would hardly have noticed, at first, that there was a body in the bed, for Alice's emaciated frame scarcely raised the covers, and her skin, over the years, had yellowed to the same shade as the pillowcases and the wall: smoke-cured. The room was always full of smoke because the chimney backs were broken and the smoke from her neighbour's fire poured into the house. When she was still well enough to leave the house, she had always carried with her the smell of smoke. The smoke formed layers of soot on all the furniture. You could dust it one minute, and it would be there again the next.

Still she loved the house. Over the years it had become a refuge. Finally, almost an extension of her own body.

It hadn't always been so. For Iris King, Union Street was a move up. For Mrs Bell, it was down. At first she hated it. The house was dark and drab, and it needed so many repairs. The kitchen tap shook and juddered whenever you turned it on, producing a thin trickle of brown water and a shower of plaster from the walls.

Iris King had tried to decorate the kitchen for her, but she'd had to give up in the end.

'I'm sorry, Mrs Bell,' she'd said. 'I just daren't mess on with this paper. It's holding up the wall.'

And they'd both had a good laugh because incredibly the old music-hall joke was true.

But afterwards Mrs Bell had felt a bit depressed. She was used to better. Her last house had had a bathroom and an indoor lavatory, with a little strip of green out the back. She'd had a bay window in the front room, too.

You take these things for granted till you haven't got them. The descent to Union Street was bitter.

1983

Nora Ephron

———————

Nora Ephron was born in 1941 in New York City and grew up in Beverly Hills, California – feeling in fifth and sixth grade 'not at all like a girl', being instead 'athletic, ambitious, outspoken, competitive, noisy, rambunctious'. Ever the critic of the politics of gender, she became a columnist and a journalist after leaving Wellesley College with a BA in 1962. Much of her writing from this time is collected as published volumes of her newspaper columns. In 1983 she co-authored the award-winning screenplay for *Silkwood* which heralded the start of a prestigious career in screenwriting, with films such as *When Harry Met Sally* and *Sleepless in Seattle*, which, through Ephron's characteristic wry humour, epitomised contemporary relationships and teased out definitions of modern romance. *Heartburn* was also made into a film in 1986.

Heartburn was published by Virago in 1996.

from

Heartburn

I looked across the table at Mark. I still love you, I thought. I still look at that dopey face of yours, with that silly striped beard, and think you are the handsomest man I've ever known. I still find you interesting, even if right now you are being more boring than the Martin Agronsky show. But someday I won't anymore. And in the meantime, I'm getting out. I am no beauty, and I'm getting on in years, and I have just about enough money to last me sixty days, and I am terrified of being alone, and I can't bear the idea of divorce, but I would rather die than sit here and pretend it's okay, I would rather die than sit here figuring out how to get you to love me again, I would rather die than spend five more minutes going through your drawers and wondering where you are and anticipating the next betrayal and worrying about whether my poor, beat-up, middle-aged body with its Caesarean scars will ever turn you on again. I can't stand feeling sorry for myself. I can't stand feeling like a victim. I can't stand hoping against hope. I can't stand sitting here with all this rage turning to hurt and then to tears. I CAN'T STAND NOT TALKING!

I looked at the pie sitting right there in front of me and suddenly it began to throb. They were talking about the State Department now. If I throw this pie at him, I thought to myself, he will never love me. And then it hit me: he *doesn't* love me. It hit me with a shimmering clarity: that was all there was to it. It didn't matter if he was crazy. It didn't matter if I was innocent or guilty. Nothing mattered except that he didn't love me. *If I throw this pie at him, he will never love me. But he doesn't love me anyway. So I can throw the pie if I want to.* I picked up the pie, thanked God for the linoleum floor, and threw it. It landed mostly on the right side of Mark's face, but that was good enough. The cream and the lime filling clung to his beard and his nose and his eyelashes, and pieces of crust dropped onto his blazer. I started to laugh. Mark started to laugh, too; I must say he handled it very well. He laughed as if all this were part of a running joke we'd forgotten to let Betty and Dmitri in on. He wiped himself off. He said, 'I think it's time for us to go home.' He stood up. So did I. I turned to Betty, who was staring wide-eyed at the two of us. 'By the way,' I said, 'I'm not coming to the dance.' And we went home.

Of course I'm writing this later, much much later, and it worries me that I've done what I usually do – hidden the anger, covered the pain, pretended it wasn't there for the sake of the story. 'Why do you feel you have to turn everything into a story?' Vera once asked me. I remember when she asked me, in fact. It was right after my marriage to Charlie broke up, and I was living in an apartment where everything made into something else – the couch made into a bed, the coffee table made into a dining table, the end table made into a stool. 'How are you?' people would ask me, in that intimate way people asked the question in those days. How *are* you. I couldn't bear it. So I told them about my apartment where everything made into something else. Then a friend called and said, 'I have one piece of advice for you. I give it to all my friends whose marriages break up: Don't buy anything at Azuma.' I added that to my repertoire.

Vera said: 'Why do you feel you have to turn everything into a story?'

So I told her why:

Because if I tell the story, I control the version.

Because if I tell the story, I can make you laugh, and I would rather have you laugh at me than feel sorry for me.

Because if I tell the story, it doesn't hurt as much.

Because if I tell the story, I can get on with it.

1984

Paula Fox

———

Paula Fox was born in 1923 in New York and attended Columbia University. She is the author of over twenty children's books and six novels, including *Poor George* and *Desperate Characters*, which was made into a film starring Shirley MacLaine in 1970.

A Servant's Tale was published in the UK by Virago in 1986.

from

A Servant's Tale

Once out of the narrow hallway of the tenement we were living in at the time, my mother depended upon me to speak for her, to stand between her and the cold, racial glare of Broadway shopkeepers whose sluggish ill will never lost its power to quell me even as it aroused a desperate desire to hear, directed toward Mamá and me, the plain justice which their voices expressed when they served other customers, Irish or German, I guessed, or similar, proper folk, who so complacently placed their canned fruit and vegetables, their white bread and dusty potatoes, on the wooden counter while the grocer, with a pencil stub, rapidly added up the prices with a self-important flourish, then rang up the total on a huge cash register whose drawer shooting out with a loud bang to receive bills and coins always made Mamá start as if at that same instant she had discovered there was no money in her pocketbook to pay for our few purchases, canned milk or vinegar, or three brown eggs.

It was only in Mr Salazar's *bodega*, after a hasty, frightened run from our flat, that Mamá moved with a touch of ease as she estimated the ripeness of plantains, or slipped her hand into a sack of black beans, or touched with one finger the fleshy white roots of sweet cassava in its open wooden crate.

Here in the dim, tiny Spanish grocery store on Broadway and 158th Street, which always smelled of cat urine and cockroach poison, of spiced sausage and coconut candy, Henry Salazar, a tall, elderly, unsmiling Cuban from whose steel-framed spectacles the left lens was missing, weighed lard and onions, and, when asked for it, went to a cubicle at the back of the store and returned with what always looked to be the same grey slab of pork banded with lines of dried dark blood. From this he carved rough chunks, throwing them on his scale until a customer cried, '*bastante*!'

Below the counter, he kept a stack of lottery tickets for sale, and near a shelf of boxes of Dutch Cleanser and cakes of yellow kitchen soap, a telephone. It was this last which drew customers to the *bodega* as much, if not more, than Salazar's meager stores of what the neighbourhood Irish children called 'spic grub'.

Salazar charged two cents for each use of the telephone; he kept the pennies in large glass jars on a shelf off by themselves. Some storekeepers displayed jellybeans in jars, offering a prize to whoever could guess the correct number of candies in them. I tried to guess at the calls for help the pennies in Salazar's jars represented, how many inquiries made to remote authorities for news of lost relatives.

Once when I'd been sent for a bottle of milk, a woman was behind the counter weeping into the phone. 'Send a police – send, please –' she gasped out. Salazar was wrapping a loaf of lard for another customer who stared aghast at the weeping woman. 'Send doctor . . .'

When she had replaced the receiver, Salazar put down the lard and held out his long hand. Dazed, she stared down into it. '*Dos centavos,*' he said gravely. She stroked her cheeks, shook her head. 'He swallowed rat poison,' she said. 'He's dancing – on his back – on the floor.' The other customer put the two pennies in Salazar's hand. As I left, I heard the clink of them dropping into a jar.

After Mamá had carried her groceries in a cloth bag back to the kitchen of our tenement flat, she would sit on the edge of a stool near the sink and stare at what she had bought. She kept one foot on the floor; the other dangled like a child's. Her body was heavy and shapeless in a dress of dark material, and she slumped, exhausted after her perilous journey. Slowly, she would begin to put things away.

Nearly every day when I got home from school, I found Mamá sitting on that stool, one elbow on the counter, staring into the sink, waiting for me to lead her out into the New York streets as if she was blind and deaf.

We had been in New York City for five years. She had not learned English despite the months she had worked in a perfume factory across the Hudson River in New Jersey.

But she managed to keep the job for a year, travelling by subway, then by bus, to the bench where she sat all day long in front of a machine that stoppered bottles of scent, surrounded by women from whose mouths issued a blizzard of language, white and cold, she said

to me, like the snow, hard, she said, like the patches of ice on the sidewalk in winter before which she would shudder with dread as I yanked
at her arm or grabbed folds of her worn black coat to drag her on and
into one of the flats where Papá had moved us because of a rent con-
cession. Several times we moved because we needed more space for
boarders who would rent from us one of the linoleum-floored cubi-
cles along the hallway, each furnished with a bureau, a chair and a
spindly bed.

It was one of those boarders, Maura Cruz, who found Mamá the job
in the perfume factory, and who, with frantic insistence, tried to
compel Mamá into becoming an American. And when she was fired
from the perfume factory – as a consequence of her inattention,
many unstoppered bottles had drenched the skirts and legs of the
talkative women further on down the assembly line with the powerful
if synthetic aroma of spring flowers – it was Maura who found her
work she could do at home. This job, making beaded bags, required
only that she deliver her completed work once a month. But the
wholesale office to which she had to take the bags was so far downtown that she complained the subway ride was nearly as long as our
journey from San Pedro. I had to go with her, she said, because she
would not be able to argue with the man who was to pay her for her
labour, and whom Maura referred to as a thieving Jew.

The thieving Jew had a dingy little office at the front end of a dark
loft near Delancey Street. He was middle-aged, a tired-looking man
who barely spoke to us, taking the beaded bags, one at a time, from
the sack in which Mamá had carried them, and looking at them so
closely he seemed about to press them like handkerchiefs to his eyes.
We made thirteen trips to him. Each time, he paid Mamá exactly the
sum Maura had told her to insist upon. One late afternoon, he told us
he was bankrupt.

'No more business. No more money,' he said when he had counted
out eighteen dollars, placing the crumpled bills in Mamá's hand. 'Is
he lying?' she asked me in Spanish. I glanced at him. Before I could
answer her, he said, 'No, I'm not lying,' so diffidently, so mildly, that
I felt a rush of sympathy toward him, and surprise that he understood our language. He smiled at me abstractedly, then turned away,
placing his hands on the rough table he used for a desk and leaning
on them, a grimace of pain on his nearly hidden face.

After these trips, we returned home to find the early winter dusk
waiting for us at the top of the subway stairs, or else the long, hazy
evenings of summer when men and children gathered beneath the

street lights on our corner, shouting at each other in a language that was not Spanish or English but an agitated, harsh mingling of both. A year after Mamá lost her job in the perfume factory, she explained to me, 'I couldn't pay attention to those bottles that flew past me. How could I – with those women always talking?'

'You didn't have to listen to them.'

'Ah, but I did! They *wanted* me to know how ignorant I was. They watched me when they talked. I was drowning, I tell you.'

I knew she understood more than she let on, but Mamá's inability, or refusal, to learn to speak English was like an ailment which ate away at her nature. Even the country folk who rented rooms from us for a few months, and who often came from remote rural districts in Cuba or Puerto Rico, even those *guajiros*, so ignorant that our chain-pull toilet alarmed them as Beatriz de la Cueva's servants' toilet had once alarmed me, would press me – whom they treated in this regard as an authority because I went to school – to help them speak as Americans spoke, to teach them to unlock their tongues so they could pronounce, without that Antilles accent to which they attributed so much of their social and economic misery, those particular words which began with the treacherous *th*, or those that ended with the perverse, unspellable *ough*, or the homely *ing* which was, said a young woman from San Juan, exactly like the sound made by a *saltón*. 'In English, a *saltón* is a grasshopper,' I said. '*Que barbaridad!*' she commented.

The Great Depression was not unique to these immigrants who had experienced so much want. When Papá told one of our boarders, Enrique Machado, that there had been sixteen million unemployed people in 1933, the Cuban shrugged. 'Hombre! You get a long ride on the subway for a nickel,' he said, as though offering proof of a prosperity kept out of his reach only by his inability to sound like everyone else.

Mamá clung to the old language like a shipwrecked person might cling to a plank, caught in currents which were carrying her ever further from the shore.

1985

Janette Turner Hospital

Janette Turner Hospital was born in Melbourne, Australia, in 1942. She graduated from the University of Queensland in 1965 and became a high-school teacher. In 1967, she moved first to the USA and then to Canada to take up postgraduate study. She began writing in 1977, but it wasn't until the publication of her first novel in 1982, which won the Canadian Seal First Novel Award, that she began to write full-time. A multi-award-winning novelist, she has lived 'all over the world'.

Borderline was published by Virago in 1990.

from

Borderline

Felicity woke beside her lover in an apartment in Boston. No one lived in the apartment, though they both shared the lease; it was purely for assignations. There were plants and rugs and Marimekko cushions and a waterbed, all the usual pretenses of permanence.

Felicity woke sweating because of the dream.

She was trapped in a painting again. She fitted snugly inside her black outline but there were 144 square inches missing from the middle of her torso. Between her breasts and her pubic hair, the viewer could see straight through to the tropics: mango trees, coconut palms, white sand. A conch shell where her navel might have been. White wave crests frothing like crabs up the sand, a little breeze off the reef stirring her pubic hair. There was a hibiscus behind her ear. Jasmine in fluted letters across her thighs announced: This is not a real woman.

Felicity slipped out of her painting and moved discreetly among the navel-gazers, staring through the tropical hole in her guts along with them, listening to the comments. What does it mean? she heard on all sides. According to the guidebook, someone said, the view could be South India or the Queensland coast of Australia. Felicity considered sticking small flags into the canvas to mark the sites of her hometowns. If you scratch the crotch and sniff, someone said, you can smell papaya.

No touching, please! called a guard.

There was a stain on the floor below the painting.

Felicity mingled with the crowd as it flowed toward the exit turnstiles. Escape was at the forefront of her mind. Passports, passports, the border guard said, and people held their documents ready for showing. Scrutiny, rubber stamp, pass on, that was the routine. But there was something wrong with Felicity's passport; a visa lacking, or a hole in the middle of her photograph. Step aside, she was told. Wait here.

Once the inspector arrived, it was all over. You again, he said, back you go. The man with the brush was waiting as usual and they pasted her back on the canvas, flattening the curves, elongating here, twisting there, making free with the placing of her eyes. She had not even settled herself properly around the empty space – through which the surf hissed and writhed – when the frame was clanged shut around her. Locked. All borders in place. The man with the keys shook the bunch in front of her face.

Felicity woke in a sweat.

Her lover had turned in his sleep and flung an arm across her breasts. She was pinned beneath him. Through the grid of her lashes and across the curved foreground of her cheeks, she could see the delicate hairs, luminous from the street lamp, crosshatching his arm muscle. A novel perspective – though perhaps it had been done in one of da Vinci's anatomical sketchbooks.

1986

Grace Nichols

———

Grace Nichols was born in 1950 and educated in Georgetown, Guyana, but has lived in Britain since 1977 and now works as a free-lance writer. In 1983 she won the Commonwealth Poetry Prize with her first book of poems, *i is a long-memoried woman*, which was followed by *The Fat Black Woman's Poems* (1984) and *Lazy Thoughts of a Lazy Woman* (1989). She has also written widely for children. She lives in Sussex with her family.

Whole of a Morning Sky was first published by Virago in 1986.

from

Whole of a Morning Sky

The Duke coming. The Duke of Edinburgh.

At school the teachers talk about the visit which is all because Guiana is part of the British Empire. You preferred if it was the Queen coming though, in her gown and crown.

Nearly every night your mother would take you and Anthony to see the lighting up all over Georgetown for the visit. All the flamboyant trees on Main Street Avenue full of electric bulbs, hanging like see-through pears of every shade from every tree, right and left of the avenue as far as your eye could see. St George's Cathedral which they say is the highest wooden building in the world is washed in flood-lights, glowing tall and white as if someone had painted it in moonlight. The Town Hall looking like a lovely icing cake because it's so studded with lights. All the shops and stores bright with new lights too, the big ones and the small. Some flashing lights saying 'Welcome', others looking as if they're embroidered in lights. Only Chin grocery shop is dark.

But you're always going into Chin shop to buy fluties, sweet red-water ice blocks that turn your tongue bright pink. You'd go into Chin shop and wait patiently for him to come and sell you because his shop always full of people. People like his saltbeef and pigtail.

Chin flat, pale, smooth, always wearing a white singlet and short khaki pants, his rubber slippers flapping up behind him. The back of the shop musty and dark, full of bags of rice and sugar piled one on top the other.

One day, a boy, a little bigger than you, come into Chin shop and begin to call for a long list of things; 'Twenty-four tin carnation milk, twelve cake soap, twelve pound sugar, four pound saltbeef, six tin tomato paste, six box match, six tin sardine, four pound cheese . . .'

From the look on his face you know he only joking. Chin must be stupid not to see that the boy only joking, that he don't have money to pay for all the things Chin busy heaping on the counter, walking up and down, weighing this and that, his slippers flapping.

You begin to giggle in anticipation. When Chin finish, the boy start to laugh too: 'Man, Chin, what wrong with you man? You don't know is fun I making? Where I going get money to buy all them thing, man?'

A red flush spreading across Chin face and his eyes becoming even narrower. Chin looking now as if he's trying hard to control himself, smiling: 'Nice, nice lil boy, come give me hand a shake,' stretching out his hand across the counter.

'Don't put out yuh hand. Don't put out yuh hand, boy,' you say, still laughing. But the boy already putting out his hand into Chin hand uncertainly, not knowing whether Chin still vex or taking the whole thing as a joke. Chin grip the boy palm with his hand and begin to squeeze, squeezing and squeezing as if he want to crack every bone inside the boy hand.

But you still go into Chin shop, and another time when it was just you alone inside, Chin lean across the counter to pinch one of the small brown nipples just showing under your cotton dress. 'Eeeeh! You getting beeg,' be say.

The pinch hurt you and you hurry out of the shop, feeling Chin is a dirty old lizard.

You have to get new school uniform to march with the other schoolchildren to go and see the Duke. New yachting shoes, new socks, new navy blue kimona, new cream blouse, new beret. But you know your father won't give the money. That you'd be lucky to get anything new at all.

1987

Kaye Gibbons

———

Kaye Gibbons was born in 1960 in North Carolina and was educated there. *Ellen Foster* was her first novel, and began life as a poem when Gibbons was still at university. Influenced by the writing of the African-American poet James Weldon Johnson and his use of common speech patterns an idioms, she went on to expand the narrative voice into the creation of Ellen, the eleven-year-old narrator. Her persuasive voice made the book an instant bestseller in America, selected by Oprah Winfrey for her bookclub. Gibbons's other books include *A Virtuous Woman* (1997), *A Cure for Dreams* (1991), *Charms for the Easy Life* (1993) and *Sights Unseen* (1995).

Ellen Foster was first published in the UK by Virago in 1998.

from

Ellen Foster

When it is morning I hear my daddy come in the house. He does not sneak. If he had a horse he would have ridden in right up the steps. He has forgotten last night and he is foolish enough to think we have too.

My mama has got her own self out of the bed. I must have slept hard not to hear her. All my clothes are on that I wore yesterday. It will save me some trouble this morning.

He's got her in the kitchen by herself. I know he won't hurt her with his hands. He might throw a cup or a fork at her but he won't touch her to leave a mark.

I try not to leave her by herself with him. Not even when they are both asleep in the bed. My baby crib is still up in their bedroom so when I hear them at night I throw a fit and will not stop until I can sleep in the baby bed. He will think twice when I am around.

And I have to see now but the door is shut. There is something in the kitchen I need so I go in there to get it.

She is sitting at one end of the table and he is sitting at the other end going through her pocketbook. Some of her heart pills are on the table rolling around loose and the bottle is in her lap.

Give the bottle to me and let me put the pills back in it. They cost money, I say to her.

That's all the pills she's got left. She took almost the whole god-damn bottle, he looks at her and tells me.

Vomit them up, mama. I'll stick my finger down your throat and you can vomit them up. She looks at me and I see she will not vomit. She will not move.

Well I'll just go to the store and use the telephone.

But my daddy says he will kill me if I try to leave this house. All the time I knew he was evil and I did not have the proof.

He would kill me and my mama both with a knife. He looks at the two of us and rubs her pocketbook, patient, like he sits and waits for folks to die all the time. He wants me to put her back in the bed.

Hell, all she needs is some sleep, he says. Take her back there and see if she don't sleep it off. And he gave me a guarantee the pills would not hurt her bad.

We will rest some more. The day is early and we need some more rest.

I always love to eat a good supper, brush my teeth and go to bed early. If I am not sleepy I can always find something to do.

Lately I lay up in the bed and read old books. I told the library teacher I wanted to read everything of some count so she made me a list. That was two years ago and I'm up to the Brontë sisters now. I do not read comic books or the newspaper. I find out what news I need off the television.

I can hardly tolerate the stories we read for school. Cindy or Lou with the dog or cat. Always setting out on some adventure. They might meet a bandit or they might hop a freight but the policeman or the engineer always brings them home and they are still good children.

I myself prefer the old stories. When I started my project I enjoyed the laughing Middle Ages lady that wore red boots. She was on a trip with a group of people swapping stories, carrying on, slapping each other on the back.

What I am reading now is a little fancy for me but it is on the list. Just men and women sneaking around in a big dark house with one all into the other's business. The library teacher said the author and her sisters wrote books because in their day they could not go out and get jobs. I bet they were just well off and did not need to work.

I could lay here and read all night. I am not able to fall asleep without reading. You have that time when your brain has nothing constructive to do so it rambles. I fool my brain out of that by making it read until it shuts off. I just think it is best to do something right up until you fall asleep.

I always want to lay here. And she moves her arm up and I push my head down by her side. And I will crawl in and make room for myself. My heart can be the one that beats.

And hers has stopped.

Damn him to the bottom of hell damn him.

What to do now when the spinning starts people will come and they will want to know why and I cannot tell them why. They will not come yet no not for a while. I have her now while she sleeps but just is not breathing. I do not have to tell him so let him sit and wonder at the quiet in here. Why this house is so still and people all over everywhere are glad for the day.

Guilty and held down in his chair by God and fear of a sweet dead woman.

You can rest with me until somebody comes to get you. We will not say anything. We can rest.

I despise that dress and get your hands off me is what she needs to be told. But I push the bathroom door and leave my aunt on the other side and me to myself.

Is this my lipstick now? I do not think I should put a dab on to wear to the church. She would let me. But somebody would say something.

Put it back put it back just like it was. When I am old I can come back and wear it. When it is not for play. They didn't need this to dress her up with? Somebody must have got her another stick. She left this one at home. To be sure they don't paint everybody they do business with with the same stick.

I will just wash my mouth and sit on the toilet to look. I can see them all through the crack in the door. Everybody I have not seen since last Christmas sitting around patting their hands together.

My daddy is thinking about how good a tall glass of anything would be. Before they all got here he rounded up all his beer cans and pitched them under the back porch.

Somebody must have given him that suit. All he ever wears is grey work outfits. I want to sew a little patch over the pockets that says his name BILL. He could be like the Esso man. Can I help you, ma'am? Check your tyres? Change your oil? Throw a knife at you?

All he has done since Sunday morning is open the door for folks and shake his head yes or no. His brother Rudolph put him in the car and took him to town to pick out the coffin. I know when he got there my mama's sister chased him off. They are the ones with the taste.

He sits there with both feet on the floor and his eyes are red but not from crying. When somebody goes by and leans forward to his ear he touches them on the shoulder. Still king. Now quiet.

She finally shut him up.

1988

Lucy Ellmann

———

Lucy Ellmann was born in Evanston, Illinois, in 1956 and moved to the UK at the age of thirteen. After attending Falmouth and Canterbury art schools, Essex University and the Courtauld Institute, she started writing fiction. *Sweet Desserts* was winner of the 1988 *Guardian* Fiction Prize and was followed by *Varying Degrees of Hopelessness. Man or Mango? A Lament*, her third novel, was published in 1998. She lives in Hampshire.

Sweet Desserts was first published in the UK by Virago in 1988.

from

Sweet Desserts

My little girl wants to wear pink shoes. She has lovely little grooves in baby places and dimples at the knee, and dirty feet. She's a person, and she wants to wear pink shoes.

Cut out the shapes from Genoese, mask with hot apricot jelly, slightly warm your coloured and flavoured Marzipan, and roll out very thin. Pass a grooved rolling pin across to mark the lines, cut into strips with fluted cutter and cover the Genoese shapes. Fill in the centres with Fondant, jelly, etc., and decorate.

I took Lily to Venice. I thought streets made of water might amuse, and anyway, *I* wanted to go. My hopes for the trip were raised by the handsome Italian train conductor who gave me the eye while punching my ticket. I left Lily asleep in the compartment with a friendly fellow traveller, and went to the loo. The ticket collector was still hanging around outside, waiting for me. He'd prepared his speech: 'You're beautiful.' I said that he was too. Then he pushed his tongue into my mouth and pushed me hard against the wall of the train in an imagined fuck. Then he pushed me into the loo and pushed me down, unzipped his trousers, and pushed my head down on his prick. I was feeling tired after a night on the train and rather enjoyed this manhandling. He snuck out of the loo first, to protect his job or his reputation. I crept out a minute later after washing my hands for some reason, feeling quite content.

Lily lost her hat in the canal as soon as we got out of the train station, and cried. And once she'd realised they were the main method of transportation, she refused to go on boats. I struggled up and down the steps of the little bridges, with the pushchair which I either hauled or carried. One wheel kept falling off all over Venice, Murano, Burano and Torcello.

We entered no churches, and no museums, until I made a determined effort and got Lily to the Guggenheim collection. A storm broke out as we arrived, and Lily ran around the courtyard in the rain, taking her clothes off. When I scolded her mildly about this, she lay down on the marble floor, condensation rising almost visibly from her towards some Cubist *papiers collés*, and blocked a doorway. When she finally fell asleep in her pushchair, I wheeled her into Peggy Guggenheim's bedroom and went to the loo for a few moments' peace. Sixty seconds later, two or three of the bilingual, pre-parental, American Art History-major guards were knocking on the loo door, scared to death that the child had been abandoned to Peggy Guggenheim's care forever.

I trudged, Lily complained, my money ran low, and meanwhile, the heat and the handsome men continued to make me feel randy. Even the male pigeons I found sexy, stalking females in St Mark's Square, with their necks all puffed out, though I noted that they were easily swayed from this quest whenever Lily threw them corn. I was approached in restaurants every night by their human equivalent, loose men who were strangely indifferent to my reaction to them – they bounced back or took off, with the same blank expression either way. They all had teddy-bear names, like Nildo, Naldo, Bepe and Pepe.

A restaurant-owner called Mimmo gave Lily some nice noodles and freshly squeezed orange juice, for which I was grateful, since all the other restaurants were shutting. He placed a tiny TV in front of her which she happily watched, undeterred by the language barrier. I relaxed. I rather liked Mimmo – he knew too little English to put me off. We started kissing. It was not bad. At least he showed determination.

He wanted me to come back and see his flat. I explained that this was out of the question with Lily around. He said, just come see it so I would know where it was and could then come to lunch some time. It made no sense to me. But Lily wanted to go, so we went. We saw his raggedy carpet and his unmade bed and the bits of cotton wool on the floor. I had never thought before about the fact that they had cotton wool in Italy too.

He started to straighten it all up a bit. I started to go. I called Lily, but she was sitting down on a little stool in Mimmo's bedroom, too tired to move. I was heading back to go pick her up, when Mimmo grabbed me and pressed me against the wall, kissing my closed lips. I suddenly realised that he felt he had a right to do anything to me, because I'd had the audacity to go to his flat. When I tried to push at the arms holding me, he pushed harder. I made myself cold and stiff, saying, 'Stop. Stop it,' again and again. I wondered how I could explain even to good friends, much less the police, that I hadn't intended to fuck this person. He suddenly relented – he must have realised it would be quite hard to rape me, and perhaps he even grasped the fact that it would be no fun.

I wandered, trembling and furious, back to his bedroom to collect my whimpering child. Mimmo escorted us back to our *pensione*, pretending that nothing had happened. He asked me to come for lunch the next day. I was too scared to say anything.

I could no longer cope with Venice. I kept crying. I wept almost continually on the train home. Lily offered me sweets, and waited for me to recover. Back in London, she still wants pink shoes, and I keep seeing Mimmo's face everywhere.

Don't Say YES When You Want To Say NO

Yes, now you too can break from a self-limiting way of life, as countless graduates of Assertiveness Training can testify, launching yourself on a life-changing programme which is easier than you think!

1989

Margaret Atwood

Margaret Atwood was born in Ottawa in 1939. She spent much of her childhood in the northern Ontario and Quebec bush country, and started writing, she says, at the age of five. She was eleven before she attended school full-time, but went on to graduate from the University of Toronto and obtain a master's degree from Radcliffe College. She has travelled extensively.

She has published poetry, short stories, literary criticism (including *Survival* 1972, a study of Canadian literature) and novels, including *The Edible Woman* (1969), *Surfacing* (1972), *Cat's Eye* and *The Robber Bride* (1993). *The Handmaid's Tale* (1985) won the Governor-General's Award, sold over a million copies in the USA and was filmed in 1990. Atwood says she started out as 'a profoundly apolitical writer, but then began to do what all novelists and some poets do: I began to describe the world around me'. She lives in Toronto, the city which provides the emotional landscape for *Cat's Eye*.

Cat's Eye was published by Virago in 1989.

from

Cat's Eye

It's the middle of March. In the schoolroom windows the Easter tulips are beginning to bloom. There's still snow on the ground, a dirty filigree, though the winter is losing its hardness and glitter. The sky thickens, sinks lower.

We walk home under the low thick sky that is grey and bulging with dampness. Moist soft flakes are falling out of it, piling up on roofs and branches, sliding off now and then to hit with a wet cottony thunk. There's no wind and the sound is muffled by the snow.

It isn't cold. I undo the ties on my blue knitted wool hat, let it flap loose on my head. Cordelia takes off her mittens and scoops up snowballs, throwing them at trees, at telephone poles, at random. It's one of her friendly days; she puts her arm through my arm, her other arm through Grace's, and we march along the street, singing *We don't stop for anybody*. I sing this too. Together we hop and slide.

Some of the euphoria I once felt in falling snow comes back to me; I want to open my mouth and let the snow fall into it. I allow myself to laugh, like the others, trying it out. My laughter is a performance, a grab at the ordinary.

Cordelia throws herself backwards onto a blank front lawn, spreads her arms out in the snow, raises them above her head, draws them down to her sides, making a snow angel. The flakes fall onto her face, into her laughing mouth, melting, clinging to her eyebrows. She blinks, closing her eyes against the snow. For a moment she looks like someone I don't know, a stranger, shining with unknown, good possibilities. Or else a victim of a traffic accident, flung onto the snow.

She opens her eyes and reaches up her hands, which are damp and reddened, and we pull her upwards so she won't disturb the image she's made. The snow angel has feathery wings and a tiny pin-head. Where her hands stopped, down near her sides, are the imprints of her fingers, like little claws.

We've forgotten the time, it's getting dark. We run along the street that leads to the wooden footbridge. Even Grace runs, lumpily, calling 'Wait up!' For once she is the one left behind.

Cordelia reaches the hill first and runs down it. She tries to slide but the snow is too soft, not icy enough, and there are cinders and pieces of gravel in it. She falls down and rolls. We think she's done it on purpose, the way she made the snow angel. We rush down upon her, exhilarated, breathless, laughing, just as she's picking herself up.

We stop laughing, because now we can see that her fall was an accident, she didn't do it on purpose. She likes everything she does to be done on purpose.

Carol says, 'Did you hurt yourself?' Her voice is quavery, she's frightened, already she can tell that this is serious. Cordelia doesn't answer. Her face is hard again, her eyes baleful.

Grace moves so that she's beside Cordelia, slightly behind her. From there she smiles at me, her tight smile.

Cordelia says, to me, 'Were you laughing?' I think she means, was I laughing at her because she fell down.

'No,' I say.

'She was,' says Grace neutrally. Carol shifts to the side of the path, away from me.

'I'm going to give you one more chance,' says Cordelia. 'Were you laughing?'

'Yes,' I say, 'but . . .'

'Just yes or no,' says Cordelia.

I say nothing. Cordelia glances over at Grace, as if looking for approval. She sighs, an exaggerated sigh, like a grownup's. 'Lying again,' she says. 'What are we going to do with you?'

We seem to have been standing there for a long time. It's colder now. Cordelia reaches out and pulls off my knitted hat. She marches the rest of the way down the hill and onto the bridge and hesitates for a moment. Then she walks over to the railing and throws my hat down into the ravine. Then the white oval of her face turns up towards me. 'Come here,' she says.

Nothing has changed, then. Time will go on, in the same way, endlessly. My laughter was unreal after all, merely a gasp for air.

I walk down to where Cordelia stands by the railing, the snow not crunching but giving way under my feet like cotton-wool packing. It sounds like a cavity being filled, in a tooth, inside my head. Usually I'm afraid to go so near the edge of the bridge, but this time I'm not. I don't feel anything as positive as fear.

'There's your stupid hat,' says Cordelia; and there it is, far down, still blue against the white snow, even in the dimming light. 'Why don't you go down and get it?'

I look at her. She wants me to go down into the ravine where the bad men are, where we're never supposed to go. It occurs to me that I may not. What will she do then?

I can see this idea gathering in Cordelia as well. Maybe she's gone too far, hit, finally, some core of resistance in me. If I refuse to do what she says this time, who knows where my defiance will end? The two others have come down the hill and are watching, safely in the middle of the bridge.

'Go on then,' she says, more gently, as if she's encouraging me, not ordering. 'Then you'll be forgiven.'

I don't want to go down there. It's forbidden and dangerous; also it's dark and the hillside will be slippery, I might have trouble climbing up again. But there is my hat. If I go home without it, I'll have to explain, I'll have to tell. And if I refuse to go, what will Cordelia do next? She might get angry, she might never speak to me again. She might push me off the bridge. She's never done anything like that before, never hit or pinched, but now that she's thrown my hat over there's no telling what she might do.

I walk along to the end of the bridge. 'When you've got it, count to a hundred,' says Cordelia. 'Before coming up.' She doesn't sound angry any more. She sounds like someone giving instructions for a game.

I start down the steep hillside, holding onto branches and tree trunks. The path isn't even a real path, it's just a place worn by whoever goes up and down here: boys, men. Not girls.

When I'm among the bare trees at the bottom I look up. The bridge railings are silhouetted against the sky. I can see the dark outlines of three heads, watching me.

My blue hat is out on the ice of the creek. I stand in the snow, looking at it. Cordelia is right, it's a stupid hat. I look at it and feel resentment, because this stupid-looking hat is mine, and deserving of ridicule. I don't want to wear it ever again.

I can hear water running somewhere, down under the ice. I step out onto the creek, reach for the hat, pick it up, go through. I'm up to my waist in the creek, slabs of broken ice up-ended around me.

Cold shoots through me. My overshoes are filling, and the shoes inside them; water drenches my snowpants. Probably I've screamed, or some noise has come out of me, but I can't remember hearing anything. I clutch the hat and look up at the bridge. Nobody is there. They must have walked away, run away. That's why the counting to a hundred: so they could run away.

I try to move my feet. They're very heavy, because of the water inside my boots. If I wanted to I could just keep standing here. It's true dusk now and the snow on the ground is bluish-white. The old tyres and pieces of rusted junk in the creek are covered over; all around me are blue arches, blue caves, pure and silent. The water of the creek is cold and peaceful, it comes straight from the cemetery, from the graves and their bones. It's water made from the dead people, dissolved and clear, and I am standing in it. If I don't move soon I will be frozen in the creek. I will be a dead person, peaceful and clear, like them.

I flounder through the water, the edges of the ice breaking off as I step. Walking with waterlogged overshoes is hard; I could slip, and fall all the way in. I grab a tree branch and haul myself up onto the bank and sit down in the blue snow and take off my overshoes and pour out the water. The arms of my jacket are wet to the elbows, my mittens are soaked. Now there are knives going through my legs and hands, and tears running down my face from the pain.

I can see lights along the edges of the ravine, from the houses there, impossibly high up. I don't know how I'm going to climb up the hill with my hands and feet hurting like this; I don't know how I'm going to get home.

My head is filling with black sawdust; little specks of the darkness are getting in through my eyes. It's as if the snowflakes are black, the way white is black on a negative. The snow has changed to tiny pellets, more like sleet. It makes a rustling noise coming down through the branches, like the shifting and whispering of people in a crowded room who know they must be quiet. It's the dead people, coming up invisible out of the water, gathering around me. *Hush*, is what they say.

I'm lying on my back beside the creek, looking up at the sky. Nothing hurts any more. The sky has a reddish undercolour. The bridge is different-looking; it seems higher above me, more solid, as if the railings have disappeared or been filled in. And it's glowing, there are pools of light along it, greenish-yellow, not like any light I've ever seen before. I sit up to get a better look. My body feels weightless, as it does in water.

There's someone on the bridge, I can see the dark outline. At first I think it's Cordelia, come back for me. Then I see that it's not a child, it's too tall for a child. I can't see the face, there's just a shape. One of the yellowish-green lights is behind it, coming out in rays from around the head.

I know I should get up and walk home, but it seems easier to stay here, in the snow, with the little pellets of ice caressing my face gently. Also I'm very sleepy. I close my eyes.

I hear someone talking to me. It's like a voice calling, only very soft, as if muffled. I'm not sure I've heard it at all. I open my eyes with an effort. The person who was standing on the bridge is moving through the railing, or melting into it. It's a woman, I can see the long skirt now, or is it a long cloak? She isn't falling, she's coming down towards me as if walking, but there's nothing for her to walk on. I don't have the energy to be frightened. I lie in the snow, watching her with lethargy, and with a sluggish curiosity. I would like to be able to walk on air like that.

Now she's quite close. I can see the white glimmer of her face, the dark scarf or hood around her head, or is it hair? She holds out her arms to me and I feel a surge of happiness. Inside her half-open cloak there's a glimpse of red. It's her heart, I think. It must be her heart, on the outside of her body, glowing like neon, like a coal.

Then I can't see her any more. But I feel her around me, not like arms but like a small wind of warmer air. She's telling me something.

You can go home now, she says. *It will be all right. Go home.*

I don't hear the words out loud, but this is what she says.

1990s

1990

Bharati Mukherjee

Bharati Mukherjee was born in Calcutta in 1940 and educated there. She earned a PhD at the University of Iowa, and has received grants from the National Endowment for the Arts and the Guggenheim Foundation for her fiction. She has taught creative writing at Columbia University and has taken up a distinguished professorship at the University of California at Berkeley. In addition to *Jasmine* she has written the novels *Wife* (1979), *The Tiger's Daughter* (1971) and *The Holder of the World* (1993), two works of non-fiction, *Days and Night in Calcutta* (1977) and *The Sorrow and the Terror*, and two collections of short stories, *Darkness* (1986) and *The Middleman and Other Stories*, which won the 1988 National Book Critics' Circle Award. Her later fiction has moved towards a wry critique of contemporary American culture, a shift she explains as one away from 'the aloofness of expatriation, to the exuberance of immigration'.

Virago first published *Jasmine* in the UK in 1990.

from

Jasmine

There are national airlines flying the world that do not appear in any directory. There are charters who've lost their way and now just fly, improvising crews and destinations. They serve no food, no beverages. Their crews often look abused. There is a shadow world of aircraft permanently aloft that share air lanes and radio frequencies with Pan Am and British Air and Air-India, portaging people who coexist with tourists and businessmen. But we are refugees and mercenaries and guest workers; you see us sleeping in airport lounges; you watch us unwrapping the last of our native foods, unrolling our prayer rugs, reading our holy books, taking out for the hundredth time an aerogram promising a job or space to sleep, a newspaper in our language, a photo of happier times, a passport, a visa, a *laissez-passer*.

We are the outcasts and deportees, strange pilgrims visiting outlandish shrines, landing at the end of tarmacs, ferried in old army trucks where we are roughly handled and taken to roped-off corners of waiting rooms where surly, barely wakened customs guards await their bribe. We are dressed in shreds of national costumes, out of season, the wilted plumage of intercontinental vagabondage. We ask only one thing: to be allowed to land; to pass through; to continue. We sneak a look at the big departure board, the one the tourists use. Our cities are there, too, our destinations are so close! But not yet, not so directly. We must sneak in, land by night in little-used strips. For us, back behind the rope in the corner of the waiting room, there is only a slate and someone who remembers to write in chalk, DELAYED, or TO BE ANNOUNCED, or OUT OF SERVICE. We take another of our precious dollars or Swiss francs and give it to a trustworthy-looking boy and say, 'Bring me tea, an orange, bread.'

What country? What continent? We pass through wars, through plagues. I am hungry for news, but the discarded papers are in characters or languages I cannot read.

The zigzag route is straightest.

I phantom my way through three continents. The small airports in the Middle East lit by oil fires and gas flares, the waiting rooms in Sudan with locusts banging on the glass, landing always in the smaller cities, the disused airfields.

On the first leg of my odyssey, I sit between a Filipina nurse and a Tamil auto mechanic both on their way to Bahrain. I walk my swollen feet up and down the aisles of our 747. Whole peoples are on the move! The Filipina says, 'The pay's great but I wish Bahrainis weren't Muslims.' She shows me her St Christopher medal on a blue sodality ribbon under her blouse. The Sri Lankan Tamil likes Muslims; he's not much taken with Buddhists and Christians. I keep my sandal-wood Ganpati hidden in my purse, a god with an elephant trunk to uproot anything in my path.

I sit with missionaries, with the deported, with Australian students who've fallen somehow into the same loop of desperation, which is for them adventure. 'Look,' says one, 'you'd love Owstrylia. Perth's just the plyce for you. Whatchu sye?' Hollow-eyed Muslim men in fur caps and woolen jackets, faces unshaven, make long-winded advances in Farsi and Pashto, elegant ghazals learned for the occasion, ripe with moons and figs and spurting fountains, then try out their broken Urdu when they guess I'm Indian.

In the soundproofed and windowless back room of an Indische Speishalle in Hamburg I watch on a tiny colour television set the first of many wonders in the West, with cheering Arabs and Africans, the Hamburg Hummels cream the opposition. A Ugandan lifts his Mickey Mouse T-shirt to show off his flesh wounds. 'When the American visa bastards turned me down, I tried to kill myself.' Later, in suburban Blankenese, the *Polizei* pull the Ugandan and me off a train and ask to see our travel documents. I hand over my forged, expensive passport. The *Polizei* scrutinise my inscrutables, then let me go. The Ugandan twitches and stammers. The flesh wound bleeds into Mickey Mouse as he scuffles. On the train I weep at the beauty of the visa stamps Hari-prar has bought me. I feel renewed, the recipient of an organ transplant.

In Amsterdam a railway porter, a Surinamese Indian who speaks a little bit of Hindi, puts me in touch with the captain of a trawler who cargoes contraband into Paramaribo, then outward to the States.

1991

Lisa St Aubin de Terán

———

Lisa St Aubin de Terán was born in south London in 1953. She attended school in London, married when she was sixteen, and for several years ran a sugar plantation and an avocado farm in the Venezuelan Andes. She was named as one of Britain's twenty best young novelists at the start of her career in 1983 by *The Times*; since then she has written a potent mix of poetry, fiction and memoir. She lives in Umbria, Italy.

Joanna was published by Virago in 1991.

from

Joanna

I had a lot of beaux, as Maman called them, a lot of admirers. It was the only way I could stop myself feeling bored. They used to tell me they were in love, which was all right so long as they didn't say it too often. Some of them had served in the war, some of them were too young, but they all used to talk about dying. They'd pretend they would die if I didn't kiss them, die if I didn't see them, care for them, and die if I refused to accept their presents. I kept them at bay because I knew they became excited if I let them get too close to me. Maman liked the flowers and the gold-wrapped chocolate truffles they sent and the hampers and bric-a-brac, but I liked only gramophone records and emeralds. The boyfriends who failed to notice this didn't last very long.

I heard somewhere about a queen in Egypt who had been forced to marry against her will and had built a pavilion of precious stones to mark her infidelities during her husband's absence. She let the whole of her kingdom defile her body and then bought a jewel to mark the scorn she held her husband in, making what he had had as worthless as she could. It was a strange story, although I liked it. None of my lovers ever saw or touched my nakedness, but they did all bring me stones.

There was a jeweller in Golders Green who strung them for me. He became my friend, together with his sister, Elsa Müller, who could make any dress or suit look as though it came from one of the most exclusive Paris houses, when actually she lived and worked on our street. Maman disapproved of her; she was the only one of my friends whom she tried to exclude from my life. The Müllers were Jewish, and

Maman, like most of my friends, had it in for the Jews. It didn't matter how charming they were, or even useful, Maman objected to having them in the house or near it. She minded if I so much as talked to them in the shop. She took it as another mark of our shame that I should even consider mixing with them socially. In her opinion, it was yet another twist of her penance that we should be reduced to living in the same street. Left to her own devices, she would probably have had them forcibly removed.

When it came to the redhead, although she admitted that the scarlet thatch itself was an undeniable blight and the grotesque size of the thing was what she called 'unfortunate' and the voracious appetite 'unladylike', she was always trying to make excuses for it, implying that its genetic defects were less accursed than they seemed. She claimed that Grandpapa had declared that Daddy's books and papers on hereditary flaws were often exaggerated and even wrong. Oh yes, she protected the redhead from the obvious verdict of criminal stigmata, but when it came to the Jews, she branded the whole race as evil, degenerate, repellent and practically every strong negative in her vocabulary. She tried to put me off the Müllers by assuring me that Daddy would never have spoken to them. When Elsa came to tea, bringing her cinnamon cake and huge *Pflaumentorte*, Maman either contrived to be out, or stayed in her room. Afterwards, she would invariably throw the remains of these delicious cakes to Rufus, her cringing little dog. Not surprisingly, the rich sweetness would make him ill. Maman, of course, interpreted this as a Jewish plot; while I liked Elsa all the more for it. I never could stand that dog.

Elsa had about a hundred cousins, and she had brothers and uncles scattered across the capital cities of Europe. She herself came from Vienna, and she could describe the place in such a way that it came to life with its wild music and its madness for dancing and balls and flirting and fun. All the men in her family were in what she called 'jewels', and she talked about precious stones and precious possessions quite unashamedly. Unlike most of my friends, who tended to be rather boringly modest about their things and therefore couldn't be brought into discussions about all the particularly lovely ones that used to fill Claremont, Elsa relished minute descriptions of vases and chandeliers and the thickly carved gilt frames of family portraits, and exotic treasures hauled and hoarded from all over the world. She truly admired my emeralds. She made me laugh with her quick cosmopolitan wit.

I enjoyed her infatuated stories about her cousin Dietrich getting lost at the Schönbrunn Palace and her cousin Josef waltzing in the street at midnight at the Graben and dancing so well that a crowd gathered and danced with him through the Viennese night. I almost loved her for so admiring what she had left. I cannot abide people who belittle their own past in their exile.

I am sure I would have liked Vienna, but I would probably have liked it best in the twenties. There were so many headlines and hoardings and talks about the Depression, it seemed to swallow up the whole of the thirties. If I stopped dancing for so much as a second, those years just became depressing. Everything was getting so serious; even one's friends were transformed into stodgy worried businessmen or politicians. Perpetual motion, that's the best remedy for boredom – or, rather, the best vaccination. I kept travelling, around the map of England from country house to country house, eliminating the weekends from Friday to Monday so that the weeks foreshortened and were easier to fill.

Considering that I've had half of Europe parading through my head, it shouldn't be so difficult to account for my own time. How can one lose the midweeks of twenty years? I can remember the beach at Selsey very clearly, though I can no longer remember which boyfriends did and didn't go there with me; but what else? I used to walk through the park sometimes, and sometimes we went boating. In summer there was tennis, and in winter, skating. I went to Paris several times, I enjoyed flying. I hated the cinema. I can't decide what was more depressing, the sight of a dole queue or the sight of a queue for the cinema. I went once, and I left halfway through. The whole idea of the darkness and sitting so close to people one doesn't know is quite horrid; as are the puppet movements on the screen with their endless oncoming black-and-whiteness. It reminded me of Canada. I enjoyed the opera and the odd concert, but I would often get restless and leave those too.

I don't know why all those middles have become so ephemeral. All I seem to remember are tunes.

1992

Gillian Slovo

Gillian Slovo was born in South Africa in 1952. In 1963, three years after the Sharpeville massacre and the first official state of emergency, her father, Joe Slovo, was forced underground for his opposition to apartheid and then into exile. Her mother, Ruth First, was the first woman to be detained under the Ninety-Day Detention Act and on her release after 117 days of solitary confinement, the whole family joined their father in exile in London, where Gillian still lives. Since the birth of her own daughter, she has been writing full-time, a detective-novel series featuring her intrepid heroine Kate Baeier and also *Ties of Blood*, her first novel set in South Africa, and a volume of autobiography, *Every Secret Thing*.

The Betrayal was published by Virago in paperback in 1992.

from

The Betrayal

Looking neither to left nor to right, Sarah Patterson walked straight past the police station. She walked as if she were completely unaware of her surroundings, as if familiarity had rendered them invisible. She walked, in short, like any other white South African woman who found herself walking only because she was between shopping malls.

But the truth couldn't have been more different. For Sarah had worked hard on her apparent unconcern and now she was involved in a different kind of work – she was counting. Conscientiously spacing each step so that the intervals between them were identical, she paced the pavement surrounding the police station, measuring it. Only when she had turned the corner did she stop.

She lowered her shopping to the ground as if she were giving herself a much deserved rest and then, out of her handbag she withdrew a small diary. She opened it to a day somewhere long in the future. On this page, on its extreme left underneath two numbers, she noted down two more. She used no words to remind herself of what they meant. She had no need for words. She would never forget that there written in sequence were: the distance between the police station and the building opposite it; the distance between the police station and the bus shelter; the distance between the left hand corner and the centre door of the police station; and, finally, the number of paces between this same point and the corner on the right.

Sarah knew such attention to detail was unnecessary but she was by nature a perfectionist. Whenever she did anything, she did it thoroughly, a virtue which had earned her a first-class degree in England as well as early promotion to a school's head of department. And now that she was in South Africa she continued to stick to her elevated standards, checking and rechecking her observations, constantly alert to anything she might have overlooked.

She picked up her bags again and walked full circle back to her car. Opening the boot she threw her shopping inside. She closed it again, reflecting, with relief, that this was the last time she would need these props. She climbed into the car and turned the key. The engine, along with the car's tinny radio, sparked into life. Music issued out of it, loud discordant music, accompanied by a voice singing gracelessly in Afrikaans. She flicked a switch and the voice was abruptly cancelled. She put the car into gear and moved it slightly, aiming it for a file of slow moving traffic. She allowed herself one backward glance. There it stood, the police station, a squat modern building with its long, narrow windows and high ramps, an ugly building, a place of pain. As she nudged her car into the midst of others, she shivered at the thought of the chain she'd started. It was hot inside, hot as hell. Unrolling the window, she breathed a sigh of relief. She stretched forward and flicked the radio on again, turning the volume up high. The voice had been joined by others just as loud, all repeating one short phrase over and over again. Sarah joined in, imitating their jagged pronunciation, singing without understanding the song's meaning or caring about it. It fitted her mood, that song, and the words were irrelevant.

She was singing lustily, loudly, when she noticed something, a blur on her right. Her voice faltered as she glanced to her right. She saw a motorbike, a policeman astride it. He was keeping pace with her – leaning over to look straight in.

Sarah was immediately transported into another space, into the vision of arrest and incarceration that she'd daily been expecting. She breathed in and tried to calm herself: no matter what happened she must remain in control.

The music sounded out alone, its disharmony drilling its way into her head. She wrenched at the dials, yanking the volume knob so hard that it came off in her hand. A crackle of radio interference took over. With the flat of her hand she banged at the casing and then there was silence. A silence broken only by the pulsing blood around her temples. A silence which she endured, waiting for the inevitable, her mind blank.

The policeman winked at her, only once. And then, as she continued to watch him, hypnotised, he rose in his seat, pushed himself
forward and he was gone, leaving only fumes as a reminder that he'd
once been there.

The bastard, Sarah thought, he was looking down my cleavage.

That bastard, she thought, and she laughed out loud. She
laughed again, first in relief and then in a kind of euphoria. I've finished, she thought, and I've survived. She pushed her right foot
down, gunning the engine as if she could clear the queue in front of
her this way.

But the traffic was slow and her eyes remained focused on the
image of the police station in her rear view mirror. The place tugged
at her, almost as if it were trying to pull her back. She drove automat-
ically, watching, fascinated as it grew smaller, watching until she could
no longer distinguish it from its surrounds. She need never see it
again. She need never see it again unless, of course it was chosen as a
target – in which case she would recognise its husk on the front page
of a newspaper. If the ANC did bomb it, she thought, the policeman
who's just passed, and the others – the ones I've been watching –
some of them might die.

She shook the thought away. She was only one of many involved in
similar reconnaissance and the time for armed struggle was rapidly
passing. They'll probably never bomb mine, she thought. Mine – it
wasn't so odd a thought, for the police station did feel a bit like hers.
For five days she had been watching it, working out its routine until
she felt as if she controlled it. She would stand across the street, look
at her watch and then say to herself, the next shift is due – and they
would arrive. She would see the back of a retreating officer and know
whether he would or would not stick to security drill. She knew what
time they ate breakfast, how soon 'elevenses' followed, when they had
lunch. She knew it all.

And now it was time for her to go.

I'm finished, she thought, and as she drove into the distance the
pull of the police station gradually diminished. She drove and drove,
humming to herself, thinking distractedly of this and that, without
coherence or the need for it.

She had been driving for some considerable time before she came
to. She looked up and it dawned on her that she was lost. Until that
moment Johannesburg had seemed defined by only two locations –
the one where she stayed and the one where the police station was
sited. But now she was elsewhere. She looked around her, searching

for a reference point. There was nobody in sight and the odds were that nobody would appear to help her out. She saw a name plate on a free-standing wall ahead and she kerb-crawled her way to it. Once there, she stopped and took her map from the dashboard shelf.

1993

Michèle Roberts

Michèle Roberts was born in 1949 in Bushey, Hertfordshire, and was educated at Oxford University, where she received a BA in 1970. She was a member of the Feminist Writers' Group with Zoe Fairbairns and Sara Maitland, and has collaborated on several projects with such writers as Judith Kazantsis and Michelene Wandor. She was creative writing fellow at the University of East Anglia and is the author of poetry, short stories and seven novels, including *The Visitation* (1983), *The Wild Girl* (1984), *In the Red Kitchen* (1990), *Flesh and Blood* (1994) and most recently *Impossible Saints*. *Daughters of the House* (1992) was short-listed for the Booker Prize and won the W. H. Smith Literary Award. She is also a regular book reviewer. Half-English and half-French, she lives in London and in Mayenne, France.

During Mother's Absence was first published by Virago in 1993 and contains the story 'Charity' from which this extract is taken.

from

'Charity'

I have a young erotic mother. Her hair, shiny and black, curves round her face and flops forward into her large dark eyes. She has an olive skin, olive eyelids, straight black brows. Her mouth is big and wide, her lips plump and rosy as cushions over her large white teeth. Today she's wearing a long dull green mac buttoned down one side and tightly belted around her narrow waist, high-heeled ankle boots, and a red beret, and she's slung her bag diagonally across her front like schoolchildren do.

It's raining. Neither of us has an umbrella, so we walk along arm in arm under the colonnades, up and down, up and down. It's lunchtime. Most people are inside eating. The yellow and grey city seems empty. Except for us. Talking as we pace, exchanging stories as fast as we can. Months since we've seen each other, so many words to turn over in our hands and offer each other like pieces of new bread torn off the still warm loaf. Then she makes up her mind, and invites me home.

We shake ourselves in the hallway like two wet dogs. She pulls me after her into the bedroom to find me some dry clothes. We watch each other undress. Slither of a rose-coloured slip, of seamed black stockings. She turns back the blue quilt on the bed, and I slide in next to her. My mother's flesh is warm. The sheets are cool and smooth. I lay my hands on her hips and pull her close, kiss her soft mouth, her shoulders, stroke her hair, the wet silky place between her legs. The storm drums on the roof. She kisses and caresses me. Her smell grows stronger, like a garden after the rain. She offers me her breast, round and white and fat, ardently we lie in each other's arms, touching kissing sucking biting, then my swollen cunt boils over and I come.

I wake up from this dream disconcerted, still fizzing. I'll tell it to Gabriella tomorrow when we're having breakfast together at my kitchen table, and she'll laugh. She'll be dipping a sweet biscuit into her little cup of black coffee, her feet tucked up under her, comfortable amongst the cushions of the basket chair, her profile alert against the white wall, and then she'll light a cigarette, impatient to tell me *her* dream. Her presence unleashes our words. We're off. Each time we see one another, this jostling at the start, glad galloping down the track of stories. After knowing her for twenty years.

1994

A. M. Homes

A. M. Homes was born in 1962 in Washington, DC, and graduated from Sarah Lawrence College in 1985. She attended the University of Iowa writers' workshop and is the author of one collection of short stories, *The Safety of Objects* (1990), and four novels: *Jack* (1989), *In a Country of Mothers*, *The End of Alice* (1996) – which spectacularly courted controversy in its unflinching portrayal of paedophilia – and most recently *Music for Torching* (1999). The original short story which formed the starting point for the novel *Music for Torching* was used in an art-text collaboration with the artist Rachel Whiteread. Homes is an art critic and teaches on the writing programme at Columbia University.

In a Country of Mothers was first published in the UK by Virago in 1994.

from

In a Country of Mothers

The shrink's office was on Sixth Avenue near Houston, seventy-some blocks from the location and about fifteen from Jody's apartment. She was late. Timing the two-minute-forty-second wait for the elevator, she figured how much standing in the lobby was costing her. On the way up she entertained herself with questions like: Do all the offices in the building belong to shrinks? Is everyone in this elevator crazy?

On the third floor, she found Claire's office and pushed the buzzer marked 'Roth'.

'Hello,' a muffled voice called through a small speaker in the wall.

Jody considered not going in, not meeting Claire Roth face-to-face but having the session out there in the hall, chatting it up with a hidden voice, as if talking to the Wizard of Oz. 'It's Jody Goodman.'

The door unlocked with a thick sound like a joy buzzer. Jody grabbed the knob and pushed.

The waiting room was long and thin, three doors with chairs in the spaces between the doors. Jody sat on the chair closest to the door going out, unsure whether you were supposed to sit in an assigned chair – the chair next to the door that belonged to your shrink? The whole thing felt like a puzzle, a test designed to reveal something significant about Jody's psyche. She had the urge to get up, take the subway back uptown, and call later to say she'd realised that she'd left the toaster oven on and had to hurry home. Reschedule? Well, right now I'm kind of busy. Oh, there's my other line. Gotta go.

There were two noise machines on the floor, filling the room with the rushing sound of mechanically driven air. She was proud of herself for knowing what they were: shrink technology, white noise. They sounded like a constantly droning vacuum cleaner. Jody closed her eyes and imagined holding one to her ear like a shell. More than once, when she and Barbara reached sensitive points in what Jody called their 'negotiations', she'd wanted to lean forward and say, 'Your sound machines don't do shit.'

The door at the end of the hall opened. 'See you Thursday,' a soft voice said. Because she couldn't decide who to look at, the patient or the shrink, Jody saw nothing.

'Hi, I'm Claire,' the shrink said, extending her hand.

'Hi,' Jody said, shaking hands, worried that the shrink could feel her trembling, her sweat.

'Would you like to come in?'

I must be crazy, Jody thought as she walked over the threshold into the office. There were floor-to-ceiling bookshelves, an old wooden desk, a leather sofa, a small table for the requisite box of Kleenex, and one chair. Claire sat in the chair, Jody on the sofa. It was easy, obvious.

'So,' Claire said, picking up a big yellow legal pad and resting it on her lap. 'What's going on?'

'I really shouldn't be doing this,' Jody said, laughing a little. 'I just escaped from the set of a movie, and coming here, sitting here, I feel like I'm in a movie.' Jody paused.

Two seconds had passed. Jody couldn't imagine lasting an hour. There was silence. Jody looked at Claire and noticed she was wearing a short skirt. She'd never seen a shrink in a short skirt before. She hoped it was a good sign.

'You made the appointment,' Claire said. 'There must be something on your mind.'

Jody had the sensation of auditioning to be Claire's patient. At the end of the hour, just like a casting director or a theatrical agent, Claire would stand up and say, Look, this is all very interesting, but I really don't work with people like you.

'On the phone you said you were having some difficulty making career decisions. Would you like to talk about that?'

Again Jody laughed, but it came out more like a snort. 'For as long as I can remember I wanted to go to UCLA film school, so this year I applied, got in. And now, all of a sudden, I'm not sure.'

Jody wanted Claire to like her, to choose her. She didn't want to say anything about herself that would seem too terrible, too complicated. She wanted Claire to think she was easy.

'So you're afraid? Is that the problem?'

Of course that was the problem, or at least part of it. But she wasn't ready to talk about it, so she started telling jokes. 'I'm not so sure it's the school I'm afraid of. I think it's getting there, flying. I used to love it. Up in the air, Junior Birdman. Up in the air, Victory.' It was the first session and Jody was singing at the top of her lungs, making her fingers into goggles and pressing them up to her eyes, making faces.

Claire was smiling at Jody. 'You're very funny. That's great.'

Not only did Claire understand; she appreciated, she approved. Jody felt incredible. She felt as though she could relax, could confess all the things she'd never been able to tell Barbara, all the things she'd never told anyone; anything and everything.

She closed her eyes and saw herself as a World War I flying ace. She was flying to Los Angeles in a leather jacket and goggles, a white silk scarf flapping back into her mother's face. Her mother wore a leather hood and big glasses and kept shouting directions into Jody's ear. The directions were based on a trip she'd made to California by bus thirty years before.

'Is there any other reason you might not want to go away?' Claire asked. 'Do you have a boyfriend?'

'No,' Jody said.

'Do you want one?'

It seemed like a strange question. 'Are you giving them away?' Jody asked.

Claire laughed. At the rate this was going, by the end of the session Jody could have the 'HBO Comedy Hour' all to herself.

'What about your family?' Claire asked.

Jody raised her eyebrows.

'Who's in your family?'

Oddly phrased, as though Claire wanted names, famous names, like Clark Gable and Rock Hudson. 'I have a mother, a father, and a grandfather,' she said uncertainly.

'What are they like?'

'Well,' she said, teasing, 'my aunt was Lucille Ball – you know, "I Love Lucy". It was really hard on my mom, not being the funny one.' Jody noticed Claire writing something down on her legal pad and got nervous. 'Don't write that down.'

'I didn't,' Claire said, looking up.

'Why not?' Jody asked.

'You don't look anything like Lucy.'

'I'm adopted,' Jody said, and Claire's expression changed. 'My aunt and I were very close.'

'What I'd like to do,' Claire said, 'is see you three times – then I'll have a better sense of things and we can talk about where to go from there. Does that sound okay to you?'

Jody nodded. She hated this part. Business before pleasure.

'What kind of a job do you have?'

'I work for a film production company.'

'Are your parents helping you?'

'A little.'

'Can you afford ninety-five dollars an hour?'

Jody nodded.

'Are you sure?'

Jody nodded again. There was something about Claire that made Jody think that even if she couldn't afford it, she wouldn't say no. She'd find a way.

Claire picked up her appointment book. 'Could you come the day after tomorrow at one?'

'Do you have anything later?'

'Three?'

Jody nodded.

'I'll see you then,' Claire said, standing.

Jody couldn't believe the session was over. Okay, so she'd been a few minutes late, but this had to be the fastest fifty minutes in history.

'Have you got the time?' Jody asked, getting up, noticing that Claire was quite tall, at least five nine or ten – model material.

'It's one-thirty-five, we ran a few minutes over.'

'Wow.'

'See you Thursday,' Claire said, closing the door behind her.

Instead of waiting for the elevator, Jody ran down the stairs, hailed a cab, and raced back uptown.

1995

Maxine Clair

———

Maxine Clair grew up in Kansas City, a place she returned to in the linked story sequence that makes up her first novel, *Rattlebone*. She currently teaches at George Washington University and lives with her four children in Washington, DC. Her stories have appeared in many American magazines.

Rattlebone was first published in the UK by Virago in 1995.

from

Rattlebone

It is dusk. You could say that every time Pearlean has come out to sit on her front porch, every time she has sat in the flamingo-pink glider that, with every rocking glide, squawks from its warp of metal on metal, every time she has brought her comb and brush and sat in the glider combing her just-washed hair, every evening that she has painted her toenails pink on the porch while she watched the children play hopscotch, every single evening after ironing tablecloths and pinafores all day, after laying white shirts out on the table to sprinkle and roll like white jelly rolls to be ironed and on hangers all turned the same way by six o'clock when cars drive up and collect the blouses and skirts, the white shirts with not too much starch and, Lord no, no blueing, no bleach – all those evenings after all those days, you could say that she has been waiting.

In the first long wish with the whole world, she waited for him to come home from the jungle in New Guinea where some men died and others went crazy over the native women. But she waited for him and went one better. Still a girl herself, she waited for their baby girl, waited for the baby that came wailing into the world proclaiming that here and now their lives would begin together.

But she had to wait for him to get a steady job, maybe in Sedalia, or else they couldn't eat. While she waited she made baby clothes, curtains for their one window, vanity skirts, made dough-cakes to save money, and lemon meringue pies to sell, whittled stick-men from birch branch, made do and waited. And when they were paying double for bricklayers in Olathe, and paying next to nothing for hauling coal here, she said, sure, it was all right, she would wait.

Surely it was only a matter of months until they got on with living, until the company got the building built, or the sidewalk laid, or the retaining wall finished. He was a good husband, paid three months' rent in advance, bought them a new bed. Sweet man, hot love, couldn't keep his hands off when he was home. When he was home. Sure, she could wait. She had the baby to play with. But what does a woman do with the feelings that bubble up when she's rubbing herself in the tub, or listening to Billy Eckstine on the radio? 'I love you,' she said. 'Wait until I get on my feet,' he said. 'Won't be long.'

Then there was the next baby. A long wait for a fertile body to make little legs and fingers, good eyes, and the best-shaped head. A long wait.

And every one of those hundreds of days filled itself up with small waits – for the iron to heat up, the skillet to sizzle, the child to get home from school, Sunday to come, payday, a word, a glance, the truth.

She's wondering this evening, now that the iron is standing cold on the board in the kitchen, and she's sitting in the glider that rocks like a squawking flamingo on the porch. She looks at her long legs. What good is love when you sit alone and wait?

Sure she waited. Because the woman she heard he was going with was pretty. Smarter than the two of them put together, really. She waited because he belonged to her, because the woman probably didn't want him anyway, because no man can keep a woman and a wife happy at the same time, because whatever goes over the Devil's back has got to come under his belly, because he was a decent man who would always do right by his kids, because what else could she do but wait?

And he came back. But since the best work was either on the railroad runs from Chicago, where he would have to live, or at the packing house across the river, where he would have to work the late shift, there was nothing to do except sit on the porch. And since every friend she ever had was busy and nothing good was on the radio, she went to church. Sunday. Morning, afternoon, evening Baptist Training Union. Singing in the women's chorus. Singing 'Christ Is All' at prayer meeting Wednesday night, Friday night Circle. What does a woman say when a nice man who has a nice job at the Post Office says that a young woman like her ought not to wait alone?

What was a husband, really? What good was a hip-husband-jitterbug with a wide-brim hat and stitched-sole Florsheim shoes? What kind of man-child-husband was this smooth talker who knew every word the

King Cole Trio ever sang but didn't know his wife had a birthmark on her behind? What kind of husband-hands couldn't go slow in the fresh sheets, what kind of husband-mouth laughed at her when she put her foot down about out-of-town jobs?

The eventide falls fast and she's waiting on the porch thinking about all that time. And isn't this the Post Office coming now, showing off his new used Chevrolet? Smiling and waving, isn't this him? And around the block to smile and wink one more time. She ought to hard-press her hair with the new bangs they are wearing. What if she winks back and recrosses her legs? What if she goes into the house to wait by the party-line phone for this Post Office man to call?

He had promised her a Mixmaster. He swears that nobody will know. And even if someone discovers their secret, who would blame them? His wife is old. Forty already. Frigid, he says. He needs a real woman. He can smell the wait getting short in her, he has seen her on the porch with her bowl of ice cream.

It is dusk. Everything is suspended. A day that started brilliantly and burned along a steady course, now treks so deeply into darkness that it has lost its way. Pearlean combs her hair. Her husband is working late. Who does she love? What is love, anyway, but a silly, groundless thing she made up in her head. Once it was handsome, tender, kind, rich, smart. Once it could sing sweet, talk good, pray out loud, and surely dance. What is it made of? What is there to love? What is there in anyone to love?

1996

Gail Anderson-Dargatz

Gail Anderson-Dargatz grew up in rural British Columbia. She has published a collection of short stories, and won the Canadian Broadcasting Company's fiction prize for the story that gave rise to *The Cure for Death by Lightning*, her first novel, published in 1996. The book became a bestseller in Britain and Canada and won many prizes, including the Betty Trask Award. Her second novel, *A Recipe for Bees*, was published in 1999. She lives on a farm in Alberta with her husband.

The Cure for Death by Lightning was first published in the UK by Virago in 1997.

from

The Cure for Death by Lightning

I took the birch branch from the spruce and walked with it, driving myself that fingernails-on-blackboard crazy with the feel of birch bark under my callused fingers. I followed the pointers out of listlessness and boredom more than curiosity. At first, the forest was quiet. Then I began hearing the noises that made up the quiet: trees aching, birds whistling, someone chopping wood way off. There was something else, too. A metal sound, a tinkling or clanking, like the sound of a horse harness, but it was too far off and receding to hear clearly. I branched off the many trails, following the sound, and when I was about ready to give up and turn back I came on the girl with the bell necklace, Bertha Moses's granddaughter, walking some distance ahead of me in the bush. She was dressed as she always was when she came to the house, in boy's jeans, a western shirt that was too small for her, and of course she wore the bell necklace; that was the sound I'd heard. The sight of her slim back in that clearing lit me up inside. She was bending over, working with something very tiny in her hands. She turned and I ducked down behind a wild rose bush.

'Beth Weeks, I see you,' she called out.

I stood up from behind the bush and grinned, all shyness and delight.

'You were sneaking up on me,' she said.

I took a few steps forward, holding my syrup tin with both hands.

'Scared me too!' she said.

She looked sideways at my wool skirt and shook her head. My eyes were drawn to the necklace. It was made from bells of many sizes, all cheap and a little tarnished, and strung on one thread of red yarn. I was tempted to pull the necklace because one good yank would send the bells tinkling into the air. She jingled the necklace.

'Like it?' she said. 'I made it.'

I nodded, then noticed the bloody cuts on her arm.

'What happened to your arm?' I said.

She pulled her sleeve down. 'Nothing.'

'Let's see.' I reached to take her wrist but she pulled her arm away. 'You did that, didn't you?' I said.

'So what if I did?'

'Doesn't it hurt?'

'Mind your own business.' She buttoned her shirtsleeves. 'What're you doing out here anyway?'

'Walking. What're you doing?'

'Nothing.'

'No, really. What's that you've got in your hand?'

The girl tried to hide what she had in her hand, but I pried her fingers open. She had two live crickets, tied together with a blond hair. She let them go and they struggled on the ground for a time, to free themselves.

'What're you doing?' I said again.

'Nothing.'

'You killing them?'

'No!'

'What then?'

She nudged the struggling crickets with her toe. 'It's a love charm,' she said finally. 'You tie two crickets together with the hair of whoever you love.'

'Who are you in love with?' I said.

The girl shrugged and went shy. She looked up and around at the sky through the trees. I flicked a ladybug off my skirt.

'I never seen you in pants,' she said. 'You don't ever wear pants?'

'When I do chores. Under a skirt!' I giggled.

'Your dad say so?' she said.

'My mum doesn't let me wear pants.'

'Granny says your father's gone stupid.'

I was immediately angry and felt my face flush, but I said nothing.

'I'm sorry,' she said. 'Granny says that about a lot of people.'

I shrugged.

'Is it true he's got metal in his head?'

'A bomb blew up right next to him. In the war. Covered him right up. Left bits of stuff in him. Mum says they couldn't get it all out. She nursed him for a while, after. That's how they met.'

'Is that what makes him like that?' she said.

The anger lit up like a match. 'Like what?'

'I don't know. Yelling all the time. Or not even that. Like when he's all nice one minute and then he's crazy. Like how he gets so jealous if a man even touches his cap at your mother.'

The fire licked around inside me and sputtered out. I kicked the ground in silence for a while. 'He wasn't always like that. You seen him. Even last spring he wasn't like that. After that bear attacked our camp, after we sold the sheep, he wasn't right after that.'

'Bet it was Coyote. Granny says that. She's scared Coyote's back, sneaking around. Granny says if a man's got something wrong with him, if he's a drunk or got hit on the head or bushed or something, then Coyote can get inside him and make him crazy, make him do stuff. Bad stuff.'

I laughed. 'Like Coyote Jack. I heard that. Dan told me you guys think he's a shape-shifter.'

'Yea, like him.'

'You really believe that?'

The girl shrugged. 'Granny's stories. Sometimes she swears it's the truth. Sometimes she says it's just stories.'

I kicked the ground. The girl looked down at the crickets and then back up at me.

'I like your hair,' she said. She reached out and ran her fingers through my hair for some time without speaking. It felt good and calming, like my mother brushing my hair before bed. After a minute I closed my eyes and enjoyed it.

'You're beautiful, like an angel,' she said, and just then, I felt that way. She stopped stroking my hair and sunk both hands into her jean pockets. I tried to think if there was something in my lunch can fit to give her; I tried to think of something to say. I felt silly asking her name because I already sort of knew her. She'd been at the house with the rest of Bertha's family so many times, drinking coffee, looking at the walls.

'Want to come to my place?' she said.

I nodded and began walking with her before I thought about where it was she lived. She lived in Bertha's house on the reserve road with all the other women in Bertha's clan. At that realisation, all the name-calling Parker and Lily Bell and the other kids from school did rose up in a hot wave that burned my cheeks and made me sulky.

Indian lover. Squaw. I walked on with her anyway with my fear of the reserve making me silent. The girl with the bell necklace walked ahead of me, breaking off branches now and again and sticking them in the crotches of trees. Her walk wasn't a walk at all; it was a skip, a dance. I found myself copying her. She put another branch in the crotch of a tree.

'What are you doing?' I asked.

She shrugged and kept walking.

'I saw Filthy Billy the other night tying his pants legs together before he went to sleep,' I said. 'And he jumped over the fire because a lizard chased him.'

'So the lizard don't come eat his heart.'

'Yeah.'

'My great-uncle did that too before he died. Some of the old people are still scared of those lizards. Filthy Billy's just plain crazy. Granny says she's seen a man die from his heart getting eaten that way, by one of them lizards. Can't believe half what Granny says.'

'I like her,' I said. 'I still have that velvet she gave me.'

We walked on a little longer in silence. The girl put branches in the crotches of trees now and again, and I found myself doing the same.

'I'll show you something,' said the girl.

'What?'

'You'll see.'

1997

Karin Cook

———

Karin Cook graduated from Vassar College and the creative writing programme at New York University. An activist and health educator, she currently works in New York. She lives in Brooklyn.

What Girls Learn was first published in the Virago V series in 1997.

from

What Girls Learn

On Wednesday, Ms Zimmerman stopped me on my way to lunch and asked how I was feeling. She removed her dark-rimmed glasses, leaving a red indentation on the bridge of her nose. 'Now, Tilden,' she said, quietly in a no-nonsense voice, 'you may not realise this, but this kind of thing has an effect on the whole family. Have you felt the effects? Any pain?'

I shook my head and tried to listen. All the while, I was watching over her shoulder for a sign of my classmates. I wanted someone to interrupt, to make her stop talking.

'Sometimes it hurts those of us on the outside even more because we feel helpless. Sometimes we blame ourselves. Was it something I did? But it's not.' Ms Zimmerman forced a smile. 'It's nothing anyone can control. That's what's so hard about it.' There was a strange, far-away look on her face.

At lunch, the girls at my table suggested just the opposite. They all watched *Charlie's Angels* on TV, had even adopted the hairstyles. They were looking for causes, for clues. Somehow, somewhere along the way, someone was culpable. If they could pin it down, they could prevent a procedure from happening in their families.

Jill Switt wanted to know if we had been drinking the water. Her reddish brown hair was brushed back in a Farrah Fawcett feather. 'Do you have asbestos in your cellar?' she asked.

Susie Rhombus's jet black hair was half-feathered, half-rolled back like Jaclyn Smith's. She asked how much red meat we ate a week. She'd heard that hot dogs were particularly bad.

'And catsup,' someone added.

'And coffee,' Libbie Gorin chimed in from the next table. 'Anything with caffeine.'

Jill continued. 'Did your mother smoke? Did anyone around her smoke?'

Susie shifted in her seat. Her father and her two older brothers all smoked.

'Cigarette smoke is definitely the worst,' Christy Diamo added, tossing her stick straight hair – a longer version of the Kate Jackson wedge.

Jill wanted to know if I had been breast fed.

'Oh give me a break, Jill, that has nothing to do with cancer,' Samantha said.

It was the first I'd heard the word *cancer*. A slow panic grew inside me, like gallons of toxic tap water sloshing up and choking me. Grandma had once smoked. I had been breast fed. We probably did have asbestos in our cellar. If not now, then at one of those places down South. We'd been remiss. Other families drank bottled water. Ate cauliflower and broccoli. My eyes welled up.

The table got quiet. We picked carefully through our lunches. I willed myself not to cry by counting the butter pats on the ceiling. But the sight of Elizabeth in the lunch line brought my attention back. She waved from across the cafeteria. It was a low wave from the hip. Usually we weren't nice to each other in public, and at school, we acknowledged each other only to point out what the other one was wearing that did not belong to her. But now, our eyes locked for an extra-long second before she clasped her fingers tight around the tray and headed for the milk cart.

In the girls' room, I locked myself safely inside the stall, sat down on the toilet with my clothes on and waited. The smell from the green linoleum floors was of wet chlorine and muddy shoes. I heard the outer door open and slam. One navy Ked appeared under the bathroom stall, a smilie face on the toe. Samantha. She slid a large book wrapped in a plastic shopping bag under the door.

'It's my mom's,' she said. 'Don't let anyone see it.'

I pulled the book out of the bag and set it on my lap. *Our Bodies, Ourselves*, it was called. The cover was white with a large black-and-white photograph of older and younger women standing together, holding signs. Inside, was a collage of women with severe parts in their hair: women running, studying, hugging, jumping rope, crossing the finish line, doing backbends and self-defence. Slowly, I turned to the table of contents and realised that I didn't know what I was looking for. I flipped through the pages looking at the diagrams and sketches of naked women, some with their legs spread wide enough to see their insides. There were photos of real women, unlike the paper dolls in the menstruation pamphlet. On one page was a picture of a bloody woman, dead on the floor of a motel room. On another, a woman with only one breast and a tattoo as a scar. All around me walls were turning, the lights buzzed. I put my head on my knees.

'Are you okay?' Samantha asked.

'Uh huh,' I said.

'My mom says you could come with us to the movie on Saturday,' she said. 'If you want.'

1998

Alice Thompson

———

Alice Thompson was born in 1961. She read English at Oxford, and studied for a PhD on Henry James at London University. She has been a writer in residence in Shetland, and at St Andrews University, and was also the keyboard player for the eighties pop group The Woodentops. Her novella *Killing Time* was published in 1991, and *Justine*, her first novel, won the James Tait Black Memorial Prize and a Scottish Arts Council Book Award. *Pandora's Box* is her second novel. It was shortlisted for the Stakis Prize in 1998.

Pandora's Box was first published by Virago in 1998.

from

Pandora's Box

Noah was in love with the empirical world. The physicality of the world, the building blocks of cities, as well as the rhythms of the natural world, offered him constant pleasure. In spite of the obsession he had for his work, Noah was not unaware of the seasons changing outside the hospital and he appreciated the mechanics of the world as he did the mechanics of the body. He didn't need an imagination as the world was mysterious enough for him.

Even though Noah had a sense of wonder for reality, he was always certain that if he collected enough information he could get to the bottom of the wonder. Just as every time Noah built up the body, dealt in its physical realities, he felt in some way he might get to the bottom of the mystery of what it was to be human. His life ran in a straight line from beginning to end and he walked along it, unaware of the drop on either side.

In his bedroom, a photograph of the Hale-Bopp comet was pinned to his wall. Late at night, he would get into bed and continue reading from his collection of encyclopaedia, pleased that he had reached a new letter before falling asleep. The facts of the world were like jewels he collected. He did not bother to thread the facts together, he just piled them up like a magpie piled up pieces of silver foil in its nest.

Noah had decided to leave the operations on the patient's face until last. For he knew that the face would prove the most challenging part of her body to regraft. While the rest of her body continued to heal wondrously quickly and perfectly, her head remained band-aged up. Her face had been so badly burnt that there was nothing of the original structure left. He would have to rebuild the bones themselves.

Noah started to draw diagrams and work out the measurements of the reconstruction. Using a textbook photograph of an idealised woman's face, he set out a face on paper of symmetrical proportions. He would give her a model face. He realised the overlying result would still look like a raw concertina of scars and blemishes but at least he could give her face's basic structure a proportion that bore some underlying semblance to perfection.

Reconstructing her face took many weeks of painstaking operations. A few weeks after surgery Noah bent down over his patient's head to unravel the bandages. Her eyes just flickered from between the swathing, as his hands expertly and slowly pulled off the fabric. He could not stop his heart beating more quickly than usual. The result would be a testament to all his powers.

But he could not believe his eyes when he saw what his hands were gradually revealing to him. Appearing beneath the bandages, inch by inch, was a beautiful young woman's face, a face so white and soft that the skin seemed as if it had never seen the light of day. This was not a face that had been so badly disfigured its features had been unrecognisable. It was a face that was the exact replica of the textbook photograph upon which Noah had based his structural measurements.

Her cool, pale, reflective eyes looked at him, in the same speculative trance with which she had stared at the ceiling all these months. She still hadn't uttered a word. What kind of woman was she? he thought. That night he dreamt of her decapitated head floating down a river, her mouth opening and shutting singing voicelessly.

The next morning he told the matron to fetch the patient some clothes and discharge her immediately. Noah wanted nothing more to do with this aberration of nature. Later that afternoon, when he walked past her bed, it was empty, the white sheet pulled tightly back over the grey blanket, the regulatory six inches, smooth and flat.

Although he had dedicated himself intensively and over a period of time to only one patient, he did not miss her, as might have been expected. On the contrary, he was relieved that she had gone. At first, Noah had been pleased by the initial speed of her body's recovery, which he took as a reflection of his medical powers. It was only when her recovery ran against all Noah's notion of what was possible, that he began to feel disturbed.

He kept his own private fears to himself – she had been his patient and no one else's, and he alone felt responsible for her. After all, it was his doorstep that she had landed on. He felt her recovery was all part of her inexplicable appearance outside his home, something peculiarly specific to him and he wanted to forget all about it. A few doctors had remarked to him on her uncanny recovery and then, as completely as she was healed, she was as completely forgotten.

Noah returned to his work on other patients, shortening noses, enlarging breasts and using prostheses to replace amputated limbs. But it was noticed in the hospital that since the arrival and departure of the anonymous patient something about Noah had changed. It was difficult to pin-point. Something to do with the way he walked, the way he talked. He was slightly more vehement, as a character slightly less controlled, but it was barely perceptible.

Noah did not expect to see her again. Nor did he wish to. He had the rest of his life to be getting on with. Noah's world was certain and complete. His new patients slotted into this world like pieces into a jigsaw.

1999

Sarah Waters

―――――

Sarah Waters was born in Wales in 1966. She has a PhD in English literature, has published articles on lesbian and gay writing, and is currently an associate lecturer with the Open University. In 1998 she received a London Arts Board New London Writers Award. Her first novel, *Tipping the Velvet*, was published in 1997. *Affinity* is her second novel.

Affinity was first published in 1999 as part of the Virago V series.

from

Affinity

30 May 1873

Last night I had an awful dream. I dreamed that I woke up & all my limbs were stiff & I could not move them, & my eyes had a paste on them that kept them shut & it had run into my mouth & kept my lips shut too. I longed to call out to Ruth or to Mrs Brink but, because of the paste, I could not, I heard the sound I was making & it was only a groan. I began to be afraid then that I should have to lie like that until I choked or starved, & when I thought that I began to cry. Then my tears began to wash away the paste from over my eyes until finally there was a little space that I might just peep through, & thought, 'Now I shall look & see my own room, at least.' The room, however, that I expected to see, was not my room at Sydenham, it was my room at Mr Vincy's hotel.

But when I did look, I saw only that the place I lay in was entirely dark, & then I knew that I was buried in my own coffin, that they had put me in it thinking I was dead. I lay crying in my coffin until the tears melted the paste from my mouth, & then I did call out, thinking 'If I only call hard enough someone is sure to hear me & let me out.' But no-one came, & when I lifted my head it knocked upon the wood that was above me & by the sound of that knock I knew that there was earth above the coffin, & that I was already in my grave. Then I knew that no-one would hear me however loudly I called.

I lay very still then, wondering what I should do, & as I did that there came a whispering voice beside me, it came against my ear & made me shiver. The voice said 'Did you think you were alone? Didn't you know that I was here?' I looked for the person that spoke, but it was too dark for me to see them, there was only the feeling of the mouth close to my ear. I couldn't tell if it was Ruth's mouth, or Mrs Brink's, or Aunty's, or someone else entirely. I only knew, from the sound of the words, that the mouth was smiling.

2000

Grace Paley

Grace Paley was born in the Bronx in 1922. Her stories have appeared in *The New Yorker*, and *The Atlantic Monthly*, among other publications. Her highly acclaimed collections of stories are: *The Little Disturbances of Man* (1959), *Enormous Changes at the Last Minute* (1974), and *Later the Same Day* (1985); she is also the author of two books of poetry and one collection of poems and prose pieces, *Long Walks and Intimate Talks* (1991). Actively involved in anti-war, feminist and anti-nuclear movements, she has been a member of the War Resisters' League, Resist, and Women's Pentagon Action, was one of the founders of the Greenwich Village Peace Center in 1961 and is a member of the executive board of PEN; she regards herself as a 'somewhat combative pacifist and cooperative anarchist.' Much of her political thinking and experience is described in her collected writings, *Just as I Thought* (1998). She has taught at Columbia University, Sarah Lawrence, Dartmouth, and City College, and in 1987, she was awarded a Senior Fellowship by the National Endowment for the Arts, in recognition of her lifetime contribution to literature. Included among her many awards and honors are: the 1994 Jewish Cultural Achievement Award for Literary Arts; the 1993 Vermont Award for Excellence in the Arts; the 1992 REA Award for Short Stories; and the 1989 Edith Wharton Award. In 1989 she was declared the first official New York State Writer. She divides her time between New York City and Vermont.

This is the first British publication of *Midrash on Happiness*.

from

Midrash on Happiness

What she meant by happiness, she said, was the following: she meant having (or having had) (or continuing to have) everything. By everything she meant, first, the children, then a dear person to live with, preferably a man, but not necessarily (by live with, she meant for a long time, but not necessarily). Along with and not in preferential order, she required three or four best women friends to whom she could tell every personal fact and then discuss on the widest, deepest, and most hopeless level the economy, the constant, unbeatable, cruel war economy, the slavery of the American worker to the idea of that economy, the complicity of male people in the whole structure, the dumbness of men (including her preferred man) on this subject. By dumbness, she meant everything dumbness has always meant: silence and stupidity. By silence, she meant refusal to speak; by stupidity, she meant refusal to hear. For happiness, she required women to walk with. To walk in the city arm in arm with a woman friend (as her mother had with aunts and cousins so many years ago) was just plain essential. Oh! those long walks and intimate talks, better than standing alone on the most admirable mountain or in the handsomest forest or hay-blown field (all of which were certainly splendid occupations for the wind-starved soul). More important even (though maybe less sweet because of age) than the old walks with boys she'd walked with as a girl, that nice bunch of worried left-wing boys who flew (always slightly handicapped by that idealistic wing) into a dream of paid-up mortgages with a small room for opinion and solitude in the corner of home. Oh, do you remember those fellows, Ruthy?

Remember? Well, I'm married to one.

But she had, Faith continued, democratically tried walking in the beloved city with a man, but the effort had failed since from about that age – twenty-seven or -eight – he had felt an obligation, if a young woman passed, to turn abstractedly away, in the middle of the most personal conversation, or even to say confidentially, Wasn't she something? – or clasping his plaid shirt, at the heart's level, Oh my God! The purpose of this: perhaps to work a nice quiet appreciation into thunderous heartbeat as he had been taught on pain of sexual death.

For happiness, she also required work to do in this world and bread on the table. By work to do, she included the important work of raising children righteously up. By righteously, she meant that along with being useful and speaking truth to the community, they must do no harm. By harm, she meant not only personal injury to the friend the lover the co-worker the parent (the city the nation) but also the stranger; she meant particularly the stranger in all her or his difference, who, because we were strangers in Egypt, deserves special goodness for life, or at least until the end of strangeness. By bread on the table, she meant no metaphor but truly bread, as her father had ended every single meal with a hunk of bread. By hunk, she was describing one of the attributes of good bread.

Suddenly she felt she had left out a couple of things: love. Oh yes, she said, for she was talking, talking all this time, to patient Ruth, and they were walking for some reason in a neighbourhood where she didn't know the children, the pizza places, or the vegetable markets. It was early evening and she could see lovers walking along Riverside Park with their arms around one another, turning away from the sun, which now sets among the new apartment houses of New Jersey, to kiss. Oh, I forgot, she said, now that I notice, Ruthy I think I would die without love. By love, she probably meant she would die without being *in* love. By *in* love, she meant the acuteness of the heart at the sudden sight of a particular person or the way over a couple of years of interested friendship one is suddenly stunned by the lungs' longing for more and more breath in the presence of that friend, or nearly drowned to the knees by the salty spring that seems to beat for years on our vaginal shores. Not to omit all sorts of imaginings which assure great spiritual energy for months and, when luck follows truth, years.

Oh sure, love. I think so, too, sometimes, said Ruth, willing to hear Faith out since she had been watching the kissers, too, but I'm really not so sure. Nowadays it seems like pride, I mean overweening pride, when you look at the children and think we don't have time to do much (by time, Ruth meant both her personal time and the planet's time). When I read the papers and hear all this boom-boom bellicosity, the guys outdaring each other, I see we have to change it all – the world – without killing it absolutely – without killing it, that'll be the trick the kids'll have to figure out. Until that begins, I don't understand happiness – what you mean by it.

Then Faith was ashamed to have wanted so much and so little all at the same time – to be so easily and personally satisfied in this terrible place, when everywhere vast public suffering rose in reeling waves from the round earth's nation-states – hung in the satellite-watched air and settled in no time at all into TV sets and newsrooms. It was all there. Look up and the news of halfway round the planet is falling on us all. So for all these conscientious and technical reasons, Faith was ashamed. It was clear that happiness could not be worthwhile, with so much conversation and so little revolutionary change. Of course, Faith said, I know all that. I do, but sometimes walking with a friend I forget the world.